Formative Assessment Framework for Teaching and Learning PreK–12

The Independent Reading Level Assessment (IRLA) is a unified standards-based framework for student assessment, text leveling, and curriculum and instruction. The IRLA includes every Common Core State Standard for Reading, both in literature and informational text, as well as those Language standards key to reading success, for students in grades PreK through 12.

Establish Baseline Level for Every Student

The IRLA will help you establish a baseline proficiency level for each of your students. The baseline level is the highest level at which a student can demonstrate proficiency without teacher help. This is the level at which you can expect the student to perform at proficiency on high stakes testing.

Develop an Action Plan to Ensure Reading Proficiency for Every Student

The IRLA will help you show students where they are, where they should be, and what skills and behaviors lie in between. Through regular conferences, you will be able to outline and track a course of correction, acceleration, or maintenance, for each student and his or her family.

Monitor Progress Towards Goal

The IRLA allows you to track progress in real-time. Each standard has been assigned a points value relative to the amount of time it should take a student to acquire that skill or concept. In each formative assessment conference, teachers score students on any standards they have mastered, allowing teachers and schools to track rate of reading growth for every student.

Spanish

The Evaluación del nivel independiente de lectura.(ENIL) parallels the IRLA while reflecting the different developmental stages of learning to read in Spanish.

Built on Common Core State Standards for Reading

Comprehension: Literature and Informational Text

- Active Reading Strategies
- Key Ideas and Details: Using Text Evidence to Support Conclusions
- Craft and Structure: Analyzing the Effects of Authors' Choices
- Integration of Knowledge and Ideas: Comparing Different Presentations

Range of Reading and Level of Text Complexity

- Engagement and Independence
- Home Reading Routines
- Reading Across Genres

Foundational Skills: Reading Standards K-5

- Print Concepts
- Sequential Phonics/Decoding Skills
- Word Recognition (Power Words and Tricky Words)
- Fluency and Self-Monitoring

Vocabulary: Language Standards 2-12

- Word Recognition
- Literary and Technical Vocabulary
- Word Structures and Etymology
- Figurative Language
- Domain-Specific Information

Written by Jane Hileman and Gin
Introduction to the 2nd Edition written by Suz

Published in the United States by American Readi
www.americanreading.com 1-866-810-BOOK ISBN: 1
MW01691011

Introduction

The goal of all our work as educators is to nurture and develop sophisticated thinkers—thinkers who synthesize and analyze information and ideas for multiple reasons. All the reading, writing, talking, and content study we (American Reading Company) support is in service of the development of this kind of thinking. Our work is to tap into children's natural and innate creativity, inquisitiveness, and motivation—to use that as the fuel to support them in developing the skills to think critically about non-personal, text dependent or text focused ideas. We are on a quest for thinking for understanding, not performance on a bubble test. Crucial to this quest is the use of evidence from text—in other words, sophisticated thinkers use evidence from multiple sources beyond their own experiences to interpret, guide, shape, reshape, and realign their own stances, beliefs, judgments and indeed the nature of their interactions with the world.

- Reading lays the foundation for the background knowledge, experience, mental stamina and journeys, synthesis of new information, access to unfamiliar worlds and experiences that sophisticated thinking requires.
- Talking provides the practice for the mental organizing, social collaboration, factual and opinion dissonance, and oral argumentation that sophisticated thinking requires.
- Writing provides the organizational framework, mental stamina, mental rehearsal time, and written practice in both organizing thoughts and amending beliefs that sophisticated thinking requires. Sophisticated and complex thinking actually requires writing—the writing time is the time when people sort out what and how they're actually thinking and check to see if it makes sense.
- Content study provides the interesting topics, background knowledge, access to unfamiliar information, and the necessary modifications of belief as a result of new information and schema required by sophisticated thinking.

Table of Contents

Phonics Infrastructure for Leveling

This … bout a rea… tor is inte… when det… st imp… ading lev… lity to un…

Read across first then down when level established

Have the reader:

1. Read across a few rows until it becomes clear which column contains words the student is unable to handle independently. Do not provide any help of any kind.
2. Back up to the highest column the student has been able to read independently and have him or her read down that column.

The highest level at which the student can read at least 70–80% (14–16) of the words is his or her phonics level. This is not necessarily his or her reading level, because you haven't checked comprehension in actual text.

	1G/2G	1B	2B	1R	2R
am	am	ham	hammer	hammering	Samuel
an	an	man	candle	candlelight	piano
and	and	sand	sandy	understand	handicapped
at	at	bat	battle	scratchy	attention
ow	down	frown	howling	Mrs. Dowerdy	touchdown
et	get	met	wetter	stretch	McGettigan
in	in	skin	Kevin	invited	skinnier
it	it	pit	quitter	splitting	situation
up	up	pup	puppies	upsetting	Tupperware
as	as	ask	basket	basketball	Alaska
or	or	for	force	forgotten	original
aw	saw	draw	drawing	strawberry	Mr. Awbrighten
ee	see	seed	sweeping	screen	McKeesport
ill	will	Bill	chilly	Hillary	William
all	all	tall	tallest	Dr. Wallington	altogether
ig	big	wig	ignore	ignorant	figures
ame	came	blame	blaming	shameful	Mrs. Amesworthy
ay	day	clay	player	playfully	payable
ake	make	bake	taking	mistaken	shakeable
oo	too	moo	tooth	toothache	foolishly

COMMON CORE STANDARDS • AMERICAN READING COMPANY

Vocabulary Infrastructure for Leveling

This locator provides information about a reader's vocabulary acquisition. The locator is intended to be used as a supplement when determining a reader's level. These lists are neither comprehensive nor sufficient, but as long as the student hasn't practiced them, they will give you an idea of whether his or her working vocabulary is sufficient to comprehend text at each level. The most important indicator of a student's reading level should always be his or her ability to understand the meaning of the text.

DO NOT give copies of this page to students.
DO NOT teach or drill these words out of context.

To confirm a reader's level:
Have the student select 3 words from a column, providing a synonym or short definition for each word. Repeat with 3 words selected by the teacher.

DO NOT allow students to use the word in a sentence in lieu of providing a definition.

	WT	BK	OR	PU	1BR	2BR	SI	GL
1	amateur	abandoned	barrier	abruptly	abolish	adjacent	alluvial	aberration
2	betray	absorbed	bellowed	abundant	audible	affirmative	amnesty	agrarian
3	brilliant	astonish	beneficial	annual	chaos	ambiguous	archaic	apocalyptic
4	capture	burrow	circulate	aroma	concede	civilian	autonomy	banal
5	disbelief	central	concealed	bewildered	civilly	commerce	blatantly	capitulate
6	erupt	century	decrease	contemplate	culture	concede	condescending	charlatan
7	exclaim	confided	defiantly	decade	dialect	controversial	crescendo	disconcerted
8	glared	corridor	departed	elevated	economy	currency	deplete	idiosyncrasy
9	gazing	destination	diminish	emerge	edible	dissent	enmity	incredulous
10	glimmer	dim	estimate	equivalent	humility	domesticated	gaunt	infrastructure
11	muttered	dwelling	extend	flee	instinctively	federation	heresy	languid
12	pleaded	enviously	frequently	frail	irregular	finite	heterogeneous	nebulous
13	prey	fragments	glimpse	gesture	kinship	inaugurated	ironic	ostentatious
14	probe	glanced	horizon	hastily	legendary	intermittent	martyr	ostracize
15	protested	hesitate	inhabit	horizontal	monotony	ominous	monotheism	propitious
16	provide	humiliated	marine	massive	mutely	precedent	paradox	queue
17	quiver	images	mythical	native	perpendicular	premeditated	peripheral	reiterate
18	recently	inquired	partially	perpetual	parallel	raucous	reconcile	rudimentary
19	scowled	peered	previous	propaganda	perilous	skeptical	subtle	venerable
20	shallow	rarely	vast	vicinity	vague	sparse	synthesis	vicissitudes

An entry-level Wt reader may not know these words, yet (see Wt Entry Requirements: Vocabulary Check).

To enter a color level, a student should correctly define 5-6 words.

Student Action Planner: Goal Setting

0	**Is this level easy enough for this student?**	Can the student read the words and ideas fluently and problem-solve 99% of challenges without teacher help of any kind?	___No. Stop and re-focus the conference on identifying the student's correct level. ___Yes. Continue to work on creating Student Action Plan.
1	**Where should I coach this student?**	Does this student need more coaching in this level or is s/he ready for coaching towards the next level?	___This level. ___Next level.
2	**What one area of reading should I focus on?**	What one area of reading most needs improvement so s/he can progress? (from the IRLA)	__ Comprehension __ Range of Reading/Reading Lifestyle __ Phonics/Word Solving __ Word Recognition __ Fluency and Self-Monitoring __ Vocabulary and Language
3	**What essential skill/strategy or concept/habit should I narrow in on?**	What one thing must the student do better in order to progress? (from the IRLA)	Student Power Goal:
4	ACTION PLAN	How will the student achieve this goal? -Constant Practice -Expert Coaching	C.P.: E.C.:

Student Action Planner: Goal Setting

Conferencing Chart for student to know what to work on
295

0	**Is this level eas[...] enough for this student?**	kind?	[...]top and re-focus the [...]ce on identifying the student's [...]vel. [...]ontinue to work on creating Student Action Plan.
1	**Where should I coach this student?**	Does this student need more coaching in this level or is s/he ready for coaching towards the next level?	___This level. ___Next level.
2	**What one area of reading should I focus on?**	What one area of reading most needs improvement so s/he can progress? (from the IRLA)	__ Comprehension __ Range of Reading/Reading Lifestyle __ Phonics/Word Solving __ Word Recognition __ Fluency and Self-Monitoring __ Vocabulary and Language
3	**What essential skill/strategy or concept/habit should I narrow in on?**	What one thing must the student do better in order to progress? (from the IRLA)	Student Power Goal:
4	ACTION PLAN	How will the student achieve this goal? -Constant Practice -Expert Coaching	C.P.: E.C.:

RTM Independent Reading Level Overview .00 - .09

I LOVE BOOKS and BOOKS LOVE ME

The RTM Reader

Readers at the Read-to-Me level must learn to LOVE books. They need to learn how books work and why people enjoy reading them. They learn to enjoy sitting by themselves and pointing to the words in picture books as they "pretend read" the books to themselves. RTM students need to experience thousands of books shared in enjoyable settings in preparation for learning to read. There is no shortcut to the vocabulary, background knowledge, language experience, reading identity, attention span, genre exposure, and phonemic awareness that come through being read to, one-on-one, for the 2,000 hours that is typical of the successful readiness reader. Organize your daily schedule and recruit helpers (adults and older students) to make sure every RTM student falls in love with books and becomes a 500-Book Kid.

RTM Learning Focus

Interactive Language: Using language to explore, negotiate, and express ideas, opinions, and feelings.

Story-Making: Creating narratives to help structure and explain their daily activities.

Active Listening to Read-Aloud: Listening and responding to books read aloud to them.

Emergency

Read-to-Me students are unable to use the pattern in 2Y books to figure out how to "read" the rest of the book. This indicates that they are not yet ready to learn to read, almost always because they haven't been read to and don't understand the way books work or why people would want to read them. This is an emergency, and they need immediate intervention. This skill deficiency is the tip of a cognitive underdevelopment which skill instruction alone will not address. Academically successful kindergartners arrive at school with well-stocked and well-organized minds, developed through extensive experience with books and conversation with interested and attentive adults. There is no shortcut for children who come without these things. Each RTM student must be read 500 books within the first month of kindergarten, much of it one-to-one.

Entry Requirements: NONE

Exit Requirements

2Y Stage 1: Sentence Pattern and Picture Reading (Entry to 2Y)

- Remember a repeated sentence stem.
- Read the main idea of the picture.
- Say a word that matches the picture.

RTM Independent Reading Level Assessment .00 - .09

Cumulative Record

Student ______________________ Teacher ______________________ Room ________ Date Started ________

RTM Foundational Skills

	Evidence		Pts.
500-Book Kid Background: Have listened to 500+ books read aloud and have a wide background and range of experience with many different kinds of books. (See *500-Book Kid Reading Log.*)		.01	
Active Listening to Read-Aloud: Enjoy being read to in school and at home. Be attentive during group read-aloud.		.01	
Interactive Language: Use language to explore, negotiate, and express ideas, opinions, and feelings.		.01	
Story-Making: Make up a story using the book and "pretend" reading. Demonstrate an obvious understanding of the materials (e.g., laugh at funny parts, comment on the material).		.01	
Text Awareness: When "reading" alone, point to the words and pretend to read them. Know that the printed words are what people read.		.01	
Book Handling: Hold the book correctly—the cover is toward the front and right side up; turn pages from right to left.		.01	
Background Knowledge: Have enough background knowledge to name and talk about pictures common to beginning books.		.01	
Listening Comprehension: Finish the sentence in a predictable book.		.01	
Foundational Skills Total		.08	

Transition to 2Y

RTM Foundational Skills Points							.08	
2Y Transition			**Evidence/Date**				**Points**	
Stage			**Yes** or **No**	Titles	Dates			
1	**Sentence Pattern and Picture Reading**	**Pattern/Picture Integration:** After the first sentence or two of a 2Y book is read aloud, remember it and use the pictures to "read" the rest of the book so that it makes sense. (The "reading" does NOT need to match the words or letters on the page to enter 2Y, but it should make sense given the pictures.)					.01	
2Y Transition Total							**.01**	
Grand Total: Student should transition to 2Y with .09 points (maximum) and demonstrated proficiency at 2Y prerequisites.							**.09**	

2Y Independent Reading Level Overview .10 - .59
Active Reading Strategies

2Y Learning Focus
Active Reading Strategies

Training Wheels
2Y readers do not actually read any words. 2Y readers use the repeated sentence stem, like training wheels, to learn to integrate the three cueing systems: phonics, syntax, and meaning. They learn to read 2Y books proficiently and fluently, sustaining concentration, monitoring comprehension, and when useful, rereading, before actually having to read any individual words.

Key Common Core Standards
Foundational Skills
Stage 1
Use the repeated sentence stem and pictures to read a 2Y book.
Stage 2/CCSF 1c
Understand that words are separated by spaces in print.
Stage 3/CCSF 3a
Demonstrate basic knowledge of one-to-one letter-sound correspondences by producing the primary or most frequent sound for each consonant.

Entry Requirement: Proficiency at St
Stage 1, Sentence Pattern and Picture Rea
- Remember a repeated sentence stem
- Read the main idea of the picture.
- Say a word that matches the picture.

Stage 2, Tracking/One-to-One Corre
- Point to each word while saying one wo page. CCSF 1c.

°Follow pattern
②track progression
help match
sounds to pics.
③

Stage 3, Initial Consonants
- When trying to figure out an unfamiliar word, get mouth into the ready position for (or say the sound of) the initial consonant, and then figure out what would make sense given the context clues. CCSF 3a. Be able to do this with 14 consonants.
- Back up and try again if the word supplied doesn't make sense given the picture (meaning), the initial consonant (phonics), and the sentence pattern (syntax).
- After someone reads the first page or two to the student, read 2Y text with purpose and understanding, proficiently, fluently, sustaining concentration, monitoring comprehension, and when useful, rereading.

Exit Requirements
Must be in place before earning 1G designation.
- Read 25 Power Words at flash speed. CCSF 3c.
- Make the primary or most frequent sound for each consonant. (Minimum 14.) CCSF 3a.
- Read and comprehend unfamiliar 1G text (successfully apply Foundational Skills and Reading Standards). CCSF 4, CCSR 1-3.

2Y Independent Reading Level Assessment .10 - .59

Entry Requirements: Cumulative Record

Student ______________________ Teacher ______________________ Room ________ Date Started ________

Stage			Evidence/Date			Date Completed
			Yes or **No**	Titles	Dates	
1	Sentence Pattern and Picture Reading	**Pattern/Picture Integration:** After the first sentence or two of a 2Y book is read aloud, remember it and use the pictures to "read" the rest of the book so that it makes sense. (The "reading" does NOT need to match the words or letters on the page to enter 2Y, but it should make sense given the pictures.)				
	A reader who is proficient at the above enters 2Y Stage 1 with .10 points.					**.10**
			Yes or **No**	Titles	Dates	
2	Tracking/ One-to-One Correspondence	**Tracking:** Use a finger to point to each word while reading, jumping over the spaces between words. Understand that words are separated by spaces in print. CCSF 1c.				
	A reader who is proficient at all of the above enters 2Y Stage 2 with .11 points.					**.11**
			Yes or **No**	Titles	Dates	
3	Initial Consonants	**Initial Consonant Sounds:** When coming to the one new word on each page of a 2Y book, before scanning the pictures for clues, produce the sound of (or get mouth into the ready position for) the initial consonant. Then scan the picture for the main idea that starts with that letter sound. Say a word that matches both the picture and the initial consonant sound without reminders or other help. Reread to correct, when necessary. (Teachers are watching the mouths and lips of students to see if they are in the correct position for the first letter of the unknown word as they scan the picture for clues.) CCSF 3a.				
	A reader who is proficient at all of the above enters 2Y Stage 3 with .16 points.					**.16**

2Y Entry Requirements: Pattern/Picture Integration Check

Student Must be Stage 1 to Enter 2Y

Text/Picture		Teacher Actions	Unsuccessful Student
The text below is an example. Any 2Y text, including any of the Cold Read Texts, can be used for this entry check.		Teacher hands the student one of the 2Y Cold Read Texts (or any 2Y text). *Will you please read this to me?* If the student can read the first sentence independently, STOP and re-level the student. The student is probably 1G or higher.	
I see the dollar.		If the student can't read the words independently, teacher reads the first sentence to the student, pointing to each word as she reads it. *This says, I see the dollar.*	
I see the frog.		Teacher reads the second sentence to the student, pointing to each word as she reads it. *This says, I see the frog.* *Now you try it. What does the next one say?*	
I see the cat.	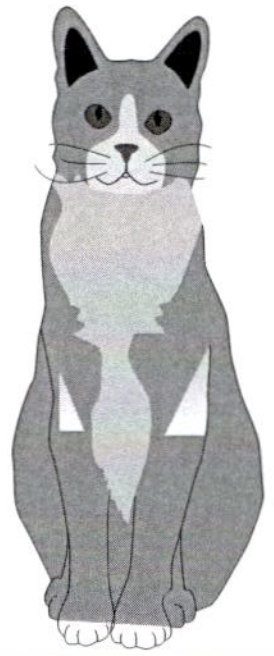	If student says, *I see the (anything reasonable, e.g., cat, kitten, little baby cat, toy, black and white toy, big eyes),* praise him and have him continue. DO NOT CORRECT FOR ANY READING OF INITIAL CONSONANT SOUNDS, WORD ACCURACY, ONE-TO-ONE CORRESPONDENCE, SPEECH, etc. All you want to know is whether or not the student can remember the sentence pattern and come up with a reasonable idea to go with the picture.	If the student is unsuccessful, repeat the first 2 sentences above. *There is a pattern. Can you figure it out?* Stop at this sentence again. *What does this one say?* If student still is unable to figure it out, repeat the first 2 AGAIN, and then read, *I see the cat.* *Now you try it. What does this one say?*
I see the cup.		If the student can successfully remember the pattern and come up with a reasonable idea to go with the picture on each page, the student is 2Y. Use the Cumulative Record to determine in which stage of 2Y the student is currently working. Stage 1 - Pattern/Picture Stage 2 - Tracking Stage 3 - Initial Consonant Sounds	If the student has no idea what to do, stop. The student is RTM and not ready for 2Y. See page 1 for a description of Read-to-Me and ideas for immediate, intensive intervention.

2Y Entry Requirements: Cold Read Text A

That is a blue bicycle.

That is a blue truck.

That is a blue door.

That is a blue motorcycle.

That is a blue flower.

That is a blue car.

Coaching 2Y

Stage 1. *I'll read the first two pages, then you read the rest.*

Stage 2. *Remember to point to each word as you say it.*

Stage 3. *Get your mouth/lips ready to make that first letter sound. What do you see in this picture that starts with that sound?*

Blue All Around
by Kieran Kiley
American Reading Company

2Y Entry Requirements: Cold Read Text B

You can see the wolf.

You can see the eyes.

You can see the teeth.

You can see the paws.

You can see the tongue.

You can see the babies.

Coaching 2Y

Stage 1. *I'll read the first two pages, then you read the rest.*

Stage 2. *Remember to point to each word as you say it.*

Stage 3. *Get your mouth/lips ready to make that first letter sound. What do you see in this picture that starts with that sound?*

Wolves
by Joi Washington
American Reading Company

2Y Entry Requirements: Cold Read Text C

There is ice
on the steps.

There is ice
on the roof.

There is ice
on the plant.

There is ice
on the fence.

There is ice
on the sign.

There is ice
on the bench.

Coaching 2Y

Stage 1. *I'll read the first two pages, then you read the rest.*

Stage 2. *Remember to point to each word as you say it.*

Stage 3. *Get your mouth/lips ready to make that first letter sound. What do you see in this picture that starts with that sound?*

The Ice Storm
by Kieran Kiley
American Reading
Company

2Y Entry Requirements: Cold Read Text D

I see the bat.

I see the wings.

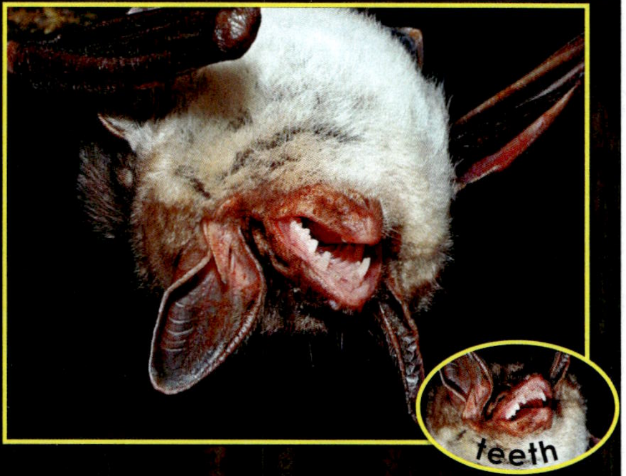

I see the teeth.

I see the bird.

I see the grasshopper.

I see the fruit.

Coaching 2Y

Stage 1. *I'll read the first two pages, then you read the rest.*

Stage 2. *Remember to point to each word as you say it.*

Stage 3. *Get your mouth/lips ready to make that first letter sound. What do you see in this picture that starts with that sound?*

Bats
by Traci Dibble
American Reading Company

2Y Foundational Skills, Stage 1

Pattern and Picture Integration

Stage 1: Sentence Pattern and Active Picture Reading

Teacher

- Read the first page or two of each book aloud until the student is able to remember the repeating sentence ste

Conf. pages for notes

Student

- Use the remembered sentence stem and picture clues to "read" the rest of the book independently (without an
- Find the main idea of the picture and use it to generate an educated guess (speculation) as to what the new wo
- Retain the sentence pattern throughout the book, substituting the one new word in the correct place.

Stage 1 students learn to "read" fluently, sustain concentration, monitor comprehension, and when useful, reread, ... akes sense. Stage 1 students are not responsible for actually reading any of the text accurately.

	Evidence/Date	Date Completed
Engagement: Actively engage in group reading activities with purpose and understanding.		
Independence: Choose to look at books independently.		
Print Concepts: Follow words from left to right, top to bottom, and page by page. CCSF 1a.		
Vocabulary/Background Knowledge: Demonstrate adequate background knowledge to name and talk about the pictures common to beginning books.		
One-to-One Correspondence: Point to objects or pictures and count them, saying one number for each object. (Doesn't have to be able to track words yet.)		
Pattern/Picture Integration: After the first sentence or two of a 2Y book is read aloud, remember it and use the pictures to "read" the rest of the book so that it makes sense. (The "reading" does NOT need to match the words or letters on the page to enter 2Y, but it should make sense given the pictures.)		
Stage 1 Total (Students must have .10 points to begin 2Y).		.10

2Y Foundational Skills, Stage 2

Tracking/Concept of Word/One-to-One Correspondence

CCSF 1c: Understand that words are separated by spaces in print.

In 2Y Stage 2, the students learn to point to one word on the page for each word they say. This is a huge step for many children. From what has been a fluid river of oral language, they must realize that there are individual words. As they say the sentence, they learn to use the spaces to point to one word at a time. 2Y readers are not processing the actual words. They are using the spaces to figure out where the words start and stop. They are still not actually decoding any words or using letter sounds. Children who can't use one-to-one correspondence to count objects will not be ready to track words as they read and should continue working at the Read-to-Me level.

	Evidence/Date	Points	
Points Brought Over From Stage 1		**.10**	
Tracking: Use a finger to point to each word while reading, jumping over the spaces between words. Understand that words are separated by spaces in print. CCSF 1c.		.01	
Self-Correcting: Say one word for each word on the page. Reread to correct for one-to-one correspondence as necessary and without prompting.		.02	
Engagement and Independence: Sustain concentration when reading independently, or with a partner, in 2Y-level materials for at least 30 minutes every day in the classroom (15 minutes per session).		.01	
Home Reading: Have established a home reading habit and read for at least 15 minutes every night or have an in-school substitute for this extra practice time.		.01	
Stage 2 Total (2Y readers must have .15 points to move to Stage 3).		**.15**	

2Y Foundational Skills, Stage 3

Using Initial Letters

CCSF 3a: Demonstrate basic knowledge of one-to-one letter-sound correspondences by producing the primary or most frequent sound for each consonant.

2Y Stage 3 students learn to use the first letter sound of the new word on each page to cross-check their picture reading. When Stage 3 students come to the one new word on each page, they must self-prompt using the first letter sound <u>before</u> they scan the picture for clues. You should see their lips in the "launch position" for the sound, or hear the letter sound, if possible, and then see them look at the picture for a main idea that starts with that sound. Now they are beginning to decode using the letters. Skilled 2Y readers read fluently, using meaning, syntax, and phonics (first letter sound only). They are developing the active reading/thinking habits essential to proficient reading at all levels. Introducing the complexity of vowel sounds at this stage disrupts and slows down the process. As students move through the levels, they will gradually and rapidly integrate the other phonics clues, but always within a context of fluency and meaning-making.

	Evidence/Date	Points	
Points Brought Over From Stage 2		.15	
Phonological Awareness: Isolate and pronounce the initial sound of a spoken word. CCSF 2d.	Consonant picture match no vowels	.05	
Phonics and Word Recognition: Demonstrate basic knowledge of letter-sound correspondences by producing the primary or most frequent sound for most consonants. CCSF 3a.		.05	
Initial Consonant Sounds: When coming to the one new word on each page of a 2Y book, before scanning the pictures for clues, produce the sound of (or get mouth into the ready position for) the initial consonant. Then scan the picture for the main idea that starts with that letter sound. (This is a very physical activity. Teachers are watching the mouths and lips of students to see if they are in the correct position for the first letter of the unknown word as they scan the picture for clues.) CCSF 3a. Be able to do this with 14 consonants.		.05	
Self-Correcting: Say a word that matches both the picture and the initial consonant sound without reminders or other help. Reread to correct, when necessary.		.05	
Print Concepts: Recognize and name most upper- and lowercase letters of the alphabet. CCSF 1d.		.05	

b	c	d	f	g	h	j	k	l	m	n	p	r	s	t	v	w	z

A	B	C	D	E	F	G	H	I	J	K	L	M	N	O	P	Q	R	S	T	U	V	W	X	Y	Z		
a	b	c	d	e	f	g	h	i	j	k	l	m	n	o	p	q	r	s	t	u	v	w	x	y	z		

Stage 3 Total (must be added to Comprehension, below).	**.40**	

2Y Comprehension

Reading Standards for Literature and Informational Text

Most of the comprehension standards below will be demonstrated during Read-Aloud. Although they are developed and scored during all 4 stages of 2Y, do not add them to a student's 2Y score until Stage 3. In order to move to 1G, students must earn .10 Comprehension Points from any combination of the standards below. Although a student may demonstrate proficiency in more than 10 of the standards, only .10 may be earned from this category. Students will continue to work on the same standards in 1G.

With prompting and support

Key Ideas and Details: Basic Understanding Understand, think about, and discuss <u>what</u> the author said.		Evidence/Date	Points	
	Have adequate background knowledge to talk and think about the pictures and ideas common to 2Y books.		**.01**	
	Read actively. Demonstrate an obvious understanding of the materials (e.g., laugh at the funny parts, comment on the material, make personal connections).		**.01**	
CCSR 1	Ask and answer questions about key details of a text. *Who, what, when, where, why...* • *What are some different kinds of animals in this story?* • *Where did the little girl want to go?*		**.01**	
CCSR 2	<u>After Read-Aloud:</u> Retell familiar stories, including key details. • *Retell the story to me. (Prompt for key details of story, if necessary.)*		**.01**	
	Identify the main topic and retell key details of a text. • *What was this mostly about? What were the most important things the author told us?*		**.01**	
CCSR 3	<u>After Read-Aloud:</u> Identify characters, settings, and major events in a story. • *Who were the characters in the story?* • *Where (and when) did it take place?* • *What happened?*		**.01**	
	Describe the connection between two individuals, events, ideas, or pieces of information in a text. • *How are____and____in this book alike (or different)?* • *How are____and____connected?*		**.01**	

Craft and Structure: **Vocabulary, Text Organization, Literary Elements** Understand and discuss the way(s) the author(s) said what was said.			Points	
CCSR 4	**Vocabulary** After Read-Aloud: Ask and answer questions about unknown words in a text. • *Are there any words in this book that you haven't heard before? What do you think they might mean?*		**.01**	
CCSR 5	Recognize common types of texts (e.g., storybooks, poems). • *Is this a story, a poem, or an informational book? Why?*		**.01**	
CCSR 6	Name the author and illustrator of a text and define the role of each in telling the story. • *Who is the author of this book? What does an author do?* • *Who is the illustrator of this book? What does an illustrator do?*		**.01**	
	Evaluate an author's work and support opinion with evidence from the text. • *Show me something you liked about this book.*		**.01**	

Integration of Knowledge and Ideas: Compare/Contrast, Analyze, Synthesize, Evaluate Discuss how the ideas in a book connect to each other and to the larger world.				
	Make predictions based on title, cover, illustrations, and text. • *Looking at the cover, what do you think this book might be about? Why?*		.01	
	Make text-to-self connections. • *What in this book reminds you of something in your own life?*		.01	
CCSR 7	Describe the relationship between illustrations and the text in which they appear (e.g., what person, place, idea, or moment in a story an illustration depicts). • *What can you learn about____from the pictures in this book?*		.01	
CCSR 8	<u>After Read-Aloud:</u> Identify the reasons an author gives to support points in a text. • *The author is telling us that_______. What reasons does he give to convince us?*		.01	
CCSR 9	Compare and contrast the adventures and experiences of characters in familiar stories. • *What happened to____ in this story?* • *What happened to____ in this story (or another story)?* • *How were their experiences the same? How were they different?*		.01	
	Identify basic similarities in and differences between two texts on the same topic (e.g., in illustrations, descriptions, or procedures). Give students 2 books on the same topic. • *How are they alike? How are they different? Which do you like better and why?*		.01	
2Y Comprehension Total (Maximum of .10)			**.10**	
2Y Foundational Skills Total			**.40**	
Stage 3 Total			**.50**	

2Y Running Record

Stage:________

Student ____________ Teacher____________ Grade______ Room______ Date________

Title:____________	**Error/Miscue Analysis**		
	Not in Background Knowledge	Needs work on this initial letter sound	Needs to learn this Power Word

Was able to self-prompt

	Yes	No		Yes	No
b	☐	☐	**m**	☐	☐
c	☐	☐	**n**	☐	☐
d	☐	☐	**p**	☐	☐
f	☐	☐	**r**	☐	☐
g	☐	☐	**s**	☐	☐
h	☐	☐	**t**	☐	☐
j	☐	☐	**v**	☐	☐
k	☐	☐	**w**	☐	☐
l	☐	☐	**z**	☐	☐

Active Reading

- ☐ Use title or first page (read by coach) to figure out the rest of the book.
- ☐ Use picture clues to figure out the one new word on each page.
- ☐ Have most of the words in the book in his or her speaking vocabulary.
- ☐ Can point to each word as she reads (voice-print match).
- ☐ Get ready to read the new word on each page by putting mouth into first letter position or by making the sound of the first letter.
- ☐ Take time to check that the new word fits both the picture and the first letter.

Power Goal

Power Word Bank

Was able to read the following words without contextual support:

Transition to 1G: Power Words

In 1G, the training wheels come off. 1G books no longer have one repeated sentence stem. 1G readers will substitute automatic recognition of the most frequently used words (Power Words) for the support previously provided by the repeated sentence stems. Power Words provide "islands of certainty" from which 1G readers use their 2Y active reading strategies to navigate the unknown. Before they move to 1G, students must recognize at least 25 of these Power Words quickly and easily, outside of the context of the memorized 2Y text. Young brains must learn how to store and retrieve visual images (right hemisphere) that are associated with oral language/naming (left hemisphere). For many students, this requires drill and practice, not just repeated reading. Some students find this exceedingly difficult and will need skilled coaching and extensive additional support—immediately—to prevent frustration and delay. **CCSF 3c:** Read (at least 25) high-frequency words by sight (e.g., *the, of, to, you, she, my, is, do*).

Points Brought Over From Stage 3							**.50**	
Power Words: Read at least 25 high-frequency words by sight. CCSF 3c.					**Date**	**# Words**	.09	

Given an unfamiliar 1G text (Cold Read) and no help of any kind:

Successfully Read and Comprehend 1G Text
Use a combination of initial sounds, sight words, and context clues to read 1G text with purpose and understanding. A transitional 1G reader may be working out the words, rather than reading fluently; however, she is insistent that what she reads make sense, stopping and trying again if something doesn't look right, sound right, or make sense. CCSF 4

1G Transition Points (Students should transition to 1G with .59 and demonstrated proficiency at 1G prerequisites.)	**.59**	

1G Independent Reading Level Overview .60 - .99
Power Words

1G Learning Focus
Power Words
1G readers will know and use 25-85 very high-frequency sight words as a reliable and familiar support framework when reading. They will be able to read these words in books they have never seen before and out of context (lists, flash cards, etc.) at Flash Speed. Power Words provide "islands of certainty" from which emergent readers can navigate the unknown. Although there are other skills involved with success at 1G, the acquisition of a bank of sight words is fundamental. They will use these words at the Blue levels as a foundation for learning the basic vowel patterns.

Key Common Core Standards
Foundational Skills
3c. Read common high-frequency words by sight (*the, of, to, you, she, my, is, are, do*).

Power Words
The 60 Power Words on the back of the 1G Skills Card are the highest-frequency sight words. These words make up more than one-third of the words used in English text. (The combined sight words in 1G and 2G make up 50% of all adult and student writing.)

Entry Requirements
Must be in place before earning 1G designation.

- Read 25 Power Words at Flash Speed. CCSF 3c.
- Make the primary or most frequent sound for each consonant. (Minimum 14.) CCSF 3a.
- Read and comprehend unfamiliar 1G text (successfully apply Foundational Skills and Reading Standards). CCSF 4, CCSR 1-3.

Exit Requirements
M[illegible]ing 2G designation.

- [illegible] Speed. CCSF 3g.
- [illegible]ants, blends, and digraphs. CCSF 3a.
- [illegible]iliar 2G text (successfully apply [illegible]ng Standards). CCSF4, CCSR 1-3.

Exit matches entry of next level

1G Independent Reading Level Assessment .60 - .99

Entry Requirements: Cumulative Record

Student ______________ Teacher ______________ Room ______ Date Started ______

<table>
<tr><td></td><td></td><td colspan="7">Evidence/Date</td><td>Date Completed</td></tr>
<tr><td rowspan="2">Word Recognition</td><td rowspan="2">Know 25 Power Words at Flash Speed
Read at least 25 high-frequency words by sight (out of context). CCSF 3c.</td><td rowspan="2">See Power Words Check on page 23. Minimum score of 25.</td><td colspan="3">Scores</td><td colspan="3">Dates</td><td rowspan="2"></td></tr>
<tr><td colspan="3"></td><td colspan="3"></td></tr>
<tr><td rowspan="6">Phonics</td><td rowspan="6">Make the Primary or Most-Frequent Sound for Each Consonant.
When trying to figure out an unfamiliar word, get mouth into the ready position for, or say the sound of, the initial consonant, then figure out what would make sense given the context clues, self-correcting when necessary. CCSF 3a.</td><td rowspan="6">Can get mouth ready to make the sound for a minimum of 14 consonants.</td><td>b</td><td>c</td><td>d</td><td>f</td><td>g</td><td>h</td><td rowspan="6"></td></tr>
<tr><td></td><td></td><td></td><td></td><td></td><td></td></tr>
<tr><td>j</td><td>k</td><td>l</td><td>m</td><td>n</td><td>p</td></tr>
<tr><td></td><td></td><td></td><td></td><td></td><td></td></tr>
<tr><td>r</td><td>s</td><td>t</td><td>v</td><td>w</td><td>z</td></tr>
<tr><td></td><td></td><td></td><td></td><td></td><td></td></tr>
<tr><td rowspan="2">Comprehension</td><td rowspan="2">Read and Comprehend 1G Text
Apply Foundational Skills (Word-Solving)
Use a combination of initial sounds, sight words, and context clues to read 1G text with purpose and understanding. A transitional 1G reader may be working out the words, rather than reading fluently; however, she is insistent that what she reads make sense, stopping and trying again if something doesn't look right, sound right, or make sense. CCSF 4

Apply Reading Standards (Comprehension)
Determine what a 1G text says explicitly and make logical inferences from it. CCSR 1-3.</td><td rowspan="2">See Cold Read Record on page 24. Minimum score of 6 on one Cold Read Text.</td><td colspan="2">Scores</td><td colspan="3">Titles</td><td>Dates</td><td rowspan="2"></td></tr>
<tr><td colspan="2"></td><td colspan="3"></td><td></td></tr>
<tr><td colspan="9">A reader who is proficient at all of the above enters 1G with .60 points.</td><td>.60</td></tr>
</table>

1G Entry Requirements: Power Words Check

To begin 1G, know 25 of these words at Flash Speed. By the end of 1G, know ALL 60 words.

Student													Dates		
a				get				lots				this			
all				go				love				to			
am				had				me				up			
an				has				my				want			
and				have				no				was			
are				he				of				we			
at				here				on				went			
be				I				one				what			
big				in				said				where			
can				is				see				who			
can't				it				she				why			
come				like				that				will			
do				little				the				with			
down				live				there				yes			
for				look				they				you			
												Totals			

Common Core Standard Foundational Skills 3c: Read common high-frequency words by sight.

1G Entry Requirements: Cold Read Record

Title:____________________ Date:____________

Given an unfamiliar 1G text (Cold Read), and NO help of any kind:

Running Record Record all errors as the student reads the passage. Indicate self-corrections.	Error/Miscue Analysis		
	Needs work on this initial letter sound	Needs to learn this Power Word	Not in background knowledge

Apply Foundational Skills

Active Reading Strategies	Yes or No
Read with purpose and understanding. Stop and try again if something doesn't look right, sound right, or make sense. Self-correct ALL errors that interfere with meaning. (Example: In most contexts, reading "like" for "love" doesn't change the meaning and still matches the initial letter sound, while reading "little" for "love" would not make sense.)	

If the answer to the above question is No, STOP and move student to an easier level.
If the answer is Yes, continue on to Reading Standards. (See specific questions on Cold Read Text Pages.)

Apply Reading Standards

Comprehension	Student Response	Score Weak.........Strong
Basic Understanding Support basic understanding with evidence from the text. CCSR 1.		1 2 3 4
Interpretation Support an interpretation or analysis with evidence from the text. CCSR 2 & 3.		1 2 3 4
Total Points (A minimum score of 6 is required in order to enter 1G.)		

1G Entry Requirements: Cold Read Text A

Let Me In by
Marilyn Pitt and Jane Hileman
American Reading Company

I want to come in.

Are you there? Le

If move through
1G successfully
have them pull
more for practice

come in. I want

There you are. Do you want to come in?

I want to go out. Let me out.

Word Solving

"Let" and "out" are not Power Words. Students who understand what they are reading will be able to figure these words out using the initial sound, picture clues, and syntax.

1G Power Words

I want to come in are you there me do go

Basic Understanding

What happened in this story?

Interpretation

Why is this funny?

1G Entry Requirements: Cold Read Text B

My Babies by
Marilyn Pitt and Jane Hileman
American Reading Company

This is my baby.
This is my little baby.

I love you.
I love you, little baby.

Go to sleep.
Go to sleep, little baby.

Do you want to be my baby?
You can be my baby.

This is my baby.
This is my little baby.

Word Solving

"Baby" is not a Power Word. Students who understand what they are reading will be able to figure out this word (and any other words they don't yet know) using the initial sound, picture clues, and syntax.

1G Power Words

this is my little I love you go to do want to be can

Basic Understanding

What happened in this story?

Interpretation

Why is this funny?

1G Entry Requirements: Cold Read Text C

Colors

The wolf can look like this.

The wolf can look like that.

Camouflage

There are wolves on the rocks.

This wolf is in the trees.

There are wolves in the grass.

Here are wolves in the snow.

The Gray Wolf
by Trace Taylor
American Reading Company

1G

1G Power Words

the can look like this that
there are on is in here

Basic Understanding

Tell me three things the text says about wolves.

Interpretation

Why do you think that some wolves look different from others?

1G Entry Requirements: Cold Read Text D

Wolf Spiders by Michelle Lynch
American Reading Company

This is a wolf.

This is a wolf spider.

Wolf spiders can live here.

They can live here.

Wolf spiders look like where they live.

They look like the rocks.

They look like the sticks.

They look like the flower.

Word Solving

"Wolf," "spider," and "rocks" are not Power Words. Students who understand what they are reading will be able to figure out these words using the initial sound, picture clues, and syntax.

1G Power Words

this is a can live here they look like where the

Basic Understanding

Tell me three things the text says about wolf spiders.

Interpretation

Do you think wolf spiders are good hunters? How do you know?

1G Comprehension

Reading Standards for Literature and Informational Text

Many of the comprehension standards below will be demonstrated during Read-Aloud, since few 1G books are complicated enough to have a narrative structure. In order to move to 2G, students must earn .10 Comprehension Points from any combination of the standards below.

With prompting and support:

	Key Ideas and Details: Using Text Evidence to Support Conclusions Understand, think about, and discuss what the author said.	Evidence/Date	Points	
	Have adequate background knowledge to talk and think about the pictures and ideas common to 1G books.		.01	
	Read actively. Demonstrate an obvious understanding of the materials (e.g., laugh at the funny parts, comment on the material, make personal connections).		.01	
	Make predictions based on title, cover, illustrations, and text. • *Looking at the cover, what do you think this book might be about? Why?*		.01	
	Make text-to-self connections. • *What in this book reminds you of something in your own life?*		.01	
CCSR 1	Ask and answer questions about key details of a text. *Who, what, when, where, why...* • *What are some different kinds of animals in this story?* • *Where did the little girl want to go?*		.01	
CCSR 2	After Read-Aloud: Retell familiar stories, including key details. • *Retell the story to me.* (Prompt for key details of story, if necessary.)		.01	
	Identify the main topic and retell key details of a text. • *What was this mostly about?* • *What were the most important things the author told us?*		.01	
CCSR 3	After Read-Aloud: Identify characters, settings, and major events in a story. • *Who were the characters in the story?* • *Where (and when) did it take place?* • *What happened?*		.01	
	Describe the connection between two individuals, events, ideas, or pieces of information in a text. • *How are ____ and ____ in this book alike (or different)?* • *How are ____ and ____ connected?*		.01	

Craft and Structure: Analyzing the Effects of Authors' Choices

Understand and discuss the way(s) the author(s) said what was said.

CCSR 4	**Vocabulary** After Read-Aloud: Ask and answer questions about unknown words in a text. • *Are there any words in this book that you haven't heard before? What do you think they might mean?*		**.01**	
CCSR 5	Recognize common types of texts (e.g., storybooks, poems). • *Is this a story, a poem, or an informational book?*		**.01**	
CCSR 6	Name the author and illustrator of a story or informational text and define the role of each in telling the story (or creating the book). • *Who is the author of this book? What does an author do?* • *Who is the illustrator of this book? What does an illustrator do?*		**.01**	
	Evaluate an author's work and support opinion with evidence from the text. • *Show me something you liked about this book.*		**.01**	

Integration of Knowledge and Ideas: Comparing Different Presentations

Discuss how the ideas in a book connect to each other and to the larger world.

CCSR 7	Describe the relationship between illustrations and the text in which they appear (e.g., what person, place, idea, or moment in a story an illustration depicts). • *What can you learn about ____ from the pictures in this book?*		**.01**	
CCSR 8	<u>After Read-Aloud:</u> Identify the reasons an author gives to support points in a text. • *The author is telling us that* ______ (teacher supplies this).*What reasons does he give to convince us?*		**.01**	
CCSR 9	<u>After Read-Aloud:</u> Compare and contrast the adventures and experiences of characters in familiar stories. • *What happened to ____ in this story?* • *What happened to ____ in this story (or another story)?* • *How were their experiences the same? How were they different?*		**.01**	
	Identify basic similarities in and differences between two texts on the same topic (e.g., in illustrations, descriptions, or procedures). Give student 2 books on same topic. • *How are they alike? How are they different? Which do you like better and why?*		**.01**	
1G Comprehension Total (Maximum of .10)			**.10**	

1G Foundational Skills

Range of Reading and Level of Text Complexity	Evidence/Date	Points	
Engagement and Independence Read regularly and independently, or with a partner, sustaining engagement in 1G level text for at least 30 minutes every day in the classroom (15 minutes per session).		.01	
Actively engage in group reading activities with purpose and understanding. CCSR 10.		✓	
Home Reading Have established a home reading habit and read for at least 30 minutes every night or has extra time in school to make it up.		.01	
Range of Reading and Level of Text Complexity Total		.02	

Print Concepts

Recognize and name **<u>all</u>** upper- and lower-case letters of the alphabet. CCSF 1d.																										✓	
A	B	C	D	E	F	G	H	I	J	K	L	M	N	O	P	Q	R	S	T	U	V	W	X	Y	Z		
a	b	c	d	e	f	g	h	i	j	k	l	m	n	o	p	q	r	s	t	u	v	w	x	y	z		
Recognize that spoken words are represented in written language by specific sequences of letters. CCSF 1b.																										✓	
Print Concepts Total																										.00	

Phonological Awareness

Orally produce groups of words that start with the same initial sound.		.01	
The following kindergarten standards are **not essential** for successful reading in either 1G or 2G, so **they are not scored or required here**. However, they will be essential at the Blue levels, so they should be taught and practiced now in preparation for application to reading at 1B.			
Recognize and produce rhyming words (orally only). CCSF 2a. *Give me some words that rhyme with:*			
Count, pronounce, blend, and segment syllables in spoken words. CCSF 2b.			
Blend and segment onsets and rimes of single-syllable spoken words. (/g/ - /oat/, /bl/- /ack/). CCSF 2c.			
Isolate and pronounce the initial, medial vowel, and final sounds (phonemes) in three-phoneme (CVC) words (e.g., /save/, /ham/). CCSF 2d.			
Add or substitute individual sounds (phonemes) in simple, one-syllable words to make new words (e.g., "at" → /sat/ → /mat/ → /map/). CCSF 2e.			
Phonological Awareness Total		**.01**	**.01**

cat	make	it	fun	book

Phonics

Initial Consonants: Use initial consonant sounds when reading.			
Demonstrate basic knowledge of one-to-one letter-sound correspondences by producing the primary or most frequent sound for each consonant. CCS 3a.		✓	
Say a word that matches both the picture and the initial consonant sound without reminders or other help. Reread to correct when necessary.		✓	
Associate the long and short sounds with common spellings (graphemes) for the five major vowels. CCSF 3b. (Will need for 1B, but not for Green levels.)			
Phonics Total		**.00**	**.00**

b	c	c	d	f	g	g	h	j	k	l	m	n	p	q	r	s	t	v	w	z

1G Foundational Skills Cont'd

Word Recognition

Word Recognition	Evidence/Date		
Power Words: Use bank of Power Words when reading.			
Read at least 25 high-frequency words by sight (e.g., *the, of, to, you, she, my, is, are, do*). CCSF 3c. (Ready to begin 1G.)		✓	
Read at least 60 high-frequency words by sight. CCSF 3c.		.10	
Word Recognition Total		**.10**	

Fluency

When handed a book at the 1G level that s/he has never seen before, be able to read it with sufficient accuracy and fluency to enable good comprehension without any help.			
Fluency Read unfamiliar 1G level text independently, sustaining concentration, monitoring comprehension, with 95-100% word accuracy, and when useful, rereading.		.03	
Monitor Comprehension • Notice, stop reading, and use repair strategies when something doesn't look right, sound right, or make sense. • When stuck, back up and try again. • When stuck, continue reading and come back to correct after gaining more information.		.03	
Fluency Total		**.06**	
1G Foundational Skills Total		**.20**	

1G Running Record

Student ______________ Teacher ______________ Grade______ Room________ Date______________

Title:______________	Error/Miscue Analysis		
	Needs work on this initial letter sound	Needs to learn this Power Word	Not in background knowledge

Was able to self-prompt

	Yes	No		Yes	No
b	☐	☐	n	☐	☐
c	☐	☐	p	☐	☐
d	☐	☐	r	☐	☐
f	☐	☐	s	☐	☐
g	☐	☐	t	☐	☐
h	☐	☐	v	☐	☐
j	☐	☐	w	☐	☐
k	☐	☐	y	☐	☐
l	☐	☐	z	☐	☐
m	☐	☐			

Active Reading

- ☐ Have automatic recall of Power Words and read them in context.
- ☐ Use picture clues to figure out unfamiliar words.
- ☐ Self-prompt a new word by putting mouth into first letter position or by making the sound of the first letter.
- ☐ Have most of the words in the book in his or her speaking vocabulary.
- ☐ Stop and try again if something doesn't look right, sound right, or make sense. Self-correct ALL errors that interfere with meaning.
- ☐ Can point to each word as he or she reads.
- ☐ Determine what a text says explicitly and makes logical inferences from it. (*What is this about so far? How do you know? Why...?*)

Power Words

a	get	lots	this
all	go	love	to
am	had	me	up
an	has	my	want
and	have	no	was
are	he	of	we
at	here	on	went
be	I	one	what
big	in	said	where
can	is	see	who
can't	it	she	why
come	like	that	will
do	little	the	with
down	live	there	yes
for	look	they	you

Power Goal

Transition to 2G

1G Entry Points	.60	
1G Foundational Skills Points	.17	
1G Comprehension Points	.10	

<table>
<tr><th colspan="2">2G Transition Points. With NO help of any kind, student must demonstrate ability to:</th><th colspan="2">Evidence/Date</th><th>Points</th><th></th></tr>
<tr><td>Word Recognition</td><td>Read 2G Power Words
Recognize and read grade-appropriate irregularly spelled words (were, could, would, does, some). CCSF3g.</td><td>See Power Words Check on page 39. Minimum score of 25.</td><td>Scores | Dates</td><td></td><td></td></tr>
<tr><td>Phonics</td><td>Self-Prompt for Initial Blends and Digraphs
Know the spelling-sound correspondences for common consonant digraphs (sh–, ch–, th–, wh–). CCSF3a.</td><td>Can make the initial sound for a minimum of 13 blends/digraphs.</td><td>br cr dr fr gr pr tr wr bl
cl fl gl pl sl sc sk sm sn
sp st sw tw ch sh th wh</td><td></td><td></td></tr>
<tr><td>Comprehension</td><td>Read and Comprehend Unfamiliar 2G Text
Apply Foundational Skills (Word-Solving)
Use a combination of initial sounds/blends, sight words, and context clues to read 2G text with purpose and understanding. A transitional 2G reader may be working out the words, rather than reading fluently; however, she is insistent that what she reads make sense, stopping and trying again if something doesn't look right, sound right, or make sense. CCSF 4
Apply Reading Standards (Comprehension)
Determine what a text says explicitly and make logical inferences from it. CCSR 1-3.</td><td>See Cold Read Record on page 40. Minimum score of 6 on one cold Read Text.</td><td>Scores | Titles | Dates</td><td></td><td></td></tr>
<tr><td colspan="4">2G Transition Points</td><td>.12</td><td></td></tr>
<tr><td colspan="4">GRAND TOTAL: Student should transition to 2B with .99 points and demonstrated proficiency at 2g prerequisites.</td><td>.99</td><td></td></tr>
</table>

2G Independent Reading Level Overview 1.00 - 1.29
Accumulating 120 Power Words. Initial Blends & Digraphs.

2G Learning Focus
Power Words, Initial Blends & Digraphs

Power Words: 2G readers will know and use 120 very high-frequency Power Words as a reliable and familiar support framework when reading. They will be able to read these words in books they have never seen before and out of context (lists, flash cards, etc.) at Flash Speed. Power Words provide "islands of certainty" from which emergent readers can navigate the unknown. The combined Power Words in G and GG make up 50% of all adult and student writing.

Initial Blends & Digraphs: When students come to a word they don't know, they will successfully use initial blends and digraphs as clues.

Key Common Core Standards

Foundational Skills

3g. Recognize and read grade-appropriate irregularly spelled words (*were, could, would, does, some*).

3a. Know the spelling-sound correspondences for common consonant digraphs (*sh–, ch–, th–, wh–*).

Entry Requirements

Must be in place before earning 2G designation.

- Read 85 Power Words at Flash Speed. CCSF 3g.
- Self-prompt for initial consonants, blends, and digraphs. CCSF 3a.
- Read and comprehend unfamiliar 2G text (successfully apply Foundational Skills and Reading Standards). CCSF4, CCSR 1-3.

Exit Requirements

Must be in place before earning 1B designation.

- Manipulate onsets and rimes. CCSF 2ce (K).
- Decode most one-syllable words. CCSF 3abc.
- Read 1B tricky words. CCSF 3g.
- Read and comprehend unfamiliar 1B text (successfully apply Foundational Skills and Reading Standards). CCSF4, CCSR 1-3.

2G Independent Reading Level Assessment 1.00 - 1.29

Entry Requirements: Cumulative Record

Student ______________________ Teacher ______________________ Room ________ Date Started ________

2G Entry Requirements

<table>
<tr><th></th><th></th><th colspan="10">Evidence/Date</th><th>Date Completed</th></tr>
<tr><td rowspan="2">Word Recognition</td><td rowspan="2">Read 2G Power Words
Recognize and read grade-appropriate irregularly spelled words (were, could, would, does, some). CCSF3g.</td><td rowspan="2">See Power Words Check on page 39. Minimum score of 25.</td><td colspan="5">Scores</td><td colspan="4">Dates</td><td rowspan="2"></td></tr>
<tr><td colspan="5"></td><td colspan="4"></td></tr>
<tr><td rowspan="6">Phonics</td><td rowspan="6">Self-Prompt for Initial Blends and Digraphs
Know the spelling-sound correspondences for common consonant digraphs (sh–, ch–, th–, wh–). CCSF3a.</td><td rowspan="6">Can make the initial sound for a minimum of 13 blends/ digraphs.</td><td>br</td><td>cr</td><td>dr</td><td>fr</td><td>gr</td><td>pr</td><td>tr</td><td>wr</td><td>bl</td><td rowspan="6"></td></tr>
<tr><td></td><td></td><td></td><td></td><td></td><td></td><td></td><td></td><td></td></tr>
<tr><td>cl</td><td>fl</td><td>gl</td><td>pl</td><td>sl</td><td>sc</td><td>sk</td><td>sm</td><td>sn</td></tr>
<tr><td></td><td></td><td></td><td></td><td></td><td></td><td></td><td></td><td></td></tr>
<tr><td>sp</td><td>st</td><td>sw</td><td>tw</td><td>ch</td><td>sh</td><td>th</td><td>wh</td><td></td></tr>
<tr><td></td><td></td><td></td><td></td><td></td><td></td><td></td><td></td><td></td></tr>
<tr><td rowspan="2">Comprehension</td><td rowspan="2">Read and Comprehend Unfamiliar 2G Text
Apply Foundational Skills (Word-Solving)
Use a combination of initial sounds/blends, sight words, and context clues to read 2G text with purpose and understanding. A transitional 2G reader may be working out the words, rather than reading fluently; however, she is insistent that what she reads make sense, stopping and trying again if something doesn't look right, sound right, or make sense. CCSF 4
Apply Reading Standards (Comprehension)
Determine what a text says explicitly and make logical inferences from it. CCSR 1-3.</td><td rowspan="2">See Cold Read Record on page 40. Minimum score of 6 on one cold Read Text.</td><td colspan="3">Scores</td><td colspan="4">Titles</td><td colspan="2">Dates</td><td rowspan="2"></td></tr>
<tr><td colspan="3"></td><td colspan="4"></td><td colspan="2"></td></tr>
<tr><td colspan="12">A reader who is proficient at all of the above enters 2G with 1.00 points.</td><td>1.00</td></tr>
</table>

2G Entry Requirements: Power Words Check

To begin 2G, know 25 of these words at Flash Speed. By the end of 2G, know ALL 60 words.

Name:												Dates			
about				fun				if				put			
animal				gave				into				ran			
as				girl				jump				saw			
be				give				make				says			
beside				goes				many				some			
boy				going				new				stop			
but				good				not				take			
by				got				now				then			
came				happy				off				these			
could				her				oh				too			
day				him				or				under			
did				his				our				were			
does				home				out				when			
eat				house				over				would			
from				how				play				your			
												Totals			

Common Core Standard Foundational Skills 3g: Read common high-frequency words by sight.

2G Entry Requirements: Cold Read Record

Title:______________________ Date:______________

Given an unfamiliar 2G text (Cold Read), and NO help of any kind:

Running Record Record all errors as the student reads the passage. Indicate self-corrections.	**Error/Miscue Analysis** Needs work on this initial blend/digraph	Needs to learn this Power Word	Not in background knowledge

Apply Foundational Skills

Active Reading Strategies	**Yes** or **No**
Read with purpose and understanding. Stop and try again if something doesn't look right, sound right, or make sense. Self-correct ALL errors that interfere with meaning. (Example: In most contexts, reading "like" for "love" doesn't change the meaning and still matches the initial letter sound, while reading "little" for "love" would not make sense.)	

If the answer to the above question is No, STOP and move student to an easier level.
If the answer is Yes, continue on to Reading Standards. (See specific questions on Cold Read Text Pages.)

Apply Reading Standards

Comprehension	**Student Response**	**Score** Weak.........Strong
Basic Understanding Support basic understanding with evidence from the text. CCSR 1.		1 2 3 4
Interpretation Support an interpretation or analysis with evidence from the text. CCSR 2 & 3.		1 2 3 4
Total Points (A minimum score of 6 is required in order to enter 2G.)		

2G Entry Requirements: Cold Read Text A

Let's Eat by Jane Hileman and Marilyn Pitt American Reading Company

2G

1G/2G Power Words

come have some I don't want it how many do you no a big not now here's of what for me to eat

Word Solving

For all other words, students should make the sound of the initial letter or blend/digraph, then look at the picture for something that makes sense.

Basic Understanding

What happened in this story?

Interpretation

How do you think the dad feels at the end of the story? How do you know?

2G Entry Requirements: Cold Read Text B

Camping
by Jane Hileman
American Reading Company

1G/2G Power Words

put up the come we'll then we can play in it now here the are and what

Word Solving

For all other words, students should make the sound of the initial letter or blend/digraph, then look at the picture for something that makes sense.

Basic Understanding

What happened in this story?

Interpretation

Why did the children go inside? How do you know?

2G Entry Requirements: Cold Read Text C

Soccer
by Trace Taylor
American Reading Company

1G/2G Power Words

this is a too many girls play boys they in the with no some

Word Solving
For all other words, students should make the sound of the initial letter or blend/digraph, then look at the picture for something that makes sense.

Basic Understanding
Tell me three things the text says about soccer.

Interpretation
How do people play soccer differently depending on where they live? How do you know?

This is a soccer ball.

This is a soccer ball, too.

Many girls play soccer.

Many boys play soccer, too.

They play soccer in the grass.

They play it in the mud.

Some play with no shoes.

Some play with shoes.

2G Entry Requirements: Cold Read Text D

This is an eagle.

The eagle loves to eat fish.

It can see a fish under the water.

Here are its claws.

Its claws are big and black.

The eagle will get the fish with its claws.

Bald Eagles
by Jayson Fleischer
American Reading Company

1G/2G Power Words

this is an they love to eat it can see a under the here are its big and black will get with

Word Solving

For all other words, students should make the sound of the initial letter or blend/digraph, then look at the picture for something that makes sense.

Basic Understanding

Tell me three things this text says about eagles.

Interpretation

What body parts are the most important for the bald eagle? Why?

2G Comprehension

Reading Standards for Literature and Informational Text

Many of the comprehension standards below will be demonstrated during Read-Aloud, since few 2G books are complicated enough to have a narrative structure. In order to move to 1B, .10 Comprehension Points must be earned from any combination of the standards below.

Key Ideas and Details: **Using Text Evidence to Support Conclusions** Understand, think about, and discuss what the author said.		Evidence/Date	Points	
	Demonstrate adequate background knowledge to name and talk about the pictures and ideas common to 2G books. Students who do not know basic vocabulary need extensive read-aloud and real-life experiences to be successful 2G readers.		.01	
	Demonstrate an obvious understanding of the materials (e.g., laugh at the funny parts, comment on the material, make personal connections). Read actively, making comments and connections without prompting.		.01	
CCSR 1	Ask and answer questions about key details in a text. • *What were some different kinds of animals in this story?* • *Where did the little girl want to go?*		.01	
CCSR 2	After Read-Aloud: Retell stories in correct sequence, including key details, and demonstrate understanding of their central message or lesson. • *Retell the story to me.* (Prompt for key details as necessary.) • *What was the lesson of this story?*		.01	
	Identify the main topic and retell key details of a text. • *What was this book mostly about?* • *What were the most important things the author told us?*		.01	
	Evaluate an author's work and support opinion with evidence from text. • *Show me something you liked about this book.*		.01	
CCSR 3	After Read-Aloud: Describe characters, settings, and major events in a story using key details.		.01	
	Describe the connection between two individuals, events, ideas, or pieces of information in a text. • *How are _______ and ______ in this book alike (or different)?* • *How are _______ and ______ in this book connected?*		.01	

Craft and Structure: Analyzing the Effects of Authors' Choices Understand and discuss the way(s) the author(s) said what was said.				
CCSR 4	Identify words and phrases in stories or poems that suggest feelings or appeal to the senses. • *What word tells how ____ feels (smells, tastes, etc.)?*		.01	
	After Read-Aloud: Ask and answer questions to help determine or clarify the meaning of words and phrases in a text. • *Is there a word in this book that you never heard before? What do you think it means?*		.01	
CCSR 5	Explain major differences between books that tell stories and books that give information, drawing on a wide reading of a range of text types. Give student a pile of books: • *Which of these books are informational?* • *Which tell stories?* • *How do you know which is which?*		.01	
	After Read-Aloud: Know and use various text features (headings, tables of contents, glossaries, electronic menus, icons) to locate key facts or information in a text.		.01	
CCSR 6	After Read-Aloud: Identify who is telling the story at various points in a text.		.01	
	Distinguish between information provided by pictures or other illustrations and information provided by the words in a text. • *What can you learn about ____ from the pictures in this book?*		.01	

Integration of Knowledge and Ideas: **Comparing Different Presentations**

Discuss how the ideas in a book connect to each other and to the larger world.

CCSR 7	After Read-Aloud: Use illustrations and details in a story to describe its characters, setting, or events. • *Tell me everything you know about _____.*		**.01**	
CCSR 7	Use the illustrations and details in a text to describe its key ideas. • *Looking at the picture, what is this page mainly about?*		**.01**	
CCSR 8	After Read-Aloud: Identify the reasons an author gives to support points in a text. • *The author is telling us that* _____(teacher supplies this). • *What reasons does he give to convince us?*		**.01**	
CCSR 9	Identify basic similarities in and differences between two texts on the same topic (e.g., in illustrations, descriptions, or procedures). Give student two books on same topic: • *How are these two books alike? How are they different?* • *Which do you like better? Why?*		**.01**	
CCSR 9	After Read-Aloud: Compare and contrast the adventures and experiences of characters in stories. • *What happened to ______ in this story?* • *What happened to ______ in this story (or another story)?* • *How were their experiences the same? How were they different?*		**.01**	
2G Comprehension Total (Maximum of .10)			**.10**	

2G Foundational Skills

Range of Reading and Level of Text Complexity	Evidence/Date	Points	
Engagement and Independence Read regularly and independently, or with a partner, sustaining engagement in 2G-level materials for at least 30 minutes (15 minutes per session) every day in the classroom.		.01	
Home Reading Have established a home reading habit and read for at least 30 minutes every night, or make up the extra reading time in school.			
Genres Enjoy both informational and literary text at 2G level. CCSR 10. Informational [ ] Literary [ ]		✓	
Range of Reading and Level of Text Complexity Total		.01	

Print Concepts

Sentences Recognize and respond to punctuation (commas, periods, question marks) while reading. CCSF 1a.		.01	
Print Concepts Total		.01	

Phonics

Initial Consonant Blends & Digraphs: Use <u>all</u> initial consonant blends and digraphs as clues to unfamiliar words without prompting. When they come to an unfamiliar word, students should automatically say the sound of the blends or digraphs while they look for meaning clues. Do not have them sound out the rest of the word.

- Know the spelling-sound correspondences for common consonant digraphs (*wr, sh*). CCSF 3a.
- <u>Student should be able to tell you the sounds for each of these:</u>

br	cr	dr	fr	gr	pr	tr	wr	bl	cl	fl	gl	pl	sl	sc	sk	sm	sn	sp	st	sw	tw	ch	sh	th	wh

Points: .01

Phonics Total .01

Word Recognition

Power Words Recognize and read high-frequency words by sight. CCSF 3g. Student can read ALL 2G Power Words at Flash Speed.		.02	
Know the following category words by sight: colors (*red, blue…*), numbers (*one, two…*), family members (*mom, brother…*), days of the week (*Monday, Tuesday…*), shapes (*circle, square…*), prepositions (*over, under, around…*). Student can read the 2G Category Words at Flash Speed.		.01	
Word Recognition Total		.03	

Vocabulary

Use and explain common antonyms frequently found in 2G-level books. Say one of the words below and ask the student to tell you the opposite. They don't need to be able to read the word, just give its opposite orally.

big or large/small or little	over/under	old/young or new	up/down	empty/full	near/far	happy/sad or unhappy	good/bad	tall/short	day/night		
										.01	

Read and identify the words that compose contractions (*can't = cannot*). (See 2G Category Words.)			
Vocabulary and Background Knowledge Total		.01	

Fluency

Read 2G text independently, sustaining concentration, monitoring comprehension, and when useful, rereading, without help from the teacher.			
Monitor Comprehension: CCSF 4abc • Use context to confirm or self-correct word recognition and understanding, rereading as necessary. CCSF 4c. • When stuck, back up and try again. • When stuck, continue reading and come back to correct after gaining more information.		.01	
Fluency Read 2G text orally with 95-100% accuracy, appropriate rate, and expression without prompting or support. CCSF 4b.		.01	
Fluency Total		.02	
2G Foundational Skills Total		.09	

2G Category Words

Student Practice Page: By the end of 2G, know ALL of these words at Flash Speed.

Name				Date		Total			
Numbers		**Days**		**Family**		**Contractions**		**Colors**	
two		Saturday		mom		can't		red	
six		Wednesday		mommy		don't		yellow	
five		Sunday		mother		won't		pink	
nine		Thursday		dad		didn't		green	
one		Monday		daddy		wasn't		purple	
seven		Friday		father		aren't		orange	
four		Tuesday		sister		couldn't		blue	
ten		**Directions**		brother		shouldn't		black	
eight		over		aunt		wouldn't		white	
three		under		uncle		she's		brown	
		around		grandmother		he's		gray	
Shapes		through		grandfather		it's			
triangle		across		baby		I'll			
rectangle		above		family		I'm			
square		inside				you're			
circle		outside				they're			

2G Running Record

Student ______________ Teacher ______________ Grade ________ Room ________ Date ______________

Title: ______________	Error/Miscue Analysis		
	Needs work on this initial letter sound	Needs to learn this Power Word	Not in background knowledge

Active Reading

- ☐ Have automatic recall of 85 Power Words and can read them in context.
- ☐ Have control of next 60 Power Words (2G Skills Card).
- ☐ Use picture clues to figure out unfamiliar words.
- ☐ Self-prompt a new word by using the first two letter sounds (blends, digraphs).
- ☐ Stop when something doesn't make sense, match the letters, or sound right.
- ☐ Go back and try again if reading doesn't make sense, match the letters, or sound right.
- ☐ Determine what a text says explicitly and make logical inferences from it. (*What is this about so far? How do you know? Why...?*)

Power Words

about	fun	if	put
animal	gave	into	ran
as	girl	jump	saw
be	give	make	says
beside	goes	many	some
boy	going	new	stop
but	good	not	take
by	got	now	then
came	happy	off	these
could	her	oh	too
day	him	or	under
did	his	our	were
does	home	out	when
eat	house	over	would
from	how	play	your

Power Goal

Transition to 1B

2G Entry Points	**1.00**	
2G Foundational Skills Points	**.10**	
2G Comprehension Points	**.09**	

1B Transition Points. With NO help of any kind, student must demonstrate ability to:			**Evidence/Date**			**Points**	
Phonics	**Manipulate Onsets and Rimes** Combine initial sounds and Power Words to make new words. CCSF 2ce (K).	See **Chunking Check** on page 55. Minimum score of 18.	Scores		Dates	.02	
	Decode Most One-Syllable Words Use a combination of sight words, rhyming, initial sounds/blends, and chunking to decode most regularly spelled one-syllable words. CCSF 3abc.	See **One-Syllable Decoding Check** on page 56. Minimum score of 18.	Scores		Dates	.03	
Word Recognition	**Read 1B Tricky Words** Recognize and read grade-appropriate irregularly spelled words. CCSF 3g.	See **Tricky Words** on page 57. Minimum score of 25.	Scores		Dates	.01	
Comprehension	**Read and Comprehend Unfamiliar 1B Text** **Apply Foundational Skills (Word-Solving)** Use a combination of decoding skills, sight words, and context clues to read 1B text with 98-100% accuracy. Stop and try again if something doesn't look right, sound right, or make sense. CCSF 4. **Apply Reading Standards (Comprehension)** Determine what a text says explicitly and make logical inferences from it. CCSR 1, CCSR 2, CCSR 3.	See **Cold Read Record** on page 58. Minimum score of 6 on one Cold Read Text.	Scores	Titles	Dates	.04	
1B Transition Points						**.10**	
GRAND TOTAL: Student should transition to 1B with 1.29 points and demonstrated proficiency at 1B prerequisites.						**1.29**	

1B Independent Reading Level Overview 1.30 -1.59
Decode Regularly Spelled 1-Syllable Words: Chunking

1B Learning Focus
Decode Regularly Spelled 1-Syllable Words: Vowel Family Chunking

1B readers take a huge jump forward in reading. Not only do they have a sight word bank of 200-300 high frequency words, they are now able to use these known words, and knowledge of regular vowel patterns, to figure out unknown words (e.g., *ride/pride*). 1B readers have their fingers out, covering parts of unfamiliar words to find something they know inside them. Once they find a chunk that looks familiar, they have to recall what known word it is part of, take off the first letter of the known word in their mind, vocalize the isolated chunk, add the beginning sound of the new word to the chunk, and see if it works out to be a sensible word. If it doesn't work out they have to start all over again. The phonological awareness skills required for this level are tremendous.

Key Common Core Standards

Foundational Skills

3b. Decode regularly spelled one-syllable words.

3c. Know final -e and common vowel team conventions for representing long vowel sounds.

3g. Recognize and read grade-appropriate irregularly spelled words.

Blend and segment onsets and rimes of single-syllable spoken words (*/g/-/oat/, /bl/-/ack/*). CCSF 2c(K)

Add or substitute individual sounds (phonemes) in simple, one-syllable words to make new words (*/at/ – /sat/ – /mat/ – /map/*). CCSF 2e(K).

Entry Requirements

Must be in place before earning 1B designation.

- Manipulate onsets and rimes. CCSF 2ce (K).
- Decode most one-syllable words. CCSF 3abc.
- Read 1B tricky words. CCSF 3g.
- Read and comprehend unfamiliar 1B text (successfully apply Foundational Skills and Reading Standards). CCSF4, CCSR 1-3.

Exit Requirements

Must be in place before earning 2B designation.

- Decode most two-syllable words. CCSF 3ef.
- Read 2B tricky words (minimum 25). CCSF 3g.
- Read and comprehend unfamiliar 2B text (successfully apply Foundational Skills and Reading Standards). CCSF4, CCSR 1-3.

1B Independent Reading Level Assessment 1.30-1.59

Entry Requirements: Cumulative Record

Student ______________________ Teacher ______________________ Room ________ Date Started ________

1B Entry Requirements

		Evidence/Date				Date Completed
Phonics	**Manipulate Onsets a…** Combine initial s… make new words.	…on …e	Scores	Dates		
	Decode Most One-… Use a combination o… initial sounds/blends, decode most regularly words. CCSF 3abc.		Scores	Dates		
Word Recognition	**Read 1B Tricky Words** Recognize and read grade-a… irregularly spelled words. CC…	…core	…s	Dates		
Comprehension	**Read and Comprehend Unfamiliar 1B Text** **Apply Foundational Skills (Word-Solving)** Use a combination of decoding skills, sight words, and context clues to read 1B text with 98-100% accuracy. Stop and try again if something doesn't look right, sound right, or make sense. CCSF 4. **Apply Reading Standards (Comprehension)** Determine what a text says explicitly and make logical inferences from it. CCSR 1, CCSR 2, CCSR 3.	See **Cold Read Record** on page 58. Minimum score of 6 on one Cold Read Text.	Scores	Titles	Dates	

Run Copies for ea level & kid

each kid turn in

A reader who is proficient at all of the above enters 1B with 1.30 points. 1.30

1B Entry Requirements: Chunking Check

Use Words You Know to Make New Words

Entry Level: 18 1B Words

Chunk	A 1B Reader Can Combine Known Words and Letter Sounds to Make New Words				
1G-2G Sight Words	Put a __ on the front of the word. What word does it make?				
at	b	c	h	s	fl
eat	b	h	m	ch	tr
in	f	p	w	ch	sp
1G-2G Sight Words	Take off the first letter. Put a __ in its place. What word does it make?				
take	b	c	m	r	fl
went	r	s	t	v	sp
down	t	br	cl	cr	fr

Common Core Standard Foundational Skills 2ce (K): Combine initial sounds and Power Words to make new words.

1B Entry Requirements: One-Syllable Decoding Check

Use Words You Know to Figure Out Words You Don't

Entry Level: 18 1B Words

Beginning Sound Changes	Beginning Blends	Ending Sound Changes	Long Vowels	"R"-Controlled
van	plan	plant	rain	park
back	stack	stacks	bake	shark
pat	flat	chats	date	car
fed	shed	sleds	need	hers
pet	Bret	nets	treat	hurt
win	chin	grins	mine	girl
sit	quit	skits	bite	bird
hill	spill	chills	smile	dirt
mop	drop	shops	rope	storm
hot	spot	spots	float	score
Totals:				

Common Core Standard Foundational Skills 3abc: Use a combination of sight words, rhyming initial sounds/blends,

1B Entry Requirements: Tricky Words

Must Recognize On Sight

Entry Level: 25 Words

Exit Level: Know All 60 Words

Dates											
after		birthday		found		much		pretty		walk	
again		both		friend		myself		pull		which	
always		bright		full		never		read		whose	
another		buy		funny		night		right		word	
any		catch		hello		old		school		work	
away		color		help		only		something		write	
beautiful		count		know		other		surprise			
because		every		laugh		own		their			
become		fight		light		party		those			
before		find		long		people		today			
begin		first		might		please		very			
										Total	

Common Core Standard Foundational Skills 3g: Recognize and read grade-appropriate irregularly spelled words.

1B Entry Requirements: Cold Read Record

Title:________________________ Date:________________

Given an unfamiliar 1B text (Cold Read), and NO help of any kind:

Running Record Record all errors as the student reads the passage. Indicate self-corrections.	Error/Miscue Analysis Needs work on this Phonics Pattern	 Needs to learn this Tricky Word	 Not in background knowledge

Apply Foundational Skills

Active Reading Strategies	Yes or No
Read with 98 - 100% word accuracy. In 100 words, student makes no more than 2 uncorrected errors.	
Stop and try again if something doesn't look right, sound right, or make sense. Self-correct ALL errors that interfere with meaning.	

If answer to either of the above questions is No, STOP and move student to an easier level.
If the answer to both is Yes, continue on to Reading Standards. (See specific questions on Cold Read Text Pages.)

Apply Reading Standards

Comprehension	Student Response	Score Weak.........Strong
Basic Understanding Support basic understanding with evidence from the text. CCSR 1.		1 2 3 4
Interpretation Support an interpretation or analysis with evidence from the text. CCSR 2 & 3.		1 2 3 4
Total Points (A minimum score of 6 is required in order to enter 1B.)		

1B Entry Requirements: Cold Read Text A

I am a little black puppy.
I live in a pet store.
Soon I will have
a kid of my own.

Many kids come.

This one pulls my tail.

This one kisses too much.

They are not for me.

Here is another kid.
He says hello.
He pats my head.
Woof! Woof!
This is the boy for me!

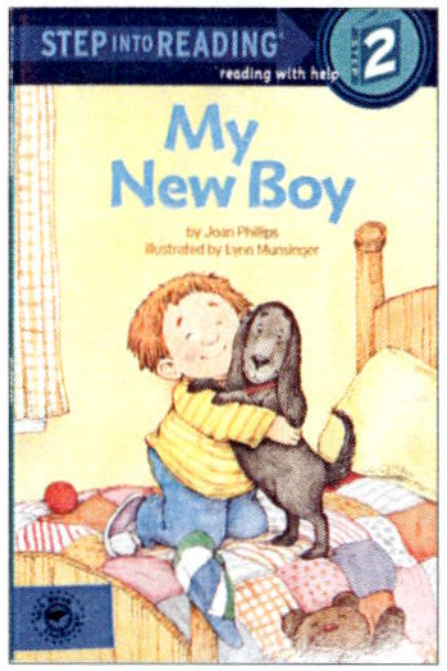

My New Boy
by Joan Phillips
Random House

1B

Basic Understanding
What is happening so far in this story?

Interpretation
Who is telling the story? How do you know?

1B Entry Requirements: Cold Read Text B

Are You My Mother?
by P. D. Eastman
Random House

A mother bird sat on her egg.

The egg jumped.

"Oh oh!" said the mother bird. "My baby will be here! He will want to eat."

"I must get something for my baby bird to eat!" she said. "I will be back!"

So away she went.

Out came the baby bird!

Basic Understanding

What is happening so far in this story?

Interpretation

What do you think the problem in the story will be? Why?

1B Entry Requirements: Cold Read Text C

The Elephant's Trunk
by Gina Cline
American Reading Company

This is an elephant.

Look at her trunk.

Her trunk helps her eat from tall trees.

She takes leaves from the trees.
She puts them in her mouth.

She takes a bath with her trunk.

She gets water with her trunk.
She spits the water on her back.

Basic Understanding

Tell me three things the text says about elephant trunks.

Interpretation

Why is the elephant's trunk important? How do you know?

1B Entry Requirements: Cold Read Text D

Rattlesnakes
by Jane Hileman
American Reading Company

Rattlesnakes kill and eat small animals. They bite them with their fangs.

The snakes open up their jaws and down goes the prey in one bite.

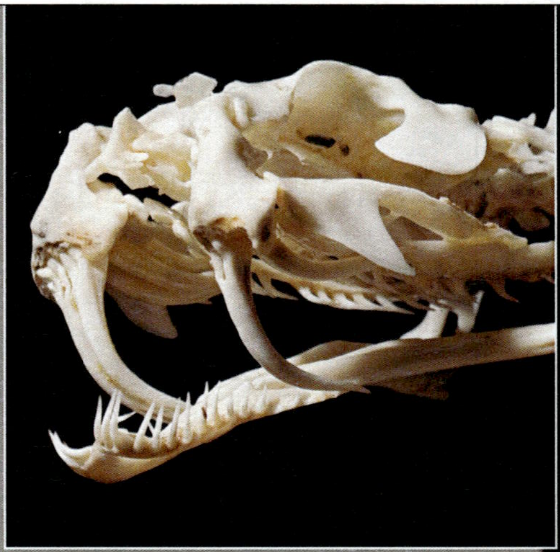

Rattlesnakes have teeth but they can't chew. After they eat, they sleep for 2 or 3 days.

Rattlesnakes eat mice, rats, small birds and other small animals.

Basic Understanding

Tell me three things the text says about rattlesnakes.

Interpretation

Compare rattlesnakes to another animal. Use evidence from the text to support your answer.

1B Comprehension

Reading Standards for Literature and Informational Text

Some of the comprehension standards below will be demonstrated during Read-Aloud, since few 1B books are complicated enough to have a narrative structure. In order to move to 2B, students must earn .10 Comprehension Points from any combination of the standards below. Do not score students higher than .10 for Comprehension. Students will work on the same standards in 2B, so whatever standard they don't master in 1B should be completed in 2B.

Key Ideas and Details: **Using Text Evidence to Support Conclusions** Understand, think about, and discuss what the author said.		Evidence/Date	Points	
	Have adequate background knowledge to name and talk about the content common to 1B books (middle of 1st grade).		.01	
	Demonstrate an obvious understanding of the materials (e.g., laugh at the funny parts, comment on the content).		.01	
	Make predictions based on title, cover, illustrations, and text.		.01	
CCSR 1	Ask and answer questions about key details in a text. • *What were some different kinds of animals in this story?* • *Where did the little girl want to go?*		.01	
CCSR 2	Retell stories in correct sequence, including key details, and demonstrate understanding of their central message or lesson. • *Retell the story to me.* (Prompt for key details, as necessary.) • *What was the lesson of this story?*		.01	
	Identify the main topic and retell key details of a text. • *What was this book mostly about?* • *What were the most important things the author told us?*		.01	
CCSR3	Describe characters, settings, and major events in a story, using key details. • *Tell 3 things about the main character.* • *Compare him/her to other characters or people.* • *Where does this story take place? When?* • *What are the main things that happen?*		.01	
	Describe the connection between two individuals, events, ideas, or pieces of information in a text. • *How are ______ and _____ in this book alike (or different)?* • *How are _____ and _____ in this book connected?*		.01	

Craft and Structure: Analyzing the Effects of Authors' Choices

Understand and discuss the way(s) the author(s) said what was said.

CCSR 4	Identify words and phrases in stories or poems that suggest feelings or appeal to the senses. • *What word tells how ____ feels (smells, tastes, etc.)?*		.01	
	Ask and answer questions to help determine or clarify the meaning of words and phrases in a text. • *Is there a word in this book that you never heard before? What do you think it means?*		.01	
CCSR 5	Explain major differences between books that tell stories and books that give information, drawing on a wide reading of a range of text types. Give student a pile of books: • *Which of these books are informational?* • *Which tell stories?* • *How do you know which is which?*		.01	
	Know and use various text features (headings, tables of contents, glossaries, electronic menus, icons) to locate key facts or information in a text. • *Where in this book would you look to find information about ____ (what tigers eat; what makes a seed grow)?*		.01	
CCSR 6	After Read-Aloud: Identify who is telling the story at various points in a text.		.01	
	Distinguish between information provided by pictures or other illustrations and information provided by the words in a text. • *What can you learn about ____ from the pictures in this book?*		.01	

Integration of Knowledge and Ideas: Comparing Different Presentations

Discuss how the ideas in a book connect to each other and to the larger world.

CCSR 7	Use illustrations and details in a story to describe its characters, setting, or events. • *Tell me everything you know about _____ (characters, setting, events).*		.01	
	Use the illustrations and details in a text to describe its key ideas. • *Looking at the picture, what is this page mainly about?* • *What were the most important things that the author taught us about bears? Why?*		.01	
CCSR 8	After Read-Aloud: Identify the reasons an author gives to support points in a text. • *The author is telling us that _____*(teacher supplies this). *What reasons does he give to convince us?*		.01	
CCSR 9	Compare and contrast the adventures and experiences of characters in stories. • *What happened to _____ in this story?* • *What happened to _____ in this story (or another story)?* • *How were their experiences the same? How were they different?*		.01	
	Identify basic similarities in and differences between two texts on the same topic (e.g., in illustrations, descriptions, or procedures). Give student two books on same topic: • *How are these two books alike? How are they different?* • *Which do you like better? Why?*		.01	
1B Comprehension Total			**.10**	

1B Foundational Skills

Range of Reading and Level of Text Complexity	Evidence/Date	Points	
Engagement and Independence Read regularly and independently, sustaining engagement, in 1B-level materials for at least 30 minutes every day in the classroom (15 minutes per session).		.01	
Home Reading Have established a home reading habit and read for at least 30 minutes every night without prompting.		.01	
Genres Choose to read both informational and literary text at the 1B level. Informational ☐ Literary ☐		✓	
Range of Reading and Level of Text Complexity Total		.02	

Print Concepts

Sentences Recognize and respond to punctuation (commas, periods, question marks) while reading. CCSF 1a. First Word ☐ Capitalization ☐ Ending Punctuation ☐		✓	
Print Concepts Total		✓	

Phonological Awareness

Distinguish long from short vowel sounds in spoken single-syllable words (e.g., */tap/* vs. */tape/*, */sock/* vs. */soak/*, */sit/* vs. */sight/*. CCSF 2a.			
Orally produce single-syllable words by blending sounds (phonemes) including consonant blends. (*/bl/-/a/-/st/*). CCSF 2b.			
Isolate and pronounce initial, medial vowel, and final sounds (phonemes) in spoken single-syllable words. CCSF 2c.			
Segment spoken single-syllable words into their complete sequence of individual sounds (phonemes) (e.g., *lap* — */l/-/a/-/p/* to *flap* — */f/-/l/-/a/-/p/*). CCSF 2d.			
Phonological Awareness Total			

<table>
<tr><th>Phonics: 1-Syllable Word Families, Long and Short Vowels, Final Consonants</th><th>Evidence/Date</th><th colspan="2">Points</th></tr>
<tr><td>Cover parts of unfamiliar words with finger and look for familiar chunks inside.</td><td></td><td>.01</td><td></td></tr>
<tr><td>Use familiar rhyming words to decode unfamiliar words. (See 1B Skills Card.)</td><td></td><td>.01</td><td></td></tr>
<tr><td>Decode almost any one-syllable word that follows a regular vowel pattern (hid/hide) or is built from a familiar chunk (lift). CCSF 3b. (See 1B Skills Card.)</td><td></td><td>.01</td><td></td></tr>
<tr><td>Decode words containing –e and common vowel team conventions for representing long vowel sounds. CCSF 3c. (See 1B Long Vowel Patterns.)
<table>
<tr><td>a-e</td><td></td><td>e-e</td><td></td><td>i-e</td><td></td><td>o-e</td><td></td><td>u-e</td><td></td><td>ay</td><td></td><td>oy</td><td></td></tr>
<tr><td>sale</td><td></td><td>Pete</td><td></td><td>smile</td><td></td><td>pole</td><td></td><td>June</td><td></td><td>gray</td><td></td><td>boy</td><td></td></tr>
<tr><td>ee</td><td></td><td>ea</td><td></td><td>ai</td><td></td><td>oa</td><td></td><td>ui</td><td></td><td>ow</td><td></td><td>ow</td><td></td></tr>
<tr><td>meet</td><td></td><td>seal</td><td></td><td>pain</td><td></td><td>load</td><td></td><td>suit</td><td></td><td>grow</td><td></td><td>cow</td><td></td></tr>
</table></td><td></td><td>.01</td><td></td></tr>
<tr><td>Decode words beginning with these sounds:
<table>
<tr><td>wr-</td><td></td><td>kn-</td><td></td><td>ph-</td><td></td><td>qu-</td><td></td><td>wh-</td><td></td></tr>
</table></td><td></td><td>.01</td><td></td></tr>
<tr><td>Use final blends and digraphs to figure out unfamiliar words (desk, wish). CCSF 3a
<table>
<tr><td>-sh</td><td></td><td>-st</td><td></td><td>-nd</td><td></td><td>-nt</td><td></td><td>-lk</td><td></td></tr>
<tr><td>-ch</td><td></td><td>-sk</td><td></td><td>-ng</td><td></td><td>-nch</td><td></td><td>-lf</td><td></td></tr>
<tr><td>-th</td><td></td><td>-ft</td><td></td><td>-nk</td><td></td><td>-mp</td><td></td><td>-lp</td><td></td></tr>
</table></td><td></td><td>.01</td><td></td></tr>
<tr><td>Decode words containing “r”-controlled vowels. (See 1B "R"-Controlled Pattern.)
<table>
<tr><td>ar</td><td></td><td>er</td><td></td><td>ir</td><td></td><td>or</td><td></td><td>ur</td><td></td></tr>
</table></td><td></td><td>.01</td><td></td></tr>
<tr><td colspan="2">1B Phonics Total</td><td>.07</td><td></td></tr>
</table>

1B Foundational Skills Cont'd

Word Recognition

Power Words Know 100-300 high-frequency words (e.g., *their, laugh, friend*) and use them as "islands of certainty" while reading in 1B level materials (including 1G and 2G Power Words, 2G Category Words, 1B Tricky Words, and 1B Word Family Key Words). CCSF 3g.		.01	
Word Recognition Total		.01	

Fluency and Self-Monitoring

Fluency Read 1B text comfortably, with confidence, purpose, and understanding. CCSF 4a.		✓	
Read 1B text orally with 95-100% accuracy, appropriate rate, and expression on initial readings. CCSF 4b.		.01	
Read in whisper voice.		.01	
Self-Monitoring Use context to confirm or self-correct word recognition and understanding, rereading as necessary. CCSF 4c.		✓	
When stuck, back up and try again.		✓	
When stuck, continue reading and come back to correct after gaining more information.		✓	
Fluency Total		.02	
1B Foundational Skills Total		.10	

1B 1-Syllable Key Words

This key word list includes the 37 most useful word families. Students who memorize these key words use the chunks in them to decode unfamiliar words. When they encounter a new word in their reading, they first find a chunk that looks like a word they already know, in their mind take off the first letter(s) of the known word, replace them with the beginning sound(s) of the new word, and see if this combination makes a sensible word. Students who are able to do this with these 37 chunks will have access to hundreds of other words. (Wylie & Durrell, 1970)

Student Practice Page

Name Dates

a				e		i				o		u	
back		thank		eat		ice		sing		rock		luck	
tail		cap		tell		sick		pink		joke		bug	
rain		cash		best		ride		chip		stop		jump	
make		at				light		it		more		junk	
sale		ate				will				got			
came		saw				in							
can		day				nine							
												Total	

Common Core Standard Foundational Skills 3g: Read common high-frequency words by sight.

1B Short Vowels

Student Practice Page

Name Dates

1B Easy		1B Hard		2B
ham	jam	swam	champ	stamper
pan	tan	plan	thank	channel
mat	pat	flat	chats	platter
net	set	Bret	frets	better
den	hen	glen	spent	bending
hill	pill	skill	grills	chilly
tin	win	thin	drink	printer
fit	mit	slit	switch	itchy
hot	pot	slot	spots	rotting
hut	rut	shut	crutch	nutty
dump	lump	stump	thumps	grumpy

1B Final "E" Pattern

Student Practice Page

Name Dates

a				*i*				*e, o, u*			
at		ate		kit		kite		pet		Pete	
rat		rate		bit		bite		not		note	
tap		tape		hid		hide		rod		rode	
cap		cape		slid		slide		hop		hope	
pan		pane		pin		pine		rob		robe	
can		cane		shin		shine		tub		tube	
back		bake		Tim		time		cut		cute	
tack		take		dim		dime		us		use	
rack		race		pick		pike		fuss		fuse	
track		trace		lick		like		luck		Luke	
										Total	

Common Core Standard Foundational Skills 3c: Know final –e (*take, side*) convention.

1B Long Vowel Teams

Student Practice Page

Name   Dates

Long "a"		Long "e"				Long "o"		Long "i"	
rain		eat		feel		road		pie	
wait		ear		queen		coat		fly	
paid		teach		deer		soak		child	
mail		read		feet		goal		light	
paint		real		sleep		foam		find	
air		sneak		feed		Joe		**Long "u"**	
stay		dream		week		toe		suit	
gray		clean		sheep		cold		fruit	
grey		cheap		tree		roll		glue	
eight		please		bee		both			
								Total	

1B 1-Syllable "R"-Controlled Pattern

Student Practice Page

Name Dates

ar		er		ir		or		ur	
car		her		girl		or		hurt	
cart		herd		dirt		fort		purple	
chart		herds		fir		cord		burn	
card		germ		sir		Ford		turn	
yard		germs		stir		more		curl	
park		fern		birth		chore		blur	
shark		clerk		chirp		fork		spur	
sparks		over		bird		cork		fur	
sharp		perch		third		storm		purr	
smart		Bert		shirts		shorts		surf	
								Total	

Common Core Standard Foundational Skills 3b: Decode regularly spelled one-syllable words (*lock, much, bring*).

1B Running Record

Student ______________ Teacher ______________ Grade ______ Room ______ Date ______________

Title: ______________	Error/Miscue Analysis		
	Needs work on this Phonics Pattern	Needs to learn this Tricky Word	Not in Background Knowledge

Active Reading

- ☐ Have automatic recall of all Power Words.
- ☐ Stop and try again when reading doesn't make sense, match the letters, or sound right.
- ☐ Cover first letter, visualize a familiar word with the same pattern, and use rimes and onset to figure out a new word.
- ☐ Use the first few letters to self-prompt.
- ☐ Use blends at the ends of words (*desk/wish*).
- ☐ Use pictures and other meaning clues to figure out new words.
- ☐ Use syntax/sentence structure to figure out words.
- ☐ Determine what a text says explicitly and make logical inferences from it. (What is this about so far? How do you know? Why...?)

1-Syllable Decoding

- ☐ Final "–e" (*at/ate...*)
- ☐ Long vowel teams (*ea, ee...*)
- ☐ Silent letter (*wr, kn, ph, qu, wh*)
- ☐ Final blends (-*sk*, -*st*, -*nd...*)
- ☐ R-controlled vowels (*ar, er, ir, ur, or*)

Power Goal

Transition to 2B

1B Entry Points	**1.30**	
1B Foundational Skills Points	**.10**	
1B Comprehension Points	**.10**	

2B Transition Points. With NO help of any kind, student must demonstrate ability to:			**Evidence/Date**			**Points**	
Phonics	**Decode Most Two-Syllable Words** Decode compound words, e.g., baseball, sunshine. Decode two-syllable words following basic patterns by breaking the words into syllables and/or chunks, e.g., always, begin. CCSF 3e. Read words with inflectional endings. CCSF 3f.	See **Decoding Two-Syllable Words** on page 79. Minimum score of 20.	Scores		Dates	.06	
Word Recognition	**Read 2B Tricky Words** Recognize and read grade-appropriate irregularly spelled words. CCSF 3g.	See **Tricky Words** on page 80. Minimum score of 25.	Scores		Dates	.01	
Comprehension	**Read and Comprehend 2B Text** **Apply Foundational Skills (Word-Solving)** Use a combination of decoding skills, sight words, and context clues to read 2B text with 98% accuracy. Stop and try again if something doesn't look right, sound right, or make sense. CCSF 4. **Apply Reading Standards (Comprehension)** Determine what a text says explicitly and make logical inferences from it. CCSR 1, CCSR 2, CCSR 3.	See **Cold Read Record** on page 81. Minimum score of 6 on one Cold Read Text.	Scores	Titles	Dates	.02	
2B Transition Points						**.09**	
GRAND TOTAL: Student should transition to 2B with 1.59 points and demonstrated proficiency at 2B prerequisites.						**1.59**	

2B Independent Reading Level Overview 1.60 -1.99
Decode Regularly Spelled 2-Syllable Words

2B Learning Focus
Decode Two-Syllable Words

2B readers know to look for the known inside the unknown. They have their fingers on the text, covering up beginnings and endings of unfamiliar words, looking for chunks, vowel patterns, endings, little words inside bigger words, as they successfully figure out the two-syllable words common to 2B text. 2B books begin to include narratives with some characterization and simple plots. Be careful, because 2B is the first level in which readers can decode without following the meaning of the text. Be sure to check comprehension carefully. Don't allow students who are working too hard on decoding to move into 1R. Make sure students learn to be fully engaged with the message of 2B books. Catch them laughing at the stories, not just figuring out what the words say, before moving them into 1R.

Key Common Core Standards
Foundational Skills

3e. Decode two-syllable words following basic patterns by breaking the words into syllables.

3f. Read words with inflectional endings (*-ed, -er, -ing, -es, -y, -est*).

3g. Recognize and read 2B irregularly spelled words.

Entry Requirements
Must be in place before earning 2B designation.

- Decode most two-syllable words. CCSF 3ef.
- Read 2B tricky words (minimum 25). CCSF 3g.
- Read and comprehend unfamiliar 2B text (successfully apply Foundational Skills and Reading Standards). CCSF4, CCSR 1-3.

Exit Requirements
Must be in place before earning 1R designation.

- Decode most regular three-syllable words. CCSF 3.
- Decode words with three-letter blends and common suffixes. CCSF 3d.
- Read 1R Tricky Words. CCSF 3f.
- Read and comprehend unfamiliar 1R text (successfully apply Foundational Skills and Reading Standards). CCSF4, CCSR 1-3.

2B Independent Reading Level Assessment 1.60 - 1.99

Entry Requirements: Cumulative Record

Student ______________________ Teacher ______________________ Room ________ Date Started ________

2B Entry Requirements

<table>
<tr><th></th><th></th><th colspan="4">Evidence/Date</th><th>Date Completed</th></tr>
<tr><td rowspan="2">Phonics</td><td rowspan="2">Decode Most Two-Syllable Words
Decode compound words, e.g., baseball, sunshine.
Decode two-syllable words following basic patterns by breaking the words into syllables and/or chunks, e.g., always, begin. CCSF 3e.
Read words with inflectional endings. CCSF 3f.</td><td rowspan="2">See Decoding Two-Syllable Words on page 79. Minimum score of 20.</td><td>Scores</td><td colspan="2">Dates</td><td rowspan="2"></td></tr>
<tr><td></td><td colspan="2"></td></tr>
<tr><td rowspan="2">Word Recognition</td><td rowspan="2">Read 2B Tricky Words
Recognize and read grade-appropriate irregularly spelled words. CCSF 3g.</td><td rowspan="2">See Tricky Words on page 80. Minimum score of 25.</td><td>Scores</td><td colspan="2">Dates</td><td rowspan="2"></td></tr>
<tr><td></td><td colspan="2"></td></tr>
<tr><td rowspan="2">Comprehension</td><td rowspan="2">Read and Comprehend Unfamiliar 2B Text
Apply Foundational Skills (Word-Solving)
Use a combination of decoding skills, sight words, and context clues to read 2B text with 98% accuracy. Stop and try again if something doesn't look right, sound right, or make sense. CCSF 4.
Apply Reading Standards (Comprehension)
Determine what a text says explicitly and make logical inferences from it. CCSR 1, CCSR 2, CCSR 3.</td><td rowspan="2">See Cold Read Record on page 81. Minimum score of 6 on one Cold Read Text.</td><td>Scores</td><td>Titles</td><td>Dates</td><td rowspan="2"></td></tr>
<tr><td></td><td></td><td></td></tr>
<tr><td colspan="6">A reader who is proficient at all of the above enters 2B with 1.60 points.</td><td>1.60</td></tr>
</table>

2B Entry Requirements: *Decoding 2-Syllable Words*

Entry Level: 20 Words (Do not count 1B Chunk words)

Name   Date   Score

1B Chunks	2B Readers Can Figure Out These Words				
Vowel Patterns (These words do not count.)	Inflectional Endings		Compound Words	Long Vowel	Short Vowel
ten	**ended**	**enter**	**henhouse**	**maple**	**saddle**
eat	**eating**	**neatest**	**teammate**	**skater**	**scatter**
boat	**coated**	**floating**	**sailboat**	**cable**	**Scrabble**
rain	**rainy**	**drainer**	**rainbow**	**peeper**	**pepper**
see	**seeing**	**needed**	**seesaw**	**sliding**	**kidding**
day	**played**	**player**	**daytime**	**timing**	**minnow**
her	**hers**	**serving**	**herself**	**pony**	**Sonny**
girl	**girls**	**twirled**	**girlfriend**	**voter**	**otter**
car	**cars**	**farthest**	**carport**	**fuel**	**bunny**
purple	**furry**	**hurried**	**sunburn**	**cuter**	**cutter**

Common Core Standard Foundational Skills 3f: Read words with inflectional endings.

Common Core Standard Foundational Skills 3e: Decode two-syllable words following basic patterns by breaking the words into syllables.

2B Entry Requirements: Tricky Words

Must Recognize On Sight

Entry Level: 25 Words

Name Date

answer		eye		living		page		sure	
bear		friendly		lost		phone		teacher	
behind		giant		million		picture		thought	
being		gone		money		push		tiny	
body		group		monkey		quiet		together	
brought		guess		more		quit		tomorrow	
build		heard		mountain		quite		tough	
calf		high		Mr.		ready		trouble	
carry		honey		Mrs.		really		until	
carried		hurry		neighbor		sentence		upon	
caught		large		noise		shoe		watch	
cent		lamb		noisy		spring		while	
child		later		nothing		squirrel		woman	
children		learn		often		special		world	
earth		leave		once		story		young	
enough		listen		open		sugar			

2B Entry Requirements: Cold Read Record

Title:________________________ Date:________________

Given an unfamiliar 2B text (Cold Read), and NO help of any kind:

Running Record Record all errors as the student reads the passage. Indicate self-corrections.	Error/Miscue Analysis		
	Needs work on this Phonics Pattern	Needs to learn this Tricky Word	Not in background knowledge.

Apply Foundational Skills

Active Reading Strategies	Yes or No
Read with 98 - 100% word accuracy. Student makes no more than 2 uncorrected errors.	
Stop and try again if something doesn't look right, sound right, or make sense. Self-correct ALL errors that interfere with meaning.	

If the answer to either of the above questions is No, STOP and move student to an easier level.
If the answer to both is Yes, continue on to Reading Standards. (See specific questions on Cold Read Text Pages.)

Apply Reading Standards

Comprehension	Student Response	Score Weak.........Strong
Basic Understanding Support basic understanding with evidence from the text. CCSR 1.		1 2 3 4
Interpretation Support an interpretation or analysis with evidence from the text. CCSR 2&3.		1 2 3 4
Total Points (A minimum score of 6 is required in order to enter 2B.)		

2B Entry Requirements: Cold Read Text A

We went camping,
just me and my dad.
Dad drove the car
because I'm too little.

We found another
campsite nearby.
My dad was tired,
so I pitched the tent.

We made a campfire.
I found the wood,
and my dad lit the fire.

My dad took a snapshot
of the fish we caught.
Then I cooked dinner
for me and my dad.

Just Me and My Dad
by Mercer Mayer
Random House

Basic Understanding

What is happening in the story so far?

Interpretation

Why is the story funny? What in the text makes it funny?

2B Entry Requirements: Cold Read Text B

Now I Love to Read
by Jane Hileman
American Reading Company

Basic Understanding

What happened in this story?

Interpretation

What do you think might be the lesson of this story?

2B Entry Requirements: Cold Read Text C

Bears
by Jane Hileman
American Reading Company

Black bears live in the woods. They are fast runners, good swimmers, and can climb trees.

Black bears use their sense of smell and sometimes hearing to find food.

Black bears are not always black. Some are brown and some are golden. They often have a white spot on their chest.

The adult male is sometimes twice as heavy as the female.

Basic Understanding

Tell me three things the text says about bears.

Interpretation

Why might it be important for black bears to be fast runners?

2B Entry Requirements: Cold Read Text D

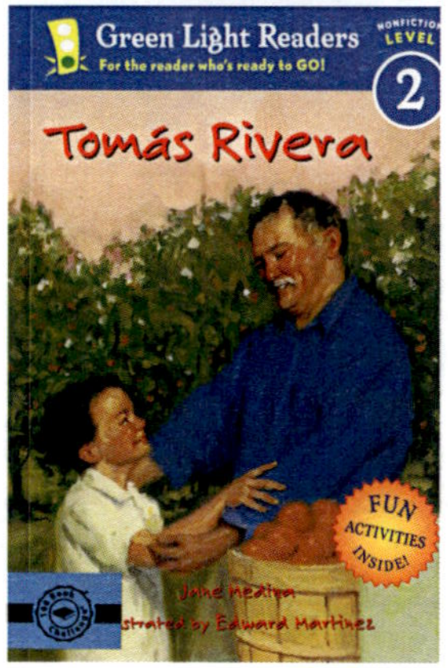

Tomás Rivera by
Jane Medina
Harcourt, Inc.

Tomás was born in Texas.
He and his family went from farm to farm picking crops.

Tomás helped pick crops all day. It was hard work. But at night, he had fun with his grandpa.

"Come quick, children!" Grandpa called. "It's time for stories!"

"You tell the best stories!" Tomás said. "I want to tell good stories, too."

Tomás started telling his stories. Then he started writing them.

When he grew up, Tomás became a teacher. He still kept writing stories.

Basic Understanding

Tell me three things the text says about Tomás Rivera.

Interpretation

Why do you think that Thomas wanted to tell stories? What in the text makes you think that?

2B

2B Comprehension

Reading Standards for Literature and Informational Text

The standards below must be demonstrated while reading independently in 2B level materials. In order to advance to 1R, students must earn .20 Comprehension Points from any combination of the standards below.

Key Ideas and Details: Using Text Evidence to Support Conclusions Understand, think about, and discuss <u>what</u> the author said.		Evidence/Date	Points	
	Demonstrate adequate background knowledge to name and talk about the pictures and ideas common to 2B books. Students who do not know basic vocabulary need extensive read-aloud and real-life experiences to be successful readers.		.02	
	Demonstrate an obvious understanding of the text (laugh at the funny parts, comment on the material, make personal connections). Student is an active reader, making comments and connections without prompting.		.02	
	Make predictions based on title, cover, illustrations, and text.		✓	
CCSR 1	Ask and answer questions about key details in a text. • *What were some different kinds of animals in this story?* • *Where did the little girl want to go?*		.02	
CCSR 2	Retell stories, including key details, and demonstrate understanding of their central message or lesson. • *Retell the story to me.* (Prompt for key details as necessary.) • *What was the lesson of this story?*		.02	
	Identify the main topic and retell key details of a text. • *What was this book mostly about?* • *What were the most important things the author told us?*		.02	
CCSR 3	Describe characters, settings, and major events in a story using key details. • *Tell 3 things about the main character.* • *Compare him/her to other characters or people.* • *Where does this story take place? When?* • *What are the main things that happen?*		.02	
	Describe the connection between two individuals, events, ideas, or pieces of information in a text. • *How are ______ and ______ in this book alike (or different)?* • *How are ______ and ______ in this book connected?*		.02	

Craft and Structure: Analyzing the Effects of Authors' Choices

Understand and discuss the way(s) the author(s) said what was said.

CCSR 4	Identify words and phrases in stories or poems that suggest feelings or appeal to the senses. • *What word tells how ____ feels (smells, tastes, etc.)?*		.02	
	Ask and answer questions to help determine or clarify the meaning of words and phrases in a text. • *Is there a word in this book that you had never heard before? What do you think it means?*		.02	
CCSR 5	Explain major differences between books that tell stories and books that give information, drawing on a wide reading of a range of text types. Give student a pile of books: • *Which of these books are informational?* • *Which tell stories?* • *How do you know which is which?*		.02	
	Know and use various text features (e.g., headings, tables of contents, glossaries, electronic menus, icons) to locate key facts or information in a text. • *Where in this book would you look to find information about ____ (what tigers eat; what makes a seed grow)?*		.02	
CCSR 6	After Read-Aloud: Identify who is telling the story at various points in a text.		.02	
	Distinguish between information provided by pictures or other illustrations and information provided by the words in a text. • *What can you learn about ____ from the pictures in this book?*		.02	

Integration of Knowledge and Ideas: Comparing Different Presentations

Discuss how the ideas in a book connect to each other and to the larger world.

CCSR 7	Use illustrations and details in a story to describe its characters, setting, or events. • *Tell me everything you know about ______.*		.02	
	Use the illustrations and details in a text to describe its key ideas. • *Looking at the picture, what is this page mainly about?* • *What were the most important things that the author taught us about bears? Why?*		.02	
CCSR 8	After Read-Aloud: Identify the reasons an author gives to support points in a text. • *The author is telling us that* ______(teacher supplies this). *What reasons does he give to convince us?*		.02	
CCSR 9	Compare and contrast the adventures and experiences of characters in stories. • *What happened to ______ in this story?* • *What happened to ______ in this story (or another story)?* • *How were their experiences the same? How were they different?*		.02	
	Identify basic similarities in and differences between two texts on the same topic (e.g., in illustrations, descriptions, or procedures.). Give student two books on same topic: • *How are these two books alike? How are they different?* • *Which do you like better? Why?*		.02	
2B Comprehension Total			**.20**	

2B Foundational Skills

Range of Reading and Level of Text Complexity	Evidence/Date	Points	
Engagement and Independence Read regularly and independently, sustaining engagement, in 2B-level materials for at least 30 minutes every day in the classroom (15 minutes per session).		.01	
Home Reading Have established a home reading habit and read for at least 30 minutes every night without prompting.		.01	
Genres Enjoy informational text, prose, and poetry at 2B level. CCSR 10.		.01	
Range of Reading and Level of Text Complexity Total		.03	

Print Concepts

Sentences Recognize and respond to punctuation (commas, periods, question marks) while reading. CCSF 1a.		✓	
Print Concepts Total		✓	

Phonological Awareness

Distinguish long from short vowel sounds in spoken single-syllable words (e.g., */tap/* vs. */tape/*, */sock/* vs. */soak/*, */sit/* vs.*/sight/*). CCSF 2a.		✓	
Orally produce single-syllable words by blending sounds (phonemes) including consonant blends. (*/bl/-/a/-/st/*). CCSF 2b.		✓	
Isolate and pronounce initial, medial vowel, and final sounds (phonemes) in spoken single-syllable words. CCSF 2c.		✓	
Segment spoken single-syllable words into their complete sequence of individual sounds (phonemes) (e.g., *lap* — */l/-/a/-/p/* to *flap* — */f/-/l/-/a/-/p/*). CCSF 2d.		✓	
Phonological Awareness Total		✓	

Phonics: Two-Syllable Words, Inflectional Endings, Compound Words	Evidence/Date	Points	
Vowel Families (Chunks) in Two-Syllable Words Cover parts of unfamiliar words with finger and look for familiar chunks inside.		✓	
Know the spelling-sound correspondences for common consonant digraphs. CCSF 3a.		✓	
Decode regularly spelled one-syllable words. CCSF 3b.		✓	
Decode words containing –e and common vowel team conventions for representing long vowel sounds (*ee, ea, ai, oa, ui*). CCSF 3c.		✓	
Decode 2-syllable words following basic patterns by breaking the words into syllables. CCSF 3e.		.02	
Use single and double consonant rule to decode 2-syllable words with long or short vowels. CCSF 3c.		.01	
Decode compound words. Use knowledge of the individual words to predict the meaning of compound words. CCSL 4d (2nd).		.01	
Recognize base words and their inflections: *write, writer, writing*. Read words with inflectional endings. CCSF 3f.		.01	
2B Phonics Total		.05	

a-e		**e-e**		**i-e**		**o-e**		**u-e**		**ay**		**oy**	
sale		Pete		smile		pole		June		gray		boy	
e-e		**e-a**		**a-i**		**o-a**		**ui**		**ow**		**ow**	
meet		seal		pain		load		suit		grow		cow	

a		e		i		o		u	
-ater	-atter	-epy	-eppy	-idle	-iddle	-oping	-opping	-uter	-utter

-ed	-ing	-es	-y	-er	-est

Word Recognition

Outlaws Know 300-500 high-frequency words (e.g., *enough, instead*) and use them as "islands of certainty" while reading in 2B level materials. CCSF 3g.		.01	
Word Recognition Total		.01	

Fluency and Self-Monitoring

Fluency Read 2B text comfortably, with confidence, purpose, and understanding. CCSF 4a.		✓	
Read 2B text orally with 98-100% accuracy, appropriate rate, and expression on initial reading. CCSF 4b.		.01	
Read in a whisper voice.		✓	
Self-Monitoring Use context to confirm or self-correct word recognition and understanding, rereading as necessary. CCSF 4c.		✓	
When stuck, back up and try again and/or continue reading and come back to correct after gaining more information.		✓	
Fluency Total		.01	
2B Foundational Skills Total		.10	

2B Who Will You Call?

Student Practice Page

Name	Dates
baker roofer speller sitter plumber reader barber driver thinker lifter	
1. Your sink is clogged.	
2. Your hair is too long.	
3. You need a good book to read.	
4. You have to get to the airport.	
5. You need a birthday cake.	
6. Rain is coming into your bedroom.	
7. You want to write a hard word.	
8. You need help with a problem.	
9. You need someone to watch your baby sister.	

Common Core Standard Foundational Skills 3f: Recognize base words and their inflections: *write, writer, writing*. Read words with inflectional endings.

2B Running Record

Student ______________ Teacher______________ Grade______ Room________ Date______________

Title:______________	Error/Miscue Analysis		
	Needs work on this Phonics Pattern	Needs to learn this Tricky Word	Not in background knowledge

Active Reading

- ☐ Use finger to look for familiar parts of words inside unfamiliar words.
- ☐ Stop and try again when reading doesn't make sense, match the letters, or sound right.
- ☐ Have control of the sight words used at this level.
- ☐ Have most of the words in the book in his or her speaking vocabulary.
- ☐ Use knowledge of endings, blends, vowel patterns, compound words, and rhyming to figure out unfamiliar two-syllable words.
- ☐ Determine what a text says explicitly and makes logical inferences from it. *(What is this about so far? How do you know? Why...?)*

Two-Syllable Decoding

- ☐ Final "–e" (*cap/cape...*)
- ☐ Long vowel teams (*ea, ee...*)
- ☐ Single/double consonants *(hoping/hopping)*
- ☐ Endings (*-ed, -er, -ing...*)
- ☐ Open/closed syllable rule (*o/pen*)

Power Goal

Transition to 1R

2B Entry Points	**1.60**	
2B Foundational Skills Points	**.10**	
2B Comprehension Points	**.20**	

1R Transition Points. With NO help of any kind, student must demonstrate ability to:			**Evidence/Date**			**Points**	
Phonics	**Decode Most Regular Three-Syllable Words** Decode most three-syllable words that follow a regular vowel pattern (*wonderful*). CCSF3. **Read Words With Three-Letter Blends and Common Suffixes** Use 3-letter blends (**spl**ash, ca**tch**) to decode words. Use common suffixes (*-y, -ier, -iest, -ly*) to decode words.	See **Phonics Survey** on page 97. Minimum score of 20.	Scores		Dates	.04	
Word Recognition	**Read 1R Tricky Words** Recognize and read 1R irregularly spelled words. CCSF 3f.	See **Tricky Words** on page 98. Minimum score of 30.	Scores		Dates	.01	
Comprehension	**Read and Comprehend Unfamiliar 1R Text** **Apply Foundational Skills (Word-Solving)** Use a combination of decoding skills, sight words, and context clues to read 1R text with 98-100% accuracy. Stop and try again if something doesn't look right, sound right, or make sense. CCSF 4. **Apply Reading Standards (Comprehension)** Determine what a 1R text says explicitly and makes logical inferences from it. CCSR 1, CCSR 2, CCSR 3.	See **Cold Read Record** on page 99. Minimum score of 6 on one Cold Read Text.	Scores	Titles	Dates	.04	
1R Transition Points						**.09**	
GRAND TOTAL: Student should transition to 1R with 1.99 points and demonstrated proficiency at 1R prerequisites.						**1.99**	

1R Independent Reading Level Overview 2.00 - 2.49

Decode Regularly Spelled Three-Syllable Words

1R Learning Focus

Decode Three-Syllable Words

1R readers are able to sit for 30 minutes and enjoy one long picture book. Their focus is not on decoding, but on the content of the book. They are enjoying traditional tales, silly stories, poetry, and informational text. They should be given the opportunity to read picture books that come in series (e.g., Clifford, Arthur, Amelia Bedelia, Berenstain Bears). Picture books with the same characters and similar plot elements prepare 1R readers for the move into chapter books at 2R. As decoding 1R text becomes easier, silent reading will become the preferred mode. Allow students to spend enough time enjoying and engaging at the 1R level before moving them into the longer and more complicated books at the 2R level.

Key Common Core Standards

Foundational Skills

3b. Know spelling-sound correspondences for additional common vowel teams (e.g., *ew, oy, oi, ought*).

3c. Decode regularly spelled two-syllable words with long vowels (Ruby, even).

3d. Decode words with common suffixes (*-y, -ly, -ier, -iest*).

3e. Identify words with inconsistent but common spelling-sound correspondences.

3f. Recognize and read 1R irregularly spelled words.

Entry Requirements

Must be in place before earning 1R designation.

- Decode most regular three-syllable words. CCSF 3.
- Decode words with three-letter blends and common suffixes. CCSF 3d.
- Read 1R Tricky Words. CCSF 3f.
- Read and comprehend unfamiliar 1R text (successfully apply Foundational Skills and Reading Standards). CCSF4, CCSR 1-3.

Exit Requirements

Must be in place before earning 2R designation.

- Decode any word familiar from speech, including multisyllabic and irregularly spelled words, diphthongs, special vowel spellings, common prefixes and suffixes, plurals, and names. CCSF 3c (3rd), 3de.
- Read and comprehend unfamiliar 2R text (successfully apply Foundational Skills and Reading Standards). CCSF4, CCSR 1-3.

1R Independent Reading Level Assessment 2.00 - 2.49

Entry Requirements: Cumulative Record

Student ______________________ Teacher ______________________ Room ________ Date Started ________

1R Entry Requirements

		Evidence/Date				Date Completed
Phonics	**Decode Most Regular 3-Syllable Words** Decode most 3-syllable words that follow a regular vowel pattern (*wonderful*). CCSF3. **Read Words With 3-Letter Blends and Common Suffixes** Use 3-letter blends (**spl**ash, ca**tch**) to decode words. Use common suffixes (*-y, -ier, -iest, -ly*) to decode words.	See **Phonics Survey** on page 97. Minimum score of 20.	Scores		Dates	
Word Recognition	**Read 1R Tricky Words** Recognize and read 1R irregularly spelled words. CCSF 3f.	See **Tricky Words** on page 98. Minimum score of 30.	Scores		Dates	
Comprehension	**Read and Comprehend Unfamiliar 1R Text** **Apply Foundational Skills (Word-Solving)** Use a combination of decoding skills, sight words, and context clues to read 1R text with 98-100% accuracy. Stop and try again if something doesn't look right, sound right, or make sense. CCSF 4. **Apply Reading Standards (Comprehension)** Determine what a 1R text says explicitly and makes logical inferences from it. CCSR 1, CCSR 2, CCSR 3.	See **Cold Read Record** on page 99. Minimum score of 6 on one Cold Read Text.	Scores	Titles	Dates	
A reader who is proficient at all of the above enters 1R with 2.00 points.						2.00

1R Entry Requirements: Phonics Survey

Entry Level: 20 Words

Name Date Score

Three-Letter Blends and Digraphs	Suffixes	Vowel Teams	Two-Syllable Long Vowels	Three-Syllable Regular	
string	stringy	haunted	paper	battery	remember
splash	splashes	tour	baking	relaxing	divided
scream	screamed	ground	female	afternoon	continent
sprout	sprouting	smooth	even	powerful	probably
squirt	squirrel	hooked	nicest	invented	understand
throw	bottle	annoying	shiny	favorite	suggested
shriek	itchy	spoiled	Tony	entertain	decided
earth	itchier	obey	hoping	crocodile	example
burst	itchiest	weight	Ruby	argument	expected
scratch	thumper	chewier	tuba	Washington	explained

Common Core Standard Foundational Skills 3b: Know spelling-sound correspondences for additional common vowel teams.

Common Core Standard Foundational Skills 3c: Decode regularly spelled two-syllable words with long vowels.

Common Core Standard Foundational Skills 3d: Decode words with common prefixes and suffixes.

1R Entry Requirements: Tricky Words

Must Recognize On Sight

Entry Level: 30 Words

Name								Dates		Total	
been		clothes		front		machine		question		weigh	
believe		clothing		glove		magic		roof		weight	
bicycle		country		heavy		minute		second		whisper	
board		dollar		idea		moon		secret		whistle	
bottom		done		Indian		move		shall		wife	
brought		early		key		o'clock		shovel		wild	
bread		engine		kind		piece		sign		wind	
breakfast		feather		knew		pond		sorry		wolf	
building		field		knock		poor		stood			
city		floor		library		present		straight			
climb		frighten		life		princess		warm			

1R Entry Requirements: Cold Read Record

Title:______________________________ Date:______________

Given an unfamiliar 1R text (Cold Read), and NO help of any kind:

Running Record Record all errors as the student reads the passage. Indicate self-corrections.	Error/Miscue Analysis		
	Needs work on this Phonics Pattern	Needs to learn this Tricky Word	Not in background knowledge.

Apply Foundational Skills

Active Reading Strategies	Yes or No
Read with 98 - 100% word accuracy. Student makes no more than 2 uncorrected errors.	
Stop and try again if something doesn't look right, sound right, or make sense. Self-correct ALL errors that interfere with meaning.	
Read fluently and with expression, using punctuation.	

If the answer to any of the above questions is No, STOP and move student to an easier level.
If the answers to all are Yes, continue on to Reading Standards. (See specific questions on Cold Read Text Pages.)

Apply Reading Standards

Comprehension	Student Response	Score Weak.........Strong
Basic Understanding Support basic understanding with evidence from the text. CCSR 1.		1 2 3 4
Interpretation Support an interpretation or analysis with evidence from the text. CCSR 2&3.		1 2 3 4
Total Points (A minimum score of 6 is required in order to enter 1R.)		

1R Entry Requirements: Cold Read Text A

The plane from Mexico was landing. Sam stood at the airport window and watched. He was going to meet his cousin Marco for the first time.

5

Soon a boy Sam's size came through the door. Sam's mother hugged him. "Marco, this is Sam," she said slowly. "Sam, this is Marco."

"Hi," said Sam. Suddenly he felt shy.

"¡Hola!" said Marco softly.

6

In the car Marco was very quiet. So was Sam.

"We are happy you have come to live with us for a year," said Sam's mother.

"Sí," said Marco. But he didn't look happy. He just looked out the window.

"You like sports?" asked Sam. Sam loved sports. He was very good at them too.

Marco shrugged.

7

Soccer Sam
by Jean Marzollo
Random House

Basic Understanding

What is happening in this story so far?

Interpretation

What do you predict will be the problem in this book?

1R Entry Requirements: Cold Read Text B

It was Halloween night.
All the witches were busy.
They were busy getting ready
for their Halloween ride.

Grouchy Witch was busy
making grouchy faces
in her cracked mirror.

Nasty Witch was busy
shooting a water gun
at her cat, Bow-Wow.

Mother Witch was busy
making a new broomstick
for Little Witch.

Oh, what a wonderful Halloween
it was going to be!

All the witches were ready . . .
but where was Little Witch?
"Little Witch, what are you doing?"
called Mother Witch.

Mother Witch went upstairs
and into Little Witch's room.
"What! You made your bed again!"
screeched Mother Witch.
"Sorry, Mother. I forgot,"
said Little Witch.

Little Witch's Big Night
by Deborah Hautzig
Random House

1R

Basic Understanding

What is happening in this story so far?

Interpretation

What do you predict will be the problem in this book?

1R Entry Requirements: Cold Read Text C

Adult Snakes

There are many kinds and sizes of adult snakes. All snakes have the same basic body parts. Snakes have a tongue that is used for smelling, not tasting. A snake's entire body is covered with scales. Snakes slide along the ground using their stomach muscles.

In the winter, most adult snakes hibernate, or sleep. When they wake up they hunt for food. In the spring, they lay eggs or have babies. A new snake life cycle begins.

Parts of a Snake

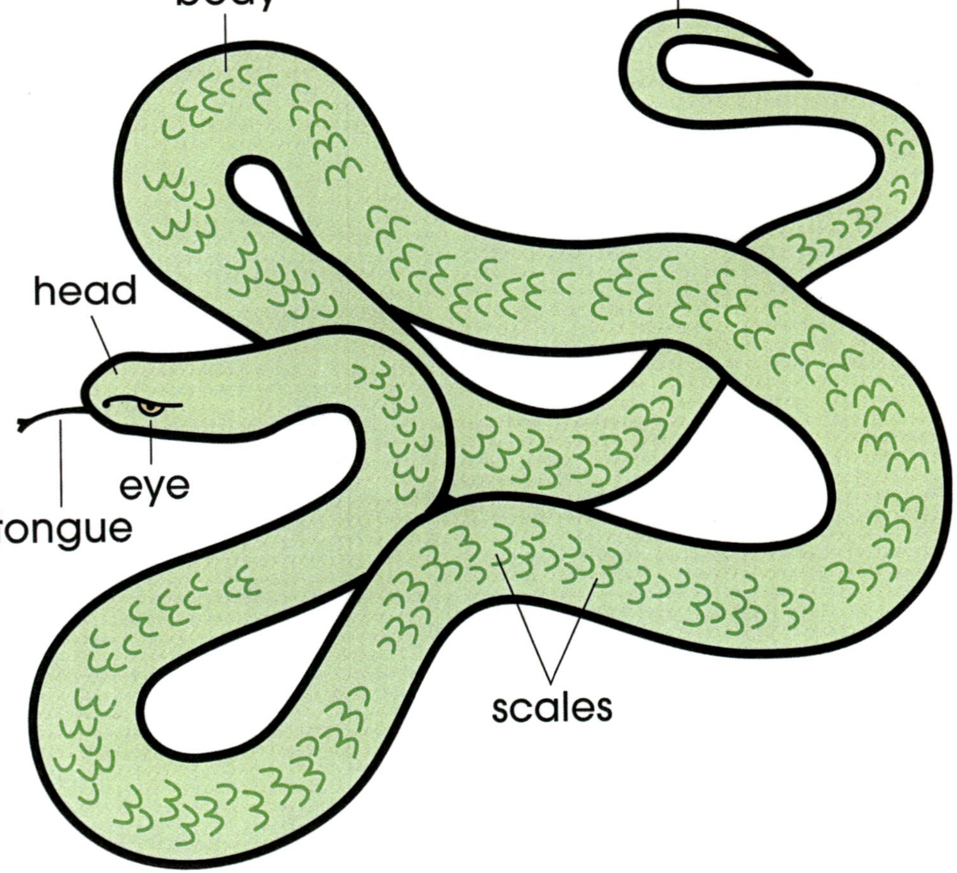

Life Cycles of Snakes by Melanie Mitchell Lerner

Basic Understanding

Tell me three things the text says about snakes.

Interpretation

What are the important events in a snake's life?

1R Entry Requirements: Cold Read Text D

You have 206 bones
in your body.

These bones fit together
perfectly.
Together, they form
your *skeleton*.

Your bones do not bend.
So they are joined
in places where
you need to bend.
These places
are called *joints*.

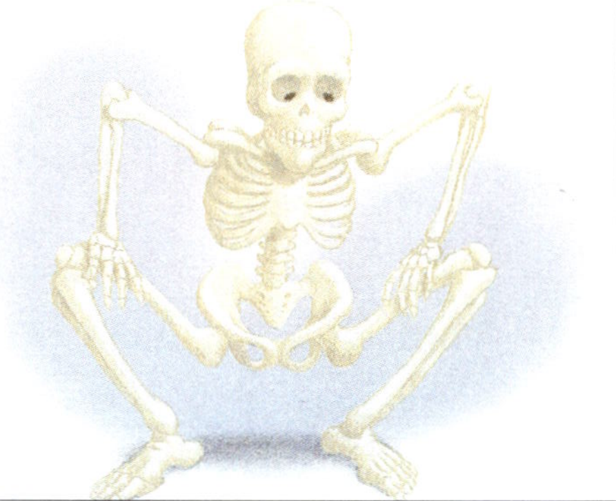

Your *spine*,
or backbone,
has many joints.
It helps you
to stand up straight
or do a somersault.

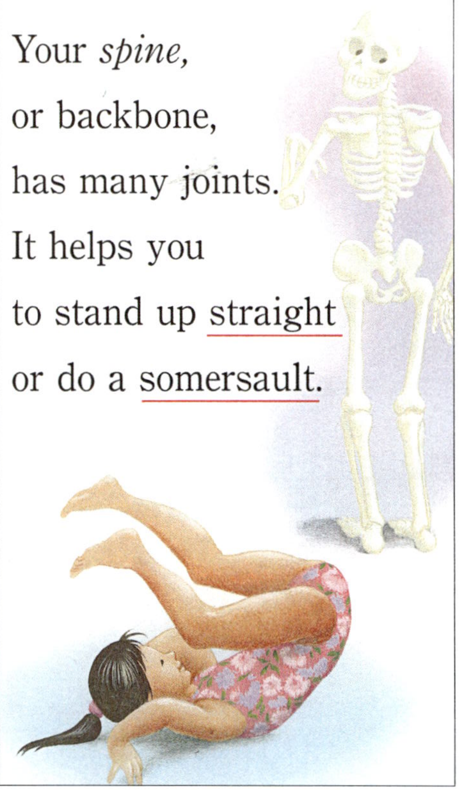

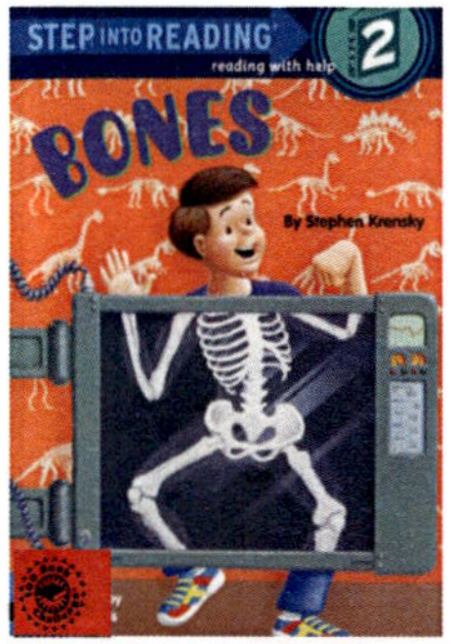

Bones by Stephen Krensky
Random House

1R

Basic Understanding

Tell me three things the text says about bones.

Interpretation

What is the most important thing you learned about bones? Why is it important?

1R Comprehension

Reading Standards for Literature and Informational Text

Proficiency in the standards below must be demonstrated while reading independently in 1R level text. In order to advance to 2R, students must earn .24 Comprehension Points.

Key Ideas and Details: **Using Text Evidence to Support Conclusions** Understand, think about, and discuss what the author said.		Evidence/Date	Points	
	Demonstrate adequate background knowledge to name and talk about the content common to 1R books.		✓	
	Read actively, demonstrate an obvious understanding of the text (laugh at the funny parts, comment on the material, make personal connections) without prompting.		.02	
CCSR 1	Ask and answer such questions as who, what, where, when, why, and how to demonstrate understanding of key details in a text. • *What were some different kinds of animals in this story? Where did the little girl want to go? Why was the dog laughing?*		.02	
CCSR 2	Recount stories, including fables and folktales from diverse cultures, and determine their central message, lesson, or moral. • *Retell the story to me. Make sure you include enough details so that I can follow what is happening.* • *What was the lesson of the story?*		.02	
	Identify the main topic of a multi-paragraph text as well as the focus of specific paragraphs within the text. • *What was this book mainly about?* • *What was this paragraph mostly about?*		.02	
CCSR 3	Describe how characters in a story respond to major events and challenges. • *How did ____ react when ____?*		.02	
	Describe the connection between a series of historical events, scientific ideas or concepts, or steps in technical procedures in a text. • *Which step comes first in a butterfly's life: the cocoon or the caterpillar? Why?* • *What were the important events in ______'s life? Which came first? How do you know?*		.02	
	Identify and describe the following literary elements in the text: plot, setting, and characters.		.02	

Craft and Structure: Analyzing the Effects of Authors' Choices

Understand and discuss the way(s) the author(s) said what was said.

CCSR 4	Describe how words and phrases (e.g., regular beats, alliteration, rhymes, repeated lines) supply rhythm and meaning in a story, poem, or song. • *Which words tell how the ______ sounds?* • *Let's clap the rhythm of this line. Which words are most important here?*		.02	
	Determine the meaning of words and phrases in a text relevant to a 1R topic or subject area. • *Is there any word in this book that you had never heard before?* • *What do you think it means?*		.02	
CCSR 5	Describe the overall structure of a story, including describing how the beginning introduces the story and the ending concludes the action. *Retell this story in three sentences that start like this:* • *In the beginning….* • *In the middle…* • *In the end….*		.02	
	Know and use various text features (e.g., captions, bold print, subheadings, glossaries, indexes, electronic menus, icons) to locate key facts or information in a text efficiently. • *Where in this book would you look to find information about ____ (what tigers eat; what makes a seed grow)?*		.02	
	Use graphic organizers to organize information and ideas from reading. • *Create a Venn diagram to compare/contrast the food of bears and foxes.*		.02	
CCSR 6	Acknowledge differences in the points of view of characters, including by speaking in a different voice for each character when reading dialogue aloud. • *Here two people are talking. Read this part so that I can tell who is speaking by changes in your voice.*		.02	
	Identify the main purpose of a text, including what the author wants to answer, explain, or describe. • *Why do you think the author wrote this book? What is the most important thing she wanted us to learn?*		.02	

Integration of Knowledge and Ideas: Comparing Different Presentations Discuss how the ideas in a book connect to each other and to the larger world.				
CCSR 7	Use information gained from the illustrations and words in a print or digital text to demonstrate understanding of its characters, setting, or plot. • *What does this illustration teach you about ___ (character, setting, or plot)?*		.02	
	Explain how specific images (e.g., a diagram showing how a machine works) contribute to and clarify a text. • *How does this diagram teach us about _____ (the life cycle of a bee; the water cycle; what wolves eat)?*		.02	
CCSR 8	Describe how reasons support specific points the author makes in a text. • *The author is telling us that ___________. What reasons does he give to convince us?*		.02	
CCSR 9	Compare and contrast two or more versions of the same story (e.g., Cinderella stories) by different authors or from different cultures. Give student two books that tell the same story/legend. • *How is this story the same in both books? How is the story different?* • *Which do you like better and why?*		.02	
	Compare and contrast the most important points presented by two texts on the same topic. Give student two books on the same topic. • *What does the author most want us to remember from this first book?* • *What does the author most want us to remember from this second book?* • *How are they alike? How are they different?* • *Which do you like better and why?*		.02	
1R Comprehension Total			.24	

1R Foundational Skills

Range of Reading and Level of Text Complexity	Evidence/Date	Points	
Engagement and Independence Read regularly and independently, sustaining engagement, in 1R-level materials for at least 30 minutes every day in the classroom (15 minutes per session).		.01	
Home Reading Have established a home reading habit and read for at least 30 minutes every night without prompting.		.01	
Genres Enjoy informational text, prose, and poetry at 1R level. CCSR 10.		.01	
Range of Reading and Level of Text Complexity Total		.03	

Phonological Awareness

Syllabication Orally segment a multisyllable word into its syllables.		✓	
Phonological Awareness Total		✓	

Phonics: Three-Syllable Words, Three-Letter Blends

Vowel Families (Chunks) in Three-Syllable Words (See 1R Phonics Survey) Cover parts of unfamiliar words with finger and look for familiar chunks inside.		✓	
Decode any three-syllable word that follows a regular vowel pattern (Washington).		.02	
Read words with common suffixes. CCSF 3d.		.01	
Use three-letter blends to figure out unfamiliar words.		.01	

-ed	-er	-ing	-es	-y	-est	-ly	-ier	-iest

str-	scr-	spl-	spr-	shr-	squ-	sch-	thr-	-tch	-rst	-rth

1R Foundational Skills Cont'd

Use silent consonants to figure out unfamiliar words. kn- / gn- / wr- / -mb / -gh		.01	
Know spelling-sound correspondences for additional common vowel teams. CCSF 3b. au / ou (you) / ou (out) / oo (too) / oo (book) / oy / oi / ey / ei / ew		.01	
Decode regularly spelled two-syllable words with long vowels (e.g., *open, Ruby, biking*). CCSF 3c.		.01	
Distinguish long and short vowels when reading regularly spelled one-syllable words. CCSF 3a.		.01	
Phonics Total		**.08**	

Word Recognition

Outlaws Recognize and read 1R irregularly spelled words and inconsistent but common spelling-sound correspondences and irregularly spelled words. (90 1R Outlaws.) CCSF 3ef.		.01	
Word Recognition Total		**.01**	

Fluency and Self-Monitoring

Fluency Read 1R text comfortably, with confidence, purpose, and understanding. CCSF 4a.		.01	
Read 1R text orally with 98%-100% accuracy, rate, and fluency, using punctuation as a guide to expression. CCSF 4b.		.01	
Read silently (with sub-vocalization, if necessary) while maintaining comprehension.		.01	
Self-Monitoring Use context to confirm or self-correct word recognition and understanding, rereading as necessary. CCSF 4c.		.01	
Fluency Total		**.04**	
1R Foundational Skills Total		**.16**	

1R Who Will You Call?

Student Practice Page

Name	Dates
artist dentist harpist realist actress actor hostess host cellist director	
1. You have a toothache.	
2. You need someone to be the king in your play.	
3. You need someone to be the fairy godmother.	
4. You want to learn to play the cello.	
5. She said she would get your table ready.	
6. He took you to your table instead.	
7. You want to learn to play the harp.	
8. You need help with a problem.	
9. You want an illustrator for the book you wrote.	
10. You need someone to take charge of the school play.	

Common Core Standard Foundational Skills 3d: Read words with common suffixes.

1R Running Record

Student ________________ Teacher ________________ Grade ______ Room ________ Date ______________

Title: ______________________________

	Error/Miscue Analysis		
	Needs work on this Phonics Pattern	Needs to learn this Tricky Word	Not in background knowledge

Active Reading Strategies

- ☐ Successfully read 98-100% of words with no help from the teacher.
- ☐ Read with expression, using punctuation.
- ☐ Stop and try again when reading doesn't make sense, match the letters, or sound right.
- ☐ Have control of the sight words used at this level.
- ☐ Have most of the words in the book in his or her speaking vocabulary.
- ☐ Look for familiar parts of words inside unfamiliar words.
- ☐ Use two-letter vowel combinations to figure out new words.
- ☐ Use knowledge of three-letter blends, vowel digraphs, and rules of syllabication to figure out regular three-syllable words.

Comprehension

☐ Determine what a text says explicitly. (*What is this about so far? How do you know?*)

☐ Support an interpretation or analysis. (*Why...? What evidence from the text supports your answer?*)

Power Goal

Transition to 2R

1R Entry Points	**2.00**	
1R Foundational Skills Points	**.16**	
1R Comprehension Points	**.24**	

2R Transition Points. With NO help of any kind, student must demonstrate ability to:			**Evidence/Date**			**Points**	
Phonics	**Decode Almost Any Word Familiar From Everyday Speech** Decode almost any word familiar from speech, including multisyllabic and irregularly spelled words, diphthongs, special vowel spellings, common prefixes and suffixes, plurals, and names. CCSF 3	See **Tricky Phonics Check** on page 115. Minimum score of 20.	Scores		Dates	.04	
Comprehension	**Read and Comprehend Unfamiliar 1R Text** **Apply Foundational Skills (Word-Solving)** Use a combination of decoding skills, sight words, and context clues to read 2R text with 98-100% accuracy. Stop and try again if something doesn't look right, sound right, or make sense. CCSF 4. **Apply Reading Standards (Comprehension)** Determine what a 1R text says explicitly and make logical inferences from it. CCSR 1, CCSR 2, CCSR 3.	See **Cold Read Record** on page 116. Minimum score of 6 on one Cold Read Text.	Scores	Titles	Dates	.05	
2R Transition Points						**.09**	
GRAND TOTAL: Student should transition to 2R with 2.49 points and demonstrated proficiency at 2R prerequisites.						**2.49**	

2R Independent Reading Level Overview 2.50 - 2.99

Finish 1 Chapter Book Each Week

2R Learning Focus

Finish 1 Chapter Book Each Week

2R readers begin 2R as picture book readers and leave as chapter book readers. They develop the habit of silent reading, the ability to sustain interest across sittings, and finally, the chapter book reading habit, where they must engage and understand without the aid of illustrations. Students should not leave 2R until they are successfully reading (and finishing) at least one chapter book a week.

Decode All Multisyllabic and Irregularly Spelled Words Familiar from Everyday Speech

2R readers are able to try various vowel/consonant sounds in unfamiliar words until they recognize the word from everyday speech. 2R books are full of irregularly spelled words, multisyllabic words, special vowel spellings, but all of the words in 2R books should be familiar to readers from their oral language (e.g., *gigantic, scientist*). Their use of decoding and context clues allows the 2R readers to get close enough to the pronunciation of any word so that as they try different possible pronunciations, they recognize one. Expect 2R readers to be able to approximate pronunciation of difficult names.

Key Common Core Standards

Foundational Skills

3d. Decode words with common prefixes (*un-, re-, mis-*) and suffixes (*-able, -ful, -ier, -iest, -tion*).

3e. Identify and read words with inconsistent but common spelling-sound correspondences (*body, cloth, ton*).

3f. Recognize and read high-frequency words common to 2R books by sight, including grade-appropriate irregularly spelled words.

- Develop the stamina, experience, and fluency to complete at least one 2R chapter book per week.
- Decode multisyllable words.

Entry Requirements

Must be in place before earning 2R designation.

- Decode almost any word familiar from speech, including multisyllabic and irregularly spelled words, diphthongs, special vowel spellings, common prefixes and suffixes, plurals, and names. (Minimum 20 correct on Tricky Phonics Check.) CCSF 3c (3rd), 3de.
- Read and comprehend unfamiliar 2R text (successfully apply Foundational Skills and Reading Standards). (Minimum 9 correct on Cold Read Record.) CCSF4, CCSR 1-3.

Exit Requirements

Must be in place before earning Wt designation.

- Notice and define literary and technical vocabulary. (Minimum 4 correct on Wt Literary Vocabulary Check.) CCSF 4c, CCSR 4.
- Decode every word encountered in Wt text (Minimum 30 correct on Phonics Gap Locator). CCSF 3bc.
- Read and comprehend unfamiliar Wt text (successfully apply Foundational Skills and Reading Standards to Wt level text). (Minimum 9 correct on Cold Read Record.) CCSR 1, CCSR 2, CCSR 3, CCSR 4, CCSF 3.
- Demonstrate ability to finish a Wt chapter book. CCSR 10.
- Demonstrate ability to read and comprehend Wt informational text. CCSR 10.

2R Independent Reading Level Assessment 2.50 - 2.99

Entry Requirements: Cumulative Record

Student ______________________ Teacher ______________________ Room _______ Date Started _______

2R Entry Requirements

		Evidence/Date				Date Completed
Phonics	**Decode Almost Any Word Familiar From Everyday Speech** Decode almost any word familiar from speech, including multisyllabic and irregularly spelled words, diphthongs, special vowel spellings, common prefixes and suffixes, plurals, and names. CCSF 3	See **Tricky Phonics Check** on page 115. Minimum score of 20.	Scores		Dates	
Comprehension	**Read and Comprehend Unfamiliar 1R Text** **Apply Foundational Skills (Word-Solving)** Use a combination of decoding skills, sight words, and context clues to read 2R text with 98-100% accuracy. Stop and try again if something doesn't look right, sound right, or make sense. CCSF 4. **Apply Reading Standards (Comprehension)** Determine what a 1R text says explicitly and make logical inferences from it. CCSR 1, CCSR 2, CCSR 3.	See **Cold Read Record** on page 116. Minimum score of 6 on one Cold Read Text.	Scores	Titles	Dates	
A reader who is proficient at all of the above enters 2R with 2.50 points.						**2.50**

2R Entry Requirements: Tricky Phonics Check

2R readers are able to try various vowel/consonant sounds in decoding unfamiliar words until they recognize the word from everyday speech.
Entry Level: 20 Words

i says e	i says long i	i says short i	vowels split	y says e	y says long i	y says short i
happier	**divide**	**ability**	**create**	**easily**	**deny**	**mystery**
curious	**decided**	**American**	**ruin**	**trophy**	**satisfy**	**crystal**
emptiness	**invited**	**imagine**	**museum**	**county**	**rely**	**gymnast**
skinnier	**replied**	**terrible**	**area**	**vocabulary**	**rhyme**	**symbol**
warrior	**polite**	**promise**	**reality**	**necessary**	**hydrant**	**system**

ch=k	ci=sh	soft c	t=tch	tion=shun	su=sh/zh	si=sh/zh
echo	**delicious**	**center**	**adventure**	**direction**	**usually**	**decision**
anchor	**musician**	**certain**	**picture**	**invitation**	**sugar**	**television**
stomach	**official**	**except**	**temperature**	**education**	**treasure**	**division**
schedule	**electrician**	**announce**	**furniture**	**combination**	**pleasure**	**conclusion**
ache	**magician**	**innocent**	**mixture**	**abbreviation**	**ensure**	**explosion**

Common Core Standard Foundational Skills 3e: Identify words with inconsistent but common spelling-sound correspondences.

2R Entry Requirements: Cold Read Record

Title:____________________ Date:____________

Given an unfamiliar 2R text (Cold Read), and NO help of any kind...

Running Record Record all errors as the student reads the passage. Indicate self-corrections.	Error/Miscue Analysis		
	Needs work on this Phonics Pattern	Needs to learn this Tricky Word	Not in background knowledge.

Apply Foundational Skills

Active Reading Strategies	Yes or No
Read with 98 - 100% word accuracy. In a text of approximately 100 words, student makes no more than 2 uncorrected errors.	
Stop and try again if something doesn't look right, sound right, or make sense. Self-correct ALL errors that interfere with meaning.	
Read fluently and with expression, using punctuation.	

If answer to any of the above questions is No, STOP and move student to an easier level.
If the answers to all are Yes, continue on to Reading Standards. (See specific questions on Cold Read Text Pages.)

Apply Reading Standards

Comprehension	Student Response	Score Weak.........Strong
Basic Understanding Support basic understanding with evidence from the text. CCSR 1.		1 2 3 4
Interpretation Support an interpretation or analysis with evidence from the text. CCSR 2 & 3.		1 2 3 4
Total Points (A minimum score of 6 is required in order to enter 2R.)		

2R Entry Requirements: Cold Read Text A

Marvin Redpost: Alone in His Teacher's House
by Louis Sachar
Random House

Basic Understanding

What is happening so far in this story?

Interpretation

Compare Nick and Marvin's reactions to having a substitute teacher.

1

Teacher's Pet

"You will have a substitute teacher tomorrow," Mrs. North told her third-grade class.

"All right!" shouted Nick.

Mrs. North stared at Nick.

Marvin Redpost looked down at his desk and smiled. Nick Tuffle was Marvin's best friend. Marvin had two best friends. His other best friend was Stuart Albright.

"I will be gone for one week," said Mrs. North. "I won't be back until next Thursday. A week from tomorrow."

"Hot dog!" exclaimed Nick.

Mrs. North glared at Nick. "I will leave detailed instructions for the substitute," she warned. "And if any of you misbehave, I will know about it. That means you, Nick."

"Hey, why pick on me?" asked Nick.

When it was time to go home, Nick and Stuart gathered around Marvin's desk.

"A substitute for a week!" said Nick, rubbing his hands together. "This is going to be great."

"Let's pretend we're each other," said Stuart. "I'll be Marvin. Marvin, you be Nick. And Nick, you can be me."

"I don't want to be *you,*" Nick said to Stuart. "I'll be Marvin, and you be me."

"I don't want to be *you!*" said Stuart.

It made Marvin feel proud that both his friends wanted to be him.

On the other hand, he wasn't sure he wanted either of them to be him.

2R Entry Requirements: Cold Read Text B

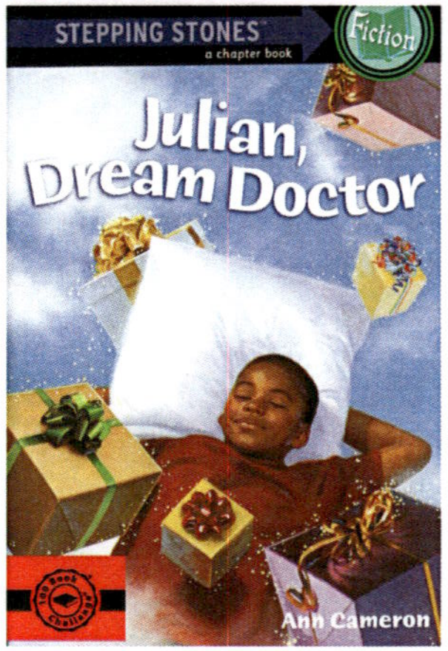

Julian, Dream Doctor
by Ann Cameron
Random House

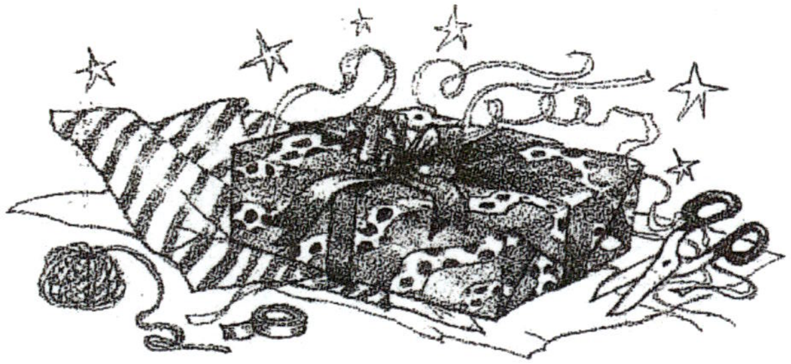

2.

My Very Good Idea

Every year we have a birthday party for my dad. Every year, the week before his birthday, my mom, Huey, and I go out and buy him a present.

This year was no different.

We went out. We got Dad a really good bowling ball. We wrapped it up and hid it in the back of the closet.

But then I started thinking. It would be nice to do something special for my dad. It would be nice to give him a surprise party and, besides the bowling ball, one special gift—something he had always dreamed of.

Once I thought of it, I could even imagine it happening. I could see myself showing Dad a mysterious box with a big bow on it, and Dad opening it and saying, "But Julian, nobody—nobody ever knew! This is what I've always dreamed of! Julian, you're a genius! This is the most unforgettable birthday that I have ever had!"

And then he would give me a big hug and be so excited he would lift me way off the ground.

Basic Understanding

What is happening so far in this story?

Interpretation

Describe how Julian's thoughts about the bowling ball change. Use evidence from the text to support your answer.

2R Entry Requirements: Cold Read Text C

Tarantulas are hairy spiders.
A big one would cover
your dinner plate.

Most tarantulas are gentle.
But some have
an unusual weapon—
their own hair.

When a coyote
tries to eat it,
the tarantula kicks
a cloud of itchy hairs
into the air.
The hairs make the coyote
cough and scratch.
Now the tarantula
can escape.

A tarantula's worst enemy
is a fierce wasp called
a tarantula hawk.
The spider tries to
fight off the wasp.
But the wasp darts in
and stings it.

Now the spider can't move.
The wasp drags it into its burrow
and lays an egg on it.
After the egg hatches,
the baby wasp
eats the tarantula alive.

Monster Bugs
by Lucille Recht Penner
Random House

2R

Basic Understanding

Tell me three things the text says about tarantulas.

Interpretation

Which is more dangerous to a tarantula: a coyote or a tarantula hawk? What evidence from the text supports your answer?

2R Entry Requirements: Cold Read Text D

Iceberg

It is April 14, 1912. The Titanic is in icy waters off the coast of Canada.

It is almost midnight. The ship is quiet. The sea is smooth as glass. The air is biting cold.

The passengers have had a good dinner. Some of them are still up playing cards. Most are asleep in their rooms.

It is a good night to be inside. But the lookout must watch for danger. He is high above the ship in the crow's-nest. He stares into the darkness.

Suddenly the lookout sees a dark shape. It is a mountain of ice! And the Titanic is heading right into it! The lookout rings an alarm. He calls, "Iceberg straight ahead!"

A seaman is below, steering the ship. He tries to turn the ship away. But it is too late.

The giant iceberg scrapes along the side of the ship.

There is a bump. A grinding noise. It doesn't seem like much. Some people do not even notice.

But the captain hurries from his room. He goes down below. He wants to see if the ship is hurt. Soon he learns the terrible truth.

The iceberg has hurt the ship badly. Water is pouring in. Five of the watertight compartments are already flooded. And that is too many. Nothing can be done now.

It seems impossible. But it is true. The Titanic is going to sink!

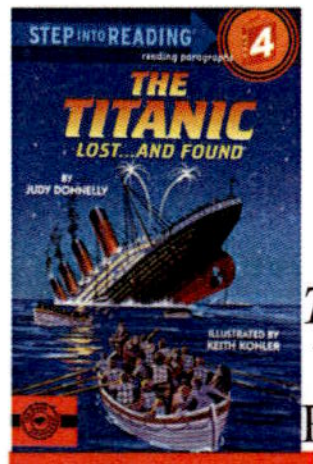

The Titanic: Lost...and Found by Judy Donnelly
Random House

Basic Understanding
Tell me three things the text says about the Titanic.

Interpretation
Using the words first, second, and third, explain what happened to make the Titanic sink.

2R Comprehension

Reading Standards for Literature and Informational Text

Proficiency in the standards below must be demonstrated while reading independently in 2R-level text. In order to advance to Wt, students must earn .24 Comprehension Points.

Key Ideas and Details: Using Text Evidence to Support Conclusions Understand, think about, and discuss what the author said.		Evidence/Date	Points	
	Demonstrate adequate background knowledge to name and talk about the content common to 2R books.		✓	
	Read actively, demonstrate an obvious understanding of the text, (laugh at the funny parts, comment on the material, make personal connections) without prompting.		.02	
CCSR 1	Ask and answer such questions as who, what, where, when, why, and how to demonstrate understanding of key details in a text. • *What were some different kinds of animals in this story?* • *Where did the little girl want to go? Why was the dog laughing?*		.02	
CCSR 2	Recount stories, including fables and folktales from diverse cultures, and determine their central message, lesson, or moral. • *Retell the story to me. Make sure you include enough details so that I can follow what is happening.* • *What was the lesson of the story?*		.02	
	Identify the main topic of a multi-paragraph text as well as the focus of specific paragraphs within the text. • *What was this book mainly about?* • *What was this paragraph mostly about?*		.02	
CCSR 3	Describe how characters in a story respond to major events and challenges. • *How did ____ react when ____?*		.02	
	Describe the connection between a series of historical events, scientific ideas or concepts, or steps in technical procedures in a text. • *Which step comes first in a butterfly's life: the cocoon or the caterpillar? Why?* • *What were the important events in _______'s life? Which came first? How do you know?*		.02	
	Identify and describe the following literary elements in the text: plot, setting, and characters.		.02	

Craft and Structure: **Analyzing the Effects of Authors' Choices** Understand and discuss <u>the way(s)</u> the author(s) said what was said.				
CCSR 4	Describe how words and phrases (e.g., regular beats, alliteration, rhymes, repeated lines) supply rhythm and meaning in a story, poem, or song. • *Which words tell how the ______ sounds?*		.02	
	Determine the meaning of words and phrases in a text relevant to a 2R topic or subject area. • *Is there any word in this book that you had never heard before?* • *What do you think it means?*		.02	
CCSR 5	Describe the overall structure of a story, including describing how the beginning introduces the story and the ending concludes the action. *Retell this story in three sentences that start like this:* • *In the beginning…* • *In the middle…* • *In the end…*		.02	
	Know and use various text features (e.g., captions, bold print, subheadings, glossaries, indexes, electronic menus, icons) to locate key facts or information in a text efficiently. • *Where in this book would you look to find information about _____ (what tigers eat; what makes a seed grow)?*		.02	
	Use graphic organizers to organize information and ideas from reading. • *Use a Venn diagram to compare/contrast the foods of bears and foxes.*		.02	
CCSR 6	Acknowledge differences in the points of view of characters, including by speaking in a different voice for each character when reading dialogue aloud. • *Here two people are talking. Read this part so that I can tell who is speaking by changes in your voice.*		.02	
	Identify the main purpose of a text, including what the author wants to answer, explain, or describe. • *Why did the author write this book? What was the most important thing she wanted us to learn?*		.02	

Integration of Knowledge and Ideas: Comparing Different Presentations

Discuss how the ideas in a book connect to each other and to the larger world.

CCSR 7	Use information gained from the illustrations and words in a print or digital text to demonstrate understanding of its characters, setting, or plot. • *What does this picture teach you about ___ (what this character is like; where this story takes place; what is happening in the story)?*		.02	
	Explain how specific images (e.g., a diagram showing how a machine works) contribute to and clarify a text. • *How does this diagram teach us about ____ (the life cycle of a bee; the water cycle; what wolves eat)?*		.02	
CCSR 8	Describe how reasons support specific points the author makes in a text. • *The author is telling us that __________. What reasons does he give to convince us?*		.02	
CCSR 9	Compare and contrast two or more versions of the same story (e.g., Cinderella stories) by different authors or from different cultures. Give student two books that tell the same story/legend. • *How is this story the same in both books? How is the story different?* • *Which do you like better and why?*		.02	
	Compare and contrast the most important points presented by two texts on the same topic. Give student two books on the same topic. • *What does the author most want us to remember from this first book?* • *What does the author most want us to remember from this second book?* • *How are they alike? How are they different?* • *Which do you like better and why?*		.02	
2R Comprehension Total			**.24**	

2R Foundational Skills

Range of Reading and Level of Text Complexity	Evidence/Date	Points	
Engagement and Independence Read regularly and independently, sustaining engagement, in 2R-level materials for at least 30 minutes every day in the classroom.		.01	
Chapter Book Habit Regularly finish 2R chapter books, at least one a week.		.02	
Home Reading Have established a home reading habit and read for at least 30 minutes every night without prompting.		.01	
Genres Enjoy informational text, prose, and poetry at 2R level. CCSR 10.		.01	
Range of Reading and Level of Text Complexity Total		.05	

Phonics: Multisyllable and Irregularly Spelled Words

Decode Multisyllable and Irregularly Spelled Words Cover parts of unfamiliar words with finger and look for familiar chunks inside.		✓	
Use rules of syllabication to approximate the pronunciation of any word, including difficult names. • Every syllable must have a vowel. • Closed syllables: End in consonant. Vowel is short (*in-sect*). • Open syllables: End in vowel. Vowel is long (*ve-to*).		.01	
Decode any word familiar from speech, including irregularly spelled words, diphthongs (two vowel sounds in the same syllable: *boy*), special vowel spellings, common endings, and multisyllabic words.		.01	
Flexibility with letter sounds. Try different sounds for the letters/chunks in an unfamiliar word until the word is recognized from everyday speech. Try different sounds for the vowels, e.g.:		.01	

short/long i	i says long e	i says long i	i is short	y says long e	y says long i
spin/spine	radio	reminder	holiday	envy	apply

Try splitting the vowels. create | museum | graduate		.01	
Try different sounds for consonants or consonant/vowel combinations, e.g., ch=k: school | si=sh/zh: decision | s=sh: sure | ti=sh: initial | t=tch: future | ci=sh: official | c=s: certain		.01	
Try making a letter silent, e.g., gn: sign | pn: pneumonia | gh: sigh | wh: white | mb: thumb		.01	
Phonics Total		.06	

Word Recognition and Vocabulary

Outlaws Read 2R words with inconsistent or irregular spelling-sound correspondences (70 of the 2R Outlaws). CCSF 3ef.		.01	
Supply words represented by common abbreviations (e.g., *Mr., St., Dec., Mon.*). Mr. | Ms. | Mrs. | Dr. | St. | Rd. | Ave. | Mon. | Jan.		✓	
Prefixes and Suffixes Decode words with common prefixes and suffixes. CCSF 3d. un- | re- | mis- | -ful | -able | -tion | -ly | -ier | -iest		.01	
Use adjectives and adverbs to describe. CCSL 6.		✓	
Word Recognition Total		.02	

2R Foundational Skills Cont'd

Fluency and Self-Monitoring

Fluency Read 2R text comfortably, with confidence, purpose, and understanding. CCSF 4a.		✓	
Read 2R books orally with 98%-100% accuracy, rate, and fluency, using punctuation as a guide to expression. CCSF 4b.		.01	
Read silently and rapidly enough to keep the plot moving in 2R chapter books.		.01	
Sustain engagement and comprehension in books with few or no illustrations.		.01	
Self-Monitoring Use context to confirm or self-correct word recognition and understanding, rereading as necessary. CCSF 4c.		✓	
Fluency Total		.03	
2R Foundational Skills Total		.16	

2R Outlaws

Must Recognize On Sight

Student Practice Page

Name								Dates		Total	
among		certain		courage		except		meadow		scene	
beauty		certainly		cousin		famous		meant		sigh	
blood		chief		curtain		fault		mirror		smooth	
blossom		chocolate		danger		forward		mischief		study	
borrow		choose		daughter		garage		necklace		swallow	
bowl		closet		diamond		gather		neither		toward	
breath		cloth		Dr.		grease		ocean		vegetable	
breathe		coffee		drawer		island		often		whole	
calendar		comb		during		juice		pleasant		wisdom	
calm		comfortable		earn		knife		police		worry	
canoe		common		eighty		loose		practice		worse	
captain		continue		either		lose		prove			
carrot		copy		English		manage		rescue			
cellar		cost		escape		marry		sandwich			

Common Core Standard Foundational Skills 3f: Recognize and read grade-appropriate irregularly spelled words.

2R Running Record

Student ______________ Teacher ______________ Grade ______ Room ________ Date ______________

Title: ______________	Error/Miscue Analysis		
	Needs work on this Phonics Pattern	Needs to learn this Tricky Word	Not in background knowledge

Active Reading

- ☐ Read fluently and with expression, using punctuation.
- ☐ Read actively: visualize, make predictions, make connections, and ask questions.
- ☐ Look for familiar parts of words inside unfamiliar words.
- ☐ Stop and try again when reading doesn't make sense, match the letters, or sound right.
- ☐ Have control of the sight words used at this level.
- ☐ Have most of the words in the book in his or her speaking vocabulary.
- ☐ Successfully decode any word used in everyday speech, including names and irregular three- and four-syllable words.

Comprehension

☐ Determine what a text says explicitly. (*What is this about so far? How do you know?*)

☐ Support an interpretation or analysis. (*Why...? What evidence from the text supports your answer?*)

Power Goal

Transition to Wt

2R Entry Points	**2.50**	
2R Foundational Skills Points	**.16**	
2R Comprehension Points	**.24**	

Wt Transition Points. With NO help of any kind, student must demonstrate ability to:			**Evidence/Date**	**Points**	
Vocabulary	**Notice and Define Literary and Technical Vocabulary** Notice unfamiliar literary, academic, and domain-specific vocabulary while reading and provide a word or phrase that could be substituted for the unfamiliar word while retaining the meaning of the sentence. CCSF 4c, CCSR 4.	See **Vocabulary Check** on page 133. Minimum score of 4.	Scores / Dates	.02	
Phonics	**Decode Every Word Encountered in Wt Text** Use rules of syllabication to approximate the pronunciation of any word, including difficult names. CCSF 3c.	See **Phonics Gap Locator** on page 134. Minimum score of 30.	Scores / Dates	.01	
Comprehension	**Read and Comprehend Unfamiliar Wt Text (Successfully Apply Reading Standards)** Determine what a text says explicitly and make logical inferences from it. Interpret vocabulary and figurative language in context. CCSR 1, CCSR 2, CCSR 3. CCSR 4.	See **Cold Read Record** on page 135. Minimum score of 9 on one Cold Read Text.	Scores / Titles / Dates	.02	
Range of Reading	**Demonstrate Ability to Finish a Wt Chapter Book** Read and finish a Wt novel, demonstrating comprehension and a command of the vocabulary used in the text. CCSR 10, CCSL 6.	After reading a Wt chapter book, student is able to tell what problem the main character faced and how the problem was resolved.	**Yes** or **No** / Titles / Dates	.02	
	Demonstrate Ability to Read and Comprehend Wt Informational Text Read a Wt informational text, demonstrating comprehension and a command of the vocabulary used in the text. CCSR 10, CCSL 6.	After reading a Wt informational text, student is able to tell what s/he learned and show where in the text s/he learned that information.	**Yes** or **No** / Titles / Dates	.02	
Wt Transition Points				**.09**	
GRAND TOTAL: Student should transition to Wt with 2.99 points and demonstrated proficiency at Wt prerequisites.				**2.99**	

Wt Independent Reading Level Overview 3.00 - 3.99
Notice and Acquire Literary Vocabulary

Wt Learning Focus
Notice and Acquire Literary Vocabulary
Wt-level books include "literary" vocabulary, language not normally used in everyday speech (e.g., *exclaimed, cautiously*). For many students this is truly a foreign language. Students who arrive at the Wt level with a vast background of listening to higher-level books will already have much of this vocabulary. Students who have not been read to will not. Students acquire literary vocabulary through immersion in text, the same way they acquired their speaking vocabulary through immersion in oral language. Wt books have 1-2 literary words per chapter-book size page of text. Wt readers must spend enough time reading at the Wt level to acquire the 1,500 new "literary" vocabulary words expected of proficient third-grade readers. This is entirely different and unrelated to decoding. At the Wt level, the major focus is on noticing these literary words and learning them through immersion in reading.

Finish One Chapter Book Each Week
Wt readers continue to develop silent reading fluency, the ability to sustain interest across sittings, and the chapter book reading habit. Students should not leave Wt unless they are successfully reading (and finishing) at least one Wt chapter book a week.

Key Common Core Standards

Language 6: Acquire and use accurately grade-appropriate conversational, general academic, and domain-specific words and phrases, including those that signal spatial and temporal relationships (e.g., *After dinner that night we went looking for them*).

Reading Informational Text 4: Determine the meaning of general academic and domain-specific words and phrases in a text relevant to a Wt topic or subject area.

Entry Requirements
Must be in place before earning Wt designation.
- Notice and define literary and technical vocabulary. (Minimum 4 correct on Wt Literary Vocabulary Check.) CCSF 4c, CCSR 4.
- Decode every word encountered in Wt text (Minimum 30 correct on Phonics Gap Locator). CCSF 3bc.
- Read and comprehend unfamiliar Bk text (successfully apply Foundational Skills and Reading Standards). (Minimum 9 correct on Cold Read Record.) CCSR 1, CCSR 2, CCSR 3, CCSR 4, CCSF 3.
- Demonstrate ability to finish a Wt chapter book. CCSR 10.
- Demonstrate ability to read and comprehend Wt informational text. CCSR 10.

Exit Requirements
Must be in place before earning Bk designation.
- Demonstrate command of a literary vocabulary of approximately 1,500 words available for comprehending Bk level text. (Minimum 5 correct on Bk Vocabulary Check.) CCSL 6.
- Read and comprehend unfamiliar Bk text (successfully apply Reading Standards). (Minimum 9 correct on Cold Read Record.) CCSR 1, CCSR 2, CCSR 3, CCSR 4, CCSF3.
- Demonstrate ability to finish a Bk chapter book in a few days. CCSR 10.
- Demonstrate ability to read and comprehend Bk informational text. CCSR 10.

Wt Independent Reading Level Assessment 3.00 - 3.99

Entry Requirements: Cumulative Record

Student ______________________ Teacher ______________________ Room ________ Date Started ________

Wt Entry Requirements

		Evidence/Date				Date Completed
Vocabulary	**Notice and Define Literary and Technical Vocabulary** Notice unfamiliar literary, academic, and domain-specific vocabulary while reading and provide a word or phrase that could be substituted for the unfamiliar word while retaining the meaning of the sentence. CCSF 4c, CCSR 4.	See **Vocabulary Check** on page 133. Minimum score of 4.	Scores		Dates	
Phonics	**Decode Every Word Encountered in Wt Text** Use rules of syllabication to approximate the pronunciation of any word, including difficult names. CCSF 3c.	See **Phonics Gap Locator** on page 134. Minimum score of 30.	Scores		Dates	
Comprehension	**Read and Comprehend Unfamiliar Wt Text (Successfully Apply Reading Standards)** Determine what a text says explicitly and make logical inferences from it. Interpret vocabulary and figurative language in context. CCSR 1, CCSR 2, CCSR 3. CCSR 4.	See **Cold Read Record** on page 135. Minimum score of 9 on one Cold Read Text.	Scores	Titles	Dates	
Range of Reading	**Demonstrate Ability to Finish a Wt Chapter Book** Read and finish a Wt novel, demonstrating comprehension and a command of the vocabulary used in the text. CCSR 10, CCSL 6.	After reading a Wt chapter book, student is able to tell what problem the main character faced and how the problem was resolved.	**Yes** or **No**	Titles	Dates	
	Demonstrate Ability to Read and Comprehend Wt Informational Text Read a Wt informational text, demonstrating comprehension and a command of the vocabulary used in the text. CCSR 10, CCSL 6.	After reading a Wt informational text, student is able to tell what s/he learned and show where in the text s/he learned that information.	**Yes** or **No**	Titles	Dates	
A reader who is proficient at all of the above enters Wt with 3.00 points.						3.00

Wt Entry Requirements: Vocabulary Check

Wt Entry Level: 4 Correct   Wt Exit Level: 10 Correct

Students should be able to offer one word or short phrase that could be substituted for the underlined word or phrase while retaining the meaning of the sentence. Do not accept examples or vague approximations. Do not help the student. Do not read the possible acceptable answers to the student. Circle the one supplied by the student, or write in their answer. Teach students the skill of being able to substitute one word or phrase for another word, but do not teach these particular words.

Literary Word	Acceptable Answers (or Anything Similar)	Check if Correct
She was extremely proud of her little dog.	very, exceptionally, really, real, highly	
Suzy was mad and muttered to herself all the way home.	grumbled, complained, growled, talked, grumped, mumbled	
"Grandpop's in a bad mood tonight," remarked Mom.	said, commented, worried, replied, answered	
The class was overjoyed about the field trip.	very happy, excited, eager, pleased, full of joy, pumped up	
They drove off into the setting sun.	sinking, disappearing, sun that was going down	
Ronald dreaded having to tell to his father the bad news.	feared, worried about, didn't want to, wasn't looking forward to	
The bully snatched the candy out of the little boy's hand.	grabbed, stole, took roughly	
Tamika was so excited, she was bouncing off the walls.	jumping up and down, all over the place	
"This new cream will work wonders on those dry hands."	fix, work miracles, make better	
After seeing the ghost, Juan was a little shaken up.	upset, nervous, anxious	

Common Core Standard Language 4a: Use sentence level context as a clue to the meaning of a word or phrase.
Common Core Standard Reading 4: Determine the meaning of words and phrases as they are used in a text.

Wt Entry Requirements: Phonics Gap Locator

Wt Entry Level: 30 Correct   Wt Exit Level: 70 Correct

4+ Syllables	i says long e	i says long i	i says y	soft c	y says long e	y says long i
interrupted	mysterious	fiery	onion	electricity	duty	satisfy
responsibility	encyclopedia	finally	champion	endurance	sugary	dryer
refrigerator	curiosity	minor	opinion	medicine	cheerfully	supply
temperature	aquarium	rival	familiar	bracelet	colony	python
combination	taxi	climate	genius	ancestor	battery	hydrant
vowels split	**si=sh/zh**	**ti=sh**	**t=ch**	**silent letters**		**cc=x**
rodeo	television	illustration	torture	pneumonia	debt	accept
react	permission	celebration	mixture	gnome	business	accent
area	measure	foundation	fracture	kneeling	folk	accident
create	mission	impatient	actually	wholesome	soften	accidentally
scientific	vision	explanation	fortunate	wrist	shepherd	vaccination

Common Core Standard Foundational Skills 3c: Use rules of syllabication to approximate the pronunciation of any word, including difficult names.

Wt Entry Requirements: Cold Read Record

Student ____________________ Teacher ____________________ Room ________ Date ________

Title: ____________________

Given an unfamiliar Wt text (Cold Read), and NO help of any kind...			
Fluently Decode Wt text	**Evidence/Student Response**		**Score**
Use combined knowledge of all letter-sound correspondences, syllabication patterns, and morphology (e.g., roots and affixes) to accurately read unfamiliar multisyllabic words, including names. CCSF 3a, CCSF 4ab.	• 99-100% word accuracy.		**Yes** or **No**
	• Appropriate rate and expression.		**Yes** or **No**
	• Stop and try again when something doesn't look right, sound right, or make sense.		**Yes** or **No**
If answer to any of the above questions is No, STOP TEST and move student to an easier level. Any student having trouble with decoding is most likely working at or below 2R.			
Reading Standards **See specific questions on Cold Read Text Pages**	**Evidence/Student Response**		**Score** Weak..........Strong
Basic Understanding Support basic understanding with evidence from the text. CCSR 1.			1 2 3 4
Interpretation Support an interpretation or analysis with evidence from the text. CCSR 2, CCSR 3.			1 2 3 4
Vocabulary Interpret vocabulary and figurative language in context. CCSR 4.			1 2 3 4
Cold Read Proficiency Total: A minimum score of 9 points on ONE Cold Read Text is required in order to enter Wt.		**Total Points**	

Wt Entry Requirements: Cold Read Text A

Beach Blues
by Diana G. Gallagher
Capstone

Basic Understanding

What is happening so far in this story?

Interpretation

What do you think Claudia's parents are trying to tell her? What evidence from the text supports your idea?

Vocabulary

What does the word dependable mean? What word could you use in its place without changing the meaning of the passage?

Tuesday Surprise

My father is **dependable** and boring. He wears a suit and goes to work before I get up, six days a week. He comes home at 6:15 **every night**. Then he reads the newspaper, eats dinner, watches TV, and goes to bed.

He does that **every day** except Sunday. Dad's computer store is closed on Sunday, but he still gets up **early**. He reads the newspaper in the morning. Then he works around the house and watches sports on TV.

Every Sunday.

Today wasn't Sunday. It was Tuesday. When I went to the kitchen, Dad was at the breakfast table reading the newspaper.

I stopped and stared. I was too surprised to talk. It was as shocking as if a **T. rex** had just squashed our kitchen.

Dad looked at his watch. "It's after eight," he said. "Aren't you late for school?"

"No school," I said. I was on winter break, but Dad doesn't take breaks. "What's wrong?" I asked.

My **mom** handed me a glass of orange juice. "Sit down, Claudia," she said. "Your father has something to tell you."

My throat closed up. I thought that something terrible must have happened. "Am I failing math?" I asked. "Are we moving? Did someone die?" I gasped. "Is something wrong with Grandma?"

"Well, she's going away for a while," Dad said.

"She can't!" I exclaimed. **Grandma** understood me. She listened to me, and she almost never yelled. She was always FAIR, even when I did something AWFUL and didn't deserve it.

"I'll miss her," I said sadly.

"You'll have **plenty of time** with her," Dad said. "It's a long drive to Florida."

Wt Entry Requirements: Cold Read Text B

Aliens for Breakfast
by Stephanie Spinner
& Jonathan Etra
Random House

Basic Understanding

What is happening so far in this story?

Interpretation

Who do you think the Dranes might be and what evidence in the text makes you think so?

Vocabulary

Find a word on the page that is new to you. What do you think it probably means? Why?

Richard eyed his bowl. Everything in it had stopped moving. Then the milk gave a tiny splash. A round pink thing the color of chewed bubblegum started to climb up the side of the bowl. Amazed, Richard touched it with his spoon.

"Stop that!" The words came directly into Richard's head. He put his spoon down very quickly. Then he took off his glasses and wiped them on his shirt sleeve. But when he put them back on, the thing was still there.

"What do you think you're doing?" asked the voice.

"Uh, eating breakfast," answered Richard. Was a piece of cereal really talking to him?

It was. "I could use some breakfast myself," it said. It crawled out of the bowl and dropped onto the table. "The trip really took it out of me."

Richard finally found his voice. "Who are you?" he asked.

"Aric. Commander of the Interspace Brigade. Our goal: to wipe out cosmic troublemakers. Our record: ninety-eight percent success."

"You're an alien?" squeaked Richard. All those books he'd read about kids meeting aliens. And now it looked like it was happening to him. Him! Richard Bickerstaff!

"I am a Ganoobian," said Aric. "*You* are the alien."

I've got to be dreaming, thought Richard. He sometimes had very exciting dreams about space travel and large but friendly creatures from other planets who made him their leader.

"Well, come on! Do not just sit there!" said Aric. His voice was awfully loud for such a little thing. It boomed inside Richard's head. "Let us get going—I am busy. I have six other planets to save. Move it or lose it! Hup-hup-hup!"

"Wait a minute," said Richard. "Where are we going? Who are we fighting? What about school? I'm going to be late!"

"Hey—it is your planet," said Aric. "And you have been chosen to help me save it. But if you do not mind the Dranes taking over, hunky-dory." He started to climb back into Richard's cereal bowl.

"Who are the Dranes?" Richard wondered.

Wt Entry Requirements: Cold Read Text C

Hungry Plants
by Mary Batten
Random House

1. Gotcha!

Everything is quiet in the bog. Or *almost* everything.

A tiny black fly buzzes around, looking for food. All of a sudden, it smells nectar, a sugary juice that plants make. The sweet smell is coming from a strange plant growing flat against the ground.

The fly lands near the plant and crawls toward a leaf. Closer, closer, closer.

The leaf slams shut, squishing the fly between two green walls.

The fly tries to get out but can't. The fly will never escape. This plant will eat it alive!

How can a plant eat a fly?

It's easy for the Venus flytrap.

The Venus flytrap is just one of more than six hundred kinds of plants that eat insects and other tiny animals. These plants are called carnivorous (kar-NIV-ur-us). This word means "meat-eating." Carnivorous plants are the T. rexes of the plant world.

Eating bugs might seem like a strange thing for a plant to do. And it is. Most plants get everything they need to be healthy from sun, rain, and soil. But insect-eating plants grow in very poor soil. They make up for this by eating bugs. For these plants, eating bugs is like taking a vitamin pill.

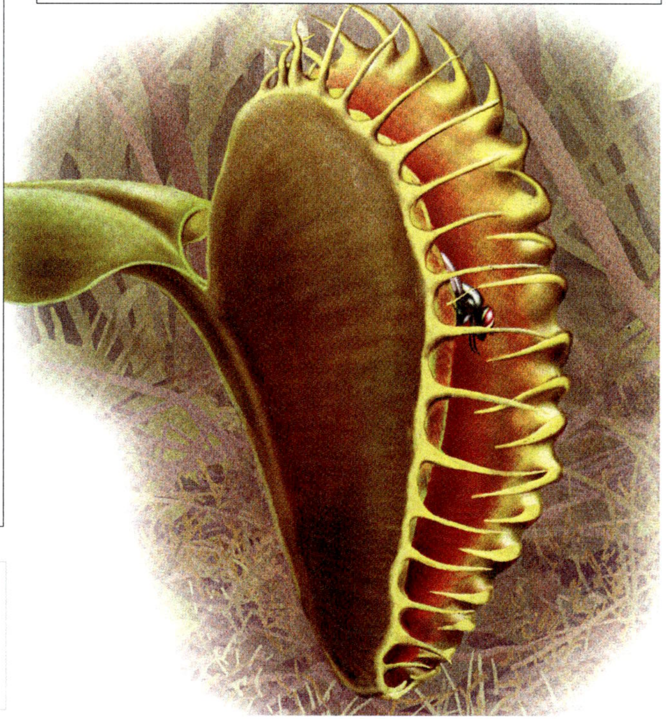

Basic Understanding

Tell me three things the text says about carnivorous plants.

Interpretation

How is a Venus flytrap like a T. rex?

Vocabulary

What does the author mean by "two green walls?"

Wt Entry Requirements: Cold Read Text D

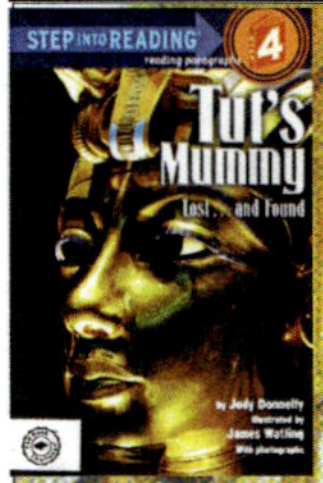

Tut's Mummy: Lost and Found
by Judy Donnelly
Random House

1
The King Is Dead

"Tutankhamen is dead! The boy king is dead!" The news travels through Egypt. King Tutankhamen (too-tonk-AH-men) was only eighteen years old. His wife and family are very sad to lose him. But the Egyptians are glad for their king.

They believe his spirit will travel to a wonderful place—the Land of the Dead.

There the king will do all the things he loved to do when he was alive. He will feast and play games. He will go hunting and fishing. His spirit will be happy forever.

Tutankhamen will need many things in the Land of the Dead. He will need food and furniture and clothing. He will need games and jewelry. All these things must be buried with him.

Most of all, the king will need his body. The Egyptians believe a spirit cannot live on without its body. So dead bodies are dried out to last forever. They are turned into mummies.

Priests come to the palace. They say prayers for the king. Then they dry out the king's body. They use a special kind of salt called natron. It takes many days. The mummy is wrapped in yards of fine cloth. More than one hundred jewels and charms are tucked in the folds. The charms will keep evil spirits away from the king.

Basic Understanding

Tell me three things the text says about King Tutankhamen.

Interpretation

The author tells us that Egyptians are happy for their king. Why? Support your answer with evidence from the text.

Vocabulary

Find a word/phrase that you don't use in speech. What do you think it probably means? Why?

Wt Comprehension

Reading Standards for Literature and Informational Text

In order to advance to Bk, students must earn a total of .48 from any combination of the standards below, demonstrated during/after reading independently in Wt-level materials.

Key Ideas and Details: Using Text Evidence to Support Conclusions Understand, think about, and discuss <u>what</u> the author said.		Evidence/Date	Points	
	Demonstrate background knowledge of a Wt-level reader, familiar with 90-100% of the vocabulary and enough of the world knowledge found in Wt-level books to ensure basic comprehension (e.g., third-grade level math, science, and social studies concepts). (Extensive reading and life experiences are required to remediate if this is a problem, not decoding or thinking skills.)		✓	
CCSR 1	Ask and answer questions to demonstrate understanding of a text, referring explicitly to the text as the basis for the answers. • *How, why, what...?* • *What connections can you make to your own life? How is it different/similar?*		.03	
CCSR 2	Recount stories, including fables, folktales, and myths from diverse cultures; determine their central message, lesson, or moral and explain how it is conveyed through key details in the text. • *Tell me the story as if I hadn't read it.* • *What is the lesson and how do you know?*		.03	
	Determine the main idea of a text; recount the key details and explain how they support the main idea. • *What is the main idea of this book and how do you know?* • *What key facts does the author use to support the main idea?*		.03	
CCSR 3	Describe characters in a story (e.g., their traits, motivations, or feelings) and explain how their actions contribute to the sequence of events. • *Who are the main characters?* • *What are they like?* • *Describe at least three qualities of the main character. How do these character traits contribute to what happens in the story?*		.03	
	Describe the relationship between a series of historical events, scientific ideas or concepts, or steps in technical procedures in a text, using language that pertains to time, sequence, and cause/effect. • **Time/Sequence:** *Using the words "first, second, third," describe the sequence of events (or steps) in the text. OR* • **Concept/Scientific Ideas/Cause and Effect:** *Using the words "because, since, as a result," explain how two ideas in the text are related.*		.03	

	Identify and describe the following literary elements in the text: plot (conflict and resolution), setting (time and place), characters (traits, roles, similarities, major and minor), narrator/point of view (first and third person), and theme (or moral). • *Where and when does the story take place?* • *Who are the main characters and what are their traits?* • *Who is the narrator? Is it told in first or second person?* • *What is the theme (lesson or moral)?*		.03	
Craft and Structure: Analyzing the Effects of Authors' Choices Understand and discuss the way(s) the author(s) said what was said.				
CCSR 4	Determine the meaning of words and phrases as they are used in a text, distinguishing literal from nonliteral language. • *Find a word you never use in your speech, or that you never saw before.* • *What do you think it probably means? Why?* • *Read the sentence again, but this time, put a word or phrase in place of the new word, without changing the meaning of the sentence.* • *Find a word or phrase that doesn't mean what it literally says: e.g., The new student began to come out of her shell.*		.03	
	Determine the meaning of general academic and domain-specific words and phrases in a text relevant to a Wt-level topic or subject area. (Same as above.)		.03	
CCSR 5	Refer to parts of stories, dramas, and poems when writing or speaking about a text, using terms such as chapter, scene, and stanza; describe how each successive part builds on earlier sections. • *Which scenes, chapters, or stanzas do you think are the most important? Why?*		.03	
	Use text features and search tools (e.g., key words, sidebars, hyperlinks) to locate information relevant to a given topic efficiently. • *Using the book you are reading, show how you can use text features to locate information quickly.*		.03	
	Distinguish among common forms of literature (e.g., poetry, novel, short story, biography, drama) using knowledge of their structural elements. • *Is this book fiction or informational? How can you tell?* • *What kind of literature is this? How can you tell?*		.03	
CCSR 6	Distinguish their own point of view from that of the narrator, the characters or the author. • *How is your point of view different or the same as the narrator, the characters, or the author?*		.03	
	Support a critical evaluation of author's craft. • *What does the author do to make the material clear or interesting?*		.03	

Integration of Knowledge and Ideas: Comparing Different Presentations

Discuss how the ideas in a book connect to each other and to the larger world.

<table>
<tr><td rowspan="2">CCSR 7</td><td>Explain how specific aspects of a text's illustrations contribute to what is conveyed by the words in a story (e.g., create mood, emphasize aspects of a character or setting).
• How do the illustrations contribute to the text?</td><td></td><td>.03</td><td></td></tr>
<tr><td>Use information gained from illustrations (e.g., maps, photographs) and the words in a text to demonstrate understanding of the text (e.g., where, when, why, and how key events occur). (Same as above.)</td><td></td><td>.03</td><td></td></tr>
<tr><td>CCSR 8</td><td>Describe the logical connection between particular sentences and paragraphs in a text (e.g. comparison, cause/effect, first/second/third in a sequence).
• What is the main idea of this paragraph? How does the next paragraph relate to it?</td><td></td><td>.03</td><td></td></tr>
<tr><td></td><td>Provide examples of facts and opinions in text.
• Does the author state any opinions? Show me.
• Give me an example of an opinion in the book. Give me an example of a fact.</td><td></td><td>.03</td><td></td></tr>
<tr><td></td><td>Differentiate essential from non-essential information.
• Give me an example of essential information.
• Give me an example of non-essential information.</td><td></td><td>.03</td><td></td></tr>
<tr><td rowspan="2">CCSR 9</td><td>Compare and contrast the themes, settings, and plots of stories written by the same author about the same or similar characters (e.g., in books from a series).
• Given two books from the same series, or about similar characters, create a matrix chart comparing them.
<table>
<tr><td></td><td>Similarities</td><td>Differences</td></tr>
<tr><td>Main Character</td><td></td><td></td></tr>
<tr><td>Minor Character</td><td></td><td></td></tr>
<tr><td>Setting</td><td></td><td></td></tr>
<tr><td>Plot</td><td></td><td></td></tr>
</table></td><td></td><td>.03</td><td></td></tr>
<tr><td>Compare and contrast the most important points and key details presented in two texts on the same topic.
<table>
<tr><td></td><td>Book A</td><td>Book B</td></tr>
<tr><td>Main Idea</td><td></td><td></td></tr>
<tr><td>Support #1</td><td></td><td></td></tr>
<tr><td>Support #2</td><td></td><td></td></tr>
<tr><td>Support #3</td><td></td><td></td></tr>
</table></td><td></td><td>.03</td><td></td></tr>
<tr><td colspan="3">Wt Comprehension Total</td><td>.48</td><td></td></tr>
</table>

Wt Foundational Skills

Range of Reading and Level of Text Complexity	Evidence/Date	Points	
Classroom Work Read regularly and independently, sustaining engagement, in Wt-level materials for at least 30 minutes every day in the classroom.		.02	
Home Reading Sustain a home reading habit, reading at Wt level for at least 30 minutes every night, or make the additional 30 minutes up in school.		.03	
Chapter Book Habit CCSR 10 • Regularly finish Wt chapter books, one per week. • Sustain engagement and comprehension in books with few or no illustrations.		.05	

Genres

Read independently and comprehend informational text at the Wt level, including:

	Evidence (List Titles or Topics Where Proficiency Was Demonstrated)	Date	Points	
History Social Studies Biography			.02	
Science			.02	

Wt Foundational Skills Cont'd

Read independently and comprehend literary text at the Wt level, including at least 4 genres:

	Evidence	Date		
Stories • Adventure • Contemporary/ Realistic Fiction • Horror • Other			.02	
Traditional Tales • Fables • Folktales • Myths			.02	
Drama or Poetry			.01	
Range of Reading and Level of Text Complexity Total			**.19**	

Phonics: Multisyllable Words, Irregularly Spelled Words

At Wt level, the following are all review (no points assigned), but they are required and may need reinforcement.

Basic Decoding Mastery
Cover parts of unfamiliar words with finger and look for familiar chunks inside.

✓

Use rules of syllabication to approximate the pronunciation of any word, including difficult names. CCSF 3c.

- Every syllable must have a vowel.
- Closed syllables: End in consonant. Vowel is short (*in-sect*).
- Open syllables: End in vowel. Vowel is long (*ve-to*).

✓

Try different sounds for the letters/chunks in an unfamiliar word. CCSF 3cd.
Try different sounds for the vowels.

long/short	i says long e	i says long i	i says y	i is short	y says long e	y says long i
Ruby/rubbish	abbreviation	reliable	convenient	ability	academy	notify

✓

Try splitting the vowels. CCSF 2cd.

create	museum	graduate

✓

Try different sounds for consonants or consonant/vowel combinations.

ch=k	si=sh	s=sh	ti=sh	t=tch	ci=sh	c=s
toothache	permission	treasure	potential	delicious	decision	certain

✓

Try taking a letter out. CCSF 3.

gnaw	pneumonia	sigh	whisper	thumb	autumn

✓

Phonics Total

✓

Word Recognition

Sight Words Read Wt level irregularly spelled words. (85 Wt Outlaws). CCSF 3d.		.01	
Word Recognition Total		.01	

Vocabulary and Language

Literary, Academic, and Technical Vocabulary Acquire and use at least 1,500 words, not familiar from everyday speech, but common to Wt-level text. Know and use words that signal spatial and temporal relationships (e.g., *After dinner that night, we went looking for them.*) CCSL 6.		.05	
Use sentence-level context clues to figure out word meaning and be able to substitute a word or phrase that means the same thing. CCSL 4a.		.01	
Prefixes and Suffixes Identify the meaning of the most common prefixes. CCSF 3a. dis- | un- | re- | mis- | over- | under- | im-/in-/il-/ir-		.02	
Identify and know the meaning of the most common derivational suffixes. CCSF 3a. (A derivational suffix is one that changes a word into a different part of speech, e.g., *happy to happiness*: from adjective to noun.) -able | -tion/-sion | -en | -ant/-ent | -ment | -less | -ful Determine the meaning of the new word formed when a known affix is added to a known word (e.g., *agreeable/disagreeable*). CCSL 4b.		.02	
Roots Use a known root word as a clue to the meaning of an unknown word with the same root (e.g., *company, companion*). CCSL 4c.		.02	
Nuance in Word Meaning Distinguish the literal and non-literal meanings of words and phrases in context (e.g., *take steps*). CCSL 5a.		.02	
Identify real-life connections between words and their use (e.g., describe people who are friendly or helpful). CCSL 5c.		.01	
Distinguish shades of meaning among related words that describe states of mind or degrees of certainty (e.g., *knew, believed, suspected, heard, wondered.*) CCSL 5d.		.01	
Vocabulary Total		.16	

Fluency, Active Reading Strategies, and Self-Monitoring for Comprehension

Fluency Read Wt text comfortably, with confidence, purpose, and understanding. CCSF 4a.		.01	
Read Wt prose and poetry orally, with 98%-100% accuracy, appropriate rate and fluency, using punctuation as a guide to expression. CCSF 4b.		.01	
Silent reading is beginning to be faster than oral and is preferred by the reader. This is essential for enjoyment of complex literature.		.01	
Active Reading Strategies Read actively: activate prior knowledge, survey, make predictions and connections, visualize, reread, and ask clarifying questions.		.01	
Adjust reading speed for various purposes. • Demonstrate aggressive self-monitoring and active reading strategies when reading difficult material. • Skim and scan to locate specific information quickly. • Read silently and rapidly for pleasure.		.01	
Self-Monitoring for Comprehension Stop when comprehension breaks down; identify specific words or passages causing comprehension difficulty and rework for clarification. Use context to confirm or self-correct word recognition and understanding, rereading as necessary. CCSF 4c.		.01	
Fluency, Active Reading Strategies, and Self-Monitoring Total		**.06**	
Wt Foundational Skills Total		**.42**	

Wt Vocabulary
Common Prefixes

Student Practice Page

Name Date Total

un-	re-	mis-	dis-	over-/under-	im-/in-/ill-/ir-
not	*again*	*wrong(ly)*	*opposite of*	*over/under*	*not*
unfriendly	remember	mistake	dishonest	underneath	incorrect
unacceptable	return	misbehave	disrespect	underwater	inactive
unbreakable	research	misplace	disagree	underground	inappropriate
unforgettable	repay	misspell	discount	undershirt	immature
unselfish	rebuild	mistreat	disappear	undersea	incapable
unequal	refill	misjudge	disappoint	underpaid	irresponsible
uncover	rebound	mishandle	distrust	overlook	irresistible
unable	recycle	mismatch	disgrace	overcome	imperfect
unknown	recharge	mistrust	discover	overnight	illegal
unexpected	retrace	misuse	disease	overpaid	improper

The prefixes *dis-*, *re-*, *in-/im-*, and *un-* account for 97% of prefixed words in printed school English.
Honig, et.al., *Teaching Reading Sourcebook*, 2000.

Common Core Standard Reading Foundations 3a: Identify and know the meaning of the most common prefixes.

Wt Vocabulary
Latin Suffixes

Student Practice Page

Name				Date	Total
-able	**-tion/-sion**	**-en**	**-ant/-ent**	**-ment**	**-less/-ful**
able to be (verb to adjective)	*the act or state of (verb to noun)*	*to make (adjective to verb)*	*having the quality of/ full of (noun to adjective)*	*the action of (verb to noun)*	*without and full of (noun to adjective)*
likable	instruction	shorten	absent	entertainment	painless
adorable	selection	lengthen	excellent	equipment	painful
comfortable	inspection	fasten	ancient	compliment	helpless
valuable	exhaustion	listen	intelligent	excitement	helpful
readable	interruption	moisten	independent	agreement	powerful
breakable	hibernation	awaken	innocent	disagreement	powerless
agreeable	exaggeration	forgotten	patient	accomplishment	careless
believable	participation	darken	impatient	improvement	voiceless
avoidable	combination	bitten	violent	requirement	flavorful
curable	discussion	weaken	brilliant	achievement	faithful

Common Core Standard Language 4b: Determine the meaning of the new word formed when a known affix is added to a known word (e.g., *agree/agreeable*).

Wt Outlaws

Must Recognize On Sight

Student Practice Page: Student should be able to read most of these on entry to Wt.

Name | Date | Total

accident		character		debt		gallon		mood		salad	
accept		chosen		death		gradually		mustache		sew	
ache		cocoa		design		guest		mystery		shawl	
actually		collar		desert		guitar		myth		square	
although		college		dessert		health		natural		statue	
anchor		cotton		disease		hoarse		nuisance		stomach	
anxious		cough		double		honesty		onion		strength	
area		couple		doubt		jealous		ought		sugar	
avenue		court		echo		journey		palm		suggest	
bacon		coyote		especially		knowledge		pearl		sword	
blond		crayon		fasten		language		persuade		tomato	
business		crooked		faint		laughter		pigeon		ton	
bruise		cruel		fortunate		league		poison		tongue	
bury		cozy		fought		leather		route		wand	
calves		cupboard		future		magician		ruin		worst	

Transition to Bk

						Points	
Wt Entry Points						**3.00**	
Wt Foundational Skills Points						**.42**	
Wt Comprehension Points						**.48**	
Bk Transition Points. With NO help of any kind, student must demonstrate ability to:			**Evidence/Date**			**Points**	
Vocabulary	**Demonstrate Command of a Literary Vocabulary of Approximately 1,500 Words** Have approximately 1,500 literary vocabulary words in reading vocabulary available for comprehending Bk level text. CCSL 6.	See **Vocabulary Check** on page 155. Minimum score of 5.	Scores		Dates	.03	
Comprehension	**Read and Comprehend Unfamiliar Bk Text (Successfully Apply Reading Standards)** Determine what a text says explicitly and make logical inferences from it. Interpret vocabulary and figurative language in context. CCSR 1, CCSR 2, CCSR 3. CCSR 4.	See **Cold Read Record** on page 156. Minimum score of 9 on one Cold Read Text.	Scores	Titles	Dates	.02	
Range of Reading	**Demonstrate Ability to Finish a Bk Chapter Book** Read and finish a Bk novel, including demonstrating comprehension and a command of the vocabulary used in the text. CCSR 10, CCSL 6.	After reading a Bk chapter book, student is able to tell what problem the main character faced and how the problem was resolved.	**Yes** or **No**	Titles	Dates	.02	
	Demonstrate Ability to Read and Comprehend Bk Informational Text Read a Bk informational text, including demonstrating comprehension and a command of the vocabulary used in the text. CCSR 10, CCSL 6.	After reading a Bk informational text, student is able to tell what s/he learned and show where in the text s/he learned that information.	**Yes** or **No**	Titles	Dates	.02	
Bk Transition Points						**.09**	
GRAND TOTAL: Student should transition to Bk with 3.99 points and demonstrated proficiency at Bk prerequisites.						**3.99**	

Bk Independent Reading Level Overview 4.00 - 4.99
Acquire a Series Reading Habit

Bk Learning Focus
Acquire a Series Reading Habit

Bk-level readers really get hooked on reading. This is when silent reading takes off and readers will sit and read for long periods of time, reluctant to stop because they want to find out what happens next. Bk is the level where good readers binge on junky series books (e.g., *Goosebumps*, *Diary of a Wimpy Kid,* Matt Christopher's sports fiction). This should be encouraged because it builds fluency, silent reading speed, endurance, and the habit of reading. Literary taste will come with experience. Require Bk-level readers to demonstrate their proficiency in both fiction and nonfiction, but otherwise let them indulge their passions. The levels that follow require students to broaden their reading into new genres. Take advantage of page-turners to have students master the narrative form: characters, settings, dialogue, point of view, theme, etc., in both reading and writing.

In Bk text, the vocabulary demands are increasing, with 3–5 words on a typical chapter book page not familiar from everyday speech. Be sure readers can define those words either from past reading experience or through the use of context clues. Bk-level readers should finish a Bk chapter book, or its equivalent, each week.

Key Common Core Standards

Reading Literature 2: Determine a theme of a story, drama, or poem from details in the text; summarize the text.

Reading Informational Text 4: Determine the meaning of general academic and domain-specific words and phrases in a text relevant to a Bk topic or subject area.

Entry Requirements

Must be in place before earning Bk designation.

- Demonstrate command of a literary vocabulary of approximately 1,500 words available for comprehending Bk level text. (Minimum 5 correct on Bk Vocabulary Check.) CCSL 6.
- Read and comprehend unfamiliar Bk text (successfully apply Reading Standards). (Minimum 9 correct on Cold Read Record.) CCSR 1, CCSR 2, CCSR 3, CCSR 4, CCSF3.
- Demonstrate ability to finish a Bk chapter book in a few days. CCSR 10.
- Demonstrate ability to read and comprehend Bk informational text. CCSR 10.

Exit Requirements

Must be in place before earning Or designation.

- Demonstrate command of a literary vocabulary of approximately 3,000 words, available for comprehending Or level text. (Minimum 5 correct on Or Vocabulary Check.) CCSL 6.
- Read and comprehend unfamiliar Or text (successfully apply Reading Standards). (Minimum 9 correct on Cold Read Record.) CCSR 1, CCSR 2, CCSR 3, CCSR 4, CCSF3.
- Demonstrate ability to finish an Or chapter book. CCSR 10.
- Demonstrate ability to read and comprehend Or informational text. CCSR 10.
- Demonstrate ability to read in a new genre (biography, historical fiction, science fiction). CCSR 9.

Bk Independent Reading Level Assessment 4.00 - 4.99

Entry Requirements: Cumulative Record

Student ____________________ Teacher ____________________ Room ________ Date Started ________

Bk Entry Requirements

		Evidence/Date				Date Completed
Vocabulary	**Demonstrate Command of a Literary Vocabulary of Approximately 1,500 Words** Have approximately 1,500 literary vocabulary words in reading vocabulary available for comprehending Bk level text. CCSL 6.	See **Vocabulary Check** on page 155. Minimum score of 5.	Scores		Dates	
Comprehension	**Read and Comprehend Unfamiliar Bk Text (Successfully Apply Reading Standards)** Determine what a text says explicitly and make logical inferences from it. Interpret vocabulary and figurative language in context. CCSR 1, CCSR 2, CCSR 3. CCSR 4.	See **Cold Read Record** on page 156. Minimum score of 9 on one Cold Read Text.	Scores	Titles	Dates	
Range of Reading	**Demonstrate Ability to Finish a Bk Chapter Book** Read and finish a Bk novel, including demonstrating comprehension and a command of the vocabulary used in the text. CCSR 10, CCSL 6.	After reading a Bk chapter book, student is able to tell what problem the main character faced and how the problem was resolved.	**Yes** or **No**	Titles	Dates	
	Demonstrate Ability to Read and Comprehend Bk Informational Text Read a Bk informational text, including demonstrating comprehension and a command of the vocabulary used in the text. CCSR 10, CCSL 6.	After reading a Bk informational text, student is able to tell what s/he learned and show where in the text s/he learned that information.	**Yes** or **No**	Titles	Dates	
A reader who is proficient at all of the above enters Bk with 4.00 points.						4.00

Bk Entry Requirements: Vocabulary Check

This page is for the teacher to use as a test of a student's vocabulary acquisition. DO NOT give copies of this page to students. DO NOT teach or drill these words out of context.

Pick a column. Student should be able to define 5 of the words to enter Bk and 12 of the words to exit. The following words are representative of the 1500 words Bk readers must acquire during their year of independent reading. This list is neither comprehensive nor sufficient, but as long as the student hasn't practiced this list, it will give you an idea of whether his/her working vocabulary is sufficient to comprehend text at the Bk level. Pick a different column each time.

Test A	Test B	Test C	Test D	Test E	Test F	Test G
(Date)						
acre	ancestor	bay	bound	canyon	cargo	cautiously
churn	citizen	clatter	continent	cottage	crop	crouch
current	dismay	dreadful	eastern	endangered	eve	fiery
flare	flock	freight	frontier	gallop	gasp	glare
gleam	glisten	gloomy	glossary	grasp	graze	harvest
hearth	hut	journey	kettle	lad	lame	lane
lantern	lawn	league	ledge	legend	lever	magnet
mane	marsh	mast	mesa	moccasin	mound	murmur
musket	myth	nation	national	northern	oasis	orbit
orchard	ornament	overhead	pasture	pilgrim	pillar	pirate
planet	plunge	polar	port	prairie	prance	preserve
quarrel	quill	rage	range	rarely	reservation	retreat
rodeo	royal	scowl	seaport	shallow	shrug	skim
stampede	sternly	stockade	stride	swamp	swarm	telescope
(Total)						

Common Core Standard Language 6: Acquire and use accurately grade-appropriate general academic and domain-specific words and phrases.

Bk Entry Requirements: Cold Read Record

Student ____________________ Teacher ____________________ Room _______ Date ______

Title: ____

Given an unfamiliar Bk text (Cold Read), and NO help of any kind:

Fluently Decode Bk text	Evidence/Student Response		
Use combined knowledge of all letter-sound correspondences, syllabication patterns, and morphology (e.g., roots and affixes) to accurately read unfamiliar multisyllabic words, including names. CCSF 3a, CCSF 4ab.	• 99-100% word accuracy.		**Yes** or **No**
	• Appropriate rate and expression.		**Yes** or **No**
	• Stop and try again if something doesn't look right, sound right, or make sense.		**Yes** or **No**

If answer to any of the above questions is No, STOP TEST and move student to an easier level. Any student having trouble with decoding is most likely working at or below 2R.

Reading Standards **See specific questions on Cold Read Text Pages**	**Evidence/Student Response**	**Score** Weak..........Strong
Basic Understanding Support basic understanding with evidence from the text. CCSR 1.		1 2 3 4
Interpretation Support an interpretation or analysis with evidence from the text. CCSR 2, CCSR 3.		1 2 3 4
Vocabulary Interpret vocabulary and figurative language in context. CCSR 4.		1 2 3 4
Cold Read Proficiency Total: A minimum score of 9 points on ONE Cold Read Text is required in order to enter Bk.	**Total Points**	

Bk Entry Requirements: Cold Read Text A

Jessi Ramsey, Pet-Sitter
by Ann M. Martin
Scholastic

Basic Understanding

What is happening so far in this story?

Interpretation

What kind of a person do you think Jessi is? Use specific details from the text to support your answer.

Vocabulary

What word could you substitute for "peered" without changing the meaning of the text? Why do you think the author chose to use "peered" instead of...?

CHAPTER 1

"Meow, meow, meow. Purr, purr."

I leaned over the edge of my bed and peered down at the floor.

"Pet me," said a small voice.

It wasn't a talking animal. It was my sister, Becca, pretending she was a cat.

I patted the top of her head but said, "Becca, I really have to do my homework."

"Then how come you're lying on your bed?" asked Becca, getting to her feet.

"Because this is a comfortable way to work."

"You're supposed to sit at your desk."

This is true. My parents believe that homework magically gets done better if you're sitting up than if you're lying down.

I sighed. Then I changed the subject, which usually distracts Becca. "Why are you a cat tonight?" I asked her.

She shrugged. "I'm trying all the animals. It's fun to pretend."

The night before, Becca had been a dog, the night before that, a horse.

"Well, kitty, let me finish my work," I said.

"Meow," replied Becca, who dropped to her hands and knees and crawled into the hallway.

Becca is eight and has a big imagination. If she weren't so shy, she'd probably make a really terrific actress, but she has awful stage fright.

I do not have stage fright, which is lucky since I'm a ballet dancer and have to perform in front of audiences all the time.

I guess I should stop and introduce myself. I am Jessi Ramsey, and I'm eleven and in sixth grade. "Jessi" is short for "Jessica." (And "Becca" is short for "Rebecca," as if you couldn't have guessed.)

Bk Entry Requirements: Cold Read Text B

Don't Close Your Eyes by
R.L. Stine
Random House

Basic Understanding

What is happening so far in this story?

Interpretation

Name two problems that Max faces in this story. What evidence from the text supports your answer?

Vocabulary

What does the phrase "head feels like a granite boulder" mean? Why do you think the author chose to use this phrase instead of...?

1

Traci Wayne and I sat across from each other at my kitchen table. Her math homework was spread out in front of me.

"Would you like me to show you how to do this equation?" I asked.

She glanced up from her *Teen People* magazine. "Max, couldn't you just *do* it for me? I have to catch up on my reading."

"Uh . . . yeah, sure," I muttered.

Yawning, I lowered my head to the page and started to scribble numbers and letters. My eyes were watering. I tried to blink them dry. I yawned again.

"Don't yawn so loud," Traci said. "How do you expect me to read?"

My eyelids drooped. They each weighed about a hundred pounds. I had to lift them up with my fingers.

I messed up the equation. I started to erase.

This doesn't sound normal, does it? This doesn't sound like Max Doyle, boy genius, the kid everyone in class calls Brainimon.

Well, it wasn't a normal afternoon. I wasn't feeling like myself at all. And I can tell you why—I hadn't slept in more than forty-eight hours.

Don't ever try staying awake for two whole days and nights. Your eyeballs burn. Your head feels like a granite boulder. And it feels as if your tongue is growing fur!

Normally, I'd be so excited to have Traci Wayne in my house, I'd do cartwheels or something. I admit it. I have a huge crush on Traci.

Whenever I see her, my heart starts to pound a hip-hop rhythm, my mouth goes as dry as talcum powder, and my knees knock together like bongos.

Traci once put her hand on my shoulder, and it gave me hiccups for three weeks.

That's true love, right?

Traci usually ignores me. It's because we're in different groups at school. She's in the way cool group. And I'm in the bottom feeders group.

My friend Aaron and I are the only ones in our group. And we're not quite sure how we got there. But we know there's no way out.

So when Traci comes over to my house, it's a big-deal thing. Even if all she wants is for me to do her math homework while she reads *Teen People*.

But tonight, yawn, yawn.

All I wanted was to put my head down and go to sleep.

But I couldn't. I had to stay awake—maybe *forever*.

I'm not joking. See, I'm a normal sixth grader. But I have a problem. I have two ghosts living in my house.

Nicky and Tara Roland are about my age. They used to live here before my family moved in. Now they're back, and they don't know how they became ghosts.

They pop in and out all the time. And they're *my* problem—because I'm the only one who can see or hear them.

Lucky me, right?

Bk Entry Requirements: Cold Read Text C

Dinosaur Hunters by
Kate McMullen
Random House

Basic Understanding

Tell me three things the text says about dinosaurs bones.

Interpretation

Using the words "first, second, third," describe the steps that turn a bone into a fossil.

Vocabulary

What word could you substitute for "seeps" without changing the meaning of the text? Why do you think the author chose to use "seeps" instead of...?

Bk

Picture a gigantic *Apatosaurus* (ah-PAT-uh-SAW-rus) walking on a riverbank. This *Apatosaurus* is old and weak. It bends its long neck and takes one last drink from the river. Then it falls on its side in the mud. It is dead.

Most of the soft flesh of the *Apatosaurus* is quickly eaten by animals. The rest rots away. In time, the hard bones sink into the mud. The mud protects the bones. They do not rot away.

For millions of years, the bones lie under the ground. Rain falls. It seeps down through the ground, dissolving minerals in the rocks. The rainwater carries these minerals along as it trickles down to the bones.

Like all bones, the *Apatosaurus* bones are filled with tiny holes. The rainwater seeps into these holes. The water evaporates. But the minerals in the water stay and harden in the bones. Little by little, what once was bone turns to stone. The bones of the *Apatosaurus* are now stone. They are fossils.

Bk Entry Requirements: Cold Read Text D

Jackie Robinson, Bravest Man in Baseball
by Margaret Davidson
Random House

Basic Understanding

Tell me three things the text says about Jackie Robinson.

Interpretation

What is the main idea of this passage? How do you know? Use details from the text to support your answer.

Vocabulary

When Jackie Robinson says that he "turned professional at an early age," what does he mean?

Pro at an Early Age

IT WAS TOWARD THE END OF A FINE FALL day on Pepper Street in Pasadena, California. Mallie Robinson had just called her children in to dinner. The first to arrive was six-year-old Jackie. "Mama, Mama, guess what?" he cried as he came skidding into the kitchen.

Mallie smiled at her youngest son. He was always bursting with some kind of hard-to-hold-in news. Now Jackie puffed out his chest and announced, "You don't have to fix lunch for me to take to school tomorrow. Or ever again!"

Mallie laughed. All five of her children had big appetites. But Jackie's was a family joke—everyone said he ate like a horse. "So what are you going to do?" she asked, still chuckling. "Go on a diet?"

"No, ma'am! We've got two softball teams at school. And the kids on one of them say they'll split their lunches with me if I promise to play on their side!"

"You might say," Jackie Robinson wrote many years later, "that I turned professional at an early age."

All the young Robinsons were natural athletes. Jackie's oldest brother, Edgar, could do all sorts of fancy tricks on his roller skates. Frank, the next oldest, was a sprinter. Mack was also a runner, but he spent more time working on his broad jump. And Willa Mae, Jackie's only sister, was good at any sport girls were allowed to play in the 1920s.

But right from the beginning it was plain that Jackie was going to be different. He wasn't just a fine athlete. He was, as a friend said, "one of a kind."

Baseball, football, relay racing, dodgeball, swimming—there didn't seem to be a sport he wasn't good at. He also had the ability to concentrate, something that all great athletes must have.

Bk Comprehension
Reading Standards for Literature and Informational Text

Proficiency in the standards below must be demonstrated while reading independently in Bk level text. In order to advance to Or, students must earn .48 Comprehension Points.

Key Ideas and Details: Using Text Evidence to Support Conclusions Understand, think about, and discuss what the author said.		Evidence/Date	Points	
	Demonstrate background knowledge of a Bk-level reader, familiar with 90-100% of the vocabulary and enough of the world knowledge found in Bk-level books to ensure basic comprehension (e.g., 4th-grade level math, science, and social studies concepts).		✓	
CCSR 1	Refer to details and examples in a text when explaining what the text says explicitly and when drawing inferences from the text. • *How, why, what...? Give an example from the text to support your answer.*		.03	
CCSR 2	Determine a theme of a story, drama, or poem from details in the text; summarize the text. (See DSI.) • *What is the most important thing that happened in this book? What lesson or moral could you get from this?* • *What is the theme of this text? What details from the text support that this is the theme?* • *A summary gives just the most important information about a text in very few words. Summarize what you've read so far in one sentence.*		.03	
	Determine the main idea of a text and explain how it is supported by key details; summarize the text. • *What was the main idea of this book and how do you know? What key facts did the author use to support the main idea? Summarize this book in just one sentence.*		.03	
CCSR 3	Describe in depth a character, setting, or event in the story or drama, drawing on specific details in the text (e.g., a character's thoughts, words, or actions). • *Describe one of the characters (settings, events) in this text. Use at least three examples from the text to support your description.*		.03	
	Explain events, procedures, ideas, or concepts in a historical, scientific, or technical text, including what happened and why, based on specific information in the text. • *Tell what happened and why it happened.* • **Time/Sequence**: *Using the words "first, second, third," describe the sequence of events (or steps) in the text. Explain why this order matters.* or • **Concept/Scientific Ideas/Cause and Effect**: *Using the words "because, since, as a result," explain how two ideas in the text are related. Explain why this relationship matters.*		.03	

	Identify and describe the following literary elements in a text: plot (conflict and resolution); setting (time and place); and characters (traits, roles, similarities, major and minor). • *What is the conflict? How is it resolved?* • *Where/when did the story take place? How does it compare to where/when you live?* • *Who are the main characters and what are their traits?*		.03	
Craft and Structure: Analyzing the Effects of Authors' Choices Understand and discuss the way(s) the author(s) said what was said.				
CCSR 4	Determine the meaning of words and phrases as they are used in a text, including those that allude to significant characters found in mythology (e.g., Herculean). • *Find a word you never use in your speech, or that you never saw before. What do you think it probably means? Why?* • *Read the sentence again, but this time, put a word or phrase in place of the new word, without changing the meaning of the sentence.*		.03	
CCSR 5	Explain major differences between poems, drama, and prose, and refer to the structural elements of poems (e.g., verse, rhythm, meter) and drama (e.g., casts of characters, settings, descriptions, dialogue, stage directions) when writing or speaking about a text. • *Is this text a poem, drama/play, or story/prose? How do you know?*		.03	
	Describe the overall structure (e.g., chronology, comparison, cause/effect, problem/solution) of events, ideas, concepts, or information in a text or part of a text. • *How did the author organize the information in this text?*		.03	
	Distinguish among common forms of literature (e.g., poetry, short story, traditional tales, biography, historical fiction, science fiction) using knowledge of their structural elements. • *Is this book fiction or informational? How can you tell?* • *What kind of literature is this? How can you tell?* • *What are the basic structures used?*		.03	
	Create graphic organizers to categorize and analyze information and ideas from reading (T-chart, Venn diagram, matrix chart, graph, timeline, map, cycle chart, etc.).		.03	
CCSR 6	Compare and contrast the point of view from which different stories are narrated, including the difference between first- and third-person narrations. • *Is this story told in the first or third person? How do you know?* • *Compare a story told in the first person to one told in the third person. How are they different? Which do you like better? Why?*		.03	
	Compare and contrast a firsthand and secondhand account of the same event or topic; describe the differences in focus and the information provided. • *Was this text a firsthand or secondhand account of the event or topic? Retell part of the text as if it had been written the other way. What differences result?*		.03	
	Distinguish their own point of view (perspective) from that of an author's. • *How is your point of view different from or the same as the author's?*		.03	

Integration of Knowledge and Ideas: Comparing Different Presentations

Discuss how the ideas in a book connect to each other and to the larger world.

CCSR 7	Make connections between the text of a story or drama and a visual or oral presentation of the text, identifying where each version reflects specific descriptions and directions in the text. • *Read the book of a movie you have seen. How do they compare? What would you have done differently in the movie?*		.03	
	Interpret information from graphic features (charts, graphs, diagrams, time lines, animations, or interactive elements on Web pages); explain how the information contributes to an understanding of the text in which it appears. • *Select a graphic feature in your book. Why do you think it was included? What does it add to the text?*		.03	
CCSR 8	Identify the evidence (facts and details) that supports an author's main idea or argument. Explain how an author uses reasons and evidence to support particular points in a text. • *The main thing the author is telling us is that __________. What reasons does he give to convince us?*		.03	
	Provide examples of facts and opinions in text. • *Does the author state any opinions? How do you know this is an opinion?* Differentiates essential from nonessential information. • *Give me an example of essential information.* • *Give me an example of nonessential information.*		.03	
CCSR 9	Compare and contrast the treatment of similar themes and topics (e.g., opposition of good and evil) and patterns of events (e.g., the quest) in stories, myths, and traditional literature from different cultures. • *Given two traditional tales, create a T-chart comparing them.*		.03	
	Integrate information from two texts on the same topic in order to write or speak about the subject knowledgeably. *Find at least two books on _____. See how much you can learn about _____. Become an expert.*		.03	
Bk Comprehension Total			**.48**	

T-chart (CCSR 9):

	Similarities	Differences
Characters		
Setting		
Plot Events		
Theme/Moral		

Bk Foundational Skills

Range of Reading and Level of Text Complexity	Evidence/Date	Points	
Engagement and Independence Read regularly and independently, sustaining engagement, in Bk-level materials for at least 30 minutes every day in the classroom.		.02	
Home Reading Sustain a home reading habit and read in Bk-level materials for at least 30 minutes every night without prompting, or make up this additional 30 minutes during the school day.		.02	
Chapter Book Habit Regularly finish Bk chapter books, at least 1 a week.		.05	

Genres CCSR 10

Read independently and comprehend informational text at the Bk level, including these 3 genres:

	Evidence (List Titles Completed)	Date		
History Social Studies			.01	
Science			.01	
Biography/Autobiography (Journal/Speech)			.02	

Read independently and comprehend <u>literary text</u> at the Bk level, including at least 4 genres:

	Evidence (List Chapter Books Completed)	Date	Points	
Stories • Adventure • Contemporary/ Realistic Fiction • Horror • Other			.03	
	Evidence (List Steps Read/Titles Completed)			
Traditional tales • Folktales • Legends • Fables • Tall tales • Myths			.01	
Drama			.01	
Poetry			.01	
Range of Reading and Level of Text Complexity Total			.19	

Phonics and Word Recognition

Decode Multisyllable Words Cover parts of unfamiliar words with finger and look for familiar chunks inside.		✓	
Use combined knowledge of all letter-sound correspondences, syllabication patterns, and morphology (e.g., roots and affixes) to accurately read unfamiliar multisyllabic words, including names, in context and out of context. CCSF 3a. (Any student having significant trouble with this is working at the wrong level.)		✓	
Demonstrate flexibility with vowel sounds when attempting to decode an unfamiliar word, e.g., trying long "e" sound for "i" for *envious, fancier, interior*. (See Bk Phonics Gap Locator.)		✓	
Phonics and Word Recognition Total:		✓	

Vocabulary and Language

	Evidence/Date	Points	
Literary, Academic, and Technical Vocabulary Notice words that are not used in everyday speech and use context clues to substitute a word or phrase that means the same thing. CCSL 4a.		.02	
Consult reference materials (e.g., dictionaries, glossaries, thesauruses), both print and digital, to find the pronunciation and determine or clarify the precise meaning of key words and phrases. CCSL 4c.		.01	
Provide synonyms or antonyms for words encountered in text. CCSL 5c.		.02	
Know and be able to use at least 3,000 words, not familiar from everyday speech, but common to Bk-level text. CCSL 6.		.05	
Affixes and Roots Use common, grade-appropriate Greek and Latin affixes and roots as clues to the meaning of a word (e.g., *telegraph, photograph, autograph*). CCSL 4b. (see roots table below)		.03	
Figurative Language Explain the meaning of simple similes and metaphors (e.g., *as pretty as a picture*) in context. CCSL 5b.		.03	
Recognize and explain the meaning of common idioms, adages, and proverbs. CCSL 5b.		.01	
Vocabulary Total		.17	

anim	aqua, hydr	ped	spec	voc	cycle	graph	opt	phon	photo	psych	therm
life, spirit	water	foot	see	wish, will	circle	write	eye	sound	light	mind	heat

Fluency, Active Reading Strategies, and Self-Monitoring

Fluency Read Bk text comfortably, with confidence, purpose, and understanding. CCSF 4a.		.01	
Read Bk prose and poetry orally with 99%-100% accuracy, appropriate rate, and fluency, using punctuation as a guide to expression. CCSF 4b.		.01	
Silent reading is faster than oral and is preferred by the reader. This is essential for enjoyment of complex literature.		.01	
Active Reading Strategies Read actively: activate prior knowledge, survey, make predictions and connections, visualize, reread, and ask clarifying questions.		.01	
Adjust reading speed for various purposes. • Demonstrate aggressive self-monitoring and active reading strategies when reading difficult material. • Skim and scan to locate specific information quickly. • Read silently and rapidly for pleasure.		.01	
Self-Monitoring for Comprehension Stop when comprehension breaks down; identify specific words or passages causing comprehension difficulty and rework for clarification. Use context to confirm or self-correct word recognition and understanding, rereading as necessary. CCSF 4c.		.01	
Fluency, Active Reading Strategies, Self-Monitoring Total		**.06**	
Bk Foundational Skills Total		**.42**	

Bk Outlaws

Must Recognize On Sight

Student Practice Page

Name | Date | Total

aisle		delicate		hymn		numb		rely		synonym	
bouquet		double		iodine		occasion		restaurant		syrup	
brilliant		dough		jewelry		orphan		rhyme		system	
burglar		doughnut		journal		oxygen		rhythm		taxi	
cafe		drought		kneel		patience		salmon		theater	
century		exhaust		knob		physical		satellite		timid	
cereal		exhausted		lily		pierce		scheme		tortillas	
chalk		foreign		limb		pineapple		scholar		trial	
cocoon		fountain		llama		pleasure		sergeant		vacuum	
college		guinea pig		machinery		poem		shield		value	
conquer		gym		mammoth		prey		soul		vehicle	
conscious		gymnastics		miracle		public		souvenir		vinegar	
cough		height		mosquito		pudding		spaghetti		whisk	
crystal		horrible		muscle		purchase		spinach		wreath	
deaf		horror		niece		rehearse		symbol		wrestle	

Common Core Standard Foundational Skills 3a: Use combined knowledge of all letter-sound correspondences, syllabication patterns, and morphology (e.g., roots and affixes) to read accurately unfamiliar multisyllabic words in context and out of context.

Bk Vocabulary
Latin Suffixes

Student Practice Page

Name:								Date		Total	
-able/-ible		**-ery/-ary/-ory**		**-tion/-cion/-sion**		**-ance/-ence**		**-ant/-ent**		**-ment**	
able to be		*relating to*		*verb to noun*		*adjective to noun*		*adjective*		*verb to noun*	
avoidable		**military**		**invention**		**importance**		**permanent**		**government**	
dependable		**temporary**		**affection**		**absence**		**decent**		**nourishment**	
adjustable		**literary**		**contradiction**		**evidence**		**convenient**		**employment**	
disagreeable		**voluntary**		**expression**		**distance**		**distant**		**treatment**	
removable		**satisfactory**		**suspicion**		**fragrance**		**elegant**		**amazement**	
respectable		**category**		**extinction**		**obedience**		**obedient**		**compliment**	
acceptable		**introductory**		**reflection**		**nuisance**		**ignorant**		**department**	
remarkable		**extraordinary**		**emotion**		**brilliance**		**constant**		**disagreement**	
visible		**imaginary**		**reaction**		**innocence**		**pleasant**		**enjoyment**	
digestible		**anniversary**		**revision**		**impatience**		**vacant**		**experiment**	

Common Core Standard Foundational Skills 3a: Use roots and affixes to read accurately unfamiliar multisyllabic words in context and out of context.

Common Core Standard Language 4a: Use common, grade-appropriate Greek and Latin affixes and roots as clues to the meaning of a word.

Latin Roots

Student's Name: ____________________

Most modern English words originated in other languages. Many of our words come from Latin, the language of Ancient Rome and its empire. Learning the meaning of these common Latin roots will help you with English vocabulary. Use the back of this card to test yourself.

Common Root	Meaning	Examples
act	do	actor, action, react, transact, enact
anim	life, spirit	animal, animate, animosity, inanimate
aqua	water	aquarium, aquatic, aquamarine, aquifer
aud	hear	audience, auditorium, auditorium, audiovi-sual, audible
cap	head	cap, captain, capital, decapitate, caput
dent	tooth	dentist, dental, denture, trident, indent
man	hand	manual, manufacture, manipulate, manu-script
opt	best	optimum, optimist, optimal, optimize
ped	foot	pedal, pedestrian, biped, pedestal
ques	ask, seek	question, quest, request
rupt	break	rupture, ,erupt, interrupt, abrupt, bankrupt
san	health	sanitary, sanitation, sanitarium, sane, insane, insanity
spec	see	spectacles, inspect, suspect, respect, specta-tor
spir	breathe	spirit, inspire, respiration, perspire, conspire
voc	voice	voice, vocal, advocate, evoke, vociferous
vol	wish, will	volition, volunteer, voluntary, benevolent

How many of these common Latin roots can you correctly define? Spell? How many examples of each can you name and define? Spell?

Common Root	Meaning	Examples
act		
anim		
aqua		
aud		
cap		
dent		
man		
opt		
ped		
ques		
rupt		
san		
spec		
spir		
voc		
vol		

Greek Roots

Student's Name: ______________________

Most modern English words originated in other languages. Many of our words come from Ancient Greece. Learning the meaning of these common Greek roots will help you with English vocabulary. Use the back of this card to test yourself.

Common Root		Examples
ast	star	astronaut, astronomer, disaster, asterisk, asteroid
biblio	book	bibliography, Bible, bibliotherapy
bio	life	biology, biography, biochemistry, biopsy, bio-sphere
chron	time	chronological, synchronize, chronicle, chronic
cycle	circle, ring	bicycle, cyclone, cycle, encyclopedia, recycle
gram	letter, writ-ten	telegram, diagram, grammar, epigram, monogram
graph	write	photograph, phonograph, autograph, biography, graphite
hydr	water	fire hydrant, hydroplane, hydraulic, hydrogen, dehydrate, hydroelectric
mech	machine	mechanic, mechanical, mechanism, mechanize
meter	measure	thermometer, centimeter, diameter, barometer
opt	eye	optician, optometrist, optic, optical
phon	sound	phonograph, symphony, telephone, microphone, phonics
photo	light	photograph, telephoto, photosynthesis, photo-genic
pysch	mind, soul	psychology, psyche, psychopath, psychiatrist
sci	know	science, conscience, conscious, omniscient
therm	heat	thermometer, thermal, thermostat, Thermos

How many of these common Greek roots can you correctly define? Spell? How many examples of each can you name and define? Spell?

Common Root	Meaning	Examples
ast		
biblio		
bio		
chron		
cycle		
gram		
graph		
hydr		
mech		
meter		
opt		
phon		
photo		
pysch		
sci		
therm		

Transition to Or

Bk Entry Points	**4.00**	
Bk Foundational Skills Points	**.42**	
Bk Comprehension Points	**.48**	

Or Transition Points. With NO help of any kind, student must demonstrate ability to:			Evidence/Date	Points	
Vocabulary	**Demonstrate Command of a Literary Vocabulary of Approximately 3,000 Words** Have approximately 3,000 literary vocabulary words in reading vocabulary available for comprehending Or level text. CCSL 6.	See **Vocabulary Check** on page 175. Minimum score of 5.	Scores / Dates	.02	
Comprehension	**Read and Comprehend Unfamiliar Or Text (Successfully Apply Reading Standards)** Determine what a text says explicitly and make logical inferences from it. Interpret vocabulary and figurative language in context. CCSR 1, CCSR 2, CCSR 3, CCSR 4.	See **Cold Read Record** on page 176. Minimum score of 9 on one Cold Read Text.	Scores / Titles / Dates	.02	
Range of Reading	**Demonstrate Ability to Finish an Or Chapter Book** Read and finish an Or novel, including demonstrating comprehension and a command of the vocabulary used in the text. CCSR 10, CCSL 6.	After reading an Or chapter book, student is able to tell what problem the main character faced and how the problem was resolved.	**Yes** or **No** / Titles / Dates	.02	
	Demonstrate Ability to Read and Comprehend Or Informational Text Read an Or informational text, including demonstrating comprehension and a command of the vocabulary used in the text. CCSR 10, CCSL 6.	After reading an Or informational text, student is able to tell what s/he learned and show where in the text s/he learned that information.	**Yes** or **No** / Titles / Dates	.02	
	Demonstrate Ability to Read in a New Genre Read an Or Biography, Historical Fiction, or Science Fiction text. CCSR 9.	After finishing an Or biography, historical fiction or science fiction book, student is able to tell what the main character faced and how the problem was resolved.	**Yes** or **No** / Titles / Dates	.01	
Or Transition Points				**.09**	
GRAND TOTAL: Student should transition to Or with 4.99 points and demonstrated proficiency at Or prerequisites.				**4.99**	

Or Independent Reading Level Overview 5.00-5.99

Proficiency and Comfort in New Genres

Or Learning Focus

Proficiency and Comfort in New Genres (Historical Fiction, Realistic Fiction, Biography, Poetry, etc.)

Or readers should demonstrate proficiency in at least five very different kinds of text. Encourage students to expand their reading experience through literacy circles, read-aloud, book clubs, sharing time, modeling, book talks and having enough of the right books in these genres. Proficient Or-level readers are comfortable in realistic/contemporary fiction, poetry, plays, informational writing, a variety of traditional tales, historical fiction, and biography.

In Or text, the vocabulary demands are increasing, with 6–10 words on a typical chapter book page not familiar from everyday speech. Or-level readers already know all but 1 or 2 of these literary words from their extensive reading at the earlier levels. Students who have not read widely will not know most of the words and will have comprehension difficulty because of the literary vocabulary load. These students must go back to the color level where they can define all (or almost all) of the words used and read from there, or they may develop the habit of "reading" without comprehension.

Or-level readers should finish an Or chapter book, or its equivalent, each week.

Key Common Core Standards

Reading Literature 9: Compare and contrast stories in the same genre (e.g., mysteries and adventure stories) on their approaches to similar themes and topics.

Reading Informational Text 9: Integrate information from several texts on the same topic in order to write or speak about the subject knowledgeably.

Entry Requirements

Must be in place before earning Or designation.

- Demonstrate command of a literary vocabulary of approximately 3,000 words, available for comprehending Or level text. (Minimum 5 correct on Or Vocabulary Check.) CCSL 6.
- Read and comprehend unfamiliar Or text (successfully apply Reading Standards). (Minimum 9 correct on Cold Read Record.) CCSR 1, CCSR 2, CCSR 3, CCSR 4, CCSF3.
- Demonstrate ability to finish an Or chapter book. CCSR 10.
- Demonstrate ability to read and comprehend Or informational text. CCSR 10.
- Demonstrate ability to read in a new genre (biography, historical fiction, science fiction). CCSR 9.

Exit Requirements

Must be in place before earning Pu designation.

- Demonstrate command of a literary vocabulary of approximately 4,500 words available for comprehending Pu level text. (Minimum 5 correct on Pu Vocabulary Check). CCSL 6.
- Read and comprehend unfamiliar Pu text (successfully apply Reading Standards). (Minimum score of 9 on Cold Read Record.) CCSR 1, CCSR2, CCSR3, CCSR4.
- Demonstrate ability to finish a Pu chapter book. CCSR 10.
- Demonstrate ability to read and comprehend Pu informational text. CCSR 10.
- Demonstrate ability to read in a new genre (fantasy, autobiography, biography, historical fiction, science fiction). CCSR 9.

Or Independent Reading Level Assessment 5.00 - 5.99

Entry Requirements: Cumulative Record

Student ______________________ Teacher ______________________ Room ________ Date Started ________

Or Entry Requirements

		Evidence/Date				Date Completed
Vocabulary	**Demonstrate Command of a Literary Vocabulary of Approximately 3,000 Words** Have approximately 3,000 literary vocabulary words in reading vocabulary available for comprehending Or level text. CCSL 6.	See **Vocabulary Check** on page 175. Minimum score of 5.	Scores		Dates	
Comprehension	**Read and Comprehend Unfamiliar Or Text (Successfully Apply Reading Standards)** Determine what a text says explicitly and make logical inferences from it. Interpret vocabulary and figurative language in context. CCSR 1, CCSR 2, CCSR 3, CCSR 4.	See **Cold Read Record** on page 176. Minimum score of 9 on one Cold Read Text.	Scores	Titles	Dates	
Range of Reading	**Demonstrate Ability to Finish an Or Chapter Book** Read and finish an Or novel, including demonstrating comprehension and a command of the vocabulary used in the text. CCSR 10, CCSL 6.	After reading an Or chapter book, student is able to tell what problem the main character faced and how the problem was resolved.	**Yes** or **No**	Titles	Dates	
	Demonstrate Ability to Read and Comprehend Or Informational Text Read an Or informational text, including demonstrating comprehension and a command of the vocabulary used in the text. CCSR 10, CCSL 6.	After reading an Or informational text, student is able to tell what s/he learned and show where in the text s/he learned that information.	**Yes** or **No**	Titles	Dates	
	Demonstrate Ability to Read in a New Genre Read an Or Biography, Historical Fiction, or Science Fiction text. CCSR 9.	After finishing an Or biography, historical fiction or science fiction book, student is able to tell what the main character faced and how the problem was resolved.	**Yes** or **No**	Titles	Dates	
A reader who is proficient at all of the above enters Or with 5.00 points.						5.00

Or Entry Requirements: Vocabulary Check

This page is for the teacher to use as a test of a student's vocabulary acquisition. DO NOT give copies of this page to students. DO NOT teach or drill these words out of context.

Pick a column. Student should be able to define 5 of the words to enter Or and 12 of the words to exit. The following words are representative of the 1,500 words Or readers must acquire during their year of independent reading. This list is neither comprehensive nor sufficient, but as long as the student hasn't practiced this list, it will give you an idea of whether his/her working vocabulary is sufficient to comprehend text at the Or level. Pick a different column each time. Each column is used as a separate test.
5 words correct in any column = Or Entry. 12 words correct in any column = Or Exit.

Test A	Test B	Test C	Test D	Test E	Test F	Test G
(Date)						
adapt	alter	altitude	angle	annual	apprentice	arch
arctic	armor	astonishment	astound	atmosphere	balcony	bin
blunder	bog	boulder	brisk	bud	burden	captive
casual	central	century	chamber	chaos	chemical	cinder
cloak	cluster	coarse	cocoon	coil	colonial	colonist
column	compact	condense	congress	crater	crest	cycle
daily	deafen	declaration	decree	dense	descend	device
drought	dune	establish	export	ferry	flee	flexible
fling	foster	furnish	fury	gale	galleon	gape
garment	grant	gravity	grim	gruff	harbor	hasty
hover	increase	inhabitant	interval	irrigate	junction	jut
keen	kernel	lair	magnify	manufacture	marvel	mass
meek	merchant	miser	muffle	parallel	patrol	peasant
peer	perch	peril	perish	physical	plume	pouch
profit	ransom	refuge	revolution	sibling	summit	unidentified
(Total)						

Common Core Standard Language 6: Acquire and use accurately grade-appropriate general academic and domain-specific words and phrases.

Or Entry Requirements: Cold Read Record

Student ____________________ Teacher ____________________ Room ________ Date ______

Title: ____________________

Given an unfamiliar Or text (Cold Read), and NO help of any kind:			
Fluently Decode Or text	**Evidence/Student Response**		**Score**
Use combined knowledge of all letter-sound correspondences, syllabication patterns, and morphology (e.g., roots and affixes) to accurately read unfamiliar multisyllabic words, including names. CCSF 3a, CCSF 4ab.	• 99-100% word accuracy.		**Yes** or **No**
	• Appropriate rate and expression.		**Yes** or **No**
	• Stop and try again when something doesn't look right, sound right, or make sense.		**Yes** or **No**
If answer to any of the above questions is No, STOP TEST and move student to an easier level. Any student having trouble with decoding is most likely working at or below 2R.			
Reading Standards **See text-specific questions on Cold Read Text Pages**	**Evidence/Student Response**		**Score** Weak..........Strong
Basic Understanding Support basic understanding with evidence from the text. CCSR 1.			1 2 3 4
Interpretation Support an interpretation or analysis with evidence from the text. CCSR 2, CCSR 3.			1 2 3 4
Vocabulary Interpret vocabulary and figurative language in context. CCSR 4.			1 2 3 4
Cold Read Proficiency Total: A minimum score of 9 points on ONE Cold Read Text is required in order to enter Or.		**Total Points**	

Or Entry Requirements: Cold Read Text A

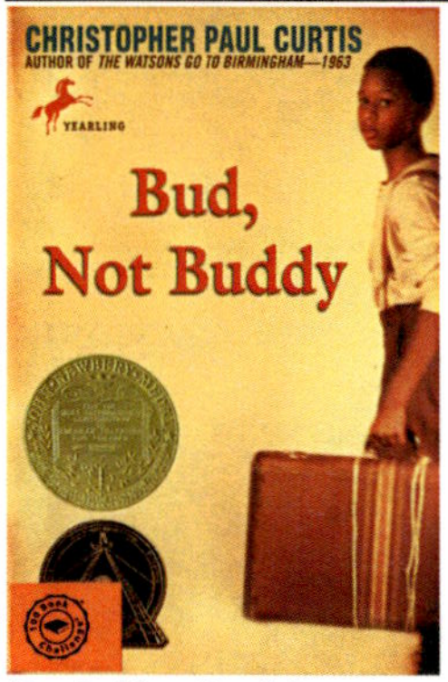

Bud, Not Buddy
by Christopher Paul Curtis
Random House

Basic Understanding

What is happening in this story so far?

Interpretation

How does Bud feel about going to a new foster family? What evidence from the text supports your answer?

Vocabulary

What does the phrase "sounding like little firecrackers going off" mean? How does this phrase contribute to the feeling of the text?

Or

CHAPTER 1

HERE WE GO AGAIN. We were all standing in line waiting for breakfast when one of the caseworkers came in and *tap-tap-tapped* down the line. Uh-oh, this meant bad news, either they'd found a foster home for somebody or somebody was about to get paddled. All the kids watched the woman as she moved along the line, her high-heeled shoes sounding like little firecrackers going off on the wooden floor.

Shoot! She stopped at me and said, "Are you Buddy Caldwell?"

I said, "It's Bud, not Buddy, ma'am."

She put her hand on my shoulder and took me out of line. Then she pulled Jerry, one of the littler boys, over. "Aren't you Jerry Clark?" He nodded.

"Boys, good news! Now that the school year has ended, you both have been accepted in new temporary-care homes starting this afternoon!"

Jerry asked the same thing I was thinking. "Together?"

She said, "Why, no. Jerry, you'll be in a family with three little girls . . ."

Jerry looked like he'd just found out they were going to dip him in a pot of boiling milk.

". . . and Bud . . ." She looked at some papers she was holding. "Oh, yes, the Amoses, you'll be with Mr. and Mrs. Amos and their son, who's twelve years old, that makes him just two years older than you, doesn't it, Bud?"

"Yes, ma'am."

She said, "I'm sure you'll both be very happy."

Me and Jerry looked at each other.

The woman said, "Now, now, boys, no need to look so glum. I know you don't understand what it means, but there's a depression going on all over this country. People can't find jobs and these are very, very difficult times for everybody. We've been lucky enough to find two wonderful families who've opened their doors for you. I think it's best that we show our new foster families that we're very . . ."

Or Entry Requirements: Cold Read Text B

Local News
by Gary Soto
Houghton Mifflin

Basic Understanding

What is happening in this story so far?

Interpretation

Describe Weasel in depth. Use at least 3 specific details from the text to support your answer.

Vocabulary

What word could you substitute for "hordes" without changing the meaning of this text?

BLACKMAIL

LIKE MOST OF HIS FRIENDS at school, Angel had an older, mean brother who pushed him around and played dirty tricks on him. One time his brother, Javier, nicknamed "Little Weasel" because he had a long, skinny neck, stuck Angel's bike up in the tree. With the help of his *vato loco* friends, all laughing and spitting sunflower seeds, Weasel hauled the bike to the top of the palm tree that stood in front of their pink stucco house.

"Get it down, Weasel!" Angel screamed, fists clenched and upper lip quivering from anger.

"You accusing me, *ese?*" his brother said, laughing. He spat on the ground and said, "Swim in it, *ese*."

Javier did not take the bike down until their *papi* drove his squeaky truck into the driveway. Their father, a carpenter, didn't like dealing with arguing kids when

he came home from work, tired from whacking nails for eight hours.

Another time, when Angel was real young, just out of the stroller, Little Weasel purposefully lost him at the Fresno Fair. Weasel snuck away on noiseless Air Jordans, and when Angel turned around, his face sticky with cotton candy, his brother was out of sight. Tears welled up in Angel's eyes and his mouth pulled down like a fish's. He wandered through hordes of people, crying, "Weasel, where are you?", a torrent of tears sprinkling his cotton candy. When Angel stopped a woman and asked if she had seen Weasel, she pointed to a tall white building and said, "Check the farm animals."

There had been other tricks. Early one summer morning, Angel had gone out to get the newspaper, and when he returned, shooting the rubber band at their cat, Pleitos, the front door clicked shut and Weasel's laughing *cara* appeared at the window. Angel was locked out, with only his pajama bottoms on.

Or Entry Requirements: Cold Read Text C

Great White Shark
by Sandra Markle
Lerner

Basic Understanding

Tell me three things the text says about sharks.

Interpretation

Name two parts of the shark's body described in this text and explain how each one helps her hunt. Use details from the text to support your answer.

Vocabulary

What do the words predator and prey mean? Can an animal be both predator and prey? Why or why not?

Or

The Animal World Is Full of PREDATORS.

Predators are the hunters who find, catch, and eat other animals—their prey—in order to survive. Every environment has its chain of hunters. The smaller, slower, less able predators become prey for the bigger, faster, more cunning hunters. And everywhere, there are just a few kinds of predators at the top of the food chain. *In the oceans of the world, one of these is the great white shark.*

A big female swims along about 20 to 30 feet (6 to 9 meters) below the surface of the ocean, searching for prey. Her white belly lets her sneak up on prey looking up from deeper water toward the light of the sky. Her dark blue gray back keeps her camouflaged (hidden) as she slips up on prey looking down into the dark ocean depths from near the surface.

All of the great white's senses are alert for clues that could mean prey is nearby. This time, her sense of hearing provides the first clue. The shark has small ear openings on top of her head. These lead through canals to special sound-detecting sacs that send messages to the shark's brain.

Or Entry Requirements: Cold Read Text D

Chief Joseph
by Jane Sutcliffe
Lerner

Basic Understanding

Tell me three things the text says about Chief Joesph.

Interpretation

What is the central idea/ message of this passage? What details from the text support this main idea?

Vocabulary

What does the phrase "thief treaty" mean? How do you know? What evidence in the text helps you know that?

2 Broken Bargain

Joseph's first test as chief came at once. White cattle ranchers were moving into the Wallowa Valley. Joseph asked them to leave. The Wallowa belonged to the Nez Perce, he told them. The ranchers were puzzled. All they knew was that the U.S. government had bought the land. That was that.

So Joseph took his argument to the government. He reminded officials that his father had never signed the "thief treaty." He had never sold the Wallowa Valley.

It didn't matter, Joseph was told. Other chiefs had signed the treaty. Joseph's band no longer had any right to the Wallowa. They would have to go to the reservation in Idaho.

In Joseph's Words

"Suppose a white man should come to me and say, 'Joseph, I like your horses, and I want to buy them.' I say to him, 'No, my horses suit me; I will not sell them.' Then he goes to my neighbor and says to him, 'Joseph has some good horses. I want to buy them, but he refuses to sell.' My neighbor answers, 'Pay me the money, and I will sell you Joseph's horses.' The white man returns to me and says, 'Joseph, I have bought your horses, and you must let me have them.' If we sold our lands to the Government, this is the way they were bought."

Or Comprehension

Reading Standards for Literature and Informational Text

Proficiency in the standards below must be demonstrated while reading independently in Or level text. In order to advance to Pu, students must earn .48 Comprehension Points.

Key Ideas and Details: Using Text Evidence to Support Conclusions Understand, think about, and discuss what the author said.		Evidence/Date	Points	
	Demonstrate background knowledge of an Or-level reader, familiar with 90-100% of the vocabulary and enough of the world knowledge found in Or-level books to ensure basic comprehension (e.g., 5th-grade level math, science, and social studies concepts).		✓	
CCSR 1	Quote accurately from a text when explaining what the text says explicitly and when drawing inferences from the text. • *How, why, what if…? Give a quote from the text to support your answer.*		.03	
CCSR 2	Determine a theme of a story, drama, or poem from details in the text, including how characters in a story or drama respond to challenges or how the speaker in a poem reflects upon a topic; summarize the text. • *What is the most important thing that happened in this book?* • *What challenge does the main character face? Support answer.* • *What lesson or moral could you get from this? Support answer.* • *What is the theme of this text? What details from the text support that this is the theme?* • *Summarize what you've read so far in one sentence.*		.03	
	Determine two or more main ideas of a text and explain how they are supported by key details; summarize the text. • *What are the main ideas of this book and how do you know?* • *What key facts did the author use to support the main ideas?* • *Summarize this book in just one sentence.*		.03	
CCSR 3	Compare and contrast two or more characters, settings, or events in a story or drama, drawing on specific details in the text (e.g., how characters interact). • *Pick two characters (settings, events) from this text.* • *Explain how they are alike and how they are different using examples from the text.*		.03	
	Explain the relationships or interactions between two or more individuals, events, ideas, or concepts in a historical, scientific, or technical text based on specific information in the text. • **Time/Sequence:** *Using the words "first, second, third," describe the sequence of events (or steps) in the text. Explain why this order matters.* OR • **Concept/Scientific Ideas/Cause and Effect:** *Using the words "because, since, as a result," explain how two ideas in the text are related. Explain why this relationship matters.*		.03	

Or Comprehension Cont'd

	Identify and describe the following literary elements in a text: plot (conflict and resolution); setting (time of day or year, historical era and place, situation); characters (traits, roles, similarities, major and minor); narrator/point of view (first person/third person); and theme (or moral). • *What is the conflict? How is it resolved?* • *Where and when did the story take place? How does it compare to where you live?* • *Who are the main characters and what are their traits?* • *Who is the narrator? Is it told in first or second person?* • *What is the theme (lesson or moral)? How do you know?*		.03	

Craft and Structure: Analyzing the Effects of Authors' Choices

Understand and discuss the way(s) the author(s) said what was said.

CCSR 4	Determine and explain the meaning and effects of words and phrases as they are used in a text, including figurative language such as metaphors and similes. • *Find a word you never use in your speech, or that you never saw before.* • *What do you think it probably means? Why?* • *Read the sentence again, but this time, put a word or phrase in place of the new word, without changing the meaning of the sentence.* • *Find a word or phrase that doesn't mean what it literally says: e.g., He was as tall as a mountain. What does it mean?* • *Find a metaphor or simile. Which one is it and how do you know? What does it mean?*		.03	
	Determine the meaning of general academic and domain-specific words or phrases in a text relevant to a *Grade 5 topic or subject area.* (Same as above.)		.03	
CCSR 5	Explain how a series of chapters, scenes, or stanzas fits together to provide the overall structure of a particular story, drama, or poem. • *Which three scenes (chapters, stanzas) do you think were the most important to this story/poem? Why? How do they connect to each other?*		.03	
	Compare and contrast the overall structure (e.g., chronology, comparison, cause/effect, problem/solution, pro/con, logical order) of events, ideas, concepts, or information in two or more texts. • *How did the author organize the information in this first text?* • *How did the author organize the information in this second text?* • *How are they alike? Different?* • *Which structure do you like better? Why?*		.03	

	Distinguish among common forms of literature (e.g., poetry, novel, short story, biography, autobiography, drama, mysteries, science fiction, adventures, historical fiction, fables, myths) using knowledge of their structural elements. • *Is this book fiction or informational? How can you tell?* • *What kind of literature is this? How can you tell?*		.03	
	Create graphic organizers to categorize and analyze information and ideas from reading. (T-chart, Venn diagram, matrix chart, timeline, graphs, maps, etc.)		.03	
CCSR 6	Describe how a narrator's or speaker's point of view influences how events are described. • *What is the perspective (bias, opinion) of the narrator?* • *How does this shape the description of events?* • *How would the story be different if someone else were telling it?*		.03	
	Analyze multiple accounts of the same event or topic, noting important similarities and differences in the point of view they represent. Give student multiple accounts of the same event. *Compare these accounts on:* • *The way they tell about the event.* • *The information they provide.* • *The way they give their opinions about what happened.*		.03	
	Distinguish their own point of view (perspective) from that of an author. • *How is your point of view different from or the same as that of the author?*		.03	

Integration of Knowledge and Ideas: **Comparing Different Presentations**

Discuss how the ideas in a book connect to each other and to the larger world.

<table>
<tr><td rowspan="2">CCSR 7</td><td>Analyze how visual and multimedia elements contribute to the meaning, tone, or beauty of a text (e.g., graphic novel, multimedia presentation of fiction, folktale, myth, poem).
• How do the illustrations contribute to the text (meaning, tone, beauty)?</td><td></td><td>.03</td><td></td></tr>
<tr><td>Draw on information from multiple print or digital sources, demonstrating the ability to locate an answer to a question quickly or to solve a problem efficiently.
• Show me the fastest way to find out _____(some detail related to the topic of the book they are reading).</td><td></td><td>.03</td><td></td></tr>
<tr><td>CCSR 8</td><td>Explain how an author uses reasons and evidence to support particular points in a text, identifying which reasons and evidence support which point(s).
• The author is telling us that __________ and ________. What reasons does he give to convince us of each point?</td><td></td><td>.03</td><td></td></tr>
<tr><td rowspan="2">CCSR 9</td><td>Compare and contrast stories in the same genre (e.g., mysteries and adventure stories) on their approaches to similar themes and topics.
• Given 2 books in the same genre, create a T-chart comparing them.
<table><tr><th></th><th>Similarities</th><th>Differences</th></tr><tr><td>Characters</td><td></td><td></td></tr><tr><td>Setting</td><td></td><td></td></tr><tr><td>Plot Events</td><td></td><td></td></tr><tr><td>Theme/Moral</td><td></td><td></td></tr></table></td><td></td><td>.03</td><td></td></tr>
<tr><td>Integrate information from several texts on the same topic in order to write or speak about the subject knowledgeably.
• Find at least two books on _____. See how much you can learn about ______. Become an expert.</td><td></td><td>.03</td><td></td></tr>
<tr><td colspan="3">Or Comprehension Total</td><td>.48</td><td></td></tr>
</table>

Or Foundational Skills

Range of Reading and Level of Text Complexity	Evidence/Date	Points	
Engagement and Independence • Read regularly and independently, sustaining engagement, in Or-level materials for at least 30 minutes every day in the classroom. • Demonstrate the stamina to sustain reading for at least 45 minutes, as required for high-stakes tests.		.02	
Home Reading Sustain a home reading habit and read in Or level for at least 30 minutes every night without prompting, or make up this <u>additional</u> 30 minutes during the school day.		.02	
Chapter Book Habit Regularly finish Or chapter books, at least one a week.		.04	

Genres

Read independently and comprehend <u>informational text</u> at the Or level, including:

	Evidence (List Titles Completed)	Date	Points	
History Social Studies			.02	
Science			.02	
Biography/Autobiography (Journal/Speech)			.02	

Or Foundational Skills Cont'd

Read independently and comprehend literary text at the Or level, including:

	Evidence (List Chapter Books Completed)	Date		
Stories • Adventure • Contemporary/ Realistic Fiction • Horror • Traditional			.02	
Drama			.01	
Poetry			.01	
Historical Fiction			.02	
Science Fiction (or Fantasy)			.02	
Range of Reading and Level of Text Complexity Total			**.22**	

Phonics and Word Recognition

Phonics and Word Recognition	Evidence/Date	Points	
Decode Multisyllable Words Use combined knowledge of all letter-sound correspondences, syllabication patterns, and morphology (e.g., roots and affixes) to accurately read unfamiliar multisyllabic words, including names, in context and out of context, at the Or level. CCSF 3a. (Any student having trouble with this is working at the wrong level.)		✓	
Phonics and Word Recognition Total		✓	

Vocabulary and Language

Literary, Academic, and Technical Vocabulary Notice words that are not used in everyday speech and use context (e.g., cause/effect relationships and comparisons in text) to substitute a word or phrase that means the same thing. CCSL 4a.		.02	
Consult reference materials (e.g., dictionaries, glossaries, thesauruses), both print and digital, to find the pronunciation and determine or clarify the precise meaning of key words and phrases. CCSL 4c. Uses diacritical marks to help with pronunciation of unfamiliar words.		.01	
Use the relationship between particular words (e.g., synonyms, antonyms, homographs) to better understand each of the words. CCSL 5c.		.02	
Know and be able to use at least 3,000-6,000 words, not familiar from everyday speech, but common to Or-level text. CCSL 6.		.05	
Affixes and Roots Use common, grade-appropriate Greek and Latin affixes and roots as clues to the meaning of a word (e.g., *photograph, photosynthesis*). CCSL 4b.		.02	
Figurative Language Interpret figurative language, including similes and metaphors, in context. CCSL 5a.		.02	
Recognize and explain the meaning of common idioms, adages, and proverbs. CCSL 5b.		.01	
Compare and contrast the varieties of English (e.g., dialects, registers) used in stories, dramas, or poems. CCSL 3b.		.01	
Vocabulary and Language Total		.16	

Or Foundational Skills Cont'd

Fluency, Active Reading Strategies, and Self-Monitoring for Understanding

Fluency • Read Or text comfortably, with expression, demonstrating an understanding of both content and punctuation. CCSF 4a. • Read Or books orally with 98%-100% accuracy, appropriate rate, and expression. CCSF 4ab. • Silent reading is rapid and efficient.		.01	
Active Reading Strategies Read actively: Activate prior knowledge, survey, make predictions and connections, visualize, reread, and ask clarifying questions.		.01	
Automatically adjust reading strategies to suit text and purpose. • Demonstrate aggressive self-monitoring and active reading strategies when reading difficult material. • Skim and scan to locate specific information quickly. • Read silently and rapidly for pleasure.		.01	
Self-Monitoring for Comprehension • Stop when comprehension breaks down, identify specific words or passages causing comprehension difficulty, and rework for clarification. • Use context to confirm or self-correct word recognition and understanding, rereading as necessary. CCSF 4c.		.01	
Fluency, Active Reading Strategies, and Self Monitoring Total		.04	
Or Foundational Skills Total		.42	

Transition to Pu

Or Entry Points			5.00	
Or Foundational Skills Points			.42	
Or Comprehension Points			.48	
Pu Transition Points. With NO help of any kind, student must demonstrate ability to:		**Evidence/Date**	**Points**	
Vocabulary	**Demonstrate Command of a Literary Vocabulary of Approximately 4,500 Words** Have approximately 4,500 literary vocabulary words in reading vocabulary available for comprehending Pu level text. CCSL 6.	See **Vocabulary Check** on page 193. Minimum score of 5.	Scores / Dates	.02	
Comprehension	**Read and Comprehend Unfamiliar Pu Text (Successfully Apply Reading Standards)** Determine what a text says explicitly and make logical inferences from it. Interpret vocabulary and figurative language in context. CCSR 1, CCSR 2, CCSR 3. CCSR 4.	See **Cold Read Record** on page 194. Minimum score of 9 on one Cold Read Text.	Scores / Titles / Dates	.02	
Range of Reading	**Demonstrate Ability to Finish a Pu Chapter Book** Read and finish a Pu novel, including demonstrating comprehension and a command of the vocabulary used in the text. CCSR 10, CCSL 6.	After reading a Pu chapter book, student is able to tell what the main character faced and how the problem was resolved.	**Yes** or **No** / Titles / Dates	.02	
	Demonstrate Ability to Read and Comprehend Pu Informational Text Read a Pu informational text, including demonstrating comprehension and a command of the vocabulary used in the text. CCSR 10, CCSL 6.	After reading a Pu informational text, student is able to tell what s/he learned and show where in the text s/he learned that information.	**Yes** or **No** / Titles / Dates	. 02	
	Demonstrate Ability to Read in a New Genre Reads a Pu Fantasy, Autobiography, Biography, Historical Fiction, or Science Fiction text. CCSR 9.	After finishing a Pu fantasy, autobiography, biography, historical fiction or science fiction book, student is able to tell what problem the main character faced and how the problem was resolved.	**Yes** or **No** / Titles / Dates	.01	
Pu Transition Points			.09	
GRAND TOTAL: Student should transition to Pu with 5.99 points and demonstrated proficiency at Pu prerequisites.			5.99	

Or

Pu Independent Reading Level Overview 6.00 - 6.99
Authors Use Structure/Form/Genre to Organize and Communicate Ideas

Pu Learning Focus

Genre/Form Matters

Pu readers understand that authors use genre/form to organize and communicate ideas. Pu readers learn to identify the genre or form of a new text so they can use their understanding of the characteristics of a genre to anticipate what they will encounter and to scaffold their understanding as they read.

Proficiency and Comfort with New Genres (e.g., Historical Fiction, Science Fiction, or Fantasy)

Pu readers should demonstrate proficiency in at least six very different kinds of text. Encourage students to expand their reading experience through literacy circles, read-aloud, book clubs, sharing time, modeling, book talks, and having enough of the right books in these genres. Proficient Pu-level readers are comfortable in realistic fiction, a variety of traditional tales, informational writing, poetry, biography, historical fiction, science fiction, and fantasy, usually developing in that order. In Pu text, the vocabulary demands are increasing, with 11–15 words on a typical chapter book page not familiar from everyday speech. Pu-level readers already know most of these literary words, and they have developed comfort with a wide variety of organizational frameworks through their wide reading in various genres. Students who have not read widely will have comprehension difficulty because of the literary vocabulary load and unfamiliar genre constructs. These students must go back to the color level where they can define all (or almost all) of the words used, follow the general text structure, and increase their proficiency levels from there. Do not allow students to develop the habit of reading without comprehension. Pu-level readers should finish a Pu chapter book, or its equivalent, each week.

Key Common Core Standard

Reading Literature 9: Compare and contrast texts in different forms or genres (e.g., stories and poems; historical novels and fantasy stories; memoir and biography) in terms of their approaches to similar themes and topics.

Entry Requirements

Must be in place before earning Pu designation.

- Demonstrate command of a literary vocabulary of approximately 4,500 words available for comprehending Pu level text. (Minimum 5 correct on Pu Vocabulary Check). CCSL 6.
- Read and comprehend unfamiliar Pu text (successfully apply Reading Standards). (Minimum score of 9 on Cold Read Record.) CCSR 1, CCSR2, CCSR3, CCSR4.
- Demonstrate ability to finish a Pu chapter book. CCSR 10.
- Demonstrate ability to read and comprehend Pu informational text. CCSR 10.
- Demonstrate ability to read in a new genre (fantasy, autobiography, biography, historical fiction, science fiction). CCSR 9.

Exit Requirements

Must be in place before earning 1Br designation.

- Demonstrate command of a literary vocabulary of approximately 6,000 words available for comprehending Br-level text. (Minimum 5 correct on 1Br Vocabulary Check.) CCSL 6.
- Read and comprehend unfamiliar easy Br text (successfully apply Reading Standards). (Minimum score of 9 on Cold Read Record.) CCSR 1, CCSR2, CCSR3, CCSR4.
- Demonstrate ability to finish a Br chapter book. CCSR 10.
- Demonstrate ability to read and comprehend Br informational text. CCSR 10.

Pu Independent Reading Level Assessment 6.00 - 6.99

Entry Requirements: Cumulative Record

Student ______________________ Teacher ______________________ Room ________ Date Started ________

Pu Entry Requirements		Evidence/Date				Date Completed
Vocabulary	**Demonstrate Command of a Literary Vocabulary of Approximately 4,500 Words** Have approximately 4,500 literary vocabulary words in reading vocabulary available for comprehending Pu level text. CCSL 6.	See **Vocabulary Check** on page 193. Minimum score of 5.	Scores		Dates	
Comprehension	**Read and Comprehend Unfamiliar Pu Text (Successfully Apply Reading Standards)** Determine what a text says explicitly and makes logical inferences from it. Interpret vocabulary and figurative language in context. CCSR 1, CCSR 2, CCSR 3. CCSR 4.	See **Cold Read Record** on page 194. Minimum score of 9 on one Cold Read Text.	Scores	Titles	Dates	
Range of Reading	**Demonstrate Ability to Finish a Pu Chapter Book** Read and finish a Pu novel, including demonstrating comprehension and a command of the vocabulary used in the text. CCSR 10, CCSL 6.	After reading a Pu chapter book, student is able to tell what the main character faced and how the problem was resolved.	**Yes** or **No**	Titles	Dates	
	Demonstrate Ability to Read and Comprehend Pu Informational Text Read a Pu informational text, including demonstrating comprehension and a command of the vocabulary used in the text. CCSR 10, CCSL 6.	After reading a Pu informational text, student is able to tell what s/he learned and show where in the text s/he learned that information.	**Yes** or **No**	Titles	Dates	
	Demonstrate Ability to Read in a New Genre Reads a Pu Fantasy, Autobiography, Biography, Historical Fiction, or Science Fiction text. CCSR 9.	After finishing a Pu fantasy, autobiography, biography, historical fiction or science fiction book, student is able to tell what problem the main character faced and how the problem was resolved.	**Yes** or **No**	Titles	Dates	

A reader who is proficient at all of the above enters Pu with 6.00 points. **6.00**

Pu Entry Requirements: Vocabulary Check

This page is for the teacher to use as a test of a student's vocabulary acquisition. DO NOT give copies of this page to students. DO NOT teach or drill these words out of context. Pick a column. Student should be able to define 5 of the words to enter Pu and 12 of the words to exit. The following words are representative of the 1,500 words Pu readers must acquire during their year of independent reading. This list is neither comprehensive or sufficient, but as long as the student hasn't practiced this list, it will give you an idea of whether his/her working vocabulary is sufficient to comprehend text at the Pu level. Pick a different column each time. Each column is used as a separate test. 5 words correct in any column = Pu Entry. 12 words correct in any column = Pu Exit.

Test A	Test B	Test C	Test D	Test E	Test F	Test G
(Date)						
acquire	allegiance	architect	arouse	ascend	assure	atom
attire	avalanche	avenge	aviator	axis	barren	beacon
cease	commence	conclude	condemn	confine	correspond	cultivate
cunning	customary	cyclone	cylinder	deceive	decimal	decline
diagonal	disdain	durable	economics	elaborate	embankment	emerge
erosion	evaporate	evident	expand	feat	flit	flourish
foe	folly	forlorn	gulf	helm	hinder	hue
kindle	lance	lanky	lasso	latitude	livestock	local
lope	lull	majority	minority	mantle	manuscript	marine
mooring	naval	navigation	opposition	oral	origin	ounce
parcel	patriot	pelt	plateau	plea	plentiful	plunder
politics	ponder	portable	prevail	previous	prime	quarry
quotation	ration	rebel	remedy	remote	reservoir	slumber
solar	span	species	stow	submerge	summit	summon
surf	treason	tyrant	vegetation	vertical	warily	wrath
(Total)						

Common Core Standard Language 6: Acquire and use accurately grade-appropriate general academic and domain-specific words and phrases.

Pu Entry Requirements: Cold Read Record

Student ______________________ Teacher ____________________ Room _______ Date ______

Title: ____

Given an unfamiliar Pu text (Cold Read), and NO help of any kind, the student is able to apply Reading Standards to Pu level text.

Fluently Decode Pu text	Evidence/Student Response		Score
Use combined knowledge of all letter-sound correspondences, syllabication patterns, and morphology (e.g., roots and affixes) to accurately read unfamiliar multisyllabic words, including names. CCSF 3a, CCSF 4ab.	• 99-100% word accuracy.		**Yes** or **No**
	• Appropriate rate and expression.		**Yes** or **No**
	• Stop and try again when something doesn't look right, sound right, or make sense.		**Yes** or **No**

If answer to any of the above questions is No, STOP TEST and move student to an easier level. Any student having trouble with decoding is most likely working at or below 2R.

Reading Standards **See text-specific questions on Cold Read Text Pages**	**Evidence/Student Response**	**Score** Weak..........Strong
Basic Understanding Support basic understanding with evidence from the text. CCSR 1.		1 2 3 4
Interpretation Support an interpretation or analysis with evidence from the text. CCSR 2, CCSR 3.		1 2 3 4
Vocabulary Interpret vocabulary and figurative language in context. CCSR 4.		1 2 3 4
Cold Read Proficiency Total: A minimum score of 9 points on ONE Cold Read Text is required in order to enter Pu.	**Total Points**	

Pu Entry Requirements: Cold Read Text A

Laugh Till You Cry by Joan Lowery Nixon
Random House

Basic Understanding

What is happening so far in this story?

Interpretation

How do you think the police officer feels about Cody? Use evidence from the text to support your answer.

Vocabulary

Find a word that you never use in speech. What do you think it probably means? Why do you think the author chose to use it?

Pu

CHAPTER ONE

Dodging low tree branches, leaping over dips and cracks in the sidewalk, Cody Carter ran harder and faster down Chimney Rock than he had ever run in his entire life. Someone was chasing him and quickly closing the short gap that lay between them.

The person yelled something, but fear and his own loud gasping for breath blocked Cody's ears, and he couldn't make out what was said. The only words that bounced through his brain were his: *I'm only thirteen years old. I'm too young to die.*

Ahead of him lay San Felipe, with cars backed up, waiting for the stoplight to change. In the nearest lane was a blue and white cop car, and Cody aimed for it, knocking on the passenger-side window. As he stared into the wide, surprised eyes of the uniformed policeman behind the wheel, Cody managed to croak, "Help!"

The officer flipped on his hazard lights and jumped from the car. Cody was bent over the fender, wiping rivulets of sweat from his eyes and gulping air.

"What's the matter, kid?" the officer called as he walked around the front of his sedan. He placed a firm hand on Cody's arm. "Are you okay?"

Cody twisted to look over his shoulder. His cousin Hayden Norton had drifted back and was standing behind some of the solid, broad-limbed oak trees that lined the street. Hayden's buddy Bradley Lee was with him. They were both at least five inches taller than Cody, even though they were all the same age and in the same grade at school.

Hayden and Brad watched Cody warily, practically sniffing the air like a couple of dogs as they waited to see what would happen next. But Hayden's other sidekick, Eddie Todd, shorter and even sneakier, was quietly edging his way back along the street. It was just like Eddie to leave the others, Cody thought. If there was going to be trouble, Eddie wouldn't be in it, even though he probably started it.

"Those guys want to kill me," Cody told the officer. He straightened, able now to breathe more easily.

The officer smiled. "Take a poke at you, maybe, but are you really sure they want to kill you?"

The humor in his voice made Cody flinch. "They do," he insisted. "They said they were going to drag me back to school and stick my head in a toilet. Drowning somebody is killing them, isn't it?"

Pu Entry Requirements: Cold Read Text B

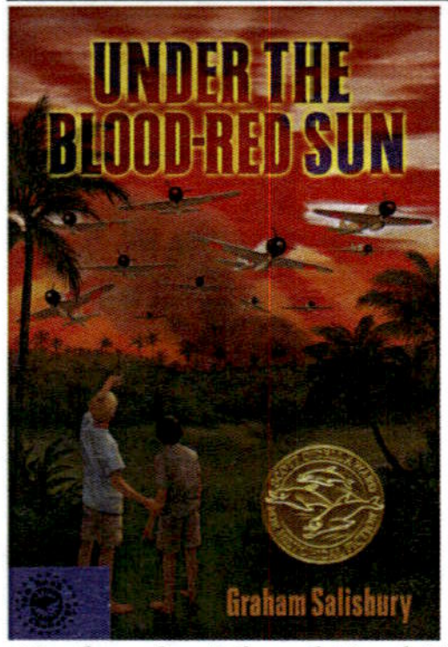

Under the Blood-Red Sun
by Graham Salisbury
Random House

Basic Understanding

What is happening so far in this story?

Interpretation

What is the central idea, so far, in this book? What do you predict the theme will be? How is it conveyed?

Vocabulary

What does the phrase "like a fisherman showing off a big one" mean? How does this phrase influence the tone of the text?

1

The Flag

It all started the day Grampa Joji decided to wash his precious flag of Japan and hang it out on the clothesline for the whole world to see. It was almost as big as the canvas tarp Papa used on his boat when it rained.

It was early September, 1941, just three weeks before the Yankees and the Dodgers started the World Series. A Sunday. Mama's day off. No breeze. The clouds, like giant white coral heads, hovered out over the ocean far beyond Honolulu harbor. In that kind of weather you stayed in the shade, at least if you were as smart as my dog Lucky, who lounged in the cool, weedless dirt under the house.

But anyway, Grampa scrubbed that flag clean. Usually, my friend Billy Davis and I thought it was pretty funny when he did something strange like that—like wash a flag, or take a bath in the stream, or laugh hysterically at Laurel and Hardy movies. Once, we got thrown out of a theater because Grampa kept on laughing, laughing, laughing, even when everyone else was quiet. Billy and I were nearly crying, Grampa was so funny. Grampa got mad and chased us. He was pretty tough about showing respect for your elders.

But a Japanese flag hanging out in the open like that was nothing to laugh about.

"Hey, Grampa," I yelled as I came up the dirt path through the trees. "Take that thing down. What if somebody *sees* it?"

Billy was with me. We'd just gotten off the bus from a trip downtown to play baseball. I threw my catcher's mitt on the ground and started walking faster. Grampa stood in front of his flag like a fisherman showing off a big one.

The white flag had a red ball in the center, with red rays like searchlights shooting out from it. Grampa waved his hand toward the clothesline. "Hey, busta, good, nah? Confonnit!"

"No! Not good! How many times do we have to tell you? This place is American, not Japanese. *American.* Didn't you hear what Papa said? Too many Japanese around here, that's what a lot of people think. . . . They don't need to see that flag to remind them."

I brushed past him and pulled the wet flag down. It soaked my shirt. Grampa's eyes got big, like he was so surprised he didn't know what to do.

"Papa's worried enough about what the Hawaiians think of us, and what the *haoles* think of us," I said. "We don't need anyone to think we're anti-*American* too. There's a war going on, you know. And Japan isn't mak-

Pu Entry Requirements: Cold Read Text C

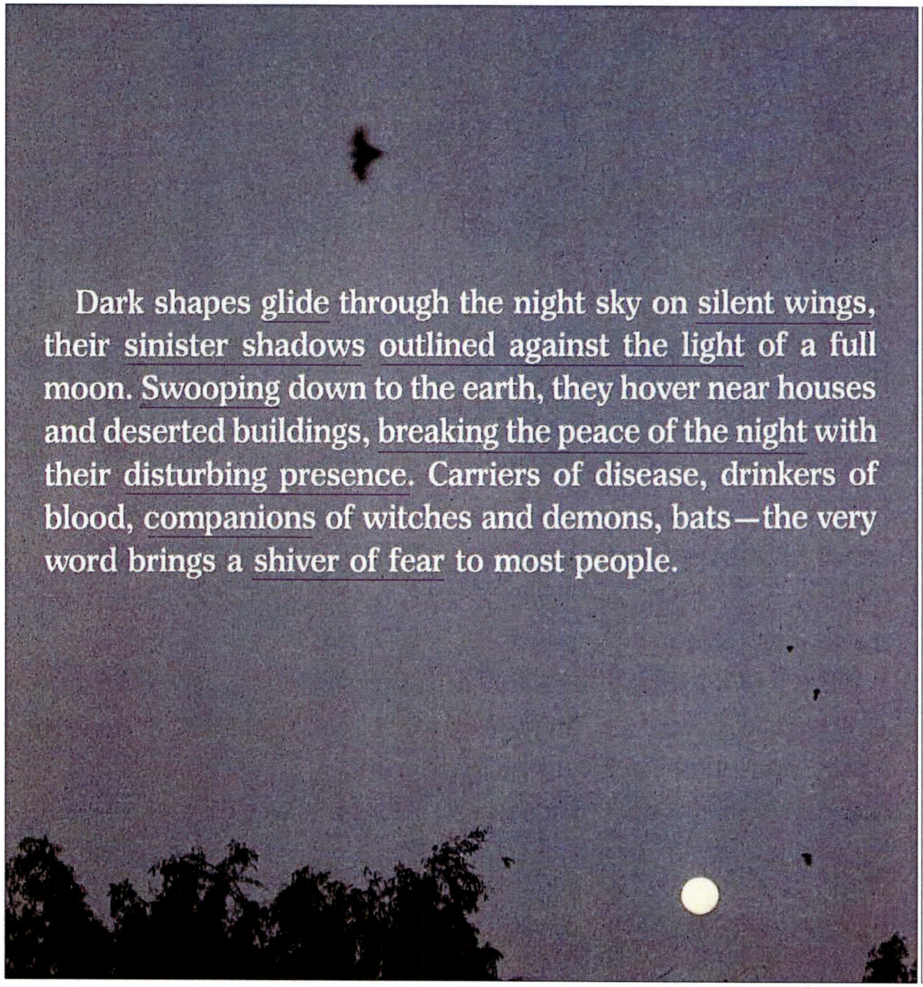

Dark shapes glide through the night sky on silent wings, their sinister shadows outlined against the light of a full moon. Swooping down to the earth, they hover near houses and deserted buildings, breaking the peace of the night with their disturbing presence. Carriers of disease, drinkers of blood, companions of witches and demons, bats—the very word brings a shiver of fear to most people.

MAMMALS THAT FLY

This popular image of bats is based on beliefs that are confused, contradictory, and almost all false. As we shall see, very few bats carry disease or feed on blood. The truth about bats, however, also tends to be confusing and full of contradictions.

Many bats are tiny animals no bigger than a hummingbird, but some bats have wing spans as wide as six feet (4 meters). Large numbers of bats eat insects, while others thrive on a diet of fruit, nectar, and even fish. Many bats make their homes in caves, attics, and other dark and hidden places, but some roost right out in the open, in the branches of trees.

Bats make up a varied group of animals, but all bats have some basic things in common. Most importantly, they are mammals and they can fly. These are the two characteristics that make bats so unique. Like dogs, horses, gorillas, and humans, bats have hairy bodies, bear live young, and feed their young on milk produced by **mammary glands.** Unlike other mammals however, they can escape the gravity of the earth and soar on widespread wings, like insects and birds.

Bats by Sylvia A. Johnson Lerner

Pu

Basic Understanding

Tell me three things the text says about bats.

Interpretation

According to this text, what is the popular image of bats?

Vocabulary

What does the phrase "escape the gravity of earth" mean? How does this phrase contribute to the tone of the text?

Pu Entry Requirements: Cold Read Text D

Rainforests
by Philip Sauvain
Lerner

Basic Understanding

Tell me three things the text says about rain forests.

Interpretation

What is the central idea or message in this section? How is it conveyed?

Vocabulary

What does the phrase "cycle of shifting cultivation" mean? How is this phrase important to the text?

Rain-forest Settlers

◀ This farmer has cleared part of the Randomafana forest in Madagascar. Rain forests may never regenerate, or grow again, after large areas are burned and cleared by farmers.

▼ Large numbers of trees are cut down to make roads like this one in French Guiana, South America. Roads encourage settlers to move into rain forests. More trees are then destroyed to make way for farmland and settlements.

The population in most rain-forest countries is growing very fast. Many of the people are very poor. Only a few wealthy landowners hold the best farmland, which they use to grow crops or to raise livestock to sell to other countries. Poor farmers are then forced to work less fertile land.

The governments of many rain-forest countries have encouraged the poor farmers to move into the forests. When they arrive in the forest, the settlers clear trees using the **slash-and-burn farming** method. Then they plant food crops, such as rice and cassavas. The settlers' crops eventually fail because the soil loses its richness. When this happens, the settlers move on. They clear and burn another area of forest to grow more crops. This cycle of shifting cultivation goes on all the time. In fact, millions of slash-and-burn farmers cut down up to 50 million acres of forestland every year.

In some places, farmers have been encouraged to settle in permanent forest villages, rather than moving from place to place. With help from their governments or other organizations, the settlers can improve the land to grow enough crops to live on.

- Slash-and-burn farming and shifting cultivation destroy more forest than any other use of the land, such as cattle ranching or logging. In 1980 half of the **deforestation** in South and Southeast Asia was the result of this type of clearing and farming.
- Fires that get out of control are a real danger in rain forests. In the early 1980s, one fire alone destroyed more than 15,000 square miles of forest on the island of Borneo.

Pu Comprehension
Reading Standards for Literature and Informational Text

Proficiency in the standards below must be demonstrated while reading independently in Pu level text. In order to advance to 1Br, students must earn .48 Comprehension Points.

Key Ideas and Details: **Using Text Evidence to Support Conclusions** Understand, think about, and discuss <u>what</u> the author said.		Evidence/Date	Points	
	Demonstrate background knowledge of a Pu-level reader, familiar with 90-100% of the vocabulary and enough of the world knowledge found in Pu-level books to ensure basic comprehension (e.g., sixth-grade level math, science, and social studies concepts).		✓	
	Automatically adjust reading strategies to suit text and purpose. • Demonstrate aggressive self-monitoring and active reading strategies when reading difficult material. • Skim and scan to locate specific information quickly. • Read silently and rapidly for pleasure.		✓	
CCSR 1	Cite textual evidence to support analysis of what the text says explicitly as well as inferences drawn from the text. • *How, why, what…? Give a citation from the text to support your answer.*		.03	
CCSR 2	Determine a theme or central idea of a text and how it is conveyed through particular details; provide a summary of the text distinct from personal opinions or judgments. • *What is the theme or central idea (central conflict, most important part) of this text? What details from the text support that this is the theme?* • *Summarize what you've read so far in one sentence. (Theme, not plot summary.)*		.03	
	Determine a central idea of a text and how it is conveyed through particular details; provide a summary of the text distinct from personal opinions or judgments. • *What is the main/central idea of this book and how do you know?* • *What key facts did the author use to support this idea?* • *Summarize this book in just one sentence.*		.03	
CCSR 3	Describe how a particular story's or drama's plot unfolds in a series of episodes as well as how the characters respond or change as the plot moves toward a resolution. • *What is the central problem of this book, and what are the key episodes that set it up? How is it resolved?* • *How do the main characters change from the beginning to the end? What inspires this change?*		.03	
	Analyze in detail how a key individual, event, or idea is introduced, illustrated, and elaborated upon in a text (e.g., through examples or anecdotes). • *Tell me everything this book has to say about ______ using examples and anecdotes from the text.*		.03	

	Identify and describe the following literary elements in the text: characters (motivations of major and minor characters); setting (time, day, year, historical period, place, situation); plot (main events, conflict, rising action, climax, falling action, resolution); narrator/point of view (first person, third person, omniscient); and theme (or moral). • *What is the conflict? How is it resolved?* • *Where and when did the story take place? How does it compare to your setting?* • *Who are the main characters and what are their traits? What are their motivations?* • *Who is the narrator? Is it told in first or third person?* • *What is the theme (lesson or moral)?*		.03	
Craft and Structure: Analyzing the Effects of Authors' Choices Understand and discuss the way(s) the author(s) said what was said				
CCSR 4	Determine the meaning of words and phrases as they are used in a text, including figurative, connotative, and technical meanings. • *Find a word you never use in your speech, or that you never saw before.* • *What do you think it probably means? Why?* • *Read the sentence again, but this time, put a word or phrase in place of the new word, without changing the meaning of the sentence.*		.03	
	Analyze the impact of a specific word choice on meaning and tone. • *How does this word/phrase influence the meaning of this section? The tone?*		.03	
CCSR 5	Analyze how a particular sentence, chapter, scene, or stanza fits into the overall structure of a text and contributes to the development of the theme, setting, or plot. • *How is this sentence (chapter, scene, stanza) important to the text as a whole?* • *How is it important to the theme (setting, plot)?*		.03	
	Analyze how a particular sentence, paragraph, chapter, or section fits into the overall structure of a text and contributes to the development of the ideas. (Same as above.)		.03	
	Identify and evaluate an author's use of various organizational structures (e.g., description, compare/contrast, cause/effect, chronological, sequential, or logical order, problem/solution, pro/con) used in a text. • *In what ways did the author organize the information in this text?* • *Which structure do you like best? Why?*		.03	
	Create graphic organizers to categorize and analyze information and ideas from reading (T-chart, Venn diagram, matrix chart, timeline, graphs, maps, etc.).		.03	
CCSR 6	Explain how an author develops the point of view (perspective) of the narrator or speaker in a text. • *How does the author develop the point of view (perspective) of the narrator? Show me an example in the text.*		.03	
	Determine an author's point of view (perspective) or purpose in a text and explain how it is conveyed in the text. • *What is the author's perspective (purpose)? How do you know? What evidence in the text supports your thinking?*		.03	

Integration of Knowledge and Ideas: Comparing Different Presentations

Discuss how the ideas in a book connect to each other and to the larger world.

CCSR 7	Compare and contrast the experience of reading a story, drama, or poem to listening to or viewing an audio, video, or live version of the text, including contrasting what they "see" and "hear" when reading the text to what they perceive when they listen or watch. • *Which did you like better: reading the story/drama/poem or listening to it/watching it be performed? Why?*		.03	
	Integrate information presented in different media or formats (e.g., visually, quantitatively) as well as in words to develop a coherent understanding of a topic or issue.		.03	
CCSR 8	Trace and evaluate the argument and specific claims in a text, distinguishing claims that are supported by reasons and evidence from claims that are not. • *What is the author's argument or claim? What evidence does the author give to support this argument?* • *Which of the author's claims have good supporting evidence? Which don't? Why?*		.03	
CCSR 9	Compare and contrast texts in different forms or genres (e.g., stories and poems; historical novels and fantasy stories) in terms of their approaches to similar themes and topics. • *Given 2 texts in different genres, create a T-chart comparing them.* (T-chart: rows Characters, Setting, Plot Events, Theme/Moral; columns Similarities, Differences)		.03	
	Compare and contrast one author's presentation of events with that of another (e.g., a memoir written by and a biography on the same person). Give student two different accounts of the same events. *Compare these two accounts on:* • *The way they tell about the events.* • *The information they provide.* • *The way they give their opinions about what happened.*		.03	
Pu Comprehension Total			**.48**	

	Similarities	Differences
Characters		
Setting		
Plot Events		
Theme/Moral		

Pu

Pu Range of Reading and Level of Text Complexity

Range of Reading and Level of Text Complexity	Evidence/Date	Points	
Engagement and Independence Read regularly and independently, sustaining engagement, in Pu-level materials for at least 30 minutes every day in the classroom. Demonstrate stamina to sustain reading for at least 60 minutes, as required for high-stakes tests.		.02	
Chapter Book Habit Regularly finish Pu chapter books, at least 1 a week.		.03	
Home Reading Sustain a home reading habit and reads in Pu-level materials for at least 30 minutes every night without prompting, or make up this <u>additional</u> 30 minutes during the school day.		.02	
Genres Identify the probable genre(s) of a new text and justify answer with evidence from the text and examples of characteristics common to that genre. • *Is this book fiction or informational? How can you tell?* • *What kind of literature is this? How can you tell?*		.01	

Read independently and comprehend <u>informational text</u> at the Pu level, including:

	Evidence (List Areas/Topics of Reading Experience)	Date	Points	
History Social Studies			.02	
Science			.02	

Pu Range of Reading and Level of Text Complexity Cont'd

	Evidence (List Areas/Topics of Reading Experience)	Date		
Biography/Autobiography (Journal/Speech)			.02	

Read independently and comprehend literary text at the Pu level, including:

	Evidence (List Chapter Books Completed)	Date		
Stories • Adventure • Contemporary/ Realistic Fiction • Horror • Traditional			.02	
Historical Fiction			.03	
Science Fiction or Fantasy			.03	
	Evidence (List Book Titles, or Steps/Time Spent Reading in the Genre.)			
Drama			.02	
Poetry			.02	
Pu Range of Reading and Level of Text Complexity Total			**.26**	

Pu Vocabulary and Language

Vocabulary and Language	Evidence/Date	Points	
Literary and Technical Vocabulary Know and be able to use at least 4,500-8,000 words, not familiar from everyday speech, but common to Pu level text. Pu readers have learned most of the literary and technical vocabulary encountered in Pu level text from their previous reading. As they spend a year reading in Pu books (minimum one hour per day), they will learn an additional 1,500 words. CCSL 6.		.05	
Notice unfamiliar words and gather vocabulary knowledge when considering a word or phrase important to comprehension or expression. CCSL 6.		.01	
Use context (e.g., the overall meaning of a sentence or paragraph; a word's position or function in a sentence) as a clue to the meaning of a word or phrase. Is able to substitute a word or phrase that means the same thing for the very few unfamiliar words in Pu level text. CCSL 4a.		.02	
Consult reference materials (e.g., dictionaries, glossaries, thesauruses), both print and digital, to find the pronunciation of a word or determine or clarify its precise meaning or its part of speech. CCSL 4c.		.01	
Verify the preliminary determination of the meaning of a word or phrase (e.g., by checking the inferred meaning in context or in a dictionary). CCSL 4d.		.01	
Use the relationship between particular words (e.g., cause/effect, part/whole, item/category) to better understand each of the words. CCSL 5b.		.01	
Distinguish among the connotations (associations) of words with similar denotations (definitions) (e.g., *stingy, scrimping, economical, unwasteful, thrifty*). CCSL 5c.		.02	
Affixes and Roots Use common, Pu-level Greek or Latin affixes and roots as clues to the meaning of a word (e.g., *audience, auditory, audible*). CCSL 4b.		.01	
Figurative Language Interpret figures of speech (e.g., personification) in context. CCSL 5a.		.02	
Decode Multisyllable Words Use combined knowledge of all letter-sound correspondences, syllabication patterns, and morphology (e.g., roots and affixes) to accurately read unfamiliar multisyllabic words, including names, in context and out of context, at the Pu level. (Any student having trouble with this is working at the wrong level.)		✓	
Pu Vocabulary and Language Total		.16	

Transition to 1Br

						Points	
Pu Entry Points						**6.00**	
Pu Comprehension Points						**.48**	
Pu Range of Reading and Level of Text Complexity Points						**.26**	
Pu Vocabulary and Language Points						**.16**	
1Br Transition Points. With NO help of any kind, student must demonstrate ability to:			**Evidence/Date**			**Points**	
Vocabulary	**Demonstrate Command of a Literary Vocabulary of Approximately 6,000 Words** Have approximately 6,000 literary vocabulary words in reading vocabulary available for comprehending Br level text. CCSL 6.	See **Vocabulary Check** on page 209. Minimum score of 5.	Scores		Dates	.03	
Comprehension	**Read and Comprehend Unfamiliar Easy Br Text** (Successfully Apply Reading Standards) Determine what a text says explicitly and makes logical inferences from it. Interpret vocabulary and figurative language in context. CCSR 1, CCSR 2, CCSR 3. CCSR 4.	See **Cold Read Record** on page 210. Minimum score of 9 on one Cold Read Text.	Scores	Titles	Dates	.02	
Range of Reading	**Demonstrate Ability to Finish a Br Chapter Book** Read and finish a Br novel, including demonstrating comprehension and a command of the vocabulary used in the text. CCSR 10, CCSL 6.	After reading a Br novel, student is able to tell what problem the main character faced and how the problem was resolved.	**Yes** or **No**	Titles	Dates	.02	
	Demonstrate Ability to Read and Comprehend Br Informational Text Read a Br informational text, including demonstrating comprehension and a command of the vocabulary used in the text. CCSR 10, CCSL 6.	After reading a Br informational text, student is able to tell what s/he learned and show where in the text s/he learned that information.	**Yes** or **No**	Titles	Dates	.02	
1Br Transition Points						**.09**	
GRAND TOTAL: Student should transition to 1Br with 6.99 points and demonstrated proficiency at 1Br prerequisites.						**6.99**	

1Br Independent Reading Level Overview 7.00 - 7.99
Authors Are Humans Who Make Choices That Can Be Evaluated

1Br Learning Focus
Authors are Human Beings Who Make Choices in Form, Content, and Organization That Can Be Evaluated

1Br versus 2Br readers are not distinguished by the difficulty of the text they read, but by the sophistication with which they can analyze author's craft across a wide range of genres and forms. Of course, some Br books are harder than others, but which Br books will be difficult for which readers is more dependent on the background knowledge, genre knowledge, and vocabulary of individual readers than on the difficulty of the text. Students entering 1Br have read widely in Pu text and can handle a few of their most familiar genres in Br. In these genres they can identify choices the author has made as a writer, compare these choices to those of another author writing in the same genre or on the same subject, and critique the effectiveness of these choices. 1Br readers can determine an author's perspective in a text and are just beginning to speculate on how the different perspectives of authors shape the choices they make.

In order to handle Br text, comfort with the 16–20 literary words per typical chapter book page and common literary constructs, extensive experience as a reader, and sufficient academic background in history and science are required.

Key Common Core Standards

Reading Informational Text 9: Analyze how two or more authors writing about the same topic shape their presentations of key information by emphasizing different evidence or advancing different interpretations of facts.

Reading Literature 9: Compare and contrast a fictional portrayal of a time, place, or character and a historical account of the same period as a means of understanding how authors of fiction use or alter history.

Entry Requirements
Must be in place before earning 1Br designation.

- Demonstrate command of a literary vocabulary of approximately 6,000 words available for comprehending Br-level text. (Minimum 5 correct on 1Br Vocabulary Check.) CCSL 6.
- Read and comprehend unfamiliar easy Br text (successfully apply Reading Standards). (Minimum score of 9 on Cold Read Record.) CCSR 1, CCSR2, CCSR3, CCSR4.
- Demonstrate ability to finish a Br chapter book. CCSR 10.
- Demonstrate ability to read and comprehend Br informational text. CCSR 10.

Exit Requirements
Must be in place before earning 2Br designation.

- Demonstrate command of a literary vocabulary of approximately 7,500 words available for comprehending Br-level text. (Minimum 5 correct on 2Br Vocabulary Check.) CCSL 6.
- Read and comprehend unfamiliar Br text (successfully apply Reading Standards). (Minimum score of 9 on Cold Read Record.) CCSR 1, CCSR2, CCSR3, CCSR4.
- Demonstrate ability to handle multiple genres of Br text by finishing a Br text in each of 3 literary genres and 3 informational genres. CCSR 10.

1Br Independent Reading Level Assessment 7.00 - 7.99

Entry Requirements: Cumulative Record

Student ____________ Teacher ____________ Room ______ Date Started ______

1Br Entry Requirements

		Evidence/Date				Date Completed
Vocabulary	**Demonstrate Command of a Literary Vocabulary of Approximately 6,000 Words** Have approximately 6,000 literary vocabulary words in reading vocabulary available for comprehending Br level text. CCSL 6.	See **Vocabulary Check** on page 177. Minimum score of 5.	Scores		Dates	
Comprehension	**Read and Comprehend Unfamiliar Easy Br Text** **(Successfully Apply Reading Standards)** Determine what a text says explicitly and make logical inferences from it. Interpret vocabulary and figurative language in context. CCSR 1, CCSR 2, CCSR 3. CCSR 4.	See **Cold Read Record** on page 178. Minimum score of 9 on one Cold Read Text.	Scores	Titles	Dates	
Range of Reading	**Demonstrate Ability to Finish a Br Chapter Book** Read and finish a Br novel, including demonstrating comprehension and a command of the vocabulary used in the text. CCSR 10, CCSL 6.	After reading a Br novel, student is able to tell what problem the main character faced and how the problem was resolved.	**Yes** or **No**	Titles	Dates	
	Demonstrate Ability to Read and Comprehend Br Informational Text Read a Br informational text, including demonstrating comprehension and a command of the vocabulary used in the text. CCSR 10, CCSL 6.	After reading a Br informational text, student is able to tell what s/he learned and show where in the text s/he learned that information.	**Yes** or **No**	Titles	Dates	
A reader who is proficient at all of the above enters 1Br with 7.00 points.						**7.00**

1Br Entry Requirements: Vocabulary Check

This page is for the teacher to use as a test of a student's vocabulary acquisition. DO NOT give copies of this page to students. DO NOT teach or drill these words out of context. Pick a column. Student should be able to define 5 of the words to enter 1Br and 12 of the words to exit. The following words are representative of the 1500 words 1Br readers must acquire during their year of independent reading. This list is neither comprehensive nor sufficient, but as long as the student hasn't practiced this list, it will give you an idea of whether his/her working vocabulary is sufficient to comprehend text at the1Br level. Pick a different column each time. Each column is used as a separate test.
5 words correct in any column = 1Br Entry. 12 words correct in any column = 1Br Exit.

Name

Test A	Test B	Test C	Test D	Test E	Test F	Test G
(Date)						
abrupt	acute	adjoining	aerial	alliance	ambush	amend
apparatus	assurance	baffle	ballad	balm	banish	bleak
blockade	blunt	cannibal	chasm	chivalry	circumference	clan
commerce	decoy	dependent	descent	dual	era	erupt
eternal	exile	falter	famine	feud	fickle	flaw
fragment	geology	gloat	glint	heave	heir	hemisphere
horizontal	improvise	initiate	infinite	institution	jeer	jubilant
laden	longitude	lure	melancholy	mirage	moderate	modify
monarch	monopoly	municipal	mutiny	narrative	neutral	objective
omen	peninsula	persecute	persist	plague	probable	precede
propel	radius	realm	reign	remnant	siege	solitary
sovereign	speculate	sphere	stifle	subdue	suburb	succession
sullen	surge	sustain	talon	tapestry	tariff	tempest
terminal	tether	torrent	trait	turbulent	typhoon	unruly
utilize	vary	vile	warp	wary	waver	wretched
(Total)						

Common Core Standard Language 6: Acquire and use accurately grade-appropriate general academic and domain-specific words and phrases.

1Br Entry Requirements: Cold Read Record

Student ______________________ Teacher ______________________ Room ________ Date ________

Title: ______________________

Given an unfamiliar Br text (Cold Read), and NO help of any kind, the student is able to apply Reading Standards to Br level text.

Fluently Decode Br text	Evidence/Student Response		Score
Use combined knowledge of all letter-sound correspondences, syllabification patterns, and morphology (e.g., roots and affixes) to read accurately unfamiliar multisyllabic words in context and out of context. (Any student having trouble with this is working at the wrong level.).	• 99-100% word accuracy.		**Yes** or **No**
	• Appropriate rate and expression.		**Yes** or **No**
	• Stop and try again when something doesn't look right, sound right, or make sense.		**Yes** or **No**

If answer to any of the above questions is No, STOP TEST and re-level student. Any student having trouble with decoding is most likely working at or below 2R.

Reading Standards **See text-specific questions on Cold Read Text Pages**	Evidence/Student Response	Score Weak..........Strong
Basic Understanding Support basic understanding with evidence from the text. CCSR 1.		1 2 3 4
Interpretation Support an interpretation or analysis with evidence from the text. CCSR 2, CCSR 3.		1 2 3 4
Vocabulary Interpret vocabulary and figurative language in context. CCSR 4.		1 2 3 4
Cold Read Proficiency Total: A minimum score of 9 points on ONE Cold Read Text is required in order to enter 1Br.	**Total Points**	

1Br Entry Requirements: Cold Read Text A

Whittington
by Alan Armstrong
Random House

Basic Understanding
What is happening so far in this story?

Interpretation
What do you think will be a theme of this book? Support your prediction with evidence from the text.

Vocabulary
What does "slack" mean in this context? If Whittington's coat is slack, what does that tell you about him?

1Br

I

Whittington Meets the Lady

SHE WAS THE UGLIEST duck he'd ever seen, purplish black with splotches of white on her wings, red wart skin around the neck, a pink bill. Her eyes were bright black dots. She was lopsided and lurched as she walked from the barn to her bathing place. She bobbled her neck to balance. Her feet were orange.

There was a cold wind. It smelled like snow. The cat hunched under a bush, wrapped tight with his ruff up.

As the duck approached, the cat eased out. He was the color of old metal, broad-faced with thick whiskers and dark lines that ran from his nose to his forehead and down his back and sides. His coat was rumpled and slack, for all he was big. His paws were black, his tail was thick and ringed with black circles. It swelled out at the end like a fox's brush. When he stood or sat, he rocked slightly from side to side like a punch-drunk fighter. He was stiff and walked low to the ground. His left ear hung down like a loose flap. He wasn't old, but he looked beaten up.

"Hello," said the cat.

The duck hadn't noticed him. She wasn't frightened, though; she was large and old and long past scaring, if that's what he had in mind.

She stopped and gave him a long look, moving her head up and down, then twisting it around, checking what she saw with each obsidian eye, which is the way it is with ducks when they have time.

"Who are you?" she asked at last.

"Whittington," he said, straightening up a little.

"So what do you want, Mr. Whittington?" asked the Lady. She settled so she was aimed into the wind and began billing her feathers to keep them lined up and fluffed. She had more than a thousand and they required a lot of care.

"A place to live."

She jerked her head around in surprise.

"You don't have a home?"

"I did," said the cat. "A boy took me in when I was a kitten. Then they sent him away because he read things backwards. They were ashamed. They'd both been to college and graduate school and here they had a child who couldn't read. They sent him to a special school out west. They said it was the best thing. He was going to take me along but they said no."

His voice trailed off.

"And?" the duck asked gently.

"They never loved me," the cat said, looking away.

1Br Entry Requirements: Cold Read Text B

Fablehaven
by Brandon Mull
Aladdin

Basic Understanding
What is happening so far in this story?

Interpretation
How do the character descriptions contribute to developing the plot in the beginning of the story?

Vocabulary
What does Kendra mean when she says she has elevated her social status?

CHAPTER ONE

The New Student

Crowding into homeroom with the other eighth graders, Kendra found her way to her desk. In a moment the bell would ring, signaling the start of the last week of school. One final week and she would leave middle school behind forever and start anew as a high school freshman, mingling with kids from two other junior highs.

A year ago that had sounded like a more exciting prospect than it did now. Kendra had been stuck in a nerd rut since around fourth grade, and a fresh start in high school might have meant an opportunity to shed the quiet, studious image. But this had been a renaissance year. Amazing how swiftly a little confidence and a more outgoing attitude could elevate your social status. Kendra no longer felt as desperate for a new beginning.

Alyssa Carter sat down in the desk next to her. "I heard we get yearbooks today," she said. She had short blonde hair and a slender build. Kendra had met Alyssa after making the soccer team back in September.

"Great, I looked hypnotized in my picture," Kendra groaned.

"Yours was adorable. Remember mine? My braces look the size of train tracks."

"Whatever. You could hardly even notice them."

The bell rang. Most of the kids were in their seats. Mrs. Price entered the room accompanied by the most disfigured student Kendra had ever seen. The boy had a bald, scabrous scalp and a face like a chapped welt. His eyes were puckered slits, his nose a malformed cavity, his mouth lipless and crusty. He scratched his arm, crooked fingers lumpy with bulging warts.

The hideous boy was otherwise nicely dressed in a black and red button-down shirt, jeans, and stylish tennis shoes. He stood in front of the class beside Mrs. Price while she introduced him.

"I'd like you all to meet Casey Hancock. His family just moved here from California. It can't be easy starting at a new school so late in the year, so please give him a warm welcome."

1Br Entry Requirements: Cold Read Text C

Exploring Mars
by D. J. Ward
Lerner

Wheels on the Ground

For studying Martian rocks, nothing beats being there. Enter *Spirit* and *Opportunity*, rolling robot geologists. *Spirit* and *Opportunity* are Mars Exploration Rovers (MERs). They are like radio-controlled cars packed with tools for studying Martian rocks and soil. The rovers' mission is to hunt for signs of water. Water leaves its mark wherever it has been. If Mars once was wet, it should be written in the rocks.

The rovers bring along a treasure chest of technology. Each MER is equipped with a panoramic camera (Pancam). Pancam is a two-eyed periscope for scanning the surrounding terrain. Because it has two eyes, Pancam can see the Martian surface in 3-D. Using Pancam, the rovers can identify hazards. This helps them move safely from place to place.

An extendable robot arm is mounted on the front of each rover. A microscope, a camera, a rock-scraping tool, and chemical sensors all are part of the arm. Each rover carries a device for detecting heat given off by rocks and soil. Power comes from solar panels that convert sunlight into electricity.

All this equipment sits atop an insect-like suspension with six multipurpose wheels. Each wheel can move up or down on its own. This flexibility allows the rovers to move over rocks and holes without tipping. The wheels can even be used to dig trenches in the soil.

Basic Understanding
Tell me three things the text says about MERs.

Interpretation
How were MERs specially designed to handle the conditions on Mars? Support your answer with evidence from the text.

Vocabulary
Explain the prase "written on the rocks." Why did the author use this phrase?

1Br

1Br Entry Requirements: Cold Read Text D

Eva Perón
by Darlen R. Stille
Compass Point

Comrades, it's said throughout the world that I am a selfish and ambitious woman; you know very well that this isn't the case. But you also know that everything I did, it was never so that I could have any political position in my country.

The crowd cheered and chanted even louder. Juan Perón was surprised. It seemed that she was more popular than he was!

Finally, Eva said, "Comrades, as General Perón has said, I will do what the people say." When Eva was finished speaking, the crowd went away, but no one was sure if Eva was going to run or not.

In the end, Eva Perón never ran for vice president.

Eva used her signature, broad gestures as she addressed the crowd on August 22, 1951.

Right after that torch-lit night, she fell ill with cancer. She died in 1952 at the age of 33. After her death, however, stories about her took on new life.

Much of Eva Perón's life was mysterious. In an attempt to keep people from learning about her past, she would not talk about her childhood. She even lied about her age and where she was born. Because they had no facts, both Eva's enemies and friends made up stories about her.

Today, people in Argentina call the stories the Black Myth and the White Myth. According to the Black Myth, Eva Perón was a ruthless woman who used Juan Perón to acquire riches and power. She was cruel to people that she did not like and forced merchants and shopkeepers to give her money.

However, according to the White Myth, Evita was a saint who sacrificed her life to help the poor of Argentina, especially poor women and children. She was devoted to fairness and justice, working tirelessly for the rights of ordinary working people.

Neither the Black Myth nor the White Myth is entirely true. Parts of each myth, however, make up Eva Perón's story. Her work helped improve the lives of the poor and humble, but her efforts were not selfless. By reaching out to the workers, she built political support for her husband and helped keep him in power. In her brief life, Eva Perón was an important, influential person in the history of her country.

Basic Understanding
Tell me three things the text says about Eva Perón.

Interpretation
What is the author's central message in this passage? What evidence from the text supports your answer?

Vocabulary
What does the author mean when he says that Perón's "efforts were not selfless?"

1Br Comprehension

Reading Standards for Literature and Informational Text

Proficiency in the standards below must be demonstrated while reading independently in Br level text. In order to advance to 2Br, students must earn .48 Comprehension Points.

	Key Ideas and Details: Using Text Evidence to Support Conclusions Understand, think about, and discuss <u>what</u> the author said.	Evidence/Date	Points	
	Demonstrate background knowledge of a 1Br-level reader, familiar with 90-100% of the vocabulary and enough of the world knowledge found in Br-level books to ensure basic comprehension (e.g., 7th-grade level math, science, and social studies concepts).		✓	
	Automatically adjust reading strategies to suit text and purpose. • Demonstrate aggressive self-monitoring and active reading strategies when reading difficult material. • Skim and scan to locate specific information quickly. • Read silently and rapidly for pleasure.		✓	
CCSR 1	Cite several pieces of textual evidence to support analysis of what the text says explicitly as well as inferences drawn from the text. • *How, why, what...? Cite at least two examples from the text to support your answer.*		.03	
CCSR 2	Determine a theme or central idea of a text and analyze its development over the course of the text; provide an objective summary of the text. • *What is the theme of this text? What details from the text support that this is the theme?* • *How does the theme develop from the beginning to the end of the text? (What is the most important thing that happened in this book? What challenge does the main character face? What lesson or moral could you get from this?)* • *Summarize what you've read so far in one sentence.*		.03	
	Determine two or more central ideas in a text and analyze their development over the course of the text; provide an objective summary of the text. • *Give two main/central ideas of this book.* • *What key facts did the author use to support each of these ideas?* • *How did each of these ideas change from the beginning to the end of the text?* • *Summarize this book in just one sentence.*		.03	
CCSR 3	Analyze how particular elements of a story or drama interact (e.g., how setting shapes the characters or plot). • *How does the setting influence the plot (or the characters)?* • *How do this character's traits shape the development of the conflict?*		.03	
	Analyze the interactions between individuals, events, and ideas in a text (e.g., how ideas influence individuals or events, or how individuals influence ideas or events). • *E.g., How did Martin Luther King shape the way people think about resistance to oppression?* • *How did __________ influence ___________?*		.03	

	Identify and describe the following literary elements in the text: characters (motivations of major and minor characters); setting (time, day, year, historical period, place, situation); plot (main events, conflict, rising action, climax, falling action, resolution). • *What is the conflict? How is it resolved?* • *Where and when did the story take place? How does it compare to your setting?* • *Who are the main characters and what are their traits? What are their motivations?*		.03	
Craft and Structure: Analyzing the Effects of Authors' Choices Understand and discuss the way(s) the author(s) said what was said.				
CCSR 4	Analyze the impact of rhymes and other repetitions of sounds (e.g., alliteration) on a specific verse or stanza of a poem or section of a story or drama. • *After reading a poem, or drama, or story, find an example of rhyme or repetition of words or sounds. How does this impact the text?*		.03	
	Determine the meaning of words and phrases as they are used in a text, including figurative, connotative, and technical meanings; analyze the impact of specific word choice on meaning and tone. • *Find a word you never use in your speech, or that you never saw before.* • *What do you think it probably means? Why?* • *Read the sentence again, but this time, put a word or phrase in place of the new word, without changing the meaning of the sentence.* • *How does this word/phrase influence the meaning of this section? The tone?*		.03	
CCSR 5	Analyze how a drama's or poem's form or structure (e.g., soliloquy, sonnet) contributes to its meaning. • *After reading a poem or drama, identify what type it is.* • *Speculate as to why the author chose that structure.* • *How does the structure contribute to this work's meaning?* • *How might another structure (prose, drama, poetic form) have influenced its meaning or effect?*		.03	
	Analyze the structure an author uses to organize a text (e.g., description, compare/contrast, cause/effect, pro/con, chronological, sequential, or logical order, problem/solution), including how the major sections contribute to the whole and to the development of the ideas. • *In what ways does the author organize the information in this text?* • *Speculate as to why the author chose this structure.* • *Which are the major sections of the text? How do they contribute to the whole?*		.03	

	Identify types of poetry (e.g., haiku, limerick, free verse) and structural elements (stanza, verse, rhyme scheme, line breaks, rhythm, alliteration). • *What kind of poetry is this? How do you know?* • *Identify an example of alliteration (etc.).*		.03	
CCSR 6	Analyze how an author develops and contrasts the points of view (perspectives) of different characters or narrators in a text. • *What do you know about the perspective of each of the main characters?* • *What in the text gives you that impression?* • *Which two characters have perspectives that differ the most? How? Why? Why did the author include both of these characters in the text?*		.03	
	Determine an author's point of view (perspective) or purpose in a text and analyze how the author distinguishes his or her position from that of others. • *What is the author's perspective or purpose? How do you know? What evidence in the text supports your thinking?* • *How does the author acknowledge other opinions or positions?*		.03	

Integration of Knowledge and Ideas: Comparing Different Presentations

Discuss how the ideas in a book connect to each other and to the larger world.

CCSR 7	Compare and contrast a written story, drama, or poem to its audio, filmed, staged, or multimedia version, analyzing the effects of techniques unique to each medium (e.g., lighting, sound, color, or camera focus and angles in a film). • *Which did you like better: reading the story/drama/poem or listening to it/watching it performed? Why?* • *Did you like the choices/interpretations of the performed version? Why or why not? What would you have done differently? What techniques were most effective in each medium? Why?*		.03	
	Compare and contrast a text to an audio, video, or multimedia version of the text, analyzing each medium's portrayal of the subject (e.g., how the delivery of a speech affects the impact of the words). (Same as above.)		.03	

<table>
<tr><th colspan="5">1Br Comprehension Cont'd</th></tr>
<tr><td>CCSR 8</td><td>Trace and evaluate the argument and specific claims in a text, assessing whether the reasoning is sound and the evidence is relevant and sufficient to support the claims.
• What is the author's main argument and what specific claims does he/she make?
• What evidence does the author give to support these?
• What reasoning does the author use?
• Which of the author's claims have good supporting evidence and/or reasoning? Which don't? Why?
• Has s/he convinced you? Why or why not? What evidence and/or reasoning would have made a stronger argument?</td><td></td><td>.03</td><td></td></tr>
<tr><td rowspan="2">CCSR 9</td><td>Compare and contrast a fictional portrayal of a time, place, or character and a historical account of the same period as a means of understanding how authors of fiction use or alter history. (See Historical Fiction Student Practice Page.)
• In this historical fiction book, what real events or characters does the author use?
• Which are fabricated? Why?
• What does the author think about this period of history? What does he/she want us to know/think/feel about it?
• Are there any historical facts that s/he changes? Why?</td><td></td><td>.03</td><td></td></tr>
<tr><td>Analyze how two or more authors writing about the same topic shape their presentations of key information by emphasizing different evidence or advancing different interpretations of facts.
• After reading 2 books on the same topic, what information do both authors include?
• What information does just one author include?
• How do their decisions influence the portrayal of the topic?
<table><tr><th></th><th>Author 1</th><th>Author 2</th></tr><tr><td>Evidence Emphasized</td><td></td><td></td></tr><tr><td>Interpretation of Facts</td><td></td><td></td></tr></table></td><td></td><td>.03</td><td></td></tr>
<tr><td></td><td>Discuss author's perspectives and biases and how these might influence the text.</td><td></td><td>.03</td><td></td></tr>
<tr><td colspan="3">1Br Comprehension Total</td><td>.48</td><td></td></tr>
</table>

1Br Range of Reading and Level of Text Complexity

Range of Reading and Level of Text Complexity	Evidence/Date	Points	
Engagement and Independence Read regularly and independently, sustaining engagement, in Br-level materials for at least 30 minutes every day in the classroom. Demonstrate stamina to sustain reading for at least 60 minutes, as required for high-stakes tests.		.02	
Chapter Book Habit Regularly finish Br chapter books, about 1 a week.		.03	
Home Reading Sustain a home reading habit and read in Br-level materials for at least 30 minutes every night without prompting, or make up this <u>additional</u> 30 minutes during the school day.		.02	
Genres Identify the probable genre(s) of a new text and justify answer with evidence from the text and examples of characteristics common to that genre. • *Is this book fiction or informational? How can you tell?* • *What kind of literature is this? How can you tell?*		.01	

Read independently and comprehend <u>informational text</u> at the Br level, including:

	Evidence (List Areas/Topics of Reading Experience)	Date	Points	
History Social Studies • American • World			.02	
Science • Life/Biological • Earth • Physical			.03	
Biography Autobiography			.02	
Expository • Journal/Newspaper Articles • Persuasive Essays • Speeches			.02	

1Br Range of Reading and Level of Text Complexity Cont'd

Read independently and comprehend literary text at the Br level, including:

	Evidence (List Chapter Books Completed)	Date		
Realistic Fiction • Adventure • Contemporary/ Realistic Fiction • Horror			.02	
Historical Fiction			.02	
Fantasy			.01	
Science Fiction			.01	
	Evidence (List Book Titles or Steps/Time Spent Reading in the Genre)			
Traditional Tales (Fables, Folktales, Myths)			.01	
Drama			.01	
Poetry			.01	
1Br Range of Reading and Level of Text Complexity Total			**.26**	

1Br Vocabulary and Language

Vocabulary and Language	Evidence/Date	Points	
Literary, Academic, and Domain Specific Vocabulary Know and be able to use 6,000-8,000 words, not familiar from everyday speech, but common to Br-level text. CCSL 6. Br readers have learned most of the literary and technical vocabulary encountered in Br-level text from their previous reading. As they spend a year reading in Br books (minimum one hour per day), they will learn an additional 1,500 words.		.05	
Notice unfamiliar words and gather vocabulary knowledge when considering a word or phrase important to comprehension or expression. CCSL 6.		.01	
Use context (e.g., the overall meaning of a sentence or paragraph; a word's position or function in a sentence) as a clue to the meaning of a word or phrase. CCSL 4a. Be able to substitute a word or phrase that means the same thing for the few unfamiliar words in Br level text.		.02	
Consult general and specialized reference materials (e.g., dictionaries, glossaries, thesauruses), both print and digital, to find the pronunciation of a word or determine or clarify its precise meaning or its part of speech. CCSL 4c.		.01	
Verify the preliminary determination of the meaning of a word or phrase (e.g., by checking the inferred meaning in context or in a dictionary). CCSL 4d.		.01	
Use the relationship between particular words (e.g., synonyms, antonyms, homographs, analogy) to better understand each of the words. CCSL 5b.		.01	
Distinguish among the connotations (associations) of words with similar denotations (definitions) (e.g., *refined, respectful, polite, diplomatic, condescending*). CCSL 5c.		.02	
Affixes and Roots Use common, grade-appropriate Greek or Latin affixes and roots as clues to the meaning of a word (e.g., *belligerent, bellicose, rebel*). CCSL 4b.		.01	
Figurative Language Interpret figurative language (e.g., similes and metaphors) and figures of speech (e.g., personification, literary, biblical, and mythological allusions) in context. CCSL 5a.		.02	
Decode Multisyllable Words Use combined knowledge of all letter-sound correspondences, syllabification patterns, and morphology (e.g., roots and affixes) to read accurately unfamiliar multisyllabic words in context and out of context. (Any student having trouble with this is working at the wrong level.)		✓	
1Br Vocabulary and Language Total		.16	

Transition to 2Br

1Br Entry Points	7.00	
1Br Comprehension Points	.48	
1Br Range of Reading and Level of Text Complexity Points	.26	
1Br Vocabulary and Language Points	.16	

2Br Transition Points. With NO help of any kind, student must demonstrate ability to:			Evidence/Date	Points	
Vocabulary	**Demonstrate Command of a Literary Vocabulary of Approximately 7,500 Words** Have approximately 7,500 literary vocabulary words in reading vocabulary available for comprehending Br-level text. CCSL 6.	See **Vocabulary Check** on page 225. Minimum score of 5.	Scores / Dates	.03	
Comprehension	**Read and Comprehend Unfamiliar Br Text (Successfully Apply Reading Standards)** Determine what a text says explicitly and make logical inferences from it. Interpret vocabulary and figurative language in context. CCSR 1, CCSR 2, CCSR 3. CCSR 4.	See **Cold Read Record** on page 226. Minimum score of 9.	Scores / Titles / Dates	.02	
Range of Reading	**Demonstrate Ability to Handle Multiple Genres of Br Level Text** Read and finish a Br text in each of 3 literary genres and 3 informational genres, including demonstrating comprehension and a command of the vocabulary used in the text. CCSR 9, CCSR 10.	After reading a Br text in each of 3 literary genres, student is able to tell what problem the main character faced and how the problem was resolved.	**Yes** or **No** / Titles / Genres (• realistic fiction • historical fiction • fantasy • science fiction • traditional tales • drama • poetry) / Dates	.02	
		After reading a Br text in each of 3 informational genres, student is able to tell what s/he learned and show where in the text s/he learned that information.	**Yes** or **No** / Titles / Genres (• history • science • biography • memoir • newspaper • persuasive/editorial • literary analysis) / Dates	.02	
2Br Transition Points				.09	
GRAND TOTAL: Student should transition to 2Br with 7.99 points and demonstrated proficiency at 2Br prerequisites.				7.99	

2Br Independent Reading Level Overview 8.00 - 8.99

Texts Reflect the Perspectives, Biases, Cultural Background, and Historical Context of Their Authors

2Br Learning Focus

Texts Reflect the Perspectives, Biases, Cultural Background, and Historical Context of Their Authors

1Br versus 2Br readers are not distinguished by the difficulty of the text they read, but by the sophistication with which they can analyze author's craft across a wide range of genres and forms. Of course, some Br books are harder than others, but which Br books will be difficult for which readers is more dependent on the background knowledge, genre knowledge, and vocabulary of individual readers than on the difficulty of the text.

2Br-level readers see the author as a writer, as a human being with his/her own biases, motivations and blind spots. They have developed a critical eye toward writing and can discuss an author's use of literary techniques. They can locate a particular book in its genre and make comparisons across texts on a wide variety of both themes and writing techniques. They read actively, talking back to the author, questioning and probing the ideas presented. Comfort with the 16–20 literary words per typical chapter book page requires extensive experience as a reader. Sentences are complex, figurative language is common, and most adults cannot handle materials written at this level of complexity. Just because a reader can read a Br text fluently doesn't mean he/she is a Br-level reader. Dig deeply into the reader's knowledge of the vocabulary, understanding of the ideas, and ability to critique the writing before assigning him/her the Br designation.

Key Common Core Standards

Reading: Informational

6: Determine an author's point of view or purpose in a text and analyze how the author acknowledges and responds to conflicting evidence or viewpoints.

8: Delineate and evaluate the argument and specific claims in a text, assessing whether the reasoning is sound and the evidence is relevant and sufficient; recognize when irrelevant evidence is introduced.

9: Analyze a case in which two or more texts provide conflicting information on the same topic and identify where the texts disagree on matters of fact or interpretation.

Entry Requirements

Must be in place before earning 2Br designation.

- Demonstrate command of a literary vocabulary of approximately 7,500 words available for comprehending Br-level text. (Minimum 5 correct on 2Br Vocabulary Check.) CCSL 6.
- Read and comprehend unfamiliar Br text (successfully apply Reading Standards). (Minimum score of 9 on Cold Read Record.) CCSR 1, CCSR2, CCSR3, CCSR4.
- Demonstrate ability to handle multiple genres of Br text by finishing a Br text in each of 3 literary genres and 3 informational genres. CCSR 10.

Exit Requirements

Must be in place before earning Si designation.

- Demonstrate command of a literary vocabulary of approximately 9,000 words available for comprehending Si-level text. (Minimum 5 correct on Si Vocabulary Check.) CCSL 6.
- "What is the book about?" is no longer answered with just a plot summary, but is answered with an analysis of the author's theme or purpose.
- Read and comprehend unfamiliar Si text (successfully apply Reading Standards). (Minimum score of 9 on Cold Read Record.) CCSR 1, CCSR2, CCSR3, CCSR4.
- Demonstrate ability to finish a Si chapter book. CCSR 10.
- Demonstrate ability to read and comprehend Si informational text. CCSR 10.

2Br Independent Reading Level Assessment 8.00 - 8.99

Entry Requirements: Cumulative Record

Student ______________ Teacher ______________ Room ______ Date Started ______

2Br Entry Requirements

		Evidence/Date					Date Completed
Vocabulary	**Demonstrate Command of a Literary Vocabulary of Approximately 7,500 Words** Have approximately 7,500 literary vocabulary words in reading vocabulary available for comprehending Br-level text. CCSL 6.	See **Vocabulary Check** on page 225. Minimum score of 5.	Scores			Dates	
Comprehension	**Read and Comprehend Unfamiliar Br Text (Successfully Apply Reading Standards)** Determine what a text says explicitly and make logical inferences from it. Interpret vocabulary and figurative language in context. CCSR 1, CCSR 2, CCSR 3. CCSR 4.	See **Cold Read Record** on page 226. Minimum score of 9.	Scores	Titles		Dates	
Range of Reading	**Demonstrate Ability to Handle Multiple Genres of Br Level Text** Read and finish a Br text in each of 3 literary genres and 3 informational genres, including demonstrating comprehension and a command of the vocabulary used in the text. CCSR 9, CCSR 10. (A student who has passed 2Br Vocabulary and Comprehension entry requirements and is working on demonstrating this range of Br reading should be considered Transitional 1Br to 2Br - or an IRLA score of 7.95.)	After reading a Br text in each of 3 literary genres, student is able to tell what problem the main character faced and how the problem was resolved.	**Yes** or **No**	Titles	Genres • realistic fiction • historical fiction • fantasy • science fiction • traditional tales • drama • poetry	Dates	
		After reading a Br text in each of 3 informational genres, student is able to tell what s/he learned and show where in the text s/he learned that information.	**Yes** or **No**	Titles	Genres • history • science • biography • memoir • newspaper • persuasive/editorial • literary analysis	Dates	

A reader who is proficient at all of the above enters 2Br with 8.00 points. **8.00**

2Br Entry Requirements: Vocabulary Check

This page is for the teacher to use as a test of a student's vocabulary acquisition. DO NOT give copies of this page to students. DO NOT teach or drill these words out of context. Pick a column. Student should be able to define 5 of the words to enter 2Br and 12 of the words to exit. The following words are representative of the 1,500 words 2Br readers must acquire during their year of independent reading. This list is neither comprehensive nor sufficient, but as long as the student hasn't practiced this list, it will give you an idea of whether his/her working vocabulary is sufficient to comprehend text at the 2Br level. Pick a different column each time. Each column is used as a separate test. 5 words correct in any column = 2Br Entry. 12 words correct in any column = 2Br Exit.

Name				Date	Total Defined	
Test A	**Test B**	**Test C**	**Test D**	**Test E**	**Test F**	**Test G**
(Date)						
accommodate	adjourn	adolescent	advocate	ambassador	amphibious	antidote
aspect	assert	atone	auxiliary	beneficial	besiege	bias
blight	breach	career	casualty	cavalry	censor	clarify
conspicuous	conspiracy	constable	contempt	void	coy	decipher
decompose	deflect	defendant	deluge	derive	dimension	doctrine
doubtless	douse	earshot	eaves	elapse	elude	emancipation
embargo	emigrant	etiquette	evade	foremost	fortify	foyer
graft	hilt	hoard	immortal	impact	inflict	inoculate
irk	jaunt	jovial	lapse	ledger	liberal	livelihood
macadam	maestro	martyr	meager	militia	mobilize	monastery
morsel	nomad	notorious	oppression	orator	outskirts	pacify
pantomime	perimeter	periodical	persistence	pious	plight	plumage
precipice	pretense	prone	provisional	quizzical	quota	ratio
recede	recoil	recur	renegade	reprieve	revelation	ruthless
saga	sentinel	sinister	sparse	subordinate	synopsis	veneer
(Total)						

Common Core Standard Language 6: Acquire and use accurately grade-appropriate general academic and domain-specific words and phrases.

2Br Entry Requirements: Cold Read Record

Student ______________________ Teacher ______________________ Room ______ Date ______

Title: ______________________

Given an unfamiliar Br text (Cold Read), and NO help of any kind, the student is able to apply Reading Standards to Br level text.

Fluently Decode Br text	**Evidence/Student Response**		**Score**
Use combined knowledge of all letter-sound correspondences, syllabication patterns, and morphology (e.g., roots and affixes) to accurately read unfamiliar multisyllabic words, including names.	• 99-100% word accuracy.		**Yes** or **No**
	• Appropriate rate and expression.		**Yes** or **No**
	• Stop and try again when something doesn't look right, sound right, or make sense.		**Yes** or **No**

If answer to any of the above questions is No, STOP TEST and re-level student. Any student having trouble with decoding is most likely working at or below 2R.

Reading Standards **See text-specific questions on Cold Read Text Pages**	**Evidence/Student Response**	**Score** Weak..........Strong
Basic Understanding Support basic understanding with evidence from the text. CCSR 1.		1 2 3 4
Interpretation Support an interpretation or analysis with evidence from the text. CCSR 2, CCSR 3.		1 2 3 4
Vocabulary Interpret vocabulary and figurative language in context. CCSR 4.		1 2 3 4
Cold Read Proficiency Total: A minimum score of 9 points on ONE Cold Read Text is required in order to enter 2Br.	**Total Points**	

2Br Entry Requirements: Cold Read Text A

The Traitor
by Laurence Yep
Harper Trophy

Basic Understanding

What is happening so far in this story?

Interpretation

What do you think the theme of this book will be? What details about the characters and setting support your prediction?

Vocabulary

Why does the author use the phrase "American justice"? How might this phrase mean different things to Father and the man?

CHAPTER | I

Joseph Young
Chinese Camp, Wyoming Territory
Sunday, June 14, 1885
Morning

Father began the morning with his usual fight.

I tried to cling to a few more minutes of sleep because it was Sunday, our one day of rest. I could hear the stranger taunting Father outside the cabin. Most Chinese did when they found out Father's identity.

"So you're the high-and-mighty Otter," the man was jeering. "What are you doing stuck here digging coal just like me?"

Father's voice was as friendly as ever. "I thought my days with a pickax were done when I left the railroad," he agreed. "But here I am again."

I kept to my bed, hoping that this time it would be different: Father would be able to make peace with the man.

"And where are all your *American* pals now?" the man sneered. "You told us they'd never let those laws pass."

"Those immigration laws passed only because of ignorance. My Western friends are fighting to overturn them right now," Father said to the man. "Westerners" was Father's polite word for *Americans*.

Calmly Father tried to assure the man that everything would work out for all of us eventually. He had such faith in *America* and in *American* justice. He never seemed to realize that his words, meant to soothe, only rubbed salt into old wounds. All the Chinese were frustrated with what was happening; but since they couldn't take it out on the *Americans*, they looked for other targets.

By now I was good at reading the tones and undercurrents of voices, so I knew that the man was getting ready to beat Father to a pulp.

With a sigh I unrolled my trousers, which I had been using as a pillow. Pulling them on, I rolled out of the bunk bed to save Father—sometimes it was hard to say who was raising whom.

The sun was just rising, so I made my way quietly past the other bunks, where our cabinmates were still snoring. When I stepped outside, I didn't recognize the man. The coal company kept upping our quotas and bringing in more Chinese to work. There were always plenty of Chinese who kept coming to the Land of the Golden Mountain—as they called *America*. And these guests—as they called themselves—were willing to do anything.

2Br Entry Requirements: Cold Read Text B

Heir Apparent by
Vivian Vande Velde
Harcourt

Basic Understanding

What is happening so far in this story?

Interpretation

What do you think the theme of this book will be? What details about the characters and setting support your prediction?

Vocabulary

What does the phrase "civil disturbance" mean? How does this phrase contribute to the tone of the text??

CHAPTER ONE

Happy Birthday to Me

It was my fourteenth birthday, and I was arguing with a bus. How pathetic is that?

Even before the bus had started in on me, my mood wasn't exactly the best it's ever been. Birthdays do that to me. This year I didn't even have a good excuse: I had actually received my birthday gift from my father on time, which might have been a sign he was making an effort to be a more considerate and involved dad. Of course, if he was really considerate and involved, he wouldn't have had his secretary call to ask me what kind of gift certificate I wanted for my birthday.

Whatever. Birthday = don't-mess-with-me mood.

So there I was, on my way to cash in my gift certificate, riding on a bus powered by artificial intelligence—emphasis on the *artificial*.

I saw the picketers just as the bus paged me: "Passenger Giannine Bellisario, you asked to disembark at the Rasmussem Gaming Center, but there is a civil disturbance at your stop. Do you wish to continue to another destination, or would you prefer to be returned to the location at which you boarded?" The voice was kind and polite and only slightly metallic.

I was not polite. I sighed. Loudly. "Are they on strike?" I asked into the speaker embedded in the armrest.

There was a brief pause while the bus's computer brain accessed Central Information. "Rasmussem employees are not on strike," the bus reassured me, at just about the same time that I could make out the picketers' signs. "The demonstration is by members of CPOC."

I sighed even louder. They pronounce it, *C pock*. It stands for Citizens to Protect Our Children. As a fourteen-year-old, I qualify—by society's definition—as a child. I am willing to accept protection from stray meteors, ecoterrorists, and my seven-year-old cousin, Todd. But I don't feel in need of protecting by CPOC, which strongly believes that only G-rated movies should be made and that libraries should stock only nice, uplifting books that promote solid family values—*nice* being defined as nothing supernatural, nothing violent, nothing scary. That about kills my entire reading list. I think there are a couple alphabet books they approve of. Still, as far as I knew, this was the first time they'd ever come after Rasmussem.

2Br Entry Requirements: Cold Read Text C

Adaptation
by Brandon Mull
Aladdin

CHANGING CONDITIONS

Conditions in a habitat are always changing. Each day the Sun rises and gives light and warmth. The weather brings changes such as wind, storms, frost, and snow. On the seashore the tides rise and fall. These are all changes in the non-living world. Changes also happen in the living world. Sometimes animals such as locusts, lemmings, or rabbits breed in vast numbers. They eat so much that other animals, who normally eat the same food, begin to starve. If living things are to survive, they must cope with all these varying conditions.

► The barnacle's life is ruled by the twice daily rise and fall of the tides.

HOT AND COLD

One of the main changes every day is the rise and fall in temperature, which happens as the Sun rises and sets. Most animals are **cold-blooded** and their activity is greatly affected by the surrounding temperature. After a cool night, a snake crawls slowly into the morning Sun and basks in its rays. Soon the snake is warm enough to move fast and pursue prey. As dusk falls and the temperature drops, the snake cools down again and can only move slowly. So it hides under a sheltering rock for the night.

SIMILAR ANIMALS, DIFFERENT ADAPTATIONS

There are many examples of similar creatures, from the same animal group, that are adapted to different habitats.

- The African hare and American jackrabbit have very long legs and ears, and short fur. These features help the hare's body lose heat in the very hot conditions of its desert home.
- The Arctic hare has shorter legs and ears, and very long, thick fur. These features help to prevent loss of body heat in the very cold habitat of the far north.

TYPES OF ADAPTATIONS

- Overall shape: A worm is long and thin to burrow through soil. A leaf is broad and flat to catch sunlight.
- Color and pattern: The green tree frog is colored to sit unnoticed among green leaves.
- Body parts: A part of the body may be adapted for a certain task, for example, the long fangs of a viper that stab venom (poison) into its prey.
- Internal workings: The chemical life processes of a living thing may show adaptations. The presence of a natural chemical **anti-freeze** in the bodies of ice worms allows them to live in the freezing temperatures inside glaciers.

SIMILAR ADAPTATIONS, DIFFERENT ANIMALS

There are many examples of varied creatures, from different animal groups, that have similar adaptations because they live in the same-habitat.

- Frogs, lizards, and squirrels that live in trees have long, slim, grasping fingers to hold on to the branches.
- Frogs, lizards, and squirrels that live on the ground have shorter, stubbier fingers for walking and running on hard surfaces.

Basic Understanding

Tell me three things the text says about animal adaptations.

Interpretation

What is the author's central message in this passage? What evidence from the text supports your answer?

Vocabulary

What are "varying conditions" and how is this phrase important to the text?

2Br Entry Requirements: Cold Read Text D

Queen of the West

Before Chicago burned, it boomed. The American Civil War ended in 1865, and since that time the city had been growing quickly. Railroads had become the dominant mode of transportation and shipping. Ten of them met in Chicago, making the city a critical hub connecting the East and West coasts and one of the most important cities in the country. One song referred to Chicago as the "Queen of the West."

The railroads prompted the creation of factories and meatpacking plants, which in turn created jobs. To fill those jobs, immigrants from Germany, Ireland, Russia, and many other countries poured into Chicago.

Chicago seemed to have everything that made a city thrive. It had a vibrant multicultural population, a large industrial district, a bustling financial district, and a location that was on the way to almost anywhere. It also boasted another feature that was not typical of Midwestern cities: a shoreline. It was situated along Lake Michigan, a body of water so large that a person might mistake it for an ocean. The Chicago River wound through the center of the city.

The Great Chicago Fire
by Marc Tyler Nobleman
Capstone

Basic Understanding

Tell me three things the text says about Chicago.

Interpretation

According to the author, how did Chicago's physical location contribute to the growth of the city?

Vocabulary

What does the phrase "dominant mode" mean? What other word or phrase could

2Br Comprehension

Reading Standards for Literature and Informational Text

Proficiency in the standards below must be demonstrated while reading independently in Br level text. In order to advance to Si, students must earn .48 Comprehension Points.

Key Ideas and Details: Using Text Evidence to Support Conclusions Understand, think about, and discuss what the author said.		Evidence/Date	Points	
	Demonstrate background knowledge of a 2Br-level reader, familiar with 90-100% of the vocabulary and enough of the world knowledge found in Br-level books to ensure basic comprehension (e.g., 8th-grade level math, science, and social studies concepts).		✓	
CCSR 1	Cite the textual evidence that most strongly supports an analysis of what the text says explicitly as well as inferences drawn from the text. • *How, why, what...? Find the example from the text that BEST supports your answer.*		.03	
CCSR 2	Determine a theme or central idea of a text and analyze its development over the course of the text, including its relationship to the characters, setting, and plot; provide an objective summary of the text. • *What is the theme of this text? What details from the text support that this is the theme? How does the theme develop from the beginning to the end of the text?* • *How do the characters, setting, and plot contribute to the theme?* • *Summarize what you've read so far in one sentence.*		.03	
	Determine a central idea of a text and analyze its development over the course of the text, including its relationship to supporting ideas; provide an objective summary of the text. • *What is the main idea of this text? What details from the text support that this is the main idea? How does the main idea develop from the beginning to the end of the text?* • *What ideas are offered to support this main idea?* • *Summarize what you've read so far in one sentence.*		.03	
CCSR 3	Analyze how particular lines of dialogue or incidents in a story or drama propel the action, reveal aspects of a character, or provoke a decision. • *What incident in this book was a turning point? Why?* • *What was the most important event in this book? Why?* • *What line of dialogue revealed something important about one of the characters?*		.04	
	Analyze how a text makes connections among and distinctions between individuals, ideas, or events (e.g., through comparisons, analogies, or categories).		.03	

	Identify and describe the following literary elements in the text: characters (motivations of major and minor characters); setting (time, day, year, historical period, place, situation); plot (main events, conflict, rising action, climax, falling action, resolution). • *What is the conflict? How is it resolved?* • *Where and when did the story take place? How does it compare to your setting?* • *Who are the main characters and what are their traits? What are their motivations?*		.03	
Craft and Structure: Analyzing the Effects of Authors' Choices Understand and discuss <u>the way(s)</u> the author(s) said what was said.				
CCSR 4	Determine the meaning of words and phrases as they are used in a text, including figurative and connotative, and technical meanings; analyze the impact of specific word choice on meaning and tone, including analogies or allusions to other texts. • *Find a word you never use in your speech, or that you never saw before.* • *What do you think it probably means? Why?* • *Read the sentence again, but this time, put a word or phrase in place of the new word, without changing the meaning of the sentence.* • *How does this word/phrase influence the meaning of this section? The tone?* • *Find an example of an analogy or a reference to another text.*		.03	
CCSR 5	Compare and contrast the structure of two or more texts and analyze how the differing structure of each text contributes to its meaning and style. • *What is the structure (genre) of this text? How does this influence the meaning or style of the book? How is it different from the structure (genre) of another literary text you've read?*		.03	
	Analyze in detail the structure of a specific paragraph in a text, including the role of particular sentences in developing and refining a key concept. • *How did the author organize this paragraph?* • *Why is each sentence included? How does each sentence contribute to developing the key concept or idea?*		.03	
	Identify types of poetry (e.g., haiku, limerick, free verse) and structural elements (stanza, verse, rhyme scheme, line breaks, rhythm, alliteration). • *What kind of poetry is this? How do you know?* • *Identify an example of alliteration (etc.).*		.03	

CCSR 6	Analyze how differences in the points of view of the characters and the audience or reader (e.g., created through the use of dramatic irony) create such effects as suspense or humor. • *What do you know about the plot or characters in this book that a character in the book doesn't know? How does this create suspense or humor?* • *Are there things characters in the book know that you don't yet? How does this create suspense?*		.03	
	Determine an author's point of view or purpose in a text and analyze how the author acknowledges and responds to conflicting evidence or viewpoints. • *What is the author's perspective (purpose)? How do you know? What evidence in the text supports your thinking?* • *How does the author acknowledge other opinions or positions?* • *How does s/he handle conflicting evidence or viewpoints?*		.03	
	Discuss author's perspectives, cultural background, and historical context and how these might influence the text.		.03	

Integration of Knowledge and Ideas: Comparing Different Presentations

Discuss how the ideas in a book connect to each other and to the larger world.

CCSR 7	Analyze the extent to which a filmed or live production of a story or drama stays faithful to or departs from the text or script, evaluating the choices made by the director or actors. • *Read the book of a movie you have seen. How do they compare? Where did the director/actors stay faithful to the book? Where did they deviate? What do you think of these choices? What would you have done differently?*		.03	
	Evaluate the advantages and disadvantages of using different media (e.g., print or digital text, video, multimedia) to present a particular topic or idea. • *If you were going to present the important information in this book to the class, what medium do you think would be most effective? Why?*		.03	

2Br Comprehension Cont'd				
CCSR 8	Delineate and evaluate the argument and specific claims in a text, assessing whether the reasoning is sound and the evidence is relevant and sufficient; recognize when irrelevant evidence is introduced. • *What is the author's argument or claim? What evidence does the author give to support this argument?* • *Which of the author's claims have good supporting evidence? Which don't? Why?* • *Is there evidence used that doesn't actually support the claim?* • *Has s/he convinced you? Why or why not? What evidence would have made a stronger argument?*		.03	
CCSR 9	Analyze how a modern work of fiction draws on themes, patterns of events, or character types from myths, traditional stories, or religious works such as the Bible, including describing how the material is rendered new. • *Make a connection between this modern novel and traditional literature on one of:* • *Common themes (good vs. evil, individual vs. society, intrinsic value vs. financial value)* • *Common patterns of events (quest, final confrontation, etc.)* • *Common character types (evil stepmother, good twin/bad twin, sacrificial figure, etc.)*		.03	
	Analyze a case in which two or more texts provide conflicting information on the same topic and identify where the texts disagree on matters of fact or interpretation. • *Find an example of two books with conflicting information. Where is the conflict? Is this a disagreement over facts or opinions? Why?*		.03	
	Discuss author's perspectives and biases and how these might influence the text.		.03	
2Br Comprehension Total			**.48**	

2Br Range of Reading and Level of Text Complexity

Range of Reading and Level of Text Complexity	Evidence/Date	Points	
Engagement and Independence Read regularly and independently, sustaining engagement, in Br-level materials for at least 30 minutes every day in the classroom. Have the stamina to sustain reading for 1-2 hours, as required on high-stakes tests.		.02	
Chapter Book Habit Regularly finish Br chapter books, about 1 a week.		.03	
Home Reading Sustain a home reading habit and read in Br-level materials for at least 30 minutes every night without prompting, or make up this <u>additional</u> 30 minutes during the school day.		.02	
Genres Identify the probable genre(s) of a new text and justify answer with evidence from the text and examples of characteristics common to that genre. • *Is this book fiction or informational? How can you tell?* • *What kind of literature is this? How can you tell?*		.01	

Read independently and comprehend <u>informational text</u> at the Br level, including:

	Evidence (List Areas/Topics of Reading Experience)	Date	Points	
History Social Studies • American • World			.03	
Science • Life/Biological • Earth • Physical			.03	
Narrative Nonfiction • Biography • Autobiography • Memoir			.02	
Essays and articles • Newspaper • Persuasive/Editorial • Literary Analysis			.02	

2Br Range of Reading and Level of Text Complexity Cont'd

Read independently and comprehend literary text at the Br level, including:

	Evidence (List Chapter Books Completed)	Date		
Realistic Fiction (Animal Stories, Adventure Stories, Horror, Mysteries, Contemporary Fiction)			.02	
Historical Fiction			.02	
Fantasy			.01	
Science Fiction			.01	
	Evidence (List Book Titles or Steps/Time Spent Reading in the Genre.)			
Traditional Tales • Fables/Folktales • Myth/Legend • Religious Text			.01	
Drama			.01	
Poetry			.01	
2Br Range of Reading and Level of Text Complexity Total			.26	

2Br Vocabulary and Language

Vocabulary and Language	Evidence/Date	Points	
Literary, Academic, and Domain Specific Vocabulary Know and be able to use 7,500-10,000 words, not familiar from everyday speech, but common to Br-level text. CCSL 6. Br readers have learned most of the literary and technical vocabulary encountered in Br-level text from their previous reading. As they spend a year reading in Br books, (minimum one hour per day), they will learn an additional 1,500 words.		.05	
Notice unfamiliar words and gather vocabulary knowledge when considering a word or phrase important to comprehension or expression. CCSL 6.		.01	
Use context (e.g., the overall meaning of a sentence or paragraph; a word's position or function in a sentence) as a clue to the meaning of the word or phrase. CCSL 4a. Be able to substitute a word or phrase that means the same thing for the very few unfamiliar words in Br-level text.		.02	
Consult general and specialized reference materials (e.g., dictionaries, glossaries, thesauruses), both print and digital, to find the pronunciation or determine or clarify its precise meaning or its part of speech. CCSL 4c.		.01	
Verify the preliminary determination of the meaning of a word or phrase (e.g., by checking the inferred meaning in context or in a dictionary). CCSL 4d.		.01	
Use the relationship between particular words (e.g., synonyms, antonyms, homographs, analogy) to better understand each of the words. CCSL 5b.		.01	
Distinguish among the connotations (associations) of words with similar denotations (definitions) (e.g., *bullheaded, willful, firm, persistent, resolute*). CCSL 5c.		.02	
Affixes and Roots Use common, grade-appropriate Greek and Latin affixes and roots as clues to the meaning of a word (e.g., *precede, recede, secede*). CCSL 4b.		.01	
Figurative Language Interpret figurative language (e.g., similes and metaphors) and figures of speech (e.g., verbal irony, puns, personification, literary, biblical, and mythological allusions) in context. CCSL 5a.		.02	
Decode Multisyllable Words Use combined knowledge of all letter-sound correspondences, syllabification patterns, and morphology (e.g., roots and affixes) to accurately read unfamiliar multisyllabic words in and out of context. (Any student having trouble with this is working at the wrong level.)		✓	
2Br Vocabulary and Language Total		.16	

Transition to Si

2Br Entry Points	**8.00**	
2Br Comprehension Points	**.48**	
2Br Range of Reading and Level of Text Complexity Points	**.26**	
2Br Vocabulary and Language Points	**.16**	

Si Transition Points. With NO help of any kind, student must demonstrate ability to:			**Evidence/Date**			**Points**	
Vocabulary	**Demonstrate Command of a Literary Vocabulary of Approximately 9,000 Words** Have approximately 9,000 literary vocabulary words in reading vocabulary available for comprehending Si text. CCSL 6.	See **Vocabulary Check** on page 241. Minimum score of 5.	Scores		Dates	.03	
Comprehension	**Read and Comprehend Unfamiliar Si Text (Successfully Apply Reading Standards)** Determine what a text says explicitly and make logical inferences from it. Interpret vocabulary and figurative language in context. CCSR 1, CCSR 2, CCSR 3. CCSR 4.	See **Cold Read Record** on page 242. Minimum score of 9.	Scores	Titles	Dates	.02	
	Author's Theme or Purpose "What is the book about?" is no longer answered with just a plot summary, but an analysis of the author's theme or purpose.	See below.	**Yes** or **No**	Titles	Dates	.02	
Range of Reading	**Demonstrate Ability to Finish a Si Chapter Book** Read and finish a Si novel, including demonstrating comprehension and a command of the vocabulary used in the text. CCSR 10, CCSL 6.	After reading a Si novel, student is able to discuss the author's theme or message using evidence from the text.	**Yes** or **No**	Titles	Dates	.02	
	Demonstrate Ability to Read and Comprehend Si Informational Text Read a Si informational text, including demonstrating comprehension and a command of the vocabulary used in the text. CCSR 10, CCSL 6.	After reading a Si informational text, student is able to discuss the author's purpose or message using evidence from the text.	**Yes** or **No**	Titles	Dates	.02	
Si Transition Points						**.09**	
GRAND TOTAL: Student should transition to Si with 8.99 points and demonstrated proficiency at Si prerequisites.						**8.99**	

Si Independent Reading Level Overview 9.00 - 10.99
Literary Analysis

Si Learning Focus
"What is the book about?" is no longer answered with a plot summary, but is answered with an analysis of the author's theme or purpose.

Si-level readers see the author as a writer, as a human being with his/her own biases, motivations, and blind spots. They have developed a critical eye toward writing and can discuss an author's use of literary techniques. They can locate a particular book in its genre and make comparisons across texts on a wide variety of both themes and writing techniques. They read actively, talking back to the author, questioning and probing the ideas presented. Comfort with the 21–25 literary words per typical chapter book page requires extensive experience as a reader. Sentences are complex, figurative language is common, and most adults cannot handle materials written at this level of complexity. Just because a reader can read a Si text fluently doesn't mean he/she is a Si-level reader. Dig deeply into the reader's knowledge of the vocabulary, understanding of the ideas, and ability to critique the writing before assigning him/her the Si designation. Si-level readers should be prepared for the marathon reading sessions (2–4 hours) required by college entrance exams.

Key Common Core Standards

Literature 6: Analyze a particular point of view or cultural experience reflected in a work of literature from outside the United States, drawing on a wide reading of world literature.

Literature 9: Analyze how an author draws on and transforms source material in a specific work (e.g., how Shakespeare treats a theme or topic from Ovid or the Bible, or how a later author draws on a play by Shakespeare).

Informational 9: Analyze seminal U.S. documents of historical and literary significance (e.g., Washington's Farewell Address, the Gettysburg Address, Roosevelt's Four Freedoms speech, King's "Letter from Birmingham Jail"), including how they address related themes and concepts.

Entry Requirements
Must be in place before earning Si designation.

- Demonstrate command of a literary vocabulary of approximately 9,000 words available for comprehending Si-level text. (Minimum 5 correct on Si Vocabulary Check.) CCSL 6.
- "What is the book about?" is no longer answered with just a plot summary, but is answered with an analysis of the author's theme or purpose.
- Read and comprehend unfamiliar Si text (successfully apply Reading Standards). (Minimum score of 9 on Cold Read Record.) CCSR 1, CCSR2, CCSR3, CCSR4.
- Demonstrate ability to finish a Si chapter book. CCSR 10.
- Demonstrate ability to read and comprehend Si informational text. CCSR 10.

Exit Requirements
Must be in place before earning Gl designation.

- Demonstrate command of a literary vocabulary of approximately 10,500 words available for comprehending Gl level text (Minimum 5 correct on Gl Vocabulary Check) CCSL 6.
- Identify the historical, political, or social context in which the author produced the text. Speculates on how this context influenced the text's themes, topics, or style. CCSR 9.
- Read and comprehend unfamiliar Gl text (successfully apply Reading Standards). (Minimum score of 9 on Cold Read Record.) CCSR 1, CCSR2, CCSR3, CCSR4.
- Demonstrate ability to finish a Gl novel. CCSR 10.
- Demonstrate ability to read and comprehend Gl informational text. CCSR 10.

Si Independent Reading Level Assessment 9.00 - 10.99

Entry Requirements: Cumulative Record

Student ______________________ Teacher ______________________ Room ________ Date Started ________

Si Entry Requirements

		Evidence/Date				Date Completed
Vocabulary	**Demonstrate Command of a Literary Vocabulary of Approximately 9,000 Words** Have approximately 9,000 literary vocabulary words in reading vocabulary available for comprehending Si text. CCSL 6.	See **Vocabulary Check** on page 259. Minimum score of 5.	Scores		Dates	
Comprehension	**Read and Comprehend Unfamiliar Si Text (Successfully Apply Reading Standards)** Determine what a text says explicitly and makedgh logical inferences from it. Interpret vocabulary and figurative language in context. CCSR 1, CCSR 2, CCSR 3. CCSR 4.	See **Cold Read Record** on page 260. Minimum score of 9.	Scores	Titles	Dates	
	Author's Theme or Purpose "What is the book about?" is no longer answered with just a plot summary, but an analysis of the author's theme or purpose.	See below.	**Yes** or **No**	Titles	Dates	
Range of Reading	**Demonstrate Ability to Finish a Si Chapter Book** Read and finish a Si novel, including demonstrating comprehension and a command of the vocabulary used in the text. CCSR 10, CCSL 6.	After reading a Si novel, student is able to discuss the author's theme or message using evidence from the text.	**Yes** or **No**	Titles	Dates	
	Demonstrate Ability to Read and Comprehend Si Informational Text Read a Si informational text, including demonstrating comprehension and a command of the vocabulary used in the text. CCSR 10, CCSL 6.	After reading a Si informational text, student is able to discuss the author's purpose or message using evidence from the text.	**Yes** or **No**	Titles	Dates	
A reader who is proficient at all of the above enters Si with 9.00 points.						**9.00**

Si Entry Requirements: Vocabulary Check

This page is for the teacher to use as a test of a student's vocabulary acquisition. DO NOT give copies of this page to students. DO NOT teach or drill these words out of context. Pick a column. Student should be able to define 5 of the words to enter Si and 12 of the words to exit. The following words are representative of the 3,000 words Si readers must acquire during their two years of independent reading. This list is neither comprehensive nor sufficient, but as long as the student hasn't practiced this list, it will give you an idea of whether his/her working vocabulary is sufficient to comprehend text at the Si level. Pick a different column each time. Each column is used as a separate test. 5 words correct in any column = Si Entry. 12 words correct in any column = Si Exit.

Test A	Test B	Test C	Test D	Test E	Test F	Test G
(Date)						
abate	abolition	abyss	accord	adversary	apex	appropriation
arbitrary	arid	benefactor	bereaved	bestow	buffer	commodity
contemporary	contour	contraband	conveyance	countenance	cultivate	curtail
dauntless	denomination	density	dire	discretion	dormant	dynasty
ebb	embellish	envoy	equilibrium	equivalent	evolution	feint
ferment	feudal	filament	fallacy	feasible	guerilla	heathen
homage	hybrid	inaccessible	inaudible	inertia	inflation	insurrection
intangible	invertebrate	invoke	isthmus	liability	liquidate	mandate
medieval	menagerie	momentum	mortify	mute	navigable	obscure
obsolete	panorama	patronize	perspective	pilfer	pinnacle	plausible
porous	predominant	prevalent	projectile	providence	quandary	ratify
recessive	reconcile	regeneration	regime	rend	revert	rift
satire	scrutinize	sediment	solubility	speculation	staunch	stealthy
strata	subordinate	superfluous	symbiosis	symmetry	tangible	theorem
translucent	tributary	ultimatum	vanquish	variable	verify	vial
(Total)						

Common Core Standard Language 6: Acquire and use accurately grade-appropriate general academic and domain-specific words and phrases.

Si Entry Requirements: Cold Read Record

Student ______________________ Teacher ____________________ Room ______ Date ______

Title: ____________________

Given an unfamiliar Si text, and NO help of any kind, the student is able to apply Reading Standards to Br level text.			
Fluently Decode Si text	**Evidence/Student Response**		**Score**
Use combined knowledge of all letter-sound correspondences, syllabication patterns, and morphology (e.g., roots and affixes) to accurately read unfamiliar multisyllabic words, including names.	• 99-100% word accuracy.		**Yes** or **No**
	• Appropriate rate and expression.		**Yes** or **No**
	• Stops and tries again when something doesn't look right, sound right, or make sense.		**Yes** or **No**
If answer to any of the above questions is No, STOP TEST and re-level student. Any student having trouble with decoding is most likely working at or below 2R.			
Reading Standards **See text-specific questions on Cold Read Text Pages**	**Evidence/Student Response**		**Score** Weak..........Strong
Basic Understanding Support basic understanding with evidence from the text. CCSR 1.			1 2 3 4
Interpretation Support an interpretation or analysis with evidence from the text. CCSR 2, CCSR 3.			1 2 3 4
Vocabulary Interpret vocabulary and figurative language in context. CCSR 4.			1 2 3 4
Cold Read Proficiency Total: A minimum score of 9 points is required in order to enter Si.		**Total Points**	

Si Entry Requirements: Cold Read Text A

The Witch of Blackbird Pond
by Elizabeth George Speare
Houghton Mifflin

Basic Understanding

What is happening so far in this story?

Interpretation

Describe the setting and the social challenges it may provide for the heroine.

Vocabulary

What does the author mean by the phrase "disheartening contrast?" How does it affect the tone of the passage?

Si

CHAPTER ONE

ON A MORNING in mid-April, 1687, the brigantine *Dolphin* left the open sea, sailed briskly across the Sound to the wide mouth of the Connecticut River and into Saybrook harbor. Kit Tyler had been on the forecastle deck since daybreak, standing close to the rail, staring hungrily at the first sight of land for five weeks.

"There's Connecticut Colony," a voice spoke in her ear. "You've come a long way to see it."

She looked up, surprised and flattered. On the whole long voyage the captain's son had spoken scarcely a dozen words to her. She had noticed him often, his thin wiry figure swinging easily hand over hand up the rigging, his sandy, sun-bleached head bent over a coil of rope. Nathaniel Eaton, first mate, but his mother called him Nat. Now, seeing him so close beside her, she was surprised that, for all he looked so slight, the top of her head barely reached his shoulder.

"How does it look to you?" he questioned.

Kit hesitated. She didn't want to admit how disappointing she found this first glimpse of America. The bleak line of shore surrounding the gray harbor was a disheartening contrast to the shimmering green and white that fringed the turquoise bay of Barbados which was her home. The earthen wall of the fortification that faced the river was bare and ugly, and the houses beyond were no more than plain wooden boxes.

"Is that Wethersfield?" she inquired instead.

"Oh, no, Wethersfield is some way up the river. This is the port of Saybrook. Home to us Eatons. There's my father's shipyard, just beyond the dock."

She could just make out the row of unimpressive shacks and the flash of raw new lumber. Her smile was admiring from pure relief. At least this grim place was not her destination, and surely the colony at Wethersfield would prove more inviting.

"We've made good time this year," Nat went on. "It's been a fair passage, hasn't it?"

"Oh, yes," she sparkled. "Though I'm glad now 'tis over."

"Aye," he agreed. "I never know myself which is best, the setting out or the coming back to harbor. Ever been on a ship before?"

"Just the little pinnaces in the islands. I've sailed on those all my life."

He nodded. "That's where you learned to keep your balance."

So he had noticed! To her pride, she had proved to be a natural sailor. Certainly she had not spent the voyage groaning and retching like some of the passengers.

"You're not afraid of the wind and the salt, anyway. At least, you haven't spent much time below."

"Not if I could help it," she laughed. Did he think anyone would stay in that stuffy cabin by choice?

Si Entry Requirements: Cold Read Text B

The Book Thief
by Markus Zusak
Random House

Basic Understanding

What is happening so far in this story?

Interpretation

Who is telling the story? How do you know? Why do you think the author chose to use this narrator?

Vocabulary

Find an example of figurative language. What does it mean? How does it contribute to the tone of the passage?

*** * * HERE IS A SMALL FACT * * ***
You are going to die.

I am in all truthfulness attempting to be cheerful about this whole topic, though most people find themselves hindered in believing me, no matter my protestations. Please, trust me. I most definitely *can* be cheerful. I can be amiable. Agreeable. Affable. And that's only the A's. Just don't ask me to be nice. Nice has nothing to do with me.

*** * * REACTION TO THE * * ***
AFOREMENTIONED FACT
Does this worry you?
I urge you—don't be afraid.
I'm nothing if not fair.

—Of course, an introduction.

A beginning.

Where are my manners?

I could introduce myself properly, but it's not really necessary. You will know me well enough and soon enough, depending on a diverse range of variables. It suffices to say that at some point in time, I will be standing over you, as genially as possible. Your soul will be in my arms. A color will be perched on my shoulder. I will carry you gently away.

At that moment, you will be lying there (I rarely find people standing up). You will be caked in your own body. There might be a discovery; a scream will dribble down the air. The only sound I'll hear after that will be my own breathing, and the sound of the smell, of my footsteps.

The question is, what color will everything be at that moment when I come for you? What will the sky be saying?

Personally, I like a chocolate-colored sky. Dark, dark chocolate. People say it suits me. I do, however, try to enjoy every color I see—the whole spectrum. A billion or so flavors, none of them quite the same, and a sky to slowly suck on. It takes the edge off the stress. It helps me relax.

As I've been alluding to, my one saving grace is distraction. It keeps me sane. It helps me cope, considering the length of time I've been performing this job. The trouble is, who could ever replace me? Who could step in while I take a break in your stock-standard resort-style vacation destination, whether it be tropical or of the ski trip variety? The answer, of course, is nobody, which has prompted me to make a conscious, deliberate decision—to make distraction my vacation. Needless to say, I vacation in increments. In colors.

Still, it's possible that you might be asking, why does he even need a vacation? What does he need distraction *from*?

Which brings me to my next point.

It's the leftover humans.

The survivors.

They're the ones I can't stand to look at, although on many occasions I still fail. I deliberately seek out the colors to keep my mind off them, but now and then, I witness the ones who are left behind, crumbling among the jigsaw puzzle of realization, despair, and surprise. They have punctured hearts. They have beaten lungs.

Which in turn brings me to the subject I am telling you about tonight, or today, or whatever the hour and color. It's the story of one of those perpetual survivors—an expert at being left behind.

It's just a small story really, about, among other things:

* A girl
* Some words
* An accordionist
* Some fanatical Germans
* A Jewish fist fighter
* And quite a lot of thievery

I saw the book thief three times.

Si Entry Requirements: Cold Read Text C

Bugs and Wonder Drugs

Bacteria are minute living organisms that can only be seen under a powerful microscope. They live almost everywhere on our planet and are essential in maintaining living systems. They decompose waste, trap nitrogen from the air for plants to use, and form part of the food chain. Millions of bacteria live inside you, helping to digest fiber from fruits and vegetables. They even manufacture some vitamins in your body.

However, some bacteria are very harmful. If they get inside your body, the conditions are perfect (warm and moist with plenty of food) for them to multiply rapidly. They release poisons called toxins. In the past, people often died as a result of infected minor injuries. Today, most infections can be cured easily.

The first antibiotic

In 1928 British scientist Alexander Fleming (1881–1955) was studying some harmful bacteria. He grew visible colonies of millions of bacteria on petri dishes. One dish became contaminated with mold, and he noticed something unusual. Where the mold grew, there were no bacteria. Fleming grew the mold and made a liquid extract that killed many types of dangerous bacteria. He called his discovery penicillin—the first **antibiotic**.

Antibiotics at work

Bacteria link molecules together into a tough barrier that becomes their cell wall. Penicillin is similar to one of the molecules used to make this barrier. As the bacterium grows, it uses penicillin along with its usual molecules. This weakens the cell wall, and eventually it bursts apart. Other antibiotics stop bacteria from reproducing, and some stop them from producing proteins.

Bacteria fight back

Bacteria can change to resist antibiotics. Sometimes the DNA in a bacterium will mutate (change) so that it makes different proteins. This might alter the bacterium so the antibiotics do not work. All offspring of that mutated bacterium will also be resistant. This means that we must be careful how we use antibiotics. If we do not finish the course of treatment given by a doctor, any bacteria not killed will be the stronger, more resistant ones. They will reproduce, which will lead to even more resistance.

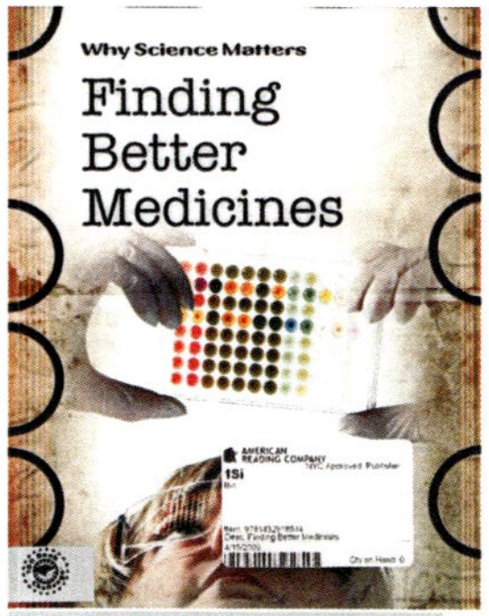

Si

Finding Better Medicines
by John Coad
Heinemann

Basic Understanding

Tell me three things the text says about antibiotics.

Interpretation

Why was penicillin an important discovery? Use evidence from the text to support your answer.

Vocabulary

What does "resistance" mean in this context? Explain the relationship between resistance and mutation.

Si Entry Requirements: Cold Read Text D

Abraham Lincoln
The Gettysburg Address
(1863)

Four score and seven years ago our fathers brought forth on this continent, a new nation, conceived in Liberty, and dedicated to the proposition that all men are created equal.

Now we are engaged in a great civil war, testing whether that nation, or any nation so conceived and so dedicated, can long endure. We are met on a great battlefield of that war. We have come to dedicate a portion of that field, as a final resting place for those who here gave their lives that that nation might live. It is altogether fitting and proper that we should do this.

But, in a larger sense, we cannot dedicate—we cannot consecrate—we cannot hallow—this ground. The brave men, living and dead, who struggled here, have consecrated it, far above our poor power to add or detract. The world will little note, nor long remember what we say here, but it can never forget what they did here. It is for us the living, rather, to be dedicated here to the unfinished work which they who fought here have thus far so nobly advanced. It is rather for us to be here dedicated to the great task remaining before us—that from these honored dead we take increased devotion to that cause for which they gave the last full measure of devotion—that we here highly resolve that these dead shall not have died in vain—that this nation, under God, shall have a new birth of freedom— and that government of the people, by the people, for the people, shall not perish from the earth.

Basic Understanding

Tell me three things the text says about the Civil War.

Interpretation

What is Abraham Lincoln's central message? What evidence from his speech supports your answer?

Vocabulary

What does Lincoln mean by the phrase "The brave men, living and dead, who struggled here, have consecrated it?"

Si Comprehension

Reading Standards for Literature and Informational Text

Proficiency in the standards below must be demonstrated while reading independently in Si level text. In order to advance to Gl, students must earn .96 Comprehension Points.

Key Ideas and Details: Using Text Evidence to Support Conclusions Understands, thinks about, and discusses <u>what</u> the author said.		Evidence/Date	Points	
	Demonstrates background knowledge of a Si-level reader, familiar with 90-100% of the vocabulary and enough of the world knowledge found in Si-level books to ensure basic comprehension (e.g., 9th/10th-grade level math, science, and social studies concepts).		✓	
	Automatically adjusts reading strategies to suit text and purpose. • Demonstrates aggressive self-monitoring and active reading strategies when reading difficult material. • Skims and scans to locate specific information quickly. • Reads silently and rapidly for pleasure.		✓	
CCSR 1	Cites strong and thorough textual evidence to support analysis of what the text says explicitly, as well as inferences drawn from the text. • *How, why, what...? Cite the evidence from the text that BEST supports your answer.*		.06	
CCSR 2	Determines a theme or central idea of a text and analyzes in detail its development over the course of the text, including how it emerges and is shaped and refined by specific details; provide an objective summary of the text. • *What is the theme or central idea of this text?* • *What details from the text support that this is the theme?* • *How does the theme develop from the beginning to the end of the text?* • *How do the characters, setting, and plot contribute to the theme?* • *Summarize what you've read so far in one sentence. (Theme, not plot summary.)*		.06	
	Determines a central idea of a text; analyzes its development over the course of the text, including how it emerges and is shaped and refined by specific details; provides an objective summary of the text. • *What is the main idea of this text?* • *What details and key ideas from the text support that this is the main idea?* • *How does the main idea develop from the beginning to the end of the text?* • *Summarize what you've read so far in one sentence.*		.06	

Si Comprehension Cont'd

CCSR 3	Analyzes how complex characters (e.g., those with multiple or conflicting motivations) develop over the course of a text, interact with other characters, and advance the plot or develop the theme. • *What is a "complex" character? Are there any in this book? Who and Why?* • *Which character in this book is most conflicted? Why? How does this internal conflict advance the plot? Develop the them?* • *Trace the development of one of the complex characters from the beginning to the end of the text.* • *How does this character interact with other characters?*		.06	
	Analyzes how the author unfolds an analysis or series of ideas or events, including the order in which the points are made, how they are introduced and developed, and the connections that are drawn between them. • *Explain, delineate, or outline how the author organizes the key ideas or events in the text.* • *How are they introduced and developed?* • *What connections are made between them?*		.06	
	Identifies and describes the following literary elements in the text: characters (motivations of major and minor characters); setting (time, day, year, historical period, place, situation); plot (main events, conflict, rising action, climax, falling action, resolution). • *What is the central conflict and how does it relate to the theme? How is it resolved? Why?* • *Describe the setting and speculate as to why the author chose it.* • *Describe the main characters and speculate as to why the author chose them.*		.06	

Craft and Structure: Analyzing the Effects of Authors' Choices

Understands and discusses the way(s) the author(s) said what they said.

CCSR 4	Determines the meaning of words and phrases as they are used in the text, including figurative and connotative meanings; analyzes the cumulative impact of specific word choices on meaning and tone (e.g., how the language evokes a sense of time and place; how it sets a formal or informal tone). • *Describe the way this author uses language. What kinds of words/phrases does he/she use? Why?* • *Show me an example of the kinds of language this author has used in this text.* • *What effect do his/her language choices have on text meaning, sense of time and place, and tone?* • *Which words/phrases struck you as important, unusual, or interesting? Why? What do they mean?*		.06	
CCSR 5	Analyzes how an author's choices concerning how to structure a text, order events within it (e.g., parallel plots), and manipulate time (e.g., pacing, flashbacks) create such effects as mystery, tension, or surprise. • *Describe the choices this author made when deciding how to organize the book (use of flashbacks, passage of time, order of events). How was it organized? Speculate as to why these choices were made. Would you have done anything differently?* • *Does the author create a sense of mystery, tension, or surprise? Where? How?*		.06	
	Analyzes in detail how an author's ideas or claims are developed and refined by particular sentences, paragraphs, or larger portions of a text (e.g., a section or chapter). • *Describe the choices this author made when deciding how to organize the ideas or claims in this book. Speculate as to why these choices were made? Were they effective?* • *How is this sentence (chapter, paragraph) important to the text as a whole?* • *How is it important to the author's claims or main idea?*		.06	

Si Comprehension Cont'd				
	Identifies types of poetry (e.g. haiku, limerick, free verse) and structural elements (stanza, verse, rhyme scheme, line breaks, rhythm, alliteration). • *What kind of poetry is this? How do you know? Discuss its structural elements and how they influence meaning, tone, effect.* • *Identify an example of alliteration (etc.).*		.06	
CCSR 6	Analyzes a particular point of view or cultural experience reflected in a work of literature from outside the United States, drawing on a wide reading of world literature. • *How does the author's cultural background/geographical location shape his/her perspective?* • *How does it shape the text (characters, setting, theme)?* • *In what ways might the book have been different had it been written by an American? By you?*		.06	
	Determines an author's point of view or purpose in a text and analyzes how an author uses rhetoric to advance it. (From *Routledge Encyclopedia of Philosophy*: Rhetoric is the art of using language to communicate effectively using three audience appeals: logos, pathos, and ethos as well as five canons of rhetoric: invention or discovery, arrangement, style, memory, and delivery.) • *What is the author's point of view (perspective/opinion) or purpose for writing? How do you know?* • *What does rhetoric mean? How does this author use rhetoric to advance his/her point of view or purpose?*		.06	
	Recognizes and evaluates use of persuasive strategies and propaganda techniques (e.g., repetition, testimonial, loaded words, bandwagon, peer pressure, transfer).		.06	

Integration of Knowledge and Ideas: Comparing Different Presentations Discusses how the ideas in a book connect to each other and to the larger world.				
CCSR 7	Analyzes the representation of a subject or a key scene in two different artistic mediums, including what is emphasized or absent in each treatment (e.g., Auden's "Musée des Beaux Arts" and Breughel's Landscape with the Fall of Icarus). • *Compare two versions of the same scene/topic. How do they compare? Where do they differ?* • *What do you think of these choices? What would you have done differently?*		**.06**	
	Analyzes various accounts of a subject told in different media (e.g., a person's life story in both print and multimedia), determining which details are emphasized in each account. • *Compare two accounts of the same event or topic. How do they compare? Where do they differ? What do you think of these choices? What would you have done differently?*		**.06**	
CCSR 8	Delineates and evaluates the argument and specific claims in a text, assessing whether the reasoning is valid and the evidence is relevant and sufficient; identifies false statements and fallacious reasoning. • *What is the author's argument or claim?* • *What reasoning does he/she use to support it? Is it valid? Is any of it fallacious?* • *What evidence does he/she give to support it? Is it relevant and sufficient?* • *Which of the author's claims have good supporting evidence? Which don't? Why?* • *Is there evidence used that doesn't actually support the claim?* • *Has s/he convinced you? Why or why not? What evidence would have made a stronger argument?*		**.06**	
CCSR 9	Analyzes how an author draws on and transforms source material in a specific work (e.g., how Shakespeare treats a theme or topic from Ovid or the Bible or how a later author draws on a play by Shakespeare). • *What other source materials (themes, characters, plots, quotes from other authors/sources) did the author use in writing this work? How do you know? Why do you think they were used? How did the author change the source material?*		**.06**	
	Analyzes seminal U.S. documents of historical and literary significance (e.g., Washington's Farewell Address, the Gettysburg Address, Roosevelt's Four Freedoms speech, King's "Letter from Birmingham Jail"), including how they address related themes and concepts. • *Read and analyze a key U.S. document. Who wrote it? Why was it written?* • *What was its basic message, theme, and central concept?* • *Why has it remained so fundamental to U.S. culture?*		**.06**	
Si Comprehension Total			**.96**	

Si Range of Reading and Level of Text Complexity

Range of Reading and Level of Text Complexity	Evidence/Date	Points	
Engagement and Independence • Reads regularly and independently, sustaining engagement, in Si-level materials for at least 30 minutes every day in the classroom. • Demonstrates the stamina to sustain reading for 1-2 hours, as required on high-stakes tests.		.02	
Home Reading • Sustains a home reading habit and reads for at least 30 minutes every night without prompting, or makes up this <u>additional</u> 30 minutes during the school day.		.02	
Full-Length Book Habit • Regularly finishes novels or full-length literary informational texts, at least 1 every other week. (Avid Si readers should be encouraged to read from a range of appropriate levels for pleasure.)		.03	
Genres CCSR 10 • Identifies the probable genre(s) of a new text and justifies their reasoning with evidence from the text and examples of characteristics common to that genre.		✓	

Reads independently and comprehends informational text at the Si level, including:

	Evidence (List Areas/Topics of Reading Experience)	Date		
American History • Early American History • 18th-Century American History • 19th-Century American History • 20th-Century American History			.08	
World History • Ancient • Medieval • Modern			.03	
Primary sources • Letter or Journal • Speech • Cartoon			.03	

Si Range of Reading and Level of Text Complexity Cont'd

Science (3 each) • Life Science • Physical Science • Earth Science			.06	
Narrative Nonfiction • Autobiography • Biography • Memoir			.06	
Essays and Articles • Newspaper • Persuasive/Editorial • Literary Analysis			.03	

Reads independently and comprehends <u>literary text</u> at the Si level, including:

	Evidence (List Chapter Books Completed)	Date		
Modern Fiction • Realistic Fiction • Historical Fiction			.05	
Classic/Canon Literature • American • British			.05	
Multicultural Literature • African American • Asian American • Latino • Native American			.05	

Si Range of Reading and Level of Text Complexity Cont'd

World Literature • Africa • Asia • Europe • Latin America • Middle East			.05	
Speculative Fiction • Fantasy • Science Fiction			.05	
	Evidence (list book titles, or Steps/Time spent reading in the genre.)			
Traditional Literature • Fable/Folktale • Myth/Legend • Religious Text			.03	
Drama			.01	
Poetry (5 Different Forms, 1 Point Each)			.05	
Shakespeare			.02	
Range of Reading and Level of Text Complexity Total			.71	

Si Vocabulary and Language

Vocabulary and Language	Evidence/Date	Points	
Literary, Academic, and Domain-Specific Vocabulary Acquires and uses accurately general academic and domain-specific words and phrases, sufficient for reading, writing, speaking, and listening at the Si level (9,000–10,500 words not familiar from everyday speech). CCSL 6. Si readers have learned most of the literary and technical vocabulary encountered in Si-level text from their previous reading. As they spend two years reading in Si books, (minimum one hour per day), they will learn an additional 3,000 words.		.10	
Uses context (e.g., the overall meaning of a sentence, paragraph, or text; a word's position or function in a sentence) as a clue to the meaning of a word or phrase. CCSL 4a. Is able to substitute a word or phrase that means the same thing for the few unfamiliar words in Si level text.		.01	
Identifies and correctly uses patterns of word changes that indicate different meanings or parts of speech (e.g., *analyze, analysis, analytical; advocate, advocacy*). CCSL 4b.		.02	
Consults general and specialized reference materials (e.g., dictionaries, glossaries, thesauruses), both print and digital, to find the pronunciation of a word or determine or clarify its precise meaning, its part of speech, or its etymology. CCSL4c.		.01	
Verifies the preliminary determination of the meaning of a word or phrase (e.g., by checking the inferred meaning in context or in a dictionary). CCSL 4d.		.01	
Analyzes nuances in the meaning of words with similar denotations. CCSL 5b.		.02	
Affixes and Roots Uses word origins to determine the meanings of specialized vocabulary. CCSL 5.		.01	
Figurative Language Interprets figures of speech (e.g., euphemism, oxymoron) in context and analyzes their role in the text. CCSL 5a.		.02	
Interprets figurative language (e.g., similes, metaphors, personification, idioms, hyperbole, symbolism) in context.		.02	
Decoding Multi-Syllable Words Uses combined knowledge of all letter-sound correspondences, syllabification patterns, and morphology (e.g., roots and affixes) to accurately read unfamiliar multisyllabic words, including names, in context and out of context, at the Si level. (Any student having trouble with this is working at the wrong level.)		√	
Si Vocabulary and Language Total		.22	

Transition to Gl

Si Entry Points	**9.00**	
Si Comprehension Points	**.96**	
Si Range of Reading and Level of Text Complexity Points	**.71**	
Si Vocabulary and Language Points	**.22**	

Gl Transition Points. With NO help of any kind, student must demonstrate ability to:			**Evidence/Date**			**Points**	
Vocabulary	**Demonstrate Command of a Literary Vocabulary of Approximately 10,500 Words** Has approximately 9,000 literary vocabulary words in reading vocabulary available for comprehending Si text. CCSL 6.	See **Vocabulary Check** on page 221. Minimum score of 5.	Scores		Dates	.02	
Comprehension	**Read and Comprehend Unfamiliar Gl Text (Successfully Apply Reading Standards)** Determine what a text says explicitly and makes logical inferences from it. Interpret vocabulary and figurative language in context. CCSR 1, CCSR 2, CCSR 3. CCSR 4.	See **Cold Read Record** on page 222. Minimum score of 12.	Scores	Titles	Dates	.02	
	Social Context Identify the historical, political, or social context in which the author produced the text. Speculate on how this context influenced the text's themes, topics, or style. CCSR 9.					.02	
Range of Reading	**Demonstrate Ability to Finish a Gl Novel** Read and finish a Br novel, including demonstrating comprehension and a command of the vocabulary used in the text. CCSR 10, CCSL 6.	After reading a Gl novel, student is able to discuss the author's theme or message using evidence from the text.	**Yes** or **No**	Titles	Dates	.02	
	Demonstrate Ability to Read and Comprehend Gl Informational Text Read a Gl informational text, including demonstrating comprehension and a command of the vocabulary used in the text. CCSR 10, CCSL 6.	After reading a Gl informational text, student is able to discuss the author's purpose or message using evidence from the text.	**Yes** or **No**	Titles	Dates	.02	
Gl Transition Points						**.10**	
GRAND TOTAL: Student should transition to Gl with 10.99 points and demonstrated proficiency at Gl prerequisites.						**10.99**	

Gl Independent Reading Level Overview 11.00 - 12.99

Texts are the products of individuals in specific historical, political, and social contexts which influence their themes, topics, and style.

Gl Learning Focus

Texts are the products of individuals in specific historical, political, and social contexts which influence their themes, topics, and style.

Gl-level readers understand that texts are a product of their times. They seek to locate the text in the literary or intellectual context of the author as a way to examine the influences on its style and themes. They have developed a critical eye toward writing and can discuss an author's use of literary techniques, propaganda, and rhetoric. They read actively, talking back to the author, locating him/her in a given social, political, or artistic moment, questioning and probing both the ideas and their presentation. Comfort with the 25+ literary words per typical chapter book page requires extensive experience as a reader. Sentences are complex, figurative language is common, and most adults cannot handle materials written at this level of complexity. Just because a reader can read a Gl text fluently doesn't mean he/she is a Gl level reader. Dig deeply into the reader's knowledge of the vocabulary, understanding of the ideas, and ability to critique the writing before assigning him/her the Gl designation. Gl-level readers should be prepared for the marathon reading sessions (2–4 hours) required by college entrance exams.

Key Common Core Standards

Reading Literature 9: Demonstrate knowledge of eighteenth-, nineteenth-, and early-twentieth-century foundational works of American literature, including how two or more texts from the same period treat similar themes or topics.

Reading Informational 9: Analyze seventeenth-, eighteenth-, and nineteenth-century foundational U.S. documents of historical and literary significance (including the Declaration of Independence, the Preamble to the Constitution, the Bill of Rights, and Lincoln's Second Inaugural Address) for their themes, purposes, and rhetorical features.

Entry Requirements

Must be in place before earning Gl designation.

- Demonstrate command of a literary vocabulary of approximately 10,500 words available for comprehending Gl level text. (Minimum 5 correct on Gl Vocabulary Check). CCSL 6.
- Identify the historical, political, or social context in which the author produced the text. Speculate on how this context influenced the text's themes, topics, or style. CCSR 9.
- Read and comprehend unfamiliar Gl text (successfully apply Reading Standards). (Minimum score of 9 on Cold Read Record.) CCSR 1, CCSR2, CCSR3, CCSR4.
- Demonstrate ability to finish a Gl novel. CCSR 10.
- Demonstrate ability to read and comprehend Gl informational text. CCSR 10.

GI Independent Reading Level Assessment 11.00 - 12.99

Entry Requirements: Cumulative Record

Student ______________ Teacher ______________ Room ______ Date Started ______

GI Entry Requirements

		Evidence/Date				Date Completed
Vocabulary	**Demonstrate Command of a Literary Vocabulary of Approximately 10,500 Words** Have approximately 9,000 literary vocabulary words in reading vocabulary available for comprehending GI text. CCSL 6.	See **Vocabulary Check** on page 221. Minimum score of 5.	Scores		Dates	
Comprehension	**Read and Comprehend Unfamiliar GI Text (Successfully Apply Reading Standards)** Determine what a text says explicitly and makes logical inferences from it. Interpret vocabulary and figurative language in context. CCSR 1, CCSR 2, CCSR 3. CCSR 4.	See **Cold Read Record** on page 222. Minimum score of 12.	Scores	Titles	Dates	
	Social Context Identify the historical, political, or social context in which the author produced the text. Speculate on how this context influenced the text's themes, topics, or style. CCSR 9.					
Range of Reading	**Demonstrate Ability to Finish a GI Novel** Read and finish a Br novel, including demonstrating comprehension and a command of the vocabulary used in the text. CCSR 10, CCSL 6.	After reading a GI novel, student is able to discuss the author's theme or message using evidence from the text.	**Yes** or **No**	Titles	Dates	
	Demonstrate Ability to Read and Comprehend GI Informational Text Read a GI informational text, including demonstrating comprehension and a command of the vocabulary used in the text. CCSR 10, CCSL 6.	After reading a GI informational text, student is able to discuss the author's purpose or message using evidence from the text.	**Yes** or **No**	Titles	Dates	
A reader who is proficient at all of the above enters GI with 11.00 points.						**11.00**

Gl Entry Requirements: Vocabulary Check

Demonstrate Depth of Literary and Academic Vocabulary

This page is for the teacher to use as a test of a student's vocabulary acquisition. DO NOT give copies of this page to students. DO NOT teach or drill these words out of context.

Pick a column. Student should be able to define 5 of the words to enter Gl and 12 of the words to exit. The following words are representative of the 10,500 words Gl readers must acquire during their year of independent reading. This list is neither comprehensive nor sufficient, but as long as the student hasn't practiced this list, it will give you an idea of whether his/her working vocabulary is sufficient to comprehend text at the Gl level. Pick a different column each time. Each column is used as a separate test. 5 words correct in any column = Gl Entry. 12 words correct in any column = Gl Exit.

Test A	Test B	Test C	Test D	Test E	Test F	Test G
(Date)						
abdicate	abridge	acclimate	accrue	acrimonious	acumen	adage
allegory	altruistic	amalgamate	amorphous	ambiguous	amplitude	analogy
anarchy	anathema	annuity	antecedent	aperture	ascertain	assimilate
atrophy	autocracy	avocation	beguile	botany	brevity	capitalist
caricature	centrifugal	concave	concur	contemptuous	capitulate	caste
circumvent	colloquial	complicity	concentric	conjecture	corollary	credulous
deify	delineation	delude	demagogue	derivative	dogmatic	duplicity
elegy	epic	emanate	equestrian	ethereal	exodus	expatriate
extemporaneous	gregarious	gossamer	gustatory	habituate	homogeneous	imminent
impervious	inalienable	incumbent	infamy	innate	innuendo	insidious
interminable	juxtaposition	meander	metamorphosis	myriad	obviate	quiescence
renaissance	requisite	restitution	reticence	retrospect	rhetoric	rudimentary
ruse	scion	secular	sedentary	socialist	somnolent	stipulate
subsequent	sustenance	synthesis	tenet	tertiary	topography	trajectory
transient	trepidation	utilitarian	veracity	vestige	vindicate	zenith
(Total)						

Common Core Standard Language 6: Acquire and use accurately grade-appropriate general academic and domain-specific words and phrases.

GI Entry Requirements: Cold Read Record

Student ______________________ Teacher ______________________ Room ________ Date ______

Title: ______________________

Given an unfamiliar GI text (Cold Read), and NO help of any kind, the student is able to apply Reading Standards to GI level text.

Fluently Decode GI text	Evidence/Student Response		Score
Use combined knowledge of all letter-sound correspondences, syllabication patterns, and morphology (e.g., roots and affixes) to accurately read unfamiliar multisyllabic words, including names.	• 99-100% word accuracy.		**Yes** or **No**
	• Appropriate rate and expression.		**Yes** or **No**
	• Stop and try again when something doesn't look right, sound right, or make sense.		**Yes** or **No**

If answer to any of the above questions is No, STOP TEST and move student to an easier level. Any student having trouble with decoding is most likely working at or below 2R.

Reading Standards **See specific questions on Cold Read Text Pages**	Evidence/Student Response	Score Weak..........Strong
Basic Understanding Support basic understanding with evidence from the text. CCSR 1.		1 2 3 4
Interpretation Support an interpretation or analysis with evidence from the text. CCSR 2, CCSR 3.		1 2 3 4
Vocabulary Interpret vocabulary and figurative language in context. CCSR 4.		1 2 3 4
Social Context *From what you have read so far, what can you tell about the historical, political, or social context in which the author wrote this text? Speculate on how this context influenced the text's themes, topics, or style.* CCSR 9.		1 2 3 4
Cold Read Proficiency Total: A minimum score of 12 points is required in order to enter GI.	**Total Points**	

GI Entry Requirements: Cold Read Text A

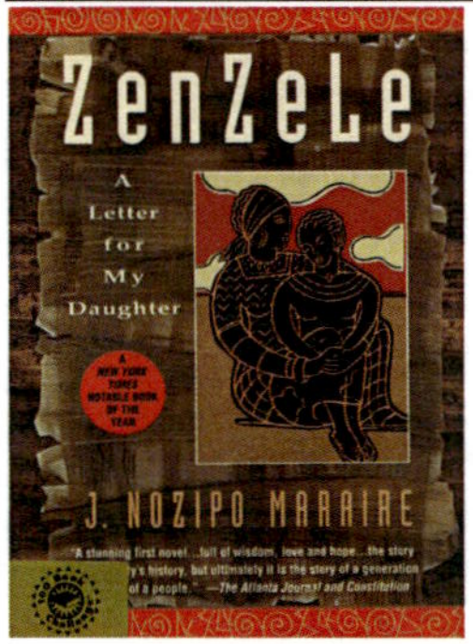

ZenZele: A Letter for My Daughter
by J. Nozipo Maraire
Random House

Basic Understanding

What is happening so far in this story?

Interpretation

What two themes might the author be setting up in these first pages. What evidence do you have for your prediction?

Vocabulary

What does "heretic" mean in this context? Why do you think the author chose to use this word?

Zenzele,

Today is the first day of winter, I believe. There is a thin frost on the ground that makes the white wall almost silver and casts a pallor on the garden. Not a single bloom remains; they all shuddered and collapsed as the air grew cool. Even the shrubs and trees are curling back their leaves in retreat, huddling together and bending low, close to the earth, to seek refuge. There is a ghostly glow and a glacial stillness all around, outside and within. There is something mournful about a winter dawn. It is a time of death, of loss, of flight.

It is still early—not even Samuel is awake—and I am sitting in the kitchen, sipping my morning tea, looking out at the backyard. As my strength falters, I love to spend the early hours of the morning in the orange glow of the dawn that fills the kitchen. I look out at the garden, whose face changes in subtle and beautiful ways every day. I have a most privileged seat at the season's opening of nature's theatrics. But perhaps the real reason that I creep quietly down in the mornings is that here I am reminded of you. This was your stage and my refuge. It is here that we encountered each other. I have a vivid image of you on the day you announced your plans: glowing brown skin that defies the indignities you subject it to (chlorine pools, Chimanimani winds, and Chakowa sun) and that lively tangle of black curls cropped short, as you insisted. You, with restless confidence, expounding on the necessity of going abroad for university. For months, you toted that bright red prospectus like a new Bible. There was undeniable proof of the merits of an American college education. During my spring cleaning, I was tempted (with fervent urging by your siblings) to discard it accidentally. We watched keenly as it grew more and more tattered from constant use. We patiently waited. It was simply a matter of time before it disintegrated and our sermons would cease. Until then, any heretic was immediately set aright by the printed word, the gospel truth of higher education, as proclaimed by that book. I became the unfortunate target of your crusade.

"Mama, they have so many subjects. Look, the psychoanalytic theories of political anthropology! I don't even know what that means. And twenty libraries, for *one* university. They even have museums, Mama, full of art, and it's *on the campus.*" You gushed, already picking up the jargon.

"Look here, Mama, the professors are from all over the world. Here's one—Professor Dao Wong Ng from Vietnam, and get this—Professor Miguel Rodrigues Carrera Maria de dos Santos from Argentina. I'll bet he thanks his parents for that! Just imagine, Mama. Oh, look, I could even learn Polish. Ha-ha. There is no limit, Mama, don't you see?"

You looking up at me, eyes wide and round like the globe you long to conquer. I heard no more. Your mind is set, I see. You are going to fly away and leave my nest.

GI Entry Requirements: Cold Read Text B

Crime and Punishment
by Fyodor Dostoevsky

Basic Understanding

What is happening so far in this story?

Interpretation

What two themes might the author be setting up in these first pages. What evidence do you have for your prediction?

Vocabulary

What does "abject" mean in this context? Why do you think the author chose to use this word?

PART ONE

CHAPTER 1

ON AN exceptionally hot evening early in July a young man came out of the garret in which he lodged in S. Place and walked slowly, as though in hesitation, towards K. Bridge.

He had successfully avoided meeting his landlady on the staircase. His garret was under the roof of a high, five-storied house, and was more like a cupboard than a room. The landlady, who provided him with garret, dinners, and attendance, lived on the floor below, and every time he went out he was obliged to pass her kitchen, the door of which invariably stood open. And each time he passed, the young man had a sick, frightened feeling, which made him scowl and feel ashamed. He was hopelessly in debt to his landlady, and was afraid of meeting her.

This was not because he was cowardly and abject, quite the contrary; but for some time past, he had been in an overstrained, irritable condition, verging on hypochondria. He had become so completely absorbed in himself, and isolated from his fellows that he dreaded meeting, not only his landlady, but any one at all. He was crushed by poverty, but the anxieties of his position had of late ceased to weigh upon him. He had given up attending to matters of practical importance; he had lost all desire to do so. Nothing that any landlady could do had a real terror for him. But to be stopped on the stairs, to be forced to listen to her trivial, irrelevant gossip, to pestering demands for payment, threats and complaints, and to rack his brains for excuses, to prevaricate, to lie—no, rather than that, he would creep down the stairs like a cat and slip out unseen.

This evening, however, on coming out into the street, he became acutely aware of his fears.

"I want to attempt a thing *like that* and am frightened by these trifles," he thought, with an odd smile. "Hm . . . yes, all is in a man's hands and he lets it all slip from cowardice, that's an axiom. It would be interesting to know what it is men are most afraid of. Taking a new step, uttering a new word is what they fear most. . . . But I am talking too much. It's because I chatter that I do nothing. Or perhaps it is that I chatter because I do nothing. I've learned to chatter this last month, lying for days together in my den thinking . . . of Jack the Giant-killer. Why am I going there now? Am I capable of *that?* Is *that* serious? It is not serious at all. It's simply a fantasy to amuse myself; a plaything! Yes, maybe it is a plaything."

The heat in the street was terrible: and the airlessness, the bustle and the plaster, scaffolding, bricks, and dust all about him, and that special Petersburg stench, so familiar to all who are unable to get out of town in summer—all worked painfully upon the young man's already overwrought nerves. The insuf-

GI Entry Requirements: Cold Read Text C

On the Revolutions of the Celestial Spheres
Nicolaus Copernicus
1543

TO HIS HOLINESS, POPE PAUL III,
From NICOLAUS COPERNICUS

A PREFACE TO HIS BOOKS ON THE REVOLUTIONS

I can readily imagine, Holy Father, that as soon as some people hear that in this volume, which I have written about the revolutions of the spheres of the universe, I ascribe certain motions to the terrestrial globe, they will shout that I must be immediately repudiated together with this belief. For I am not so enamored of my own opinions that I disregard what others may think of them. I am aware that a philosopher's ideas are not subject to the judgment of ordinary persons, because it is his endeavor to seek the truth in all things, to the extent permitted to human reason by God. Yet I hold that completely erroneous views should be shunned. Those who know that the consensus of many centuries has sanctioned the conception that the earth remains at rest in the middle of the heaven as its center would, I reflected, regard it as an insane pronouncement if I made the opposite assertion that the earth moves.

Therefore I debated with myself for a long time whether to publish the volume which I wrote to prove the earth's motion or rather to follow the example of the Pythagoreans and certain others, who used to transmit philosophy's secrets only to kinsmen and friends, not in writing but by word of mouth, as is shown by Lysis' letter to Hipparchus. And they did so, it seems to me, not, as some suppose, because they were in some way jealous about their teachings, which would be spread around; on the contrary, they wanted the very beautiful thoughts attained by great men of deep devotion not to be ridiculed by those who are reluctant to exert themselves vigorously in any literary pursuit unless it is lucrative; or if they are stimulated to the nonacquisitive study of philosophy by the exhortation and example of others, yet because of their dullness of mind they play the same part among philosophers as drones among bees. When I weighed these considerations, the scorn which I had reason to fear on account of the novelty and unconventionality of my opinion almost induced me to abandon completely the work which I had undertaken...

However, Your Holiness will perhaps not be greatly surprised that I have dared to publish my studies after devoting so much effort to working them out that I did not hesitate to put down my thoughts about the earth's motion in written form too. But you are rather waiting to hear from me how it occurred to me to venture to conceive any motion of the earth, against the traditional opinion of astronomers and almost against common sense. ...I was impelled to consider a different system of deducing the motions of the universe's spheres for no other reason than the realization that astronomers do not agree among themselves in their investigations of this subject...

For a long time, then, I reflected on this confusion in the astronomical traditions concerning the derivation of the motions of the universe's spheres. I began to be annoyed that the movements of the world machine, created for our sake by the best and most systematic Artisan of all, were not understood with greater certainty by the philosophers, who otherwise examined so precisely the most insignificant trifles of this world...

...I have no doubt that acute and learned astronomers will agree with me if, as this discipline especially requires, they are willing to examine and consider, not superficially but thoroughly, what I adduce in this volume in proof of these matters. However, in order that the educated and uneducated alike may see that I do not run away from the judgement of anybody at all, I have preferred dedicating my studies to Your Holiness rather than to anyone else. For even in this very remote corner of the earth where I live you are considered the highest authority by virtue of the loftiness of your office and your love for all literature and astronomy too. Hence by your prestige and judgement you can easily suppress calumnious attacks although, as the proverb has it, there is no remedy for a backbite.

Basic Understanding

Tell me three things this text says about the study of the universe.

Interpretation

What is one of Copernicus's central ideas in this introduction? What evidence do you have to support your answer?

Vocabulary

What does Copernicus mean by "best and most systematic Artisan?" Why do you think he chose to use this phrase?

GI Entry Requirements: Cold Read Text D

Martin Luther King, Jr.
"Letter from a Birmingham Jail"
16 April 1963

Basic Understanding

Tell me three things this text says about the conflict in Birmingham.

Interpretation

What is Dr. King's central argument in this letter, so far? What evidence do you have to support your answer?

Vocabulary

What does Dr. King mean when he says that we can not afford "to live with the narrow, provincial "outside agitator" idea?" How does this phrase support his argument in this letter?

My Dear Fellow Clergymen:

While confined here in the Birmingham city jail, I came across your recent statement calling my present activities "unwise and untimely." Seldom do I pause to answer criticism of my work and ideas. .... But since I feel that you are men of genuine good will and that your criticisms are sincerely set forth, I want to try to answer your statement in what I hope will be patient and reasonable terms.

I think I should indicate why I am here in Birmingham, since you have been influenced by the view which argues against "outsiders coming in." I have the honor of serving as president of the Southern Christian Leadership Conference, an organization operating in every southern state, with headquarters in Atlanta, Georgia. We have some eighty five affiliated organizations across the South, and one of them is the Alabama Christian Movement for Human Rights. Frequently we share staff, educational and financial resources with our affiliates. Several months ago the affiliate here in Birmingham asked us to be on call to engage in a nonviolent direct action program if such were deemed necessary. We readily consented, and when the hour came we lived up to our promise. So I, along with several members of my staff, am here because I was invited here. I am here because I have organizational ties here.

But more basically, I am in Birmingham because injustice is here. Just as the prophets of the eighth century B.C. left their villages and carried their "thus saith the Lord" far beyond the boundaries of their home towns, and just as the Apostle Paul left his village of Tarsus and carried the gospel of Jesus Christ to the far corners of the Greco Roman world, so am I compelled to carry the gospel of freedom beyond my own home town. Like Paul, I must constantly respond to the Macedonian call for aid.

Moreover, I am cognizant of the interrelatedness of all communities and states. I cannot sit idly by in Atlanta and not be concerned about what happens in Birmingham. Injustice anywhere is a threat to justice everywhere. We are caught in an inescapable network of mutuality, tied in a single garment of destiny. Whatever affects one directly, affects all indirectly. Never again can we afford to live with the narrow, provincial "outside agitator" idea. Anyone who lives inside the United States can never be considered an outsider anywhere within its bounds.

You deplore the demonstrations taking place in Birmingham. But your statement, I am sorry to say, fails to express a similar concern for the conditions that brought about the demonstrations. I am sure that none of you would want to rest content with the superficial kind of social analysis that deals merely with effects and does not grapple with underlying causes. It is unfortunate that demonstrations are taking place in Birmingham, but it is even more unfortunate that the city's white power structure left the Negro community with no alternative.

In any nonviolent campaign there are four basic steps: collection of the facts to determine whether injustices exist; negotiation; self purification; and direct action. We have gone through all these steps in Birmingham. There can be no gainsaying the fact that racial injustice engulfs this community. Birmingham is probably the most thoroughly segregated city in the United States. Its ugly record of brutality is widely known. Negroes have experienced grossly unjust treatment in the courts. There have been more unsolved bombings of Negro homes and churches in Birmingham than in any other city in the nation. These are the hard, brutal facts of the case. On the basis of these conditions, Negro leaders sought to negotiate with the city fathers. But the latter consistently refused to engage in good faith negotiation.

Gl Comprehension

Reading Standards for Literature and Informational Text

Proficiency in the standards below must be demonstrated while reading independently in Gl-level materials. In order to be prepared for college, students should earn at least .96 points.

Key Ideas and Details: Using Text Evidence to Support Conclusions Understand, think about, and discuss <u>what</u> the author said.		Evidence/Date	Points	
	Have background knowledge of a Gl-level reader, familiar with 90-100% of the vocabulary and enough of the world knowledge found in Gl-level books to ensure basic comprehension (e.g., 11th/12th-grade level math, science, and social studies concepts).		✓	
	Automatically adjust reading strategies to suit text and purpose. • Demonstrate aggressive self-monitoring and active reading strategies when reading difficult material. • Skim and scan to locate specific information quickly. • Read silently and rapidly for pleasure.		✓	
CCSR 1	Cite strong and thorough textual evidence to support analysis of what the text says explicitly as well as inferences drawn from the text, including determining where the text leaves matters uncertain. • *How, why, what...? Find the examples from the text that BEST supports your answer.* • *What is implied by this text? What makes you think this?*		.06	
CCSR 2	Determine two or more themes or central ideas of a text and analyze their development over the course of the text, including how they interact and build on one another to produce a complex account; provide an objective summary of the text. • *What are two themes (or central ideas) of this text?* • *How does each theme develop from the beginning to the end of the text?* • *How do the two themes interact and build on one another?* • *Summarize what you've read so far in one sentence.*		.06	
	Determine two or more central ideas of a text and analyze their development over the course of the text, including how they interact and build on one another to provide a complex analysis; provide an objective summary of the text. • *What are two central ideas of this text?* • *How does each idea develop from the beginning to the end of the text?* • *How do the two ideas interact and build on one another?* • *Summarize what you've read so far in one sentence.*		.06	

GI Comprehension Cont'd

CCSR 3	Analyze the impact of the author's choices regarding how to develop and relate elements of a story or drama (e.g., where a story is set, how the action is ordered, how the characters are introduced and developed). • *Why do you think the author chose to use this setting? How does this shape the plot or characters? Do you think it is an effective setting choice? Why or why not?* • *Why do you think the author chose to present the events in the order he chose? How does this shape the story? Do you think this was an effective choice? Why or why not?* • *Why do you think the author chose the characters he/she did?*		.06	
	Analyze a complex set of ideas or sequence of events and explain how specific individuals, ideas, or events interact and develop over the course of the text. • *Delineate the central set of ideas or sequence of events in your text. How do they interact and develop over the course of the text? Does the order in which they are presented matter? Why?*		.06	
	Identify and describe the following literary elements in the text: characters (motivations of major and minor characters); setting (time, day, year, historical period, place, situation); plot (main events, conflict, rising action, climax, falling action, resolution). • *What is the conflict? How is it resolved?* • *Where and when did the story take place? How does it compare to your setting?* • *Who are the main characters and what are their traits? What are their motivations?*		.06	

Craft and Structure: Analyzing the Effects of Authors' Choices

Understand and discuss <u>the way(s)</u> the author(s) said what was said.

CCSR 4	Determine the meaning of words and phrases as they are used in the text, including figurative and connotative meanings; analyze the impact of specific word choices on meaning and tone, including words with multiple meanings or language that is particularly fresh, engaging, or beautiful. (Include Shakespeare as well as other authors.) • *Which passage do you think was the most beautiful, engaging, or fresh? Why?* • *Which words make it unusually effective? What do they mean?* • *Which of this is figurative language? What is the difference between the connotations and denotations of the figurative language?*		.06	
CCSR 5	Analyze how an author's choices concerning how to structure specific parts of a text (e.g., the choice of where to begin or end a story, the choice to provide a comedic or tragic resolution) contribute to its overall structure and meaning as well as its aesthetic impact. • *How was the text structured (opening scene, handling of passage of time, introduction of characters, dialogue, narrator, ending, etc.)? Which were the most important decisions the author made about structuring this book?* • *Why do you think the author made these choices?* • *How does each choice affect the meaning of the text?* • *How does each choice affect the text's aesthetic impact?* • *What genre is this book? Why do you think the author chose to structure the text in this way?*		.06	
	Analyze and evaluatethe effectiveness of the structure an author uses in his or her exposition or argument, including whether the structure makes points clear, convincing, and engaging (e.g., compare/contrast, pro/con, chronological sequence, cause and effect). • *What kind of structure did the author use to organize his/her argument or exposition?* • *Did this work for clarity, effect, or engagement?* • *Can you identify a section where you might restructure the argument to make it more effective?*		.06	

GI Comprehension Cont'd

	Identify types of poetry (e.g. haiku, limerick, free verse) and structural elements (stanza, verse, rhyme scheme, line breaks, rhythm, alliteration). • *What kind of poetry is this? How do you know?* • *Identify an example of alliteration (etc.).*		.06	
CCSR 6	Analyze a case in which grasping a point of view (perspective) requires distinguishing what is directly stated in a text from what is really meant (e.g., satire, sarcasm, irony, or understatement). • *Find an example of where what is said is different from, or the opposite of, what is implied. Explain.*		.06	
	Determine an author's point of view or purpose in a text in which the rhetoric is particularly effective, analyzing how style and content contribute to the power, persuasiveness, or beauty of the text. • *What is the most effective/persuasive argument you have read? What made it so persuasive?*		.06	

Integration of Knowledge and Ideas: Comparing Different Presentations

Discuss how the ideas in a book connect to each other and to the larger world.

CCSR 7	Analyze multiple interpretations of a story, drama, or poem (e.g., recorded or live production of a play or recorded novel or poetry), evaluating how each version interprets the source text. (Include at least one play by Shakespeare and one play by an American dramatist.) • *Compare two presentations of the same scene/story. How do they compare? Where do they differ? What do you think of these choices? What would you have done differently?*		.06	
	Integrate and evaluate multiple sources of information presented in different media or formats (e.g., visually, quantitatively) as well as in words in order to address a question or solve a problem. (Research paper.)		.06	
CCSR 8	Delineate and evaluate the reasoning in seminal U.S. texts, including the application of constitutional principles and use of legal reasoning (e.g., in U.S. Supreme Court majority opinions and dissents) and the premises, purposes, and arguments in works of public advocacy (e.g., The Federalist, presidential addresses). • *What is the author's argument or claim? What reasoning does s/he use to support it?* • *Which of the author's claims have good supporting evidence? Which don't? Why?* • *Is there reasoning used that doesn't actually support the claim?* • *Has s/he convinced you? Why or why not? What evidence or rationale would have made a stronger argument?*		.06	
CCSR 9	Demonstrate knowledge of eighteenth-, nineteenth- and early twentieth-century foundational works of American literature, including how two or more texts from the same period treat similar themes or topics. • *Given 2 works from the same period, create a T-chart comparing them.* [T-chart: columns Similarities, Differences; rows Characters, Setting, Plot Events, Themes]		.06	
	Analyze seventeenth-, eighteenth-, and nineteenth-century foundational U.S. documents of historical and literary significance (including the Declaration of Independence, the Preamble to the Constitution, the Bill of Rights, and Lincoln's Second Inaugural Address) for their themes, purposes, and rhetorical features.		.06	
GI Comprehension Total			**.96**	

	Similarities	Differences
Characters		
Setting		
Plot Events		
Themes		

GI Range of Reading and Level of Text Complexity

Range of Reading and Level of Text Complexity	Evidence/Date	Points	
Engagement and Independence • Read regularly and independently, sustaining engagement, in GI-level materials for at least 30 minutes every day in the classroom. • Demonstrate the stamina to sustain reading for 2-4 hours, as required by college entrance exams.		.02	
Home Reading • Sustain a home reading habit and read for at least 30 minutes every night without prompting, or make up this additional 30 minutes during the school day.		.02	
Full-Length Book Habit • Regularly finish chapter books, at least 1 every other week. (Avid GI readers should be encouraged to read from a range of appropriate levels for pleasure.)		.03	
Genres CCSR 10 • Identify the probable genre(s) of a new text and justify their reasoning with evidence from the text and examples of characteristics common to that genre.		✓	

Read independently and comprehend <u>informational text</u> at the GI level, including:

	Evidence (List Areas/Topics of Reading Experience)	Date		
American History • Early American History • 18th-Century American History • 19th-Century American History • 20th-Century American History			.08	
World History • Ancient • Medieval • Modern			.03	
Primary sources • Letter or Journal • Speech • Cartoon			.03	

Gl Range of Reading and Level of Text Complexity Cont'd

Science (3 Each) • Life Science • Physical Science • Earth Science			.06	
Narrative Nonfiction • Autobiography • Biography • Memoir			.06	
Essays and articles • Newspaper • Persuasive/Editorial • Literary Analysis			.03	

Read independently and comprehend <u>literary text</u> at the Gl level, including:

	Evidence (List Chapter Books Completed)	Date		
Modern Fiction • Realistic Fiction • Historical Fiction			.04	
Classic/Canon Literature • 18th-Century American • 19th-Century American • Early 20th-Century American			.06	
Multicultural Literature • African American • Asian American • Latino • Native American			.06	

GI Range of Reading and Level of Text Complexity Cont'd

World Literature • Africa • Asia • Europe • Latin America • Middle East			.05	
Speculative Fiction • Fantasy • Science Fiction			.04	
	Evidence (List Book Titles or Steps/Time Spent Reading in the Genre.)			
Traditional Literature • Classical Mythology • Religious Text			.02	
Drama			.01	
Poetry (5 Different Forms, 1 Point each)			.05	
Shakespeare			.02	
GI Range of Reading and Level of Text Complexity Total			.71	

Gl Vocabulary and Language

Vocabulary and Language	Evidence/Date	Points	
Literary, Academic, and Domain-Specific Vocabulary Know and be able to use at least 10,500-12,000 words, not familiar from everyday speech, but common to Gl-level text. CCSL 6. Gl readers have learned most of the literary and technical vocabulary encountered in Gl-level text from their previous reading. As they spend two years reading in Gl books (minimum one hour per day), they will learn an additional 3,000 words.		.10	
Notice unfamiliar words and gather vocabulary knowledge when considering a word or phrase important to comprehension or expression. CCSL 6.		.01	
Use context (e.g., the overall meaning of a sentence, paragraph, or text; a word's position or function in a sentence) as a clue to the meaning of a word or phrase. CCSL 4a.		.01	
Identify and correctly use patterns of word changes that indicate different meanings or parts of speech (e.g., conceive, conception, conceivable). CCSL 4b.		.01	
Consult general and specialized reference materials (e.g., dictionaries, glossaries, thesauruses), both print and digital, to find the pronunciation of a word or determine or clarify its precise meaning, its part of speech, its etymology, or its standard usage. CCSL 4c.		.01	
Verify the preliminary determination of the meaning of a word or phrase (e.g., by checking the inferred meaning in context or in a dictionary). CCSL 4d.		.01	
Analyze nuances in the meaning of words with similar denotations. CCSL 5b.		.02	
Affixes and Roots Use word origins to determine the meanings of specialized vocabulary. CCSL 5.		.01	
Figurative Language Interpret figures of speech (e.g., hyperbole, paradox) in context and analyzes their role in the text. CCSL 5a.		.02	
Interpret figurative language (e.g., similes, metaphors, personification, idioms, hyperbole, symbolism) in context.		.02	
Decode Multisyllable Words Use combined knowledge of all letter-sound correspondences, syllabification patterns, and morphology (e.g., roots and affixes) to accurately read unfamiliar multisyllabic words, including names, in context and out of context, at the Gl level. (Any student having trouble with this is working at the wrong level.)		✓	
Gl Vocabulary and Language Total		.22	

Transition to College and Career

GI Entry Points	11.00	
GI Comprehension Points	.96	
GI Range of Reading and Level of Text Complexity Points	.73	
GI Vocabulary and Language Points	.20	

College and Career Transition Points. With NO help of any kind, student must demonstrate ability to:		**Evidence/Date**	**Points**	
Vocabulary	**Demonstrate Command of a Literary Vocabulary of Approximately 12,000 Words** Have approximately 12,000 literary vocabulary words in reading vocabulary available for comprehending college and career level text. CCSL 6.		.02	
Range of Reading	**Handle an Academic History Text** Read and finish a short, college-appropriate academic text in any social science field, including demonstrating comprehension and a command of the vocabulary used in the text. CCSR 10.		.02	
	Handle an Academic Science Text Read and finish a short, college-appropriate academic text in any science field, including demonstrating comprehension and a command of the vocabulary used in the text. CCSR 10.		.02	
	Handle an Academic Humanities Text Read and finish a short, college-appropriate academic text in any humanities field, including demonstrating comprehension and a command of the vocabulary used in the text. CCSR 10.		.02	
	Handle a Professional Text Read and finish a professional text in any career field, including demonstrating comprehension and a command of the vocabulary used in the text. CCSR 10.		.02	
College and Career Transition Points			.10	
GRAND TOTAL: Student should graduate with 12.99 points and demonstrated proficiency at college and career prerequisites.			12.99	

Common Core Standard: Reading 1

Read closely to determine what the text says explicitly and to make logical inferences from it; cite specific textual evidence when writing or speaking to support conclusions drawn from the text.

Grade	Literature	Informational
K	With prompting and support, ask and answer questions about key details in a text.	With prompting and support, ask and answer questions about key details in a text.
1	Ask and answer questions about key details in a text.	Ask and answer questions about key details in a text.
2	Ask and answer such questions as who, what, where, when, why, and how to demonstrate understanding of key details in a text.	Ask and answer such questions as who, what, where, when, why, and how to demonstrate understanding of key details in a text.
3	Ask and answer questions to demonstrate understanding of a text, referring explicitly to the text as the basis for the answers.	Ask and answer questions to demonstrate understanding of a text, referring explicitly to the text as the basis for the answers.
4	Refer to details and examples in a text when explaining what the text says explicitly and when drawing inferences from the text.	Refer to details and examples in a text when explaining what the text says explicitly and when drawing inferences from the text.
5	Quote accurately from a text when explaining what the text says explicitly and when drawing inferences from the text.	Quote accurately from a text when explaining what the text says explicitly and when drawing inferences from the text.
6	Cite textual evidence to support analysis of what the text says explicitly as well as inferences drawn from the text.	Cite textual evidence to support analysis of what the text says explicitly as well as inferences drawn from the text.
7	Cite several pieces of textual evidence to support analysis of what the text says explicitly as well as inferences drawn from the text.	Cite several pieces of textual evidence to support analysis of what the text says explicitly as well as inferences drawn from the text.
8	Cite the textual evidence that most strongly supports an analysis of what the text says explicitly as well as inferences drawn from the text.	Cite the textual evidence that most strongly supports an analysis of what the text says explicitly as well as inferences drawn from the text.
9-10	Cite strong and thorough textual evidence to support analysis of what the text says explicitly as well as inferences drawn from the text.	Cite strong and thorough textual evidence to support analysis of what the text says explicitly as well as inferences drawn from the text.
11-12	Cite strong and thorough textual evidence to support analysis of what the text says explicitly as well as inferences drawn from the text, including determining where the text leaves matters uncertain.	Cite strong and thorough textual evidence to support analysis of what the text says explicitly as well as inferences drawn from the text, including determining where the text leaves matters uncertain.

Common Core Standard: Reading 2

Determine central ideas or themes of a text and analyze their development; summarize the key supporting details and ideas.

Grade	Literature	Informational
K	With prompting and support, retell familiar stories, including key details.	With prompting and support, identify the main topic and retell key details of a text.
1	Retell stories, including key details, and demonstrate understanding of their central message or lesson.	Identify the main topic and retell key details of a text.
2	Recount stories, including fables and folktales from diverse cultures, and determine their central message, lesson, or moral.	Identify the main topic of a multiparagraph text as well as the focus of specific paragraphs within the text.
3	Recount stories, including fables, folktales, and myths from diverse cultures; determine the central message, lesson, or moral and explain how it is conveyed through key details in the text.	Determine the main idea of a text; recount the key details and explain how they support the main idea.
4	Determine a theme of a story, drama, or poem from details in the text; summarize the text.	Determine the main idea of a text and explain how it is supported by key details; summarize the text.
5	Determine a theme of a story, drama, or poem from details in the text, including how characters in a story or drama respond to challenges or how the speaker in a poem reflects upon a topic; summarize the text.	Determine two or more main ideas of a text and explain how they are supported by key details; summarize the text.
6	Determine a theme or central idea of a text and how it is conveyed through particular details; provide a summary of the text distinct from personal opinions or judgments.	Determine a central idea of a text and how it is conveyed through particular details; provide a summary of the text distinct from personal opinions or judgments.
7	Determine a theme or central idea of a text and analyze its development over the course of the text; provide an objective summary of the text.	Determine two or more central ideas in a text and analyze their development over the course of the text; provide an objective summary of the text.
8	Determine a theme or central idea of a text and analyze its development over the course of the text, including its relationship to the characters, setting, and plot; provide an objective summary of the text.	Determine a central idea of a text and analyze its development over the course of the text, including its relationship to supporting ideas; provide an objective summary of the text.
9-10	Determine a theme or central idea of a text and analyze in detail its development over the course of the text, including how it emerges and is shaped and refined by specific details; provide an objective summary of the text.	Determine a central idea of a text and analyze its development over the course of the text, including how it emerges and is shaped and refined by specific details; provide an objective summary of the text.
11-12	Determine two or more themes or central ideas of a text and analyze their development over the course of the text, including how they interact and build on one another to produce a complex account; provide an objective summary of the text.	Determine two or more central ideas of a text and analyze their development over the course of the text, including how they interact and build on one another to provide a complex analysis; provide an objective summary of the text.

Common Core Standard: Reading 3

Analyze how and why individuals, events, and ideas develop and interact over the course of a text.

Grade	Literature	Informational
K	With prompting and support, identify characters, settings, and major events in a story.	With prompting and support, describe the connection between two individuals, events, ideas, or pieces of information in a text.
1	Describe characters, settings, and major events in a story, using key details.	Describe the connection between two individuals, events, ideas, or pieces of information in a text.
2	Describe how characters in a story respond to major events and challenges.	Describe the connection between a series of historical events, scientific ideas or concepts, or steps in technical procedures in a text.
3	Describe characters in a story (e.g., their traits, motivations, or feelings) and explain how their actions contribute to the sequence of events.	Describe the relationship between a series of historical events, scientific ideas or concepts, or steps in technical procedures in a text, using language that pertains to time, sequence, and cause/effect.
4	Describe in depth a character, setting, or event in a story or drama, drawing on specific details in the text (e.g., a character's thoughts, words, or actions).	Explain events, procedures, ideas, or concepts in a historical, scientific, or technical text, including what happened and why, based on specific information in the text.
5	Compare and contrast two or more characters, settings, or events in a story or drama, drawing on specific details in the text (e.g., how characters interact).	Explain the relationships or interactions between two or more individuals, events, ideas, or concepts in a historical, scientific, or technical text based on specific information in the text.
6	Describe how a particular story's or drama's plot unfolds in a series of episodes as well as how the characters respond or change as the plot moves toward a resolution.	Analyze in detail how a key individual, event, or idea is introduced, illustrated, and elaborated in a text (e.g., through examples or anecdotes).
7	Analyze how particular elements of a story or drama interact (e.g., how setting shapes the characters or plot).	Analyze the interactions between individuals, events, and ideas in a text (e.g., how ideas influence individuals or events, or how individuals influence ideas or events).
8	Analyze how particular lines of dialogue or incidents in a story or drama propel the action, reveal aspects of a character, or provoke a decision.	Analyze how a text makes connections among and distinctions between individuals, ideas, or events (e.g., through comparisons, analogies, or categories).
9-10	Analyze how complex characters (e.g., those with multiple or conflicting motivations) develop over the course of a text, interact with other characters, and advance the plot or develop the theme.	Analyze how the author unfolds an analysis or series of ideas or events, including the order in which the points are made, how they are introduced and developed, and the connections that are drawn between them.
11-12	Analyze the impact of the author's choices regarding how to develop and relate elements of a story or drama (e.g., where a story is set, how the action is ordered, how the characters are introduced and developed).	Analyze a complex set of ideas or sequence of events and explain how specific individuals, ideas, or events interact and develop over the course of the text.

Common Core Standard: Reading 4

Interpret words and phrases as they are used in a text, including determining technical, connotative, and figurative meanings, and analyze how specific word choices shape meaning or tone.

Grade	Literature	Informational
K	Ask and answer questions about unknown words in a text.	With prompting and support, ask and answer questions about unknown words in a text.
1	Identify words and phrases in stories or poems that suggest feelings or appeal to the senses.	Ask and answer questions to help determine or clarify the meaning of words and phrases in a text.
2	Describe how words and phrases (e.g., regular beats, alliteration, rhymes, repeated lines) supply rhythm and meaning in a story, poem, or song.	Determine the meaning of words and phrases in a text relevant to a Grade 2 topic or subject area.
3	Determine the meaning of words and phrases as they are used in a text, distinguishing literal from nonliteral language.	Determine the meaning of general academic and domain-specific words and phrases in a text relevant to a Grade 3 topic or subject area.
4	Determine the meaning of words and phrasesas they are used in a text, including those that allude to significant characters found in mythology (e.g., Herculean).	Determine the meaning of general academic and domain-specific words or phrases in a text relevant to a Grade 4 topic or subject area.
5	Determine the meaning of words and phrases as they are used in a text, including figurative language such as metaphors and similes.	Determine the meaning of general academic and domain-specific words and phrases in a text relevant to a Grade 5 topic or subject area.
6	Determine the meaning of words and phrases as they are used in a text, including figurative and connotative meanings; analyze the impact of a specific word choice on meaning and tone.	Determine the meaning of words and phrases as they are used in a text, including figurative, connotative, and technical meanings.
7	Determine the meaning of words and phrases as they are used in a text, including figurative and connotative meanings; analyze the impact of rhymes and other repetitions of sounds (e.g., alliteration) on a specific verse or stanza of a poem or section of a story or drama.	Determine the meaning of words and phrases as they are used in a text, including figurative, connotative, and technical meanings; analyze the impact of a specific word choice on meaning and tone.
8	Determine the meaning of words and phrases as they are used in a text, including figurative and connotative meanings; analyze the impact of specific word choices on meaning and tone, including analogies or allusions to other texts.	Determine the meaning of words and phrases as they are used in a text, including figurative, connotative, and technical meanings; analyze the impact of specific word choices on meaning and tone, including analogies or allusions to other texts.
9-10	Determine the meaning of words and phrases as they are used in the text, including figurative and connotative meanings; analyze the cumulative impact of specific word choices on meaning and tone (e.g., how the language evokes a sense of time and place; how it sets a formal or informal tone).	Determine the meaning of words and phrases as they are used in a text, including figurative, connotative, and technical meanings; analyze the cumulative impact of specific word choices on meaning and tone (e.g., how the language of a court opinion differs from that of a newspaper).
11-12	Determine the meaning of words and phrases as they are used in the text, including figurative and connotative meanings; analyze the impact of specific word choices on meaning and tone, including words with multiple meanings or language that is particularly fresh, engaging, or beautiful. (Include Shakespeare as well as other authors.)	Determine the meaning of words and phrases as they are used in a text, including figurative, connotative, and technical meanings; analyze how an author uses and refines the meaning of a key term or terms over the course of a text (e.g., how Madison defines *faction* in Federalist No. 10).

Common Core Standard: Reading 5

Analyze the structure of texts, including how specific sentences, paragraphs, and larger portions of the text (e.g., a section, chapter, scene, or stanza) relate to each other and the whole.

Grade	Literature	Informational
K	Recognize common types of texts (e.g., storybooks, poems).	Identify the front cover, back cover, and title page of a book.
1	Explain major differences between books that tell stories and books that give information, drawing on a wide reading of a range of text types.	Know and use various text features (e.g., headings, tables of contents, glossaries, electronic menus, icons) to locate key facts or information in a text.
2	Describe the overall structure of a story, including describing how the beginning introduces the story and the ending concludes the action.	Know and use various text features (e.g., captions, bold print, subheadings, glossaries, indexes, electronic menus, icons) to locate key facts or information in a text efficiently.
3	Refer to parts of stories, dramas, and poems when writing or speaking about a text, using terms such as chapter, scene, and stanza; describe how each successive part builds on earlier sections.	Use text features and search tools (e.g., key words, sidebars, hyperlinks) to locate information relevant to a given topic efficiently.
4	Explain major differences between poems, drama, and prose, and refer to the structural elements of poems (e.g., verse, rhythm, meter) and drama (e.g., casts of characters, settings, descriptions, dialogue, stage directions) when writing or speaking about a text.	Describe the overall structure (e.g., chronology, comparison, cause/effect, problem/solution) of events, ideas, concepts, or information in a text or part of a text.
5	Explain how a series of chapters, scenes, or stanzas fits together to provide the overall structure of a particular story, drama, or poem.	Compare and contrast the overall structure (e.g., chronology, comparison, cause/effect, problem/solution) of events, ideas, concepts, or information in two or more texts.
6	Analyze how a particular sentence, chapter, scene, or stanza fits into the overall structure of a text and contributes to the development of the theme, setting, or plot.	Analyze how a particular sentence, paragraph, chapter, or section fits into the overall structure of a text and contributes to the development of the ideas.
7	Analyze how a drama's or poem's form or structure (e.g., soliloquy, sonnet) contributes to its meaning.	Analyze the structure an author uses to organize a text, including how the major sections contribute to the whole and to the development of the ideas.
8	Compare and contrast the structure of two or more texts and analyze how the differing structure of each text contributes to its meaning and style.	Analyze in detail the structure of a specific paragraph in a text, including the role of particular sentences in developing and refining a key concept.
9-10	Analyze how an author's choices concerning how to structure a text, order events within it (e.g., parallel plots), and manipulate time (e.g., pacing, flashbacks) create such effects as mystery, tension, or surprise.	Analyze in detail how an author's ideas or claims are developed and refined by particular sentences, paragraphs, or larger portions of a text (e.g., a section or chapter).
11-12	Analyze how an author's choices concerning how to structure specific parts of a text (e.g., the choice of where to begin or end a story, the choice to provide a comedic or tragic resolution) contribute to its overall structure and meaning as well as its aesthetic impact.	Analyze and evaluate the effectiveness of the structure an author uses in his or her exposition or argument, including whether the structure makes points clear, convincing, and engaging.

Common Core Standard: Reading 6

Assess how point of view or purpose shapes the content and style of a text.

Grade	Literature	Informational
K	With prompting and support, name the author and illustrator of a story and define the role of each in telling the story.	Name the author and illustrator of a text and define the role of each in presenting the ideas or information in a text.
1	Identify who is telling the story at various points in a text.	Distinguish between information provided by pictures or other illustrations and information provided by the words in a text.
2	Acknowledge differences in the points of view of characters, including by speaking in a different voice for each character when reading dialogue aloud.	Identify the main purpose of a text, including what the author wants to answer, explain, or describe.
3	Distinguish their own point of view from that of the narrator or those of the characters.	Distinguish their own point of view from that of the author of a text.
4	Compare and contrast the point of view from which different stories are narrated, including the difference between first- and third-person narrations.	Compare and contrast a firsthand and secondhand account of the same event or topic; describe the differences in focus and the information provided.
5	Describe how a narrator's or speaker's point of view influences how events are described.	Analyze multiple accounts of the same event or topic, noting important similarities and differences in the point of view they represent.
6	Explain how an author develops the point of view of the narrator or speaker in a text.	Determine an author's point of view or purpose in a text and explain how it is conveyed in the text.
7	Analyze how an author develops and contrasts the points of view of different characters or narrators in a text.	Determine an author's point of view or purpose in a text and analyze how the author distinguishes his or her position from that of others.
8	Analyze how differences in the points of view of the characters and the audience or reader (e.g., created through the use of dramatic irony) create such effects as suspense or humor.	Determine an author's point of view or purpose in a text and analyze how the author acknowledges and responds to conflicting evidence or viewpoints.
9-10	Analyze a particular point of view or cultural experience reflected in a work of literature from outside the United States, drawing on a wide reading of world literature.	Determine an author's point of view or purpose in a text and analyze how an author uses rhetoric to advance that point of view or purpose.
11-12	Analyze a case in which grasping point of view requires distinguishing what is directly stated in a text from what is really meant (e.g., satire, sarcasm, irony, or understatement).	Determine an author's point of view or purpose in a text in which the rhetoric is particularly effective, analyzing how style and content contribute to the power, persuasiveness, or beauty of the text.

Common Core Standard: Reading 7

Integrate and evaluate content presented in diverse media and formats, including visually and quantitatively, as well as in words.

Grade	Literature	Informational
K	With prompting and support, describe the relationship between illustrations and the story in which they appear (e.g., what moment in a story an illustration depicts).	With prompting and support, describe the relationship between illustrations and the text in which they appear (e.g., what person, place, thing, or idea in the text an illustration depicts).
1	Use illustrations and details in a story to describe its characters, setting, or events.	Use the illustrations and details in a text to describe its key ideas.
2	Use information gained from the illustrations and words in a print or digital text to demonstrate understanding of its characters, setting, or plot.	Explain how specific images (e.g., a diagram showing how a machine works) contribute to and clarify a text.
3	Explain how specific aspects of a text's illustrations contribute to what is conveyed by the words in a story (e.g., create mood, emphasize aspects of a character or setting).	Use information gained from illustrations (e.g., maps, photographs) and the words in a text to demonstrate understanding of the text (e.g., where, when, why, and how key events occur).
4	Make connections between the text of a story or drama and a visual or oral presentation of the text, identifying where each version reflects specific descriptions and directions in the text.	Interpret information presented visually, orally, or quantitatively (e.g., in charts, graphs, diagrams, time lines, animations, or interactive elements on Web pages) and explain how the information contributes to an understanding of the text in which it appears.
5	Analyze how visual and multimedia elements contribute to the meaning, tone, or beauty of a text (e.g., graphic novel, multimedia presentation of fiction, folktale, myth, poem).	Draw on information from multiple print or digital sources, demonstrating the ability to locate an answer to a question quickly or to solve a problem efficiently.
6	Compare and contrast the experience of reading a story, drama, or poem to listening to or viewing an audio, video, or live version of the text, including contrasting what they "see" and "hear" when reading the text to what they perceive when they listen or watch.	Integrate information presented in different media or formats (e.g., visually, quantitatively) as well as in words to develop a coherent understanding of a topic or issue.
7	Compare and contrast a written story, drama, or poem to its audio, filmed, staged, or multimedia version, analyzing the effects of techniques unique to each medium (e.g., lighting, sound, color, or camera focus and angles in a film).	Compare and contrast a text to an audio, video, or multimedia version of the text, analyzing each medium's portrayal of the subject (e.g., how the delivery of a speech affects the impact of the words).
8	Analyze the extent to which a filmed or live production of a story or drama stays faithful to or departs from the text or script, evaluating the choices made by the director or actors.	Evaluate the advantages and disadvantages of using different mediums (e.g., print or digital text, video, multimedia) to present a particular topic or idea.
9-10	Analyze the representation of a subject or a key scene in two different artistic mediums, including what is emphasized or absent in each treatment (e.g., Auden's "Musée des Beaux Arts" and Breughel's *Landscape with the Fall of Icarus*).	Analyze various accounts of a subject told in different media (e.g., a person's life story in both print and multimedia), determining which details are emphasized in each account.
11-12	Analyze multiple interpretations of a story, drama, or poem (e.g., recorded or live production of a play or recorded novel or poetry), evaluating how each version interprets the source text. (Include at least one play by Shakespeare and one play by an American dramatist.)	Integrate and evaluate multiple sources of information presented in different media or formats (e.g., visually, quantitatively) as well as in words in order to address a question or solve a problem.

Common Core Standard: Reading 8

Delineate and evaluate the argument and specific claims in a text, including the validity of the reasoning as well as the relevance and sufficiency of the evidence.

Grade	Literature	Informational
K	(Not applicable to literature)	With prompting and support, identify the reasons an author gives to support points in a text.
1	(Not applicable to literature)	Identify the reasons an author gives to support points in a text.
2	(Not applicable to literature)	Describe how reasons support specific points the author makes in a text.
3	(Not applicable to literature)	Describe the logical connection between particular sentences and paragraphs in a text (e.g., comparison, cause/effect, first/second/third in a sequence).
4	(Not applicable to literature)	Explain how an author uses reasons and evidence to support particular points in a text.
5	(Not applicable to literature)	Explain how an author uses reasons and evidence to support particular points in a text, identifying which reasons and evidence support which point(s).
6	(Not applicable to literature)	Trace and evaluate the argument and specific claims in a text, distinguishing claims that are supported by reasons and evidence from claims that are not.
7	(Not applicable to literature)	Trace and evaluate the argument and specific claims in a text, assessing whether the reasoning is sound and the evidence is relevant and sufficient to support the claims.
8	(Not applicable to literature)	Delineate and evaluate the argument and specific claims in a text, assessing whether the reasoning is sound and the evidence is relevant and sufficient; recognize when irrelevant evidence is introduced.
9-10	(Not applicable to literature)	Delineate and evaluate the argument and specific claims in a text, assessing whether the reasoning is valid and the evidence is relevant and sufficient; identify false statements and fallacious reasoning.
11-12	(Not applicable to literature)	Delineate and evaluate the reasoning in seminal U.S. texts, including the application of constitutional principles and use of legal reasoning (e.g., in U.S. Supreme Court majority opinions and dissents) and the premises, purposes, and arguments in works of public advocacy (e.g., *The Federalist*, presidential addresses).

Common Core Standard: Reading 9

Analyze how two or more texts address similar themes or topics in order to build knowledge or to compare the approaches the authors take.

Grade	Literature	Informational
K	With prompting and support, compare and contrast the adventures and experiences of characters in familiar stories.	With prompting and support, identify basic similarities in and differences between two texts on the same topic (e.g., in illustrations, descriptions, or procedures).
1	Compare and contrast the adventures and experiences of characters in stories.	Identify basic similarities in and differences between two texts on the same topic (e.g., in illustrations, descriptions, or procedures).
2	Compare and contrast two or more versions of the same story (e.g., Cinderella stories) by different authors or from different cultures.	Compare and contrast the most important points presented by two texts on the same topic.
3	Compare and contrast the themes, settings, and plots of stories written by the same author about the same or similar characters (e.g., in books from a series).	Compare and contrast the most important points and key details presented in two texts on the same topic.
4	Compare and contrast the treatment of similar themes and topics (e.g., opposition of good and evil) and patterns of events (e.g., the quest) in stories, myths, and traditional literature from different cultures.	Integrate information from two texts on the same topic in order to write or speak about the subject knowledgeably.
5	Compare and contrast stories in the same genre (e.g., mysteries and adventure stories) on their approaches to similar themes and topics.	Integrate information from several texts on the same topic in order to write or speak about the subject knowledgeably.
6	Compare and contrast texts in different forms or genres (e.g., stories and poems; historical novels and fantasy stories) in terms of their approaches to similar themes and topics.	Compare and contrast one author's presentation of events with that of another (e.g., a memoir written by and a biography on the same person).
7	Compare and contrast a fictional portrayal of a time, place, or character and a historical account of the same period as a means of understanding how authors of fiction use or alter history.	Analyze how two or more authors writing about the same topic shape their presentations of key information by emphasizing different evidence or advancing different interpretations of facts.
8	Analyze how a modern work of fiction draws on themes, patterns of events, or character types from myths, traditional stories, or religious works such as the Bible, including describing how the material is rendered new.	Analyze a case in which two or more texts provide conflicting information on the same topic and identify where the texts disagree on matters of fact or interpretation.
9-10	Analyze how an author draws on and transforms source material in a specific work (e.g., how Shakespeare treats a theme or topic from Ovid or the Bible or how a later author draws on a play by Shakespeare).	Analyze seminal U.S. documents of historical and literary significance (e.g., Washington's Farewell Address, the Gettysburg Address, Roosevelt's Four Freedoms speech, King's "Letter from Birmingham Jail"), including how they address related themes and concepts.
11-12	Demonstrate knowledge of eighteenth-, nineteenth- and early twentieth-century foundational works of American literature, including how two or more texts from the same period treat similar themes or topics.	Analyze seventeenth-, eighteenth-, and nineteenth-century foundational U.S. documents of historical and literary significance (including the Declaration of Independence, the Preamble to the Constitution, the Bill of Rights, and Lincoln's Second Inaugural Address) for their themes, purposes, and rhetorical features.

Common Core Standard: Reading 10

Read and comprehend complex literary and informational texts independently and proficiently.

Grade	Literature	Informational
K	Actively engage in group reading activities with purpose and understanding.	Actively engage in group reading activities with purpose and understanding.
1	With prompting and support, read prose and poetry of appropriate complexity for Grade 1.	With prompting and support, read informational texts appropriately complex for Grade 1.
2	By the end of the year, read and comprehend literature, including stories and poetry, in the Grades 2–3 text complexity band proficiently, with scaffolding as needed at the high end of the range.	By the end of year, read and comprehend informational texts, including history/social studies, science, and technical texts, in the Grades 2–3 text complexity band proficiently, with scaffolding as needed at the high end of the range.
3	By the end of the year, read and comprehend literature, including stories, dramas, and poetry, at the high end of the Grades 2–3 text complexity band independently and proficiently.	By the end of the year, read and comprehend informational texts, including history/social studies, science, and technical texts, at the high end of the Grades 2–3 text complexity band independently and proficiently.
4	By the end of the year, read and comprehend literature, including stories, dramas, and poetry, in the Grades 4–5 text complexity band proficiently, with scaffolding as needed at the high end of the range.	By the end of year, read and comprehend informational texts, including history/social studies, science, and technical texts, in the Grades 4–5 text complexity band proficiently, with scaffolding as needed at the high end of the range.
5	By the end of the year, read and comprehend literature, including stories, dramas, and poetry, at the high end of the Grades 4–5 text complexity band independently and proficiently.	By the end of the year, read and comprehend informational texts, including history/social studies, science, and technical texts, at the high end of the Grades 4–5 text complexity band independently and proficiently.
6	By the end of the year, read and comprehend literature, including stories, dramas, and poems, in the Grades 6–8 text complexity band proficiently, with scaffolding as needed at the high end of the range.	By the end of the year, read and comprehend literary nonfiction in the Grades 6–8 text complexity band proficiently, with scaffolding as needed at the high end of the range.
7	By the end of the year, read and comprehend literature, including stories, dramas, and poems, in the Grades 6–8 text complexity band proficiently, with scaffolding as needed at the high end of the range.	By the end of the year, read and comprehend literary nonfiction in the Grades 6–8 text complexity band proficiently, with scaffolding as needed at the high end of the range.
8	By the end of the year, read and comprehend literature, including stories, dramas, and poems, at the high end of Grades 6–8 text complexity band independently and proficiently.	By the end of the year, read and comprehend literary nonfiction at the high end of the Grades 6–8 text complexity band independently and proficiently.
9-10	By the end of Grade 9, read and comprehend literature, including stories, dramas, and poems, in the Grades 9–10 text complexity band proficiently, with scaffolding as needed at the high end of the range. By the end of Grade 10, read and comprehend literature, including stories, dramas, and poems, at the high end of the Grades 9–10 text complexity band independently and proficiently.	By the end of Grade 9, read and comprehend literary nonfiction in the Grades 9–10 text complexity band proficiently, with scaffolding as needed at the high end of the range. By the end of Grade 10, read and comprehend literary nonfiction at the high end of the Grades 9–10 text complexity band independently and proficiently.
11-12	By the end of Grade 11, read and comprehend literature, including stories, dramas, and poems, in the Grades 11–CCR text complexity band proficiently, with scaffolding as needed at the high end of the range. By the end of Grade 12, read and comprehend literature, including stories, dramas, and poems, at the high end of the Grades 11–CCR text complexity band independently and proficiently.	By the end of Grade 11, read and comprehend literary nonfiction in the Grades 11–CCR text complexity band proficiently, with scaffolding as needed at the high end of the range. By the end of Grade 12, read and comprehend literary nonfiction at the high end of the Grades 11–CCR text complexity band independently and proficiently.

American Reading Company Phonics References

Phonics Cards for Levels B, BB, R, and RR

The Phonics Cards were developed to highlight the phonics knowledge students need to master at the Blue and Red levels. Acquiring proficiency in letter-sound relationships is a critical task for students reading on first and second grade levels. These cards are designed to assist teachers as they conference with students, suggesting a logical sequence for phonics skill acquisition, and providing a tool to identify the sounds a student has mastered, as well as those he or she still needs to learn.

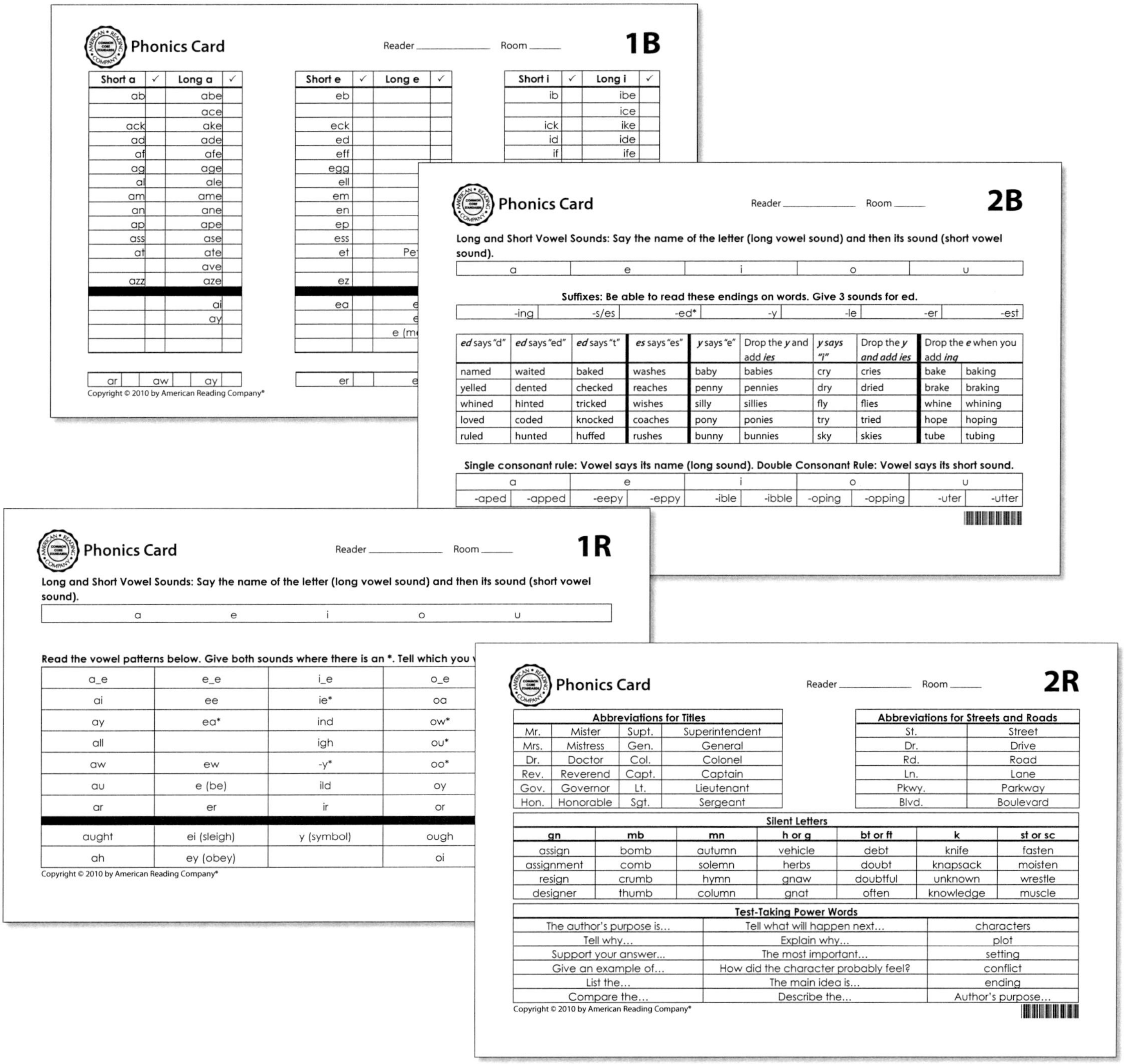

Phonics Card

Reader ______________ Room ________ **1B**

Short a	✓	Long a	✓
ab		abe	
		ace	
ack		ake	
ad		ade	
af		afe	
ag		age	
al		ale	
am		ame	
an		ane	
ap		ape	
ass		ase	
at		ate	
		ave	
azz		aze	
		ai	
		ay	

ar		aw		ay	

Short e	✓	Long e	✓
eb			
eck			
ed			
eff			
egg			
ell			
em			
en			
ep			
ess			
et		Pete	
ez			
ea		ea	
		ee	
		e (me)	

er		ew	

Short i	✓	Long i	✓
ib		ibe	
		ice	
ick		ike	
id		ide	
if		ife	
ig			
ill		ile	
im		ime	
in		ine	
ip		ipe	
iss		ise	
it		ite	
		ive	
izz		ize	
		ie	
		y (my)	
		ight	
		ild	

ir		ing	

1B

Short o	✓	Long o	✓
ob		obe	
ock			
		oke	
od		ode	
off			
og			
oll		ole	
om		ome	
on		one	
op		ope	
oss		ose	
ot		ote	
		ove*	
oz		oze	
		oa	
		ow (know)	
		old	

or		ouse	
ow (cow)		ook (book)	
ound		oy	
ould			

Short u	✓	Long u	✓
ub		ube	
uck		uce	
		uke	
ud		ude	
uff			
ug		uge	
ull		ule	
um		ume	
un		une	
up		upe	
uss		use	
ut		ute	
uzz			
		ui	
		ue	
ur			

Be able to use all of these beginnings			✓
br		bl	
cr		cl	
dr		fl	
fr		gl	
gr		pl	
pr		sl	
tr		sc	
sm		sk	
sn		sc	
sw		sp	
tw		st	
sh		th	
ch		wh	
y			
wr		kn	
qu		ph	

Be able to use all of these endings

-sh		-sk		-nk		-nch		-lf	
-th		-nd		-nt		-mp		-lk	
-st		-ng		-ch		-ft		-lp	

Phonics Card

Reader ____________ Room ________

2B

Long and Short Vowel Sounds: Say the name of the letter (long vowel sound) and then its sound (short vowel sound).

a	e	i	o	u

Suffixes: Be able to read these endings on words. Give 3 sounds for ed.

-ing	-s/es	-ed*	-y	-le	-er	-est

ed says "d"	*ed* says "ed"	*ed* says "t"	*es* says "es"	*y* says "e"	Drop the *y* and add *ies*	*y says "i"*	Drop the *y and add ies*	Drop the *e* when you add *ing*	
named	waited	baked	washes	baby	babies	cry	cries	bake	baking
yelled	dented	checked	reaches	penny	pennies	dry	dried	brake	braking
whined	hinted	tricked	wishes	silly	sillies	fly	flies	whine	whining
loved	coded	knocked	coaches	pony	ponies	try	tried	hope	hoping
ruled	hunted	huffed	rushes	bunny	bunnies	sky	skies	tube	tubing

Single consonant rule: Vowel says its name (long sound). Double Consonant Rule: Vowel says its short sound.

a		e		i		o		u	
-aped	-apped	-eepy	-eppy	-ible	-ibble	-oping	-opping	-uter	-utter

Homophone: Use each correctly in a sentence. **2B**

to too two	there their they're	it's its	be bee	deer dear	right write	no know	one won	four for	eight ate
knew new	no know	red read	blue blew	ant aunt	sent cent	here hear	hi high	by buy	which witch

Compound Words

someone	everything	football	afternoon	anything	breakfast
something	everyone	basketball	airplane	anybody	birthday
sometimes	everywhere	baseball	grandmother	hamburger	maybe

2-Syllable Words

Short vowel first	Long vowel first	Short vowel first	Long vowel first	Long and short vowels	
admit	April	magic	navy	raisin	glasses
expert	easy	lesson	pretend	teacher	sleepy
inside	icing	finish	pilot	title	hiking
Oscar	Oprah	gossip	frozen	model	sloppy
until	unit	sudden	rumor	human	ruler

R controlled	Soft c	Soft g	au	oy/oi	ou/ow
target	center	angel	August	enjoy	mountain
person	cellar	danger	autumn	royal	fountain
thirsty	circus	engine	author	destroy	power
order	decide	gentle	because	poison	allow

Phonics Card

Reader ____________ Room ______ **1R**

Long and Short Vowel Sounds: Say the name of the letter (long vowel sound) and then its sound (short vowel sound).

a	e	i	o	u

Read the vowel patterns below. Give both sounds where there is an *. Tell which you would try first.

a_e	e_e	i_e	o_e	u_e
ai	ee	ie*	oa	ui
ay	ea*	ind	ow*	ue
all		igh	ou*	
aw	ew	-y*	oo*	
au	e (be)	ild	oy	
ar	er	ir	or	ur
aught	ei (sleigh)	y (symbol)	ough	
ah	ey (obey)		oi	

Be able to use all of these beginnings. Give 2 possible sounds for c and g.			
shr-	spr-	kn-	c*-
thr-	spl-	gn-	g*-
scr-	squ-	wr-	gym
str-	sch-	ph-	dw-

Be able to use these suffixes.			**1R**
-er	-ly	-en	-est
lighter	lightly	lighten	lightest
brighter	brightly	brighten	brightest
tighter	tightly	tighten	tightest

Be able to use all of these suffixes.

-ing	-s/es	-ed	-y	-ly	-le	-er	-est	-iest	-ie

–y	–ier	–iest	–ly	–dge	–tch	–mb	–gh	
heavy	heavier	heaviest	heavily	edge	patch	numb	enough	high
easy	easier	easiest	easily	pledge	catcher	dumb	tough	thigh
lucky	luckier	luckiest	luckily	judge	pitcher	plumber	rough	sigh
busy	busier	busiest	busily	badgered	itchier	limb	cough	highway

Be able to read 3-Syllable Words

Try Long Vowel Sound First		Try Short Vowel Sound First		Try Different Sounds for the Vowels until You Recognize the Word	
Abraham	vacation	America	valentine	superman	different
electric	decided	example	several	principal	beginner
icicle	finally	important	history	bicycle	mystery
opener	potato	octopus	probably	triangle	bicycle
universe	Juniper	understand	underline	possible	Africa

Phonics Card

Reader ________________ Room ________ **2R**

Abbreviations for Titles			
Mr.	Mister	Supt.	Superintendent
Mrs.	Mistress	Gen.	General
Dr.	Doctor	Col.	Colonel
Rev.	Reverend	Capt.	Captain
Gov.	Governor	Lt.	Lieutenant
Hon.	Honorable	Sgt.	Sergeant

Abbreviations for Streets and Roads	
St.	Street
Dr.	Drive
Rd.	Road
Ln.	Lane
Pkwy.	Parkway
Blvd.	Boulevard

Silent Letters

gn	mb	mn	h or g	bt or ft	k	st or sc
assign	bomb	autumn	vehicle	debt	knife	fasten
assignment	comb	solemn	herbs	doubt	knapsack	moisten
resign	crumb	hymn	gnaw	doubtful	unknown	wrestle
designer	thumb	column	gnat	often	knowledge	muscle

Test-Taking Power Words

The author's purpose is…	Tell what will happen next…	characters
Tell why…	Explain why…	plot
Support your answer…	The most important…	setting
Give an example of…	How did the character probably feel?	conflict
List the…	The main idea is…	ending
Compare the…	Describe the…	Author's purpose…

2R Readers can figure out any word they know from everyday speech. **2R**

Be flexible with the vowel sounds. Try one. Try another. Work until you recognize the word.

i says *e*	*i* says *i*	Vowels split	soft *c*	*y* says *e*	*y* says *i*
radio	scientist	create	celebrate	celebrity	simplify
stadium	reminder	piano	certain	democracy	notify
experience	biography	museum	introduce	envy	apply
appreciate	divided	diagram	criticism	personality	identify
appreciation	excitement	graduate	medicine	nationality	multiply

Read these familiar proper nouns: people, places, and things.

Presidents	Continents	Countries	States	Football Teams
George Washington	Antarctica	United States of America	Pennsylvania	Philadelphia Eagles
John F. Kennedy	South America	Liberia	Indiana	Indianapolis Colts
Abraham Lincoln	Africa	Germany	Massachusetts	New England Patriots
Bill Clinton	Australia	Vietnam	Washington	Seattle Seahawks
Thomas Jefferson	Asia	Canada	Florida	Miami Dolphins

ch=k	si=sh	s=sh	t=tch	-able	-ate	ci=sh
schools	television	sure	future	dependable	separate	artificial
scholarship	decision	sugar	creature	breakable	fascinate	commercial
character	explosion	measure	fracture	predictable	exterminate	official
stomach	conclusion	treasure	nature	lovable	refrigerate	racial
headache	permission	pleasure	capture	acceptable	celebrate	appreciate

The Long and the Short of It—Vowel Word Family Practice

Learning the common spelling patterns, often called "word families," is one of the critical skills an emerging reader needs to master. Knowledge of these spelling patterns and syllable structures allows a child to quickly search the bank of known words in his or her head, looking for the pattern that will help unlock the new word. Children need to be able to add, remove, and substitute letters and word chunks smoothly and effortlessly, allowing them to use this process in a way that does not distract from the task of understanding text. Providing students with the word family practice they need to become proficient decoders is an important task for any teacher working with students who are reading on a primary level.

The following pages have been developed to assist teachers by providing as many useful words as possible to aid students who are learning vowel word families. The words are organized according to American Reading Company's color-coded leveling system in an effort to provide a logical sequence for learning and practice. The shaded words also appear as high-frequency sight words on our Skill Cards.

We are providing the lists in a form that can be reproduced in any fashion that works in your classroom. We hope you find the lists helpful.

Word Families

297	Short A	ab	ac/ack	act	ad	af/aft	ag	al	am/amp	
299	Short A	an	ance	anch	and	ang	ank	ant	ap	
301	Short A	ash	ask	asp	ast	ass	at	atch	ax	
303	Long A	ace	ade	age	ake	ale	ame	ane	ape	
305	Long A	are	ase	aste	ate	ave	aze			
307	Long A	aid	ail	ain	aint	air	aise	ait	ay	
309	Other Sounds A	alk	al/all	au/aught	aw	awl	awn	eigh		
311	R-Controlled A	ar	ard	ark	arm	arn	arp	art		
313	Short E	ec/eck	ed	edge	ef/eft	eg/egg	el/ell	elf/elp	elt	em
315	Short E	en	end	ent	ep	ex	es/ess	est	et	
317	Long E	ea	each	ead	eak	eal	eam	ean	eap	
319	Long E	ear	eas/east	eat						
321	Long E	ee	eed	eek	eel	een	eep	eer	eet	
323	Other E	ew	ea	ear	ei	ey				
323	R-Controlled E	er	ear							
325	Short I	ib	ic/ick	id/idge	iff	ift	ig	ilk	il/ill	
327	Short I	ilt	im	imp	in	inch/ince	ing	ink	int	
329	Short I	ip	ish	isk	is/iss	ist	it	itch	ix	
331	Long I	ibe	ice	ide	ie	ife	ike	ile	ime	
333	Long I	ine	ipe	ire	ise	ite	ive			
335	Long I	igh	ight	ild	ind	y				
337	R-Controlled I	ir	ird	irt						
339	Short O	ob	oc/ock	od	og	ol/oll	om			
341	Short O	on	op	os	ot	ox	ong			
343	Long O	obe	ode	oe	oke	ole	ome	one	ope	
345	Long O	ose	ote	ove						
347	Long O	oach	oad	oak	oal	oam	oan	oast	oat	
349	Long O	old	oll	olt	ost	ow	own			
351	Other O	oi	on	oo	ood	ood	oof	ook		
353	Other O	ool	oom	oon	oop	oose	oot	oss/ost		
355	Other O	oth	ouch	oud	ought	ould	oun	our		
357	Other O	ouse	out	ove	ow	owl	own	oy		
359	R-Controlled O	or/ord	ore	ork	orm	orn	ort/orth			
361	Short U	ub	uc/uck	ud	udge	uff	ug	um	umb	
363	Short U	ump	un	unch	ung	unc/unk	unt	up	us	
365	Short U	ush	ust	ut	utch	utt				
367	Long U	ube/upe	ue	ure	use	ute				
369	R-Controlled U	ur	url	urn	urse	urt/urth				

A—Short Vowel Word Families

Word Family	**ab**	**ac/ack**	**act**	**ad**	**af/aft**	**ag**	**al**	**am/amp**
Key Word	**cab**	**black**	**act**	**had**	**after**	**flag**	**pal**	**am**
YY								
G				had				am
GG		black		Dad				
B	cab	back	act	bad		flag	pal	ham
regular short vowel	cabs	Jack	acts	dad		flags	pals	jam
word families	jab	pack	fact	dads		gag	Al	Pam
initial consonant	jabs	packs	facts	fad		gags	gal	ram
blends/digraphs	lab	rack		fads		nag	gals	Sam
final consonant	labs	racks		mad		nags	Sal	clam
blends/digraphs	nab	sack		pad		rag		slam
word + *s*	nabs	sacks		pads		rags		swam
	blab	shack		sad		sag		lamp
	blabs	shacks		Tad		sags		lamps
	crab	smack		glad		wag		camp
	crabs	smacks		Brad		wags		damp
	grab	snack		add		brag		ramp
	grabs	snacks				brags		champ
	scab	stack				drag		cramp
	scabs	track				drags		stamp
		whack				snag		tramp
BB	jabbed	packed	acted	padded	after	gagged	Sally	camped
word endings (*-ing*, *-es*,	jabbing	packing	acting	padding	giraffe	gagging	rally	camping
-ed, *-y*, *-le*, *-er*, *-est*)	nabbed	packer	actor	address	staff	nagged	tally	camper
two-syllable words	grabbed	package	actress	radish	Daffy	nagging	valley	campfire
with regular vowels	grabbing	smacked	practice	saddle		lagged	alley	campsite
suffixes: *-ing*, *-ed*, *-y*,	grabby	snacking	tractor	paddle		wagging	gallon	slammed
-es, *-le*, *-er*, *-est*	stabbed	tackle	attract	madder		bragging	gallup	slamming
	stabbing	racket		sadder		dragging	Albert	stamped
	blabbing	jacket		madly		snagging	Alvin	stamping
	gabby	jackpot		badly		sagged	Allie	stamper
	crabby	backbone		gladly		saggy	Alice	scamper
	rabbit	backward		sadly		shaggy		rammed
	cabin	fullback		Adam		bragger		hammer
	absent	blackboard		Bradley		waggle		sample
		attack		Bradford		wagon		
R	Scrabble	Acme	factory	badge	craft	saggier	Alison	family
three-syllable words	crabbier		exactly	Madge	crafts	saggiest	allergy	hammering
three-letter blends	crabbiest		attractive		draft	shaggier	calorie	hamburger
suffixes: *-ly*, *-ier*, *-iest*					drafts	shaggiest	calendar	damaging
					afternoon		balance	camera
					afterwards		salary	example
RR	absolutely	stackable	actually	adventure	Africa	Snaggletooth	alligator	America
multisyllabic words	laboratory	bacteria	activity	advantage	cafeteria	magazine	alphabet	ambulance
from everyday speech	fabulous	acne	action	advertisement			Alabama	amphibian
irregular sounds	blabbermouth	accurate	fraction	gradual			alcohol	champion
prefixes: *un-*, *re-*, *mis-*	Jabberwocky	unpack	subtraction	graduation			calculator	familiar
suffixes: *-ful*, *-able*, *-tion*		restack		addition				restamp
Wt +	drab	lack	factor	adaptation	shaft	aggravate	algebra	ambassador
words not familiar	fabulously	cackle	activate	adjective	shafted	aggravation	aluminum	bamboo
from everyday speech	habitat	shackle	acceptance	admission	Afghanistan	magnify	Caldecott	campus
prefixes: *self-*, *over-*,	abstain	blacksmith	acrobatics	unadjustable	understaffed	agony	calcium	stampede
after-, *dis-*, *under-*, *non-*	fabric	acknowledge		disadvantage	overstaffed	agriculture	alcove	rampage
suffixes: *-ward*, *-ness*,	fabrication	unstackable				magnificent	galley	flammable
-ship, *-less*	absented					aggressive		amateur

A—Short Vowel Word Families

Word Family	an	ance	anch	and	ang	ank	ant	ap
Key Word	**can**	**dance**	**ranch**	**and**	**sang**	**thank**	**ant**	**cap**
YY								
G	an			and			can't	
	can							
GG	ran			grandfather	triangle			happy
				grandmother				
B	Dan		ranch	band	sang	thank	ant	cap
regular short vowel	fan		branch	bands	bang	bank	ants	caps
word families	fans			hand	bangs	banks	pant	gap
initial consonant	man			hands	fang	rank	pants	lap
blends/digraphs	pan			land	fangs	sank	chant	laps
final consonant	pans			lands	gang	tank	chants	nap
blends/digraphs	tan			sand	gangs	tanks	grant	naps
word + *s*	tans			sands	hang	yank	grants	rap
	van			brand	hangs	yanks	slant	raps
	vans			brands	rang	blank	slants	sap
	plan			stand	slang	blanks	plant	tap
	plans			stands	pang	drank	plants	taps
	than			grand	pangs	Frank		chap
	Stan					plank		clap
						planks		flap
						Hank		slap
						spank		snap
						spanks		trap
BB	fanned	dance	branched	handed	banging	banking	antler	napped
word endings (*-ing*, *-es*,	fanning	dances	branches	handing	banged	banker	antlers	napping
-ed, *-y*, *-le*, *-er*, *-est*)	Fanny	danced	branching	handy	banger	yanking	anthill	rapped
two-syllable words	tanned	dancing	ranches	handle	hanging	yanked	chanted	rapping
with regular vowels	tanning	dancer	rancher	landing	hanged	cranked	chanting	wrapper
suffixes: *-ing*, *-ed*, *-y*,	planned	chance	ranchers	landlord	hanger	cranky	granted	tapped
-es, *-le*, *-er*, *-est*	planning	chances		sandy	ganging	ranking	granting	tapping
	planner	glance		sandal	ganged	spanked	panted	slapped
	planets	glanced		sandwich	anger	thanking	panting	slapping
	Danny	glancing		banded	angry	thankful	planted	snapping
	pancake	fancy		Band-Aid	dangle	tanker	planter	Snapple
	panic	Nancy		Randy	jangle	ankle	planting	clapping
	panel	Clancy		branded	tangle	hankie	slanted	trapping
	channel			standing	angle	Frankie	slanting	happen
	answer				bangle	blanket		chapter
R	banana	France		strand	kangaroo	crankier	fantasy	happier
three-syllable words	manager	cancel		bandage	gangster	crankiest	constantly	happily
three-letter blends	fantastic	fancier		sandier	angrily	Thanksgiving	antenna	happening
suffixes: *-ly*, *-ier*, *-iest*	Canada	fanciest		sandiest			antelope	capital
								Rapunzel
RR	January	Lancelot	anchovy	dandelion	language	crankiness	replant	application
multisyllabic words	Anacin			handicapped		thankfulness	anniversary	appointment
from everyday speech	Daniel			handful		thankfully	cantaloupe	apostrophe
irregular sounds	Tyrannosaurus					Frankenstein		appropriate
prefixes: *un-*, *re-*, *mis-*	replan							capitalization
suffixes: *-ful*, *-able*, *-tion*								Captain Hook
Wt +	analyze	ancestor	branchless	standard	sprang	prank	anthology	capture
prefixes: *self-*, *over-*,	ransom	prance	blanch	expanded	spangled	prankster	lantern	rapidly
after-, *dis-*, *under-*, *non-*	transmit	trance	blanched	demand	gangplank	hankering	annual	trapeze
suffixes: *-ward*, *-ness*,	phantom	circumstance	blanching	grandstand	overhang	thankless	Antarctica	Japanese
-ship, *-less*	underplan	circumstances		bandana		anklet	antagonize	contraption

A—Short Vowel Word Families

Word Family	ash	ask	asp	ast	ass	at	atch	ax
Key Word	**cash**	**ask**	**grasp**	**fast**	**class**	**at**	**catch**	**ax**
YY								
G						at		
						that		
GG						Saturday		
B	cash	ask		fast	class	bat		ax
regular short vowel	bash	asks		cast	mass	bats		Max
word families	dash	mask		casts	pass	fat		tax
initial consonant	gash	masks		last	brass	hat		wax
blends/digraphs	mash	task		lasts	glass	hats		flax
final consonant	rash	tasks		past	grass	mat		axe
blends/digraphs	sash			blast		pat		
word + *s*	clash			blasts		rat		
	crash					rats		
	flash					sat		
	slash					brat		
	stash					brats		
	trash					chat		
						flat		
BB	dashes	asked	clasp	lasted	passed	batted	catch	taxed
word endings (*-ing*, *-es*,	dashed	asking	clasps	lasting	passing	batting	hatch	taxes
-ed, *-y*, *-le*, *-er*, *-est*)	dashing	asker	clasped	blasted	passes	batter	batch	taxi
two-syllable words	gashes	masked	clasping	blasting	passage	patted	match	waxed
with regular vowels	gashed	masking	gasp	faster	password	patting		waxing
suffixes: *-ing*, *-ed*, *-y*, *-es*,	crashes	basket	gasps	fastest	glasses	Patty		waxy
-le, *-er*, *-est*	crashed		gasped	nasty	glassy	pattern		waxes
	crashing		gasping	plastic	classy	matted		relax
	flashed		grasp	plaster	classroom	platter		Ex-lax
	flashing		grasps	castle	classmate	platform		
	flashy		grasped		grasses	chatted		
	flashlight		grasping		grassy	chatting		
	rashes					chatter		
	mashed					chatty		
	mashing					fatter		
	trashed					flatter		
	trashy					matter		
	trashcan					attic		
R	splash	basketball	aspirin	nastier	assembly	Atlantic	scratch	relaxing
three-syllable words	splashes	wastebasket	raspberry	nastiest	passenger	attended	scratching	taxi cab
three-letter blends	splasher			fantastic	assistant	attached	scratchy	
suffixes: *-ly*, *-ier*, *-iest*	flashier				grasshopper	battery	matched	
	flashiest				grassier	chattering	catcher	
RR	splashable	Nebraska	graspable	astronaut	casserole	natural	scratchier	galaxy
multisyllabic words		unmasked	asphalt		Massachusetts	catalog	scratchiest	saxophone
from everyday speech		askable			embarrass	category	scratchable	rewaxed
irregular sounds		Alaska			assignment	unattached	unscratched	unwaxed
prefixes: *un-*, *re-*, *mis-*					assigned	attachable	catchable	
suffixes: *-ful*, *-able*, *-tion*								
Wt +	brash	flask	aspirator	mast	ambassador	plateau	unscratchable	maximum
prefixes: *self-*, *over-*,	unsplashable	bask	aspect	vast	classify	atlas	uncatchable	maximize
after-, *dis-*, *under-*, *non-*	bashfully	basked	asp	pasture	massive	atmosphere		taxpayer
suffixes: *-ward*, *-ness*,			hasp	astronomy	assertive	flattery		axis
-ship, *-less*			ungraspable	astronomer	assassin	flattering		axle
				asteroid	assassinate			overtaxed

A—Long Vowel Word Families with Final *E*

Word Family	ace	ade	age	ake	ale	ame	ane	ape
Key Word	**ace**	**made**	**age**	**make**	**sale**	**came**	**plane**	**tape**
YY								
G								
GG				make		came		
				take				
B	face	made	age	bake	sale	name	plane	tape
regular long vowel word families	lace	fade	cage	bakes	sales	names	planes	tapes
initial consonant blends/digraphs	pace	fades	page	cake	bale	fame	cane	cape
final consonant blends/digraphs	race	wade	rage	cakes	bales	game	canes	capes
word + *s*	brace	wades	stage	fake	hale	games	Jane	drape
	grace	blade		Jake	male	lame	lane	drapes
	place	blades		lake	males	same	lanes	grape
	space	grade		rake	pale	tame	mane	grapes
	trace	grades		rakes	tale	tames	manes	shape
		shade		wake	tales	blame	pane	shapes
		shades		brake	scale	blames	panes	
		trade		brakes	scales	flame	crane	
		trades		shake	stale	flames	cranes	
				shakes	whale	frame		
				snake	whales	frames		
				stake		shame		
BB	faced	faded	caged	baked	whaling	named	airplane	taped
word endings (*-ing*, *-es*, *-ed*, *-y*, *-le*, *-er*, *-est*)	facing	fading	caging	baking	scaly	naming		taping
two-syllable words with regular vowels	faces	waded	cages	baker		blamed		draped
suffixes: *-ing*, *-ed*, *-y*, *-es*, *-le*, *-er*, *-est*	laced	wading	paged	faked		blaming		draping
	lacing	graded	paging	faking		framed		draper
	laces	grading	pages	raked		framing		shaped
	raced	grader	pager	raking		framer		shaping
	racing	shaded	staged	making		shamed		tapeworm
	races	shading	staging	taking		shaming		paper
	racer	shady	backstage	waking		tamed		
	placed	traded	stages	braking		taming		
	placing	trading	aged	shaking		tamer		
	pacing	trader	aging	shaky		nickname		
	traced			awake		became		
	tracing			cupcake				
R	gracefully	shadier	teenager	mistaken	tattletale	ashamed	windowpane	scrape
three-syllable words	bracelet	shadiest			fairytale			scraped
three-letter blends	lacier				female			scraping
suffixes: *-ly*, *-ier*, *-iest*	laciest							drapery
								paperback
								sandpaper
RR	disgraceful	invaded	courageous	shakeable		unnamed		unscraped
multisyllabic words from everyday speech	replacement	ungraded	uncaged	unbaked		untamed		unshaped
irregular sounds	traceable	unshaded		unraked		unashamed		reshaped
prefixes: *un-*, *re-*, *mis-*	untraceable	unfaded		rakeable				
suffixes: *-ful*, *-able*, *-tion*	replace	untraded						
	replaceable							
Wt +	faceless	arcade	rages	awaken	exhale	shamefully	humane	landscape
words not familiar from everyday speech	embrace	grenade	cagey	reawaken	nightingale	renamed	insane	capable
prefixes: *self-*, *over-*, *after-*, *dis-*, *under-*, *non-*	embraceable	barricade	wage	unshakeable	scalable	nameless	spontaneous	incapable
suffixes: *-ward*, *-ness*, *-ship*, *-less*	unembraceable	masquerade	enraged	underbaked	salable		deplaned	paperless
	graceless	selfmade	outrageous	undertaker				shapeless
			underage					skyscraper
			agent					

A—Long Vowel Word Families

Word Family	are	ase	aste	ate	ave	aze
Key Word	**care**	**case**	**paste**	**ate**	**gave**	**blaze**
YY						
G						
GG	square				gave	
B	care	case		ate	cave	
regular long vowel	cares	base		date	caves	
word families	bare	vase		dates	Dave	
initial consonant	dare	chase		fate	pave	
blends/digraphs	dares			gate	paves	
final consonant	fare			gates	rave	
blends/digraphs	fares			hate	raves	
word + *s*	mare			hates	save	
	mares			Kate	saves	
	rare			late	wave	
	scare			mate	waves	
	scares			rate	brave	
	share			rates	grave	
	shares			crate	graves	
	spare			plate	shave	
	stare			plates	shaves	
	stares			skate	slave	
				state	slaves	
BB	cared	based	paste	dated	caved	blaze
word endings (*-ing*, *-es*,	caring	basing	pasted	dating	caving	blazing
-ed, *-y*, *-le*, *-er*, *-est*)	careful	bases	pasting	dater	caveman	blazes
two-syllable words	dared	baseball	pastes	hated	paved	blazer
with regular vowels	daring	basement	paster	hater	paving	razor
suffixes: *-ing*, *-ed*, *-y*,	scared	chased	pasty	hating	pavement	
-es, *-le*, *-er*, *-est*	scary	chasing	waste	rated	saved	
	scarecrow	chases	wasted	rater	saving	
	shared	vases	wasting	rating	waved	
	sharing	laser	wastes	skated	waving	
	spared	staircase	waster	skating	shaved	
	stared	suitcase	taste	skater	shaving	
	staring		tasted	later	shaver	
	barefoot		tasting		bravest	
	compare		tasty		behave	
R	scarier	erase	tastier	lately	Lifesaver	amaze
three-syllable words	scariest	eraser	tastiest	create	microwave	amazed
three-letter blends	carefully	pillowcase	wastepaper	created	bravely	amazing
suffixes: *-ly*, *-ier*, *-iest*	parent		wastebasket	creating		
	prepare		toothpaste	operate		
RR	parenthood	chaseable	tasteful	creation	misbehave	
multisyllabic words	carelessly	erasable	wasteful	donated	slavery	
from everyday speech	uncaring	unreasonable		elevator	behavior	
irregular sounds				educate	shaveable	
prefixes: *un-*, *re-*, *mis-*				celebrate		
suffixes: *-ful*, *-able*, *-tion*				unrated		
Wt +	area	phrase	tastefully	debate	engrave	graze
prefixes: *self-*, *over-*,	glared	phase	baste	unevaluated	engraved	daze
after-, *dis-*, *under-*, *non-*	rarely	unphased	haste	overrated	engravable	maze
suffixes: *-ward*, *-ness*,	carelessness	baseless	hasten	underrated	crave	gazed
-ship, *-less*	aware			dedicate	haven	amazement

A—Other Vowel Sounds

Word Family	aid	ail	ain	aint	air	aise	ait	ay
Key Word	**paid**	**tail**	**rain**	**paint**	**hair**	**raise**	**wait**	**day**
YY								
G								
GG								day
								play
B	paid	tail	rain	paint	hair		wait	away
regular long vowel word families	laid	tails	rains	paints	air		waits	say
	maid	Gail	brain	faint	fair		bait	bay
initial consonant blends/digraphs	maids	bail	brains	faints	fairs		baits	gay
	raid	bails	chain	saint	pair			hay
final consonant blends/digraphs	raids	fail	chains	saints	pairs			jay
	braid	fails	drain		chair			lay
word + *s*	braids	hail	drains		chairs			may
		jail	gain		stair			pay
		jails	gains		stairs			ray
		mail	grain		Clair			rays
		mails	grains					way
		nail	main					ways
		nails	pain					clay
		pail	pains					gray
		rail	plain					pray
		sail	stain					stay
		snail	stains					sway
		snails	train					tray
		trail	trains					
		trails	vain					
BB	braided	failed	gained	fainted	aired	raise	baited	stayed
word endings (*-ing*, *-es*, *-ed*, *-y*, *-le*, *-er*, *-est*)	braiding	failing	gaining	fainting	airing	raises	baiting	staying
	braider	jailed	chained	fainter	airplane	raised	baiter	swayed
two-syllable words with regular vowels	raided	jailer	drained	painted	airbag	praise	waited	swaying
	raiding	mailed	draining	painting	airhead	praised	waiting	maybe
suffixes: *-ing*, *-ed*, *-y*, *-es*, *-le*, *-er*, *-est*	raider	mailing	drainer	painter	paired	praising	waiter	mayor
	mermaid	mailman	stained	dainty	pairing		waitress	prayer
		mailbox	staining		dairy		faith	crayon
		e-mail	trained		hairy			player
		nailed	trainer		hairdo			haystack
		railing	rainbow		staircase			hayride
		trailer	rainfall		repair			subway
		sailor	rainstorm					always
R		toenail	sprain		fairly		faithful	spray
three-syllable words			strainer		fairytale		faithfully	runaway
three-letter blends			remaining		repaired			yesterday
suffixes: *-ly*, *-ier*, *-iest*			explained		repairing			holiday
			complain		airliner			
RR	unpaid	unjailed	retrain	repaint	unfairly	unpraised	unfaithful	daydreamer
multisyllabic words from everyday speech	repaid	unmailed	untrained	unpainted		unraised	unfaithfully	expressway
irregular sounds	unbraided	remailed	painfully	paintable				bricklayer
prefixes: *un-*, *re-*, *mis-*	rebraided		Maine					respray
suffixes: *-ful*, *-able*, *-tion*			entertain					
			container					
Wt +	maiden	failure	slain	faintly	chairman	praiseworthy	strait	betray
prefixes: *self-*, *over-*, *after-*, *dis-*, *under-*, *non-*	staid	tailor	Spain	acquainted	despair		faithfulness	repayment
	bridesmaid	wail	Novocain	acquaintance	prairie		straitjacket	dismay
suffixes: *-ward*, *-ness*, *-ship*, *-less*		Braille	obtain	maintain	fairness		traitor	overstay
		detail	explainable	paintless	hairless			

A—Other Vowel Sounds

Word Family	**alk**	**al/all**	**au/aught**	**aw**	**awl**	**awn**	**eigh**
Key Word	**walk**	**all**	**because**	**saw**	**crawl**	**lawn**	**eight**
YY							
G		all					
GG				saw			eight
B	walk	ball	because	jaw		lawn	
word families based on common sight words	talk	call	caught	jaws		fawn	
	chalk	fall		law		yawn	
initial consonant blends/digraphs		hall		laws		fawns	
		mall		paw		yawns	
final consonant blends/digraphs		tall		paws			
		wall		raw			
word + *s*		small		claw			
		balls		claws			
		calls		draw			
		falls		draws			
		halls		straw			
		malls		straws			
		walls		hawk			
				hawks			
BB	talked	called	August	pawed	crawl	yawned	
word endings (*-ing*, *-es*,	talking	calling	author	pawing	crawled	yawning	
-ed, *-y*, *-le*, *-er*, *-est*)	talker	caller	autumn	clawed	crawling	yawner	
two-syllable words	walked	falling		clawing	crawler	awning	
with regular vowels	walking	taller		drawing		drawn	
suffixes: *-ing*, *-ed*, *-y*,	walker	tallest		awful			
-es, *-le*, *-er*, *-est*	sidewalk	smaller		lawyer			
	chalked	smallest		lawyers			
	chalking	hallway		seesaw			
	chalky	always		seesaws			
	chalkboard	also					
		already					
		almost					
		walnut					
		install					
R	sleepwalker		taught	strawberry		lawnmower	neighbor
three-syllable words	beanstalk		daughter	awfully			sleigh
three-letter blends			causes	drawstring			weigh
suffixes: *-ly*, *-ier*, *-iest*			caused				weight
			naughty				freight
							neighborly
RR	Alka-Seltzer	normally	untaught	lawful			
multisyllabic words		gradually	retaught	redraw			
from everyday speech		altogether	granddaughter				
irregular sounds		recall	Australia				
prefixes: *un-*, *re-*, *mis-*			audience				
suffixes: *-ful*, *-able*, *-tion*			auditorium				
Wt +	stalk	reinstall	naughtiness	gawk	shawl	dawn	weightless
words not familiar	stalking	wallop	slaughter	awkward	scrawl	dawning	
from everyday speech	stalked	allspice		rawhide	sprawl	scrawny	
prefixes: *self-*, *over-*,	baled	all-purpose		flaw	sprawled	withdrawn	
after-, *dis-*, *under-*, *non-*	alkaline	all-in		flawless	bawl		
suffixes: *-ward*, *-ness*,		all-fired					
-ship, *-less*		all fours					

A—with R

Word Family	ar	ard	ark	arm	arn	arp	art
Key Word	**car**	**card**	**park**	**farm**	**barn**	**sharp**	**part**
YY							
G	are						
GG							
B	car	card	park	farm	barn	sharp	part
regular *ar* word families	cars	cards	parks	farms	barns	harp	parts
initial consonant blends/digraphs	bar	hard	dark	arm	darn	harps	cart
final consonant blends/digraphs	bars	yard	mark	arms	yarn		carts
word + *s*	far	yards	marks	harm	yarns		chart
	jar		shark	harms			charts
	jars		sharks	charm			dart
	scar		spark	charms			darts
	scars		sparks				smart
	star		Mark				start
	stars		Clark				starts
	tar						Bart
	tars						
BB	scarred	harder	marked	armed	Arnie	sharper	darted
word endings (*-ing*, *-es*, *-ed*, *-y*, *-le*, *-er*, *-est*)	scarring	hardest	marking	army	Marnie	sharpest	darting
two-syllable words with regular vowels	starred	yardstick	marker	armchair	Barney	sharpen	parted
suffixes: *-ing*, *-ed*, *-y*, *-es*, *-le*, *-er*, *-est*	starring	backyard	market	armrest	barnyard	carpet	parting
	starry	guard	sparked	harmed	Arnold		partner
	March	guarded	sparking	harming			started
	barber	guarding	sparkle	charmed			starting
	Barbie	guards	Sparky	charming			starter
	darling	lifeguard	darker	charmer			Starbucks
	marble		parked	farmed			smarter
	Margo		parking	farming			smarty
	garlic		ballpark	farmer			charter
	arctic		barked	Marmie			farther
	charcoal		barking	alarm			artist
R	large	hardly	darkness	Armstrong	Arnoldson	carpenter	artery
three-syllable words	garage		darken			sharply	apartment
three-letter blends	charge		sparkler			sharpener	cartwheel
suffixes: *-ly*, *-ier*, *-iest*	charger		birthmark			sharpening	cartwheels
							artistic
RR	chargeable	cardboard	Arkansas	pharmacy	carnival	unsharpened	unartistic
multisyllabic words from everyday speech	recharge	unguarded	darkened	armful		resharpened	artful
irregular sounds	marvelous		darkening				artificial
prefixes: *un-*, *re-*, *mis-*	margarine		unparked				
suffixes: *-ful*, *-able*, *-tion*			reparked				
Wt +	harvest	coward	lark	armor	darned	carp	particle
words not familiar from everyday speech	cargo	cowardly	quark	alarming	darning	tarp	particular
prefixes: *self-*, *over-*, *after-*, *dis-*, *under-*, *non-*	arcade	hardy		harmless	carnivore	tarps	particularly
suffixes: *-ward*, *-ness*, *-ship*, *-less*	barter	shard		pharmacology	carnivores	harpist	startle
	varnish	hardship		pharmacist	carnage	carpentry	departure
	arson	disregard		disarm			cartilage
	starch	discard		armless			uncharted
	article	cardinal					barter
	architect						artistry

E—Short Vowel Word Families

Word Family	ec/eck	ed	edge	ef/eft	eg/egg	el/ell	elf/elp	elt	em
Key Word	**neck**	**red**	**edge**	**left**	**beg**	**tell**	**help**	**belt**	**them**
YY									
G									
GG		red							
B	neck	bed			beg	tell	help	belt	them
regular short vowel word families	necks	beds			begs	tells	helps	belts	gem
initial consonant blends/digraphs	deck	fed			leg	bell	yelp	felt	gems
final consonant blends/digraphs	decks	led			legs	bells	yelps	melt	hem
word + *s*	peck	Ned			Meg	cell	self	melts	hems
	pecks	red			peg	cells	shelf	knelt	stem
	check	Ted			pegs	fell	elf		stems
	checks	wed				sell			
	speck	weds				well			
	specks	bled				yell			
	wreck	fled				yells			
	wrecks	Fred				shell			
		shed				smell			
		sled				spell			
		sleds				swell			
		sped				Nell			
BB	pecked	wedded		left	begged	selling	helped	belted	hemmed
word endings (*-ing*, *-es*, *-ed*, *-y*, *-le*, *-er*, *-est*)	pecking	wedding		lefty	begging	spelled	helping	beltway	hemming
two-syllable words with regular vowels	checked	shedding		theft	beggar	spelling	helper	seatbelt	empty
suffixes: *-ing*, *-ed*, *-y*, *-es*, *-le*, *-er*, *-est*	checking	sledding		thefts	pegged	speller	yelped	melted	temper
	checker	bobsled		effort	Peggy	smelled	yelping	melting	memo
	checklist	bedroom		leftovers	leggings	smelling		shelter	
	paycheck	pedal			leggy	smelly			
	spellcheck	edit			eggplant	belly			
	wrecked	credit			egghead	jelly			
	wrecking	Cedric			egg role	yelled			
	wrecker	Edna			eggshell	shelled			
	necktie	Edward				swelling			
	necklace	Eddie				yellow			
	freckle	Neddie				dwelling			
	hectic	Freddie							
R	electric	shred	edge		regular	elephant			lemonade
three-syllable words		shredded	edged			relative			memorize
three-letter blends		Frederick				cellphone			remember
suffixes: *-ly*, *-ier*, *-iest*		editing				melody			memory
		editor							poem
									September
RR	electricity	education	sledgehammer	leftover		elementary	helpful		chemical
multisyllabic words from everyday speech	electrical	educate		Jefferson		Delaware	unhelpful		temperature
irregular sounds	checkable	medical		referee		television			
prefixes: *un-*, *re-*, *mis-*	uncheckable	medicine		refereed		helicopter			
suffixes: *-ful*, *-able*, *-tion*						elevator			
Wt +	gecko	federal	knowledge	hefty	nutmeg	mellow	helpless	meltdown	demonstrate
words not familiar from everyday speech	reckless	pedestrian	acknowledge	reference	segregation	cellophane	helplessly	sweltering	trembled
prefixes: *self-*, *over-*, *after-*, *dis-*, *under-*, *non-*	recklessly	editorial	hedges	effective	regulate	elegant	self-help	pelt	democracy
suffixes: *-ward*, *-ness*, *-ship*, *-less*	heckler	edition	hedgerow	efficient	overregulate	cellular	elflike	beltless	membrane
	speckled	reeducate	fledgling	effortlessly	segment				hemisphere
	electrician	dedicate	pledge	effigy	irregular				emptiness
	electrify	dedication	wedge		negative				emperor
					regulations				

E—Short Vowel Word Families

Word Family	en	end	ent	ep	ex	es/ess	est	et
Key Word	**ten**	**end**	**went**	**step**	**exit**	**yes**	**best**	**get**
YY								
G			went					get
GG	ten					yes		
	then							
	when							
B	tens	end	bent	step	flex	mess	best	bet
regular short vowel word families	Ben	ends	dent	steps	Rex	less	nest	jet
	den	bend	dents	pep	hex	bless	nests	jets
initial consonant blends/digraphs	dens	bends	lent	kept		chess	pest	let
	hen	lend	rent	crept		dress	pests	lets
final consonant blends/digraphs	hens	lends	rents	slept		press	rest	met
	Ken	mend	sent	swept		Bess	rests	net
word + *s*	men	mends	tent	prep			test	nets
	pen	send	tents				tests	set
	pens	sends	vent				vest	wet
	open	tend	vents				vests	yet
		blend	scent				west	gets
		spend	scents				chest	Mets
		spends	spent				chests	Brett
BB	tender	ended	dented	stepped	exit	dressed	rested	better
word endings (*-ing*, *-es*, *-ed*, *-y*, *-le*, *-er*, *-est*)	tennis	ending	denting	stepping	sexy	dressing	resting	betting
	kennel	bended	dentist	pepper	flexed	dresses	tested	Betty
two-syllable words with regular vowels	fence	bending	rented	peppy	text	dresser	testing	setting
	French	mended	renting	preppy	extra	dressy	tester	settle
suffixes: *-ing*, *-ed*, *-y*, *-es*, *-le*, *-er*, *-est*	bench	mending	renter	reptile	excuse	pressed	nesting	netting
	wrench	tended	center	doorstep	Exxon	presses	pester	netted
	sentence	tending	scented			blessed	question	wetting
	enjoy	tender	enter			blessing	presto	wetter
	engine	blended	entry			messes	biggest	petting
	even	blending	plenty			messy	bravest	petal
	oven	blender	twenty			message	darkest	letter
	fasten	lending	gently			lesson	honest	metal
	token	lender	gentle			essay		basket
		sending	sentence			question		bonnet
		spending	event			unless		carpet
		spender	absent			confess		planet
		friend	prevent					puppet
R	energy	calendar	invented	accept	exactly	messenger	questioning	ketchup
three-syllable words	entire	pretended	gentleman	accepted	example	stress	questioner	lettering
three-letter blends	general	suspended	entrance	except	except	stressful	wrestler	sketch
suffixes: *-ly*, *-ier*, *-iest*	quench	suspender	recently	overslept	expected	dressier	pestering	
	quenched		argument	stepmother	expensive	dressiest	honestly	
	evenly			September	explained			
RR	environment	bendable	president	peppermint	excitement	successful	digestion	violet
multisyllabic words from everyday speech	engagement	suspendable	accident	acceptable	exaggerate	successfully	restaurant	forgetful
irregular sounds	Tennessee	mendable	unscented	unacceptable	excellent	unsuccessful	estimate	
prefixes: *un-*, *re-*, *mis-*	Kentucky	surrender	rentable		examine	unsuccessfully		
suffixes: *-ful*, *-able*, *-tion*	Pennsylvania	dependable	preventable		examination			
	reenter	attendance			reexamined			
Wt +	generally	endanger	element	exception	flexible	accessory	investment	settlers
prefixes: *self-*, *over-*, *after-*, *dis-*, *under-*, *non-*	drench	endlessly	garment	reception	hexagon	professor	festival	etch
	genre	horrendous	centimeter	wept	exclaim	overdressed	siesta	wretch
suffixes: *-ward*, *-ness*, *-ship*, *-less*	envy	trend	century	represent	exhibit	underdressed	testify	metaphor
	wren	intended	gentleness		exception	overstressed	western	petrified

E—Long Vowel Word Families

Word Family	ea	each	ead	eak	eal	eam	ean	eap
Key Word	**eat**	**teach**	**read**	**beak**	**real**	**dream**	**clean**	**leap**
YY								
G								
GG	eat							
B	tea	teach	read	beak	real	dream	clean	leap
regular long vowel word families	pea	beach	reads	beaks	deal	dreams	cleans	leaps
initial consonant blends/digraphs	peas	peach	bead	leak	deals	beam	bean	cheap
final consonant blends/digraphs	sea	reach	beads	leaks	heal	beams	beans	heap
word + *s*	flea	bleach	lead	peak	heals	seam	Jean	heaps
	fleas	preach	leads	peaks	meal	seams	jeans	
	leave		plead	weak	meals	cream	lean	
	leaf		pleads	creak	peal	gleam	leans	
	plea			creaks	peals	gleams	mean	
				freak	seal	steam	means	
				freaks	seals	steams		
				sneak	steal	team		
				sneaks	steals	teams		
				speak				
				speaks				
BB	eagle	teacher	reading	leaked	healed	beamed	cleaned	leaping
word endings (*-ing, -es, -ed, -y, -le, -er, -est*)	eagles	teaches	reader	leaking	healing	beaming	cleaning	leapfrog
two-syllable words with regular vowels	beagle	teaching	leading	leaky	healer	dreamed	cleaner	cheaper
suffixes: *-ing, -ed, -y, -es, -le, -er, -est*	beagles	preacher	leader	creaked	pealed	dreaming	leaned	
	beaver	preaches	beaded	creaking	pealing	dreamer	leaning	
	beavers	preaching	beading	creaky	sealed	dreamy	leaner	
	easel	preached	pleading	freaked	sealing	daydream	meaning	
	peace	bleacher		freaking	dealing	steamed	meaner	
	peacock	bleaching		speaking	dealer	steamy	meantime	
	greasy	bleached		speaker	stealing	gleamed	beanbag	
	measles	peaches		sneaking	really	creamy	jellybean	
	weave	peachy		sneaker	oatmeal	creampuff	peanut	
	weaver	beaches		sneakers		teamwork	peanuts	
		beached		sneaky		teammate		
		reaches		weaker				
		reached		weakest				
		reaching						
R	greasier		cheerleader	streak	squeal	scream	beanstalk	cheaply
three-syllable words	greasiest			streaked	squealer	screaming	meanly	
three-letter blends				squeak	squealing	stream	cleanly	
suffixes: *-ly, -ier, -iest*				squeaky		streamers		
				weakly				
RR	beautiful	reachable	unbeaded	sneakiness			cleanable	
multisyllabic words from everyday speech	beautifully	unreachable	reread	weakness				
irregular sounds	peaceful	teachable	readable	unstreaked				
prefixes: *un-, re-, mis-*	peacefully	unteachable						
suffixes: *-ful, -able, -tion*	unpeaceful	reteach						
Wt +	league	beachcomber	beady	bleak	conceal	gleaming	meaningful	cheapskate
words not familiar from everyday speech	increase	impeach	mislead	teak	ordeal	dreamless		reap
prefixes: *self-, over-, after-, dis-, under-, non-*	cease	teacherless	pleaded	unspeakable	realistic			
suffixes: *-ward, -ness, -ship, -less*		overteach	leaderless		realize			
					realized			

E—Long Vowel Word Families

Word Family	ear	eas/east	eat
Key Word	**dear**	**beast**	**eat**
YY			
G			
GG			
B regular long vowel word families initial consonant blends/digraphs final consonant blends/digraphs word + *s*	dear		eat
	ear		eats
	ears		beat
	fear		beats
	gear		heat
	hear		heats
	hears		meat
	near		neat
	rear		seat
	tear		seats
	year		cheat
	years		cheats
	clear		pleat
	smear		pleats
	smears		treat
	spear		treats
	spears		wheat
BB word endings (*-ing*, *-es*, *-ed*, *-y*, *-le*, *-er*, *-est*) two-syllable words with regular vowels suffixes: *-ing*, *-ed*, *-y*, *-es*, *-le*, *-er*, *-est*	feared	easy	eating
	fearing	Easter	eater
	cleared		heating
	clearing		heated
	clearer		heater
	clearest		seating
	smeared		seated
	smearing		cheating
	speared		cheated
	hearing		cheater
	earring		beating
	earmuff		beater
	nearer		pleated
	appear		treating
			neater
			neatest
R three-syllable words three-letter blends suffixes: *-ly*, *-ier*, *-iest*	disappear	beast	repeating
	clearly	feast	repeater
	nearly	least	repeated
			neatly
RR multisyllabic words from everyday speech irregular sounds prefixes: *un-*, *re-*, *mis-* suffixes: *-ful*, *-able*, *-tion*	appearance	easily	anteater
	unsmeared	uneasy	mistreat
	tearful		beatable
	fearful		unseated
			unheated
			repeatable
Wt + words not familiar from everyday speech prefixes: *self-*, *over-*, *after-*, *dis-*, *under-*, *non-* suffixes: *-ward*, *-ness*, *-ship*, *-less*	fearfully	east	features
	fearless	eastward	unbeatable
	fearlessly	eastern	unrepeatable
	bleary	queasy	peatmoss
	tearstained	beastly	neatnick
	yearly	increase	
		decrease	

E—Long Vowel Word Families

Word Family	**ee**	**eed**	**eek**	**eel**	**een**	**eep**	**eer**	**eet**
Key Word	**see**	**need**	**week**	**feel**	**green**	**keep**	**deer**	**feet**
YY								
G	see							
GG	three				green			
B	sees	feed	week	feel	seen	keep	deer	feet
regular short vowel	bee	feeds	weeks	feels	teen	beep	sneer	beet
word families	bees	seed	peek	heel	teens	keeps	sneers	beets
initial consonant	seed	seeds	peeks	heels	queen	deep	steer	meet
blends/digraphs	seen	weed	seek	peel	queens	Jeep	steers	meets
final consonant	sheep	weeds	seeks	peels		peep		greet
blends/digraphs	sleep	bleed	cheek	steel		peeps		greets
word + *s*	tree	bleeds	cheeks	wheel		weep		sheet
	trees	breed	creek	wheels		weeps		sheets
	breeze	breeds	creeks	kneel		cheep		sleet
	cheese	freed		kneels		creep		sleets
	deep	greed				creeps		sweet
	free	needs				sheep		sweets
	freeze					sleep		tweet
	meet					sleeps		
	freed					steep		
	knee					sweep		
						sweeps		
BB	kneed	needy	peeked	wheeled	between	sleeping	sneered	greeted
word endings (*-ing*, *-es*,	kneecap	needed	peeking	wheeling	fifteen	sleeper	sneering	greeting
-ed, *-y*, *-le*, *-er*, *-est*)	seeing	needing	peeker	wheeler	teeny	sleepy	steered	greeter
two-syllable words	agree	needle		pinwheel	greener	keeping	steering	sweeter
with regular vowels	coffee	weeded		two-wheeler	greenest	keeper	career	meeting
suffixes: *-ing*, *-ed*, *-y*,	degree	weeding		feeling	greenhouse	deeper		sleeting
-es, *-le*, *-er*, *-est*	Frisbee	weeder		feeler		beeper		beetle
	teepee	feeding		feelers		beeping		cheetah
	treetops	feeder		Steelers		peeping		
	breezes	bleeding		peeling		weeping		
	cheezes	speeding		peeled		sweeping		
	sneezes	speedy				sweeper		
	freezes	greedy				creeping		
		agreed				creepy		
						sheepdog		
R	screech	succeed	weekly	cartwheel	screen	deeply	Cheerios	street
three-syllable words	screeched			wheelchair	teenager	deepest	reindeer	sweeten
three-letter blends	freely				sunscreen	sleepover		sweetly
suffixes: *-ly*, *-ier*, *-iest*	bumblebee				teenier	sleepiest		
	chimpanzee				teeniest	sleepier		
RR	agreeable	greedier				housekeeper	volunteer	parakeet
multisyllabic words	agreement	guaranteed					cheerfully	sweetheart
from everyday speech	dungarees							unsweetened
irregular sounds	referee							
prefixes: *un-*, *re-*, *mis-*								
suffixes: *-ful*, *-able*, *-tion*								
Wt +	Greece	proceed	Greek	eel	canteen	innkeeper	engineer	fleet
words not familiar	glee	seedling	sleek	wheelbarrow	queenly	sleepiness	peer	fleeting
from everyday speech	jamboree	feedback	cheeky	reel	teensy	sleepless	peering	sweetener
prefixes: *self-*, *over-*,	disagreement	speedometer			velveteen	oversleep	cheerily	
after-, *dis-*, *under-*, *non-*					spleen		pioneer	
suffixes: *-ward*, *-ness*,					sheen			
-ship, *-less*								

E—Other Sounds

Word Family	ew	ea	ear	ei	ey
Key Word	new	read	bear	eight	grey
YY					
G					
GG	new			eight	grey
					they
B regular word families based on common sight words initial consonant blends/digraphs final consonant blends/digraphs word + *s*	dew	read	bear		hey
	few	dead	bears		
	pew	lead	pear		
	grew	bread	pears		
	blew	breads	wear		
	chew	head	wears		
	drew	heads			
	flew				
	knew				
	stew				
	stews				
	hews				
BB word endings (*-ing*, *-es*, *-ed*, *-y*, *-le*, *-er*, *-est*) two-syllable words with regular vowels suffixes: *-ing*, *-ed*, *-y*, *-es*, *-le*, *-er*, *-est*	fewer	heading	tear		obey
	chewy	headed	tearing		
	chewing	ahead	swear		
	chewed	heavy	swearing		
	Jewish	ready	swears		
	nephew	already	wearing		
		weather	wearer		
		feather	bearhugs		
		sweat	bearlike		
		breakfast	bearskin		
		instead	footwear		
			tearaway		
R three-syllable words three-letter blends suffixes: *-ly*, *-ier*, *-iest*	screw	spread	outerwear	eighteen	
	newspaper	thread		reins	
		bedspread		reindeer	
		gingerbread		vein	
		heaven		veins	
				sleigh	
RR multisyllabic words from everyday speech irregular sounds prefixes: *un-*, *re-*, *mis-* suffixes: *-ful*, *-able*, *-tion*	unscrew	dreadlocks	bearable		
	screwdriver	pleasant	bearably		
	renew	pleasure	unbearable		
		measure	wearable		
		measurable	unwearable		
		rethread	rewearable		
Wt + words not familiar from everyday speech prefixes: *self-*, *over-*, *after-*, *dis-*, *under-*, *non-* suffixes: *-ward*, *-ness*, *-ship*, *-less*	brew	dread	overbearing		survey
	shrew	dreading	forebearer		prey
	shrewd	pheasant			
	renewable	peasant			
		widespread			
		meadow			
		deaden			

E—with R

Word Family	er	ear
Key Word	her	learn
YY		
G		
GG	over	
	her	
B regular *er* word families initial consonant blends/digraphs final consonant blends/digraphs word + *s*	hers	
	germ	
	germs	
	term	
	fern	
	ferns	
	clerk	
	jerk	
	herd	
BB word endings (*-ing*, *-es*, *-ed*, *-y*, *-le*, *-er*, *-est*) two-syllable words with regular vowels suffixes: *-ing*, *-ed*, *-y*, *-es*, *-le*, *-er*, *-est*	jerked	earn
	jerky	earns
	jersey	earning
	nerve	earned
	serve	learn
	serving	learns
	server	learning
	sermon	learned
	swerve	pearl
	swerved	pearls
	swerving	
	verse	
	person	
	perhaps	
	mermaid	
	answer	
	winner	
R three-syllable words three-letter blends suffixes: *-ly*, *-ier*, *-iest*	terrible	earth
	personal	search
	bakery	searched
	interest	searching
	wonderful	
	gerbil	
RR multisyllabic words from everyday speech irregular sounds prefixes: *un-*, *re-*, *mis-* suffixes: *-ful*, *-able*, *-tion*	certain	relearn
	certainly	rehearse
	performance	unearth
	perspiration	
	nervous	
	New Jersey	
Wt + words not familiar from everyday speech prefixes: *self-*, *over-*, *after-*, *dis-*, *under-*, *non-* suffixes: *-ward*, *-ness*, *-ship*, *-less*	sternly	yearn
	heritage	earnest
	persuasive	
	percent	
	verbal	
	errand	
	error	
	terror	

I—Short Vowel Word Families

Word Family	ib	ic/ick	id/idge	iff	ift	ig	ilk	il/ill
Key Word	**rib**	**sick**	**did**	**sniff**	**if**	**big**	**milk**	**will**
YY								
G						big		will
GG			did		if			
B	rib	pick	hid		gift	pig	milk	dill
regular short vowel	ribs	kick	kid		gifts	pigs	milks	fill
word families	bib	lick	kids		lift	dig	silk	gill
initial consonant	bibs	Nick	lid		lifts	digs	silks	hill
blends/digraphs	fib	Rick	lids		sift	fig		ill
final consonant	fibs	sick	rid		sifts	figs		kill
blends/digraphs	crib	tick	rids		drift	rig		pill
word + *s*	cribs	brick	skid		drifts	rigs		till
		chick	skids		shift	wig		chill
		flick	slid		shifts	wigs		drill
		quick				twig		grill
		slick				twigs		skill
		stick						skills
		thick						spill
		trick						spills
BB	fibbed	kicked	kidded	sniff	lifted	digging	milked	filled
word endings (*-ing*, *-es*,	fibbing	kicking	kidding	sniffs	lifting	digger	milking	filling
-ed, *-y*, *-le*, *-er*, *-est*)	fibber	picked	skidded	sniffed	lifter	trigger	milky	killed
two-syllable words	nibble	picking	skidding	sniffing	sifted	bigger	milkman	killer
with regular vowels	nibbled	picky	hidden	sniffle	sifting	biggest	milkshake	chilled
suffixes: *-ing*, *-ed*, *-y*,	nibbler	licked	middle	cliff	sifter	giggle	milkmaid	chilling
-es, *-le*, *-er*, *-est*	dribble	licking	midnight	cliffs	drifted	giggling	silky	chilly
	dribbled	ticked	width	jiffy	drifting	giggler	silkworm	drilled
	dribbling	ticking	kidnap		drifter	giggled		drilling
	ribbon	sticking	stupid		shifted	wiggle		grilled
	ribbit	sticky			shifting	wiggling		skilled
		quicker			shifty	wiggler		spilled
		quickest			fifty	wiggled		willing
		thickest			fifteen	wiggly		hillside
		Knicks			snowdrift	piggy		skillet
		nickel			forklift	ignore		pillow
		Mickey Mouse				signal		silver
		picture				zigzag		children
R	scribble	chickenpox	kidnapper	different		figure	buttermilk	thrill
three-syllable words	scribbler	quickly	midget	difficult			milkier	gorilla
three-letter blends	scribbling	strict	kidney	sheriff			milkiest	
suffixes: *-ly*, *-ier*, *-iest*		stricter	stupider	sniffling			silkier	
		strictest	stupidest	stiffly			silkiest	
		sickly	stupidly					
RR	contribute	bricklayer	video	difficulty	shoplifting	dignity		caterpillar
from everyday speech	undid	Nickelodeon	undid			cigarette		vanilla
irregular sounds	redid	dictionary				signature		spillable
prefixes: *un-*, *re-*, *mis-*		fiction						illness
suffixes: *-ful*, *-able*, *-tion*								million
Wt +	sibling	panicky	giddy	difference	swift	gigabyte	milkweed	billow
prefixes: *self-*, *over-*,	squib	flickering	humid	cliffhanger	driftwood	swig	milkless	illustrator
after-, *dis-*, *under-*, *non-*	tribute	picket	riddance	stiffness	shiftless	sprig	ilk	village
suffixes: *-ward*, *-ness*,		thicket	midship	skiff	thifty	undignified	bilk	millennium
-ship, *-less*		wickedness	widow		nifty	significant		lily
		ticklishness				significantly		military
								illegal

I—Short Vowel Word Families

Word Family	ilt	im	imp	in	inch/ince	ing	ink	int
Key Word	**quilt**	**him**	**chimp**	**in**	**inch**	**sing**	**pink**	**print**
YY								
G				in				
GG		him		into			pink	
B	quilt	Jim	chimp	fin	inch	ring	think	print
regular short vowel word families	quilts	Kim	chimps	fins	pinch	rings	thinks	prints
	tilt	Tim	limp	kin	clinch	bring	link	lint
initial consonant blends/digraphs	tilts	rim	limps	sin	cinch	brings	links	lints
	wilt	rims	skimp	sins	finch	king	mink	hint
final consonant blends/digraphs	wilts	brim	skimps	tin		kings	minks	hints
	stilt	brims	blimp	win		sing	rink	mint
word + *s*	stilts	grim	blimps	wins		sings	rinks	mints
		slim		chin		wing	sink	tint
		swim		gin		wings	wink	tints
		swims		grin		cling	winks	
		dim		grins		clings	blink	
		dims		shin		sling	blinks	
		trim		skin		sting	drink	
		trims		spin		stings	stink	
				thin		swing	stinks	
				twin		thing		
BB	tilted	rimmed	limped	grinned	inches	bringing	linked	hinted
word endings (*-ing*, *-es*,	titling	brimmed	limping	grinning	inched	ringing	linking	hinting
-ed, *-y*, *-le*, *-er*, *-est*)	wilted	brimming	skimped	skinned	inching	singing	winked	tinted
two-syllable words	wilting	trimmed	skimping	skinning	pinches	singer	winking	tinting
with regular vowels	quilting	trimming	skimpy	skinny	pinched	clinging	blinked	printed
suffixes: *-ing*, *-ed*, *-y*,	quilted	slimmer	pimple	winning	pinching	clingy	blinking	printing
-es, *-le*, *-er*, *-est*	quilter	slimming	dimple	winner	clinches	slinging	blinker	printer
	guilt	swimmer	simple	spinner	clinched	stinging	sinking	
	guilted	swimming	simpler	thinner	clinching	stingy	sinker	
	guilty	Timmy	simplest	thinnest	flinches	stinger	drinking	
		himself		princess	flinched	swinging	drinker	
		impress		window	finches	swinger	stinking	
		limit		invite	pincher	single	stinker	
				insect		jingle	stinky	
				index		finger	thinking	
				indent			thinker	
R	guiltier	animal	important	interest	flinch	spring	shrink	squints
three-syllable words	guiltiest	chimney	improve	invented		string	Tinkerbell	squinted
three-letter blends			shrimp	include		stringy	stinkier	squinting
suffixes: *-ly*, *-ier*, *-iest*			chimpanzee	inventor		stringier	stinkiest	splinter
			pimply	gingerbread		stringiest		interest
				injure				Internet
RR		swimmable	improvement	information	pinchable	singable	sinkable	interpretation
multisyllabic words		imagination	unimportant	introduce		unsingable	shrinkable	interrupt
from everyday speech		immediately		invisible				interruptible
irregular sounds		impression		Cinderella				interview
prefixes: *un-*, *re-*, *mis-*				Indiana				printable
suffixes: *-ful*, *-able*, *-tion*				intentionally				misprint
Wt +	kilt	imitate	impolite	investigate	unpinchable	mingle	brink	interrogation
prefixes: *self-*, *over-*,	guiltless	victim	import	independence		shingle	unsinkable	uninterruptible
after-, *dis-*, *under-*, *non-*		imaginative		Lincoln		wring	unthinkable	unprintable
suffixes: *-ward*, *-ness*,		unimaginative				ringless	unshrinkable	disinterested
-ship, *-less*		shimmer				springy	overthink	

I—Short Vowel Word Families

Word Family	**ip**	**ish**	**isk**	**is/iss**	**ist**	**it**	**itch**	**ix**
Key Word	**chip**	**fish**	**disk**	**this**	**list**	**it**	**witch**	**six**
YY								
G				this		it		
						little		
GG					sister			six
B	lip	fish	disk	miss	list	bit		fix
regular short vowel word families	lips	dish	disks	hiss	lists	bits		mix
	dip	wish	brisk	kiss	fist	fit		Trix
initial consonant blends/digraphs	dips	swish	risk	Swiss	fists	fits		
	hip		risks	crisp	mist	sit		
final consonant blends/digraphs	nip		whisk		twist	hit		
	rip		whisks			hits		
word + *s*	sip					kit		
	tip					knit		
	zip					pit		
	chip					wit		
	clip					skit		
	drip					quit		
	flip					slit		
	ship					spit		
	skip					twit		
BB	ripped	fished	risked	misses	listed	fitted	witch	fixes
word endings (*-ing*, *-es*, *-ed*, *-y*, *-le*, *-er*, *-est*)	ripping	fishes	risking	missed	listen	knitted	ditch	fixed
	dipped	fishing	risky	missing	twisted	fitting	ditched	fixing
two-syllable words with regular vowels	dipping	dished	whisked	Missy	twisting	hitting	ditching	fixer
	dripped	dishes	whisking	hisses	twister	quitting	hitched	mixes
suffixes: *-ing*, *-ed*, *-y*, *-es*, *-le*, *-er*, *-est*	flipped	wished	whisker	hissed	twisty	sitting	pitch	mixed
	flipping	wishing	frisky	hissing	wrist	slitting	pitches	mixing
	tipped	wishy-washy		kisses	wristwatch	spitting	pitching	mixer
	tipping	swishy		kissed	blister	hitter	pitcher	pixie
	tripped	Trisha		kissing	fistfight	quitter	stitch	pixel
	triplets	catfish		kisser	pistol	city	stitching	sixty
	gripped	finish		Disney	artist	admit	switch	Sixers
	Skippy	foolish		missile	dentist	written	switches	Dixie
	clipper	polish		wisdom	insist	kitchen	switching	sixteen
	chipmunk	rubbish		crispy	resist		itchy	Netflix
	lipstick	selfish					kitchen	
R	slippery	dishwasher	riskier	scissors	insisted	split	itchier	prefix
three-syllable words	strip	squish	riskiest	whisper	listening	splitting	itchiest	mixture
three-letter blends	stripped	squishy		crispier	history		twitch	suffix
suffixes: *-ly*, *-ier*, *-iest*	worship	squishier		crispiest				
		squishiest		prisoner				
				discuss				
RR	championship	babyish		dismissal	scientist	critical	itchiness	fixable
multisyllabic words	equipment	childish		Mississippi	exist	criticize	restitched	appendix
from everyday speech	gossiping	punishment		Wisconsin	relist	readmit		remixed
irregular sounds		selfishly		disruption				unmixed
prefixes: *un-*, *re-*, *mis-*		unselfish		mistrust				unfixed
suffixes: *-ful*, *-able*, *-tion*				discussion				unfixable
Wt +	eclipse	cherish	asterisk	admission	colonist	literary	bewitch	nix
prefixes: *self-*, *over-*,	ownership	perish	briskly	distrust	persist	literature	glitch	
after-, *dis-*, *under-*, *non-*	slipperiness	stylish		distinguish	thistle	brittle	hitchhiker	
suffixes: *-ward*, *-ness*,		unselfishly		mission	bristle	uncritical		
-ship, *-less*								

I—Long Vowel Word Families with *E*

Word Family	**ibe**	**ice**	**ide**	**ie**	**ife**	**ike**	**ile**	**ime**
Key Word	**tribe**	**ice**	**ride**	**pie**	**life**	**like**	**mile**	**time**
YY								
G						like		
GG								
B		ice	ride	pie		likes	mile	time
regular long vowel word families		dice	rides	pies		Mike	miles	times
		lice	hide	tie		bike	file	grime
initial consonant blends/digraphs		mice	hides	ties		bikes	files	slime
		nice	side	die		hike	pile	dime
final consonant blends/digraphs		rice	sides	dies		hikes	piles	dimes
		price	tide	lie		spike	tile	lime
word + *s*		slice	tides	lies		spikes	tiles	limes
		spice	wide			yikes	smile	chime
		twice	bride				smiles	chimes
			brides					crime
			glide					crimes
			glides					
			pride					
			slide					
			slides					
BB	tribe	iced	glided	cried	life	liked	filed	chimed
word endings (*-ing*, *-es*,	tribes	icy	glider	cries	wife	liking	filing	chiming
-ed, *-y*, *-le*, *-er*, *-est*)	bribe	iceberg	hiding	died	knife	biked	filer	timed
two-syllable words	bribes	slices	riding	dried	knifed	biking	piled	timer
with regular vowels	bribed	sliced	rider	fries	lifetime	biker	piling	timing
suffixes: *-ing*, *-ed*, *-y*, *-es*,	bribing	slicing	spider	fried	housewife	hiked	piler	bedtime
-le, *-er*, *-est*		slicer	cider	lied		hiking	tiled	daytime
		spices	sideways	tied		hiker	tiling	mealtime
		spiced	sidewalk	bowtie		spiked	tiler	nighttime
		spicy	sliding			spiking	smiled	sometime
		prices	hideout			spiker	smiling	anytime
		priced	inside				smiler	
		pricy	outside				smiley	
		nicer	hayride				while	
		nicest	divide				awhile	
			bedside					
R	describe	nicely	decided	butterflies		strike		
three-syllable words		advice	divided	fireflies		strikeout		
three-letter blends		icier	divider	Pied Piper		striking		
suffixes: *-ly*, *-ier*, *-iest*		iciest	insider					
		spicier	widest					
RR	hibernate	license	hideaway	satisfied	wildlife	likable	crocodile	suppertime
multisyllabic words			sidetracked	terrified		unlike	refiled	untimed
from everyday speech				applied		unlikable	unfiled	
irregular sounds				denied			retiled	
prefixes: *un-*, *re-*, *mis-*				retied			untiled	
suffixes: *-ful*, *-able*, *-tion*								
Wt +	fiber	device	collide	electrified	lifeless	hitchhiker	juvenile	prime
words not familiar from	subscribe	sacrifice	provide	identified	lifelike	dislike	hostile	timeline
everyday speech	vibration	splice	unprovided	notified	unlifelike	likely	Nile	timesaver
prefixes: *self-*, *over-*,	vibe	entice	stride	untried	nightlife	unlikely	stockpile	timeless
after-, *dis-*, *under-*, *non-*	scribe	priceless	brideless	magnified	knifeless			timely
suffixes: *-ward*, *-ness*,		deiced						
-ship, *-less*								

I—Long Vowel Word Families with *E*

Word Family	ine	ipe	ire	ise	ite	ive
Key Word	**nine**	**wipe**	**fire**	**rise**	**white**	**five**
YY						
G						
GG	nine				white	five
B	fine	wipe	fire	rise	bite	dive
regular long vowel word families	fines	wipes	fires	wise	bites	dives
initial consonant blends/digraphs	dine	pipe	hire		kite	hive
final consonant blends/digraphs	dines	pipes	hires		kites	hives
word + *s*	line	ripe	tire		site	drive
	lines	gripe	tires		quite	fives
	mine	gripes	wire		write	live
	nine	swipe	wires		writes	lives
	pine	swipes				jive
	vine					
	vines					
	wine					
	shine					
	spine					
	wine					
	whine					
BB	dined	griped	fired	rises	biter	diving
word endings (*-ing, -es, -ed, -y, -le, -er, -est*)	dining	griping	firing	rising	biting	diver
two-syllable words with regular vowels	diner	swiped	fireman	wiser	writer	driver
suffixes: *-ing, -ed, -y, -es, -le, -er, -est*	shined	swiping	fireplace	wisest	writing	driving
	shining	wiped	fireworks	sunrise	invite	alive
	shiner	wiper	firefly	surprise	polite	arrive
	shiny	wiping	hired		termite	
	whined	wipeout	campfire			
	whining	sniper	hiring			
	whiner	drainpipe	hirer			
	ninety	tailpipe	tired			
	mining		wiring			
	finer		wiretap			
	finest		siren			
	define					
	online					
	shoeshine					
R	shinier	stripe	fireproof	surprised	invited	arriving
three-syllable words	shiniest	striped		surprising	whiten	arrived
three-letter blends	recliner	ripen		unsurprised		lively
suffixes: *-ly, -ier, -iest*	porcupine	ripened				
RR	pineapple	unripe	umpire	advertise	appetite	
multisyllabic words from everyday speech		unripened	vampire	compromise	excitement	
irregular sounds		unstriped	retire	disguise	excitedly	
prefixes: *un-, re-, mis-*				exercise	uninvited	
suffixes: *-ful, -able, -tion*				surprisingly	rewrite	
				unwise		
Wt +	combine	sideswiped	bonfire	advise	recite	strive
words not familiar from everyday speech	outline	stripeless	desired	unsurprisingly	spite	thrive
prefixes: *self-, over-, after-, dis-, under-, non-*	recline		perspire	unsupervised	Web site	survival
suffixes: *-ward, -ness, -ship, -less*	shrine		retirement		trite	arrival
	spineless				item	overdrive
						revive

I—Long Vowel Word Families

Word Family	igh	ight	ild	ind	y
Key Word	**high**	**light**	**child**	**find**	**my**
YY					
G					my
GG					by
B		light	child	find	cry
regular long vowel word families		lights	mild	finds	dry
		night	wild	hind	fly
initial consonant blends/digraphs		nights		kind	fry
		might		kinds	shy
final consonant blends/digraphs		right		mind	sky
				minds	sly
word + *s*				wind	spy
				winds	try
				blind	why
				blinds	
				grind	
				grinds	
BB		sight	wilder	minded	crying
word endings (*-ing*, *-es*, *-ed*, *-y*, *-le*, *-er*, *-est*)		tight	wildest	minding	drying
		bright	wildcat	winding	flying
two-syllable words with regular vowels		brighter	wildfire	blinded	frying
		brightest	milder	blinding	spying
suffixes: *-ing*, *-ed*, *-y*, *-es*, *-le*, *-er*, *-est*		flight	mildest	blinder	
		flights		blindest	
		fright		kinder	
		knight		kindest	
		knights		finder	
		lightning		finding	
		lighted		grinder	
		lightest		grinding	
		midnight			
		sunlight			
		tonight			
		nightmare			
		moonlight			
R	high	frighten	wildly	behind	
three-syllable words	higher	tighten	mildly	remind	
three-letter blends	highway	lighten		kindly	
suffixes: *-ly*, *-ier*, *-iest*	sigh	brighten		blindly	
	sighs	nightly			
	sighed	tightly			
	sighing	brightly			
	thigh	slightly			
	thighs				
RR	highness	frightening	childhood	reminder	rely
multisyllabic words from everyday speech		lightening	wildflowers	unkind	deny
irregular sounds		untighten		unkindly	supply
prefixes: *un-*, *re-*, *mis-*				unwind	
suffixes: *-ful*, *-able*, *-tion*					
Wt +	resign	slight	mildness	mastermind	spry
words not familiar from everyday speech	design	sightless	wildness	mindless	slyly
prefixes: *self-*, *over-*, *after-*, *dis-*, *under-*, *non-*	redesign	frightful	childless	kindness	hyphen
suffixes: *-ward*, *-ness*, *-ship*, *-less*		eyesight	childlike		testify
		tightness			magnify
		brightness			

I—with R

Word Family	ir	ird	irt
Key Word	**girl**	**bird**	**dirt**
YY			
G			
GG	girl		
B	girls	bird	dirt
regular ir word families	fir	birds	flirt
initial consonant blends/digraphs	first	third	flirts
final consonant blends/digraphs	firs	thirds	shirt
word + *s*	sir		shirts
	stir		skirt
	stirs		skirts
	birth		
	births		
	chirp		
	chirps		
	firm		
BB	stirred	birdcage	flirted
word endings (*-ing*, *-es*, *-ed*, *-y*, *-le*, *-er*, *-est*)	stirring	birdseed	flirting
two-syllable words with regular vowels	twirl	birdbath	flirty
suffixes: *-ing*, *-ed*, *-y*, *-es*, *-le*, *-er*, *-est*	twirls		dirty
	twirling		thirteen
	twirled		thirty
	twirler		birthday
	girlfriend		birthdays
	circus		
	circle		
R	firmly		squirt
three-syllable words	squirrel		squirted
three-letter blends	squirm		birthstone
suffixes: *-ly*, *-ier*, *-iest*	swirling		dirtier
	thirsty		dirtiest
	thirstier		sweatshirt
	thirstiest		
RR	Virginia		unbirthday
multisyllabic words from everyday speech	whirlpool		
irregular sounds			
prefixes: *un-*, *re-*, *mis-*			
suffixes: *-ful*, *-able*, *-tion*			
Wt +	chirped	girders	shirtless
words not familiar from everyday speech	sirloin	girdle	flirtations
prefixes: *self-*, *over-*, *after-*, *dis-*, *under-*, *non-*	whirlwind	mockingbird	virtuous
suffixes: *-ward*, *-ness*, *-ship*, *-less*	circumference	hummingbird	virtue
	circulate		virtual

O—Short Vowel Word Families

Word Family	ob	oc/ock	od	og	ol/oll	om
Key Word	**job**	**rock**	**nod**	**frog**	**doll**	**mom**
YY						
G						
GG						mom
B	job	rock	nod	frog	doll	moms
regular short vowel word families	jobs	rocks	nods	frogs		Tom
	Bob	dock	God	fog		bomb
initial consonant blends/digraphs	cob	lock	odd	hog		bombs
	gob	locks	pod	hogs		prom
final consonant blends/digraphs	knob	sock	pods	jog		proms
	mob	socks	Todd	jogs		
word + *s*	mobs	block	clod	log		
	rob	blocks	clods	logs		
	sob	clock	rod	clog		
	sobs	flock	rods	clogs		
	blob	knock		smog		
	blobs	shock				
	glob	smock				
	slob	stock				
BB	mobbed	docking	nodded	fogged	follow	bombed
word endings (*-ing*, *-es*, *-ed*, *-y*, *-le*, *-er*, *-est*)	mobbing	locked	nodding	fogging	hollow	bombing
	sobbed	locking	body	foggy	holler	bomber
two-syllable words with regular vowels	sobbing	locker	model	foghorn	dollar	mommy
	robbed	socking	everybody	jogged	trolley	momma
suffixes: *-ing*, *-ed*, *-y*, *-es*, *-le*, *-er*, *-est*	robbing	blocked	nobody	jogging	solve	grandmom
	robber	blocking	somebody	jogger	Molly	Tommy
	slobber	knocked	bodysuit	logged	Polly	compare
	cobweb	knocking	oddball	logging	golly	comma
	knobby	shocked		logger		tomboy
	goblin	shocker		clogged		comet
	hobby	shocking		clogging		command
	lobster	stocking		hogging		vomit
	wobble	hockey		smoggy		
	robin	doctor		Boggle		
	lobby	pocket		progress		
	problem	rocker				
	Bobby	rocket				
R	probably	broccoli	bodies	foggier	lollipop	computer
three-syllable words	robbery	occupy	goddess	foggiest	olive	complete
three-letter blends	Robin Hood	October	godmother	smoggier	involve	common
suffixes: *-ly*, *-ier*, *-iest*	clobbered	octopus	Godzilla	smoggiest	tolerate	promise
			modern		following	company
			dodge		hollering	commander
			Dodgers			commanded
RR	observation	occupation		catalog	Colorado	comfortable
from everyday speech		unblocked		recognize	unsolved	communicate
irregular sounds		restocked		unrecognized	solvable	communication
prefixes: *un-*, *re-*, *mis-*		pocketful				
suffixes: *-ful*, *-able*, *-tion*		crocodile				
Wt +	oblong	blockbuster	product	backlog	scholarship	atomic
prefixes: *self-*, *over-*,	obstacle	stockpile	toddler	unrecognizable	colony	combine
after-, *dis-*, *under-*, *non-*	obligation	document	sod		colonial	recombine
suffixes: *-ward*, *-ness*,	obnoxious	sprocket	godless		intolerant	commencement
-ship, *-less*	observatory	aftershock			unsolvable	
	throb	mockingbird			toleration	

O—Short Vowel Word Families

Word Family	on	op	os	ot	ox	ong
Key Word	**con**	**stop**	**closet**	**got**	**box**	**long**
YY						
G						
GG		stop		got		
				not		
B	on	cop		cot	box	long
regular short vowel word families	Don	cops		cots	fox	song
initial consonant blends/digraphs		hop		dot	pox	songs
final consonant blends/digraphs		hops		dots	sox	bong
word + *s*		plop		hot		pong
		pop		lot		
		slop		lots		
		mop		pot		
		mops		pots		
		chop		rot		
		chops		blot		
		drop		plot		
		drops		shot		
		flop		shots		
		flops		slot		
		shop		spot		
BB	contest	hopped	closet	dotted	boxes	bongo
word endings (*-ing, -es, -ed, -y, -le, -er, -est*)	confess	mopped	gosling	Dottie	boxed	wrong
two-syllable words with regular vowels	connect	mopping	Cosco	rotted	boxing	belong
suffixes: *-ing, -ed, -y, -es, -le, -er, -est*	contact	chopped		rotting	boxer	
	concert	chopping		rotten	boxcar	
	Donald	chopper		blotted	mailbox	
	Donnie	chopstick		blotter	sandbox	
	Ronnie	dropped		bottle	toolbox	
	Bonnie	dropping		spotted	foxes	
	honest	shopped		spotting	foxy	
	honor	shopping		spotty		
		shopper		spotlight		
		stopped		knotted		
		stopping		knotting		
		sloppy		cotton		
		floppy		otter		
		topic		popcorn		
R	continent	sloppier		spottier	foxier	strong
three-syllable words	constantly	popular		spottiest	foxiest	belonging
three-letter blends	consider	property		forgotten	chickenpox	belonged
suffixes: *-ly, -ier, -iest*	nonsense	adopted		lottery	Magnavox	
		lollipop				
RR	considerate	cooperate	posture	unknotted		
multisyllabic words from everyday speech	Monopoly	opportunity				
irregular sounds	contraction	operation				
prefixes: *un-, re-, mis-*	congratulations	opposite				
suffixes: *-ful, -able, -tion*	consequences	rechop				
	confusion					
Wt +	Congress	opera	cosmic	spotless	approximately	throng
prefixes: *self-, over-, after-, dis-, under-, non-*	conquer	proper	cosmopolitan	pottery	chatterbox	tongs
suffixes: *-ward, -ness, -ship, -less*	contrast	copper	jostle	cottage	oxygen	songless
	dishonorable	opposition	nostril	mascot		longing
	dishonest	uncooperative	hostage	patriotic		longingly
	discontinue	unchoppable		unpatriotic		

O—Long Vowel Word Families with Final *E*

Word Family	obe	ode	oe	oke	ole	ome	one	ope
Key Word	**robe**	**rode**	**goes**	**joke**	**hole**	**home**	**bone**	**hope**
YY								
G								
GG			goes					
B	robe	rode	toe	joke	hole	home	bone	hope
regular long vowel word families	robes	code	toes	jokes	holes	homes	bones	hopes
initial consonant blends/digraphs	globe	codes	Joe	woke	mole		cone	dope
final consonant blends/digraphs	globes			broke	moles		cones	dopes
word + *s*				choke	pole		lone	mope
				smoke	poles		phone	mopes
				smokes	role		phones	nope
				spoke	roles		shone	open
				spokes	stole		stone	rope
				Coke	whole		stones	ropes
				cokes			tone	scope
				poke			tones	scopes
				pokes				slope
								slopes
BB	robed	explode	tiptoe	broken	armhole	homey	phoned	hoped
word endings (*-ing*, *-es*, *-ed*, *-y*, *-le*, *-er*, *-est*)	bathrobe		tiptoed	choked	keyhole	homeroom	phoning	hoping
two-syllable words with regular vowels	earlobe			choking	manhole	homesick	earphone	hoper
suffixes: *-ing*, *-ed*, *-y*, *-es*, *-le*, *-er*, *-est*	Globe Trotters			joked	stolen	homework	jawbone	moped
				joker	tadpole		postpone	moper
				joking			boney	moping
				poked			Tony	roped
				poking			alone	roping
				slower				roper
				slowest				sloped
				slowpoke				sloping
				smoked				dopey
				smoker				
				smoking				
				smoky				
				spoken				
				token				
R		exploded	tomatoes	stroke	buttonhole	homeless	telephone	dopier
three-syllable words		exploding	toenail	stroked	coleslaw	homier	throne	dopiest
three-letter blends			poem	strokes		homiest	lonely	opener
suffixes: *-ly*, *-ier*, *-iest*				stroking			lonelier	opened
							loneliest	opening
RR		rodeo	poetry	heartbroken	casserole	homemaker	baloney	hopefully
multisyllabic words from everyday speech		Nickelodeon	dominoes	misspoke			microphone	reopen
irregular sounds		Rhode Island						telescope
prefixes: *un-*, *re-*, *mis-*								unopened
suffixes: *-ful*, *-able*, *-tion*								
Wt +	probe	episode	doe	heatstroke	adolescent	dome	cyclone	microscope
words not familiar from everyday speech	wardrobe	mode	hoe	outspoken	blowhole	chrome	opponent	stethoscope
prefixes: *self-*, *over-*, *after-*, *dis-*, *under-*, *non-*	disrobe	strode	woe	provoke	linoleum	Rome	zone	hopeless
suffixes: *-ward*, *-ness*, *-ship*, *-less*	robeless	mother lode	woeful		wholesale		loneliness	hopelessly
		encode	woefully		cubbyhole			
		decode						

O—Long Vowel Word Families with Final *E*

Word Family	ose	ote	ove
Key Word	**nose**	**note**	**drove**
YY			
G			
GG			
B regular long vowel word families initial consonant blends/digraphs final consonant blends/digraphs word + *s*	nose	note	drove
	hose	notes	cove
	pose	vote	coves
	rose	votes	stove
	chose		stoves
	those		wove
	close		
BB word endings (*-ing*, *-es*, *-ed*, *-y*, *-le*, *-er*, *-est*) two-syllable words with regular vowels suffixes: *-ing*, *-ed*, *-y*, *-es*, *-le*, *-er*, *-est*	closed	noted	Rover
	closes	noting	clover
	closing	notepad	
	closely	notebook	
	chosen	voted	
	hosed	voter	
	hoses	voting	
	hosing	wrote	
	noses		
	nosey		
	posed		
	poses		
	posing		
	poser		
	roses		
	rosy		
	suppose		
R three-syllable words three-letter blends suffixes: *-ly*, *-ier*, *-iest*	rosier	remote	
	rosiest		
RR multisyllabic words from everyday speech irregular sounds prefixes: *un-*, *re-*, *mis-* suffixes: *-ful*, *-able*, *-tion*	supposedly	promoted	overheated
		rewrote	
Wt + words not familiar from everyday speech prefixes: *self-*, *over-*, *after-*, *dis-*, *under-*, *non-* suffixes: *-ward*, *-ness*, *-ship*, *-less*	composer	devoted	alcove
	expose	quote	woven
	propose	totem pole	overly
	opposed	voteless	grove
	unopposed	noteworthy	stovepipe
	rosewater	notable	cloverleaf

O—Long Vowel Word Families

Word Family	oach	oad	oak	oal	oam	oan	oast	oat
Key Word	**coach**	**road**	**soak**	**goal**	**foam**	**loan**	**toast**	**boat**
YY								
G								
GG								
B	coach	road	oak	goal	foam	loan	toast	coat
regular long vowel word families	roach	roads	croak	goals	foams	loans	toasts	coats
		load	croaks	coal	roam	Joan	coast	boat
initial consonant blends/digraphs		loads	soak	foal	roams	groan	coasts	boats
		toad	soak	foals		groans	roast	goat
final consonant blends/digraphs		toads				moan	roasts	goats
						moans		float
word + *s*								floats
BB	coaches	loaded	croaked	goalpost	roamed	groaned	coasted	coated
word endings (*-ing*, *-es*, *-ed*, *-y*, *-le*, *-er*, *-est*)	coached	loading	croaking	goalie	roaming	groaner	coasting	coating
	coaching	loader	soaked	charcoal	roamer	groaning	coaster	raincoat
two-syllable words with regular vowels	roaches	armload	soaking		foamed	loaned	roasted	floated
	cockroach	railroad			foaming	loaning	roasting	floating
suffixes: *-ing*, *-ed*, *-y*, *-es*, *-le*, *-er*, *-est*		roadblock			foamy	moaned	roaster	floater
		roadway				moaner	toasted	boated
		roadwork				moaning	toasting	boating
		crossroad					toaster	boater
							toasty	boathouse
								lifeboat
								sailboat
								tugboat
								speedboat
								oatmeal
R					foamier		toastier	throat
three-syllable words three-letter blends suffixes: *-ly*, *-ier*, *-iest*					foamiest		toastiest	throats
RR	approach	unload						recoat
multisyllabic words from everyday speech	approached	unloaded						recoated
irregular sounds	approaching	reload						
prefixes: *un-*, *re-*, *mis-*		reloaded						
suffixes: *-ful*, *-able*, *-tion*								
Wt +	approachable	download	cloak	goalless			boast	scapegoat
words not familiar from everyday speech	unapproachable	roadster	cloaked				boasting	moat
prefixes: *self-*, *over-*, *after-*, *dis-*, *under-*, *non-*	coachless	overload	cloakless				coastal	coatless
suffixes: *-ward*, *-ness*, *-ship*, *-less*	broach	overloaded					coastline	coattails
	stagecoach	toadstool						

O—Long Vowel Word Families

Word Family	old	oll	olt	ost	ow	ow (cont.)	own
Key Word	**old**	**roll**	**colt**	**most**	**know**	**know**	**own**
YY							
G							
GG					yellow		
B	old	roll	colt	most	know	blow	own
regular long vowel word families	bold	rolls	colts	ghost	knows	blows	blown
initial consonant blends/digraphs	cold	toll	bolt	ghosts	grow	crow	flown
final consonant blends/digraphs	colds	tolls	bolts	host	show	crows	grown
word + *s*	fold	troll	jolt	hosts	shows	flow	shown
	folds	trolls	jolts	post	bow	flows	
	gold			posts	bows	glow	
	hold				low	glows	
	holds				mow	slow	
	mold				mows	slows	
	molds				row	snow	
	sold				rows	snows	
	told				tow		
	scold				tows		
	scolds						
BB	bolder	rolled	bolted	bedpost	bowed	snowed	owner
word endings (*-ing*, *-es*, *-ed*, *-y*, *-le*, *-er*, *-est*)	boldest	rolling	bolting	hosted	bowl	Snow White	
two-syllable words with regular vowels	colder	roller	jolted	hosting	flowed	snowman	
suffixes: *-ing*, *-ed*, *-y*, *-es*, *-le*, *-er*, *-est*	coldest		jolting	posted	glowed	snowy	
	folded			posting	grower	towed	
	folder			poster	lower	borrow	
	folding			postman	mowed	below	
	golden			postpone	mower	follow	
	holder			hostess	rowed	pillow	
	holding				rower	rainbow	
	moldy				cornrow	willow	
	older				showed	arrow	
	oldest				slowed	elbow	
	scolded				slowpoke		
R	moldier	swollen			throw		thrown
three-syllable words	moldiest	collect			snowier		
three-letter blends		collector			snowiest		
suffixes: *-ly*, *-ier*, *-iest*		stroller			pillowcase		
RR	potholder	collection	thunderbolt		snowmobile		unknown
multisyllabic words from everyday speech	unfolded	controlling	unbolted		windowsill		
irregular sounds	refolded	uncontrolled	rebolted		marshmallow		
prefixes: *un-*, *re-*, *mis-*		steamroller					
suffixes: *-ful*, *-able*, *-tion*							
Wt +	boldface	collide	molt	postage	lowly	knowingly	homeowner
words not familiar from everyday speech	marigold	enroll	revolting	ghostless	shallow	unknowingly	landowner
prefixes: *self-*, *over-*, *after-*, *dis-*, *under-*, *non-*	withhold	poll	volts	ghostlike	widow	mellow	overthrown
suffixes: *-ward*, *-ness*, *-ship*, *-less*	boldness	scroll	voltage	hostless		sparrow	overgrown
		recollection				narrow	ownership
		stroll					

O—Other Word Families

Word Family	oi	on	oo	ood	ood	oof	ook
Key Word	**noisy**	**son**	**too**	**food**	**good**	**roof**	**look**
YY							
G							look
GG			too		good		
B		son	boo		goods		book
word families based on common sight words		sons	zoo		hood		books
initial consonant blends/digraphs		ton	zoos		hoods		took
final consonant blends/digraphs		tons	moo				brook
word + *s*			shoo				brooks
							cook
							cooks
							crook
							hook
							shook
BB	noisy	money	booed	food	goody	roof	cooked
word endings (*-ing*, *-es*, *-ed*, *-y*, *-le*, *-er*, *-est*)		honey	mooed	foods	goodies	roofs	cooking
two-syllable words with regular vowels		sonny	shooed	mood	goodbye	roofer	cookie
suffixes: *-ing*, *-ed*, *-y*, *-es*, *-le*, *-er*, *-est*			shooing	moods	hoodie	sunroof	cookies
			shampoo	moody	hoodies	goof	cookbook
			boo-boo	doodle	hooded	goofed	cookout
			tattoo	noodle	stood	goofing	crooked
			Scooby Doo	poodle	wood	goofy	hooked
					woods	poof	hooking
					wooded	proof	looked
					woody		looking
							booklet
							bookmark
							notebook
							logbook
							handbook
							checkbook
							rookie
R	avoid	wonderful	kangaroo	moodier	wooden	goofier	
three-syllable words	oil	consider	tattooed	moodiest	woodsy	goofiest	
three-letter blends	foil					fireproof	
suffixes: *-ly*, *-ier*, *-iest*	spoil					soundproof	
	joint					rainproof	
	boil					waterproof	
	broil						
	choice						
	moist						
	noise						
	noisier						
	noisiest						
RR	poison	continue			misunderstood	bulletproof	unhooked
multisyllabic words from everyday speech	toilet	contribute			neighborhood		uncooked
irregular sounds		considerate					recooked
prefixes: *un-*, *re-*, *mis-*		consideration					
suffixes: *-ful*, *-able*, *-tion*		tongue					
Wt +	topsoil	confide	yahoo	brood	brotherhood	spoof	mistook
prefixes: *self-*, *over-*, *after-*, *dis-*, *under-*, *non-*	boisterous	confirm	cuckoo	hoodlum	motherhood		nook
suffixes: *-ward*, *-ness*, *-ship*, *-less*	asteroid	consist	kazoo	moodily	fatherhood		outlook
	moisten	monsoon			sisterhood		overlook
		reconsider					undercooked

O—Other Word Families

Word Family	ool	oom	oon	oop	oose	oot	oss/ost
Key Word	**cool**	**room**	**soon**	**hoop**	**goose**	**boot**	**boss**
YY							
G							
GG							
B word families based on common sight words initial consonant blends/digraphs final consonant blends/digraphs word + *s*							
BB word endings (*-ing*, *-es*, *-ed*, *-y*, *-le*, *-er*, *-est*) two-syllable words with regular vowels suffixes: *-ing*, *-ed*, *-y*, *-es*, *-le*, *-er*, *-est*	cool	room	soon	hoop	goose	boot	boss
	cooled	rooms	sooner	hoops	loose	boots	bosses
	cooling	roomy	moon	loop	moose	hoot	bossed
	drool	boom	moons	loops	noose	hoots	bossing
	drooled	booms	noon	coop		hooted	bossy
	drooling	boomed	spoon	cooped		hooting	loss
	fool	booming	spoons	scoop		loot	losses
	fooled	bloom	spooned	scoops		looted	moss
	fooling	blooms	spooning	scooped		root	mosses
	foolish	bloomed	teaspoon	scooper		roots	toss
	pool	blooming	balloon	snoop		toot	tossed
	poolside	broom	baboon	snoops		scoot	tossing
	school	brooms	cartoon	snooping		scooting	cross
	schools	zoom	raccoon	Snoopy		scooter	crosses
	spool	zooms		stoop		shoot	gloss
	stool	zoomed		troop		shoots	glossy
	stools	zooming		droop		shooting	floss
	tool	gloom		drooped		shooter	frosting
	tools	gloomy					Frosty
		bedroom					across
R three-syllable words three-letter blends suffixes: *-ly*, *-ier*, *-iest*			afternoon	droopier	loosen		bossier
			tablespoon	droopiest	loosely		bossiest
				snoopier	goose bumps		
				snoopiest			
RR multisyllabic words from everyday speech irregular sounds prefixes: *un-*, *re-*, *mis-* suffixes: *-ful*, *-able*, *-tion*	schooled		honeymoon	scoopful			uncross
	unschooled						recross
	foolishly						
Wt + words not familiar from everyday speech prefixes: *self-*, *over-*, *after-*, *dis-*, *under-*, *non-* suffixes: *-ward*, *-ness*, *-ship*, *-less*	preschool	loom	harpoon	loophole	papoose	snooty	crossword
	Google	doom	lagoon	stormtrooper	caboose	bootless	crisscross
	retool	bloomless	maroon			zoot suit	
	toolless		spoonless			reboot	
	hooligan						

O—Other Word Families

Word Family	oth	ouch	oud	ought	ould	oun	our
Key Word	**cloth**	**couch**	**loud**	**thought**	**would**	**found**	**our**
YY							
G							
GG					would		our
					could		
B			loud		should	found	hour
word families based on common sight words			cloud				hours
			clouds				sour
			proud				sours
initial consonant blends/digraphs							flour
							flours
final consonant blends/digraphs							ours
word + *s*							
BB		couch	clouding	thought		bound	ourselves
word endings (*-ing*, *-es*, *-ed*, *-y*, *-le*, *-er*, *-est*)		pouch	cloudy	bought		hound	hourglass
		grouch	louder	fought		hounds	
two-syllable words with regular vowels		grouchy	prouder	ought		mound	
			aloud	brought		mounds	
suffixes: *-ing*, *-ed*, *-y*, *-es*, *-le*, *-er*, *-est*						pound	
						pounds	
						round	
						sound	
						sounds	
						ground	
						wound	
						count	
						counter	
R	cloth	grouchier	cloudier			mountain	
three-syllable words	washcloth	grouchiest	cloudiest			fountain	
three-letter blends	moth					rebound	
suffixes: *-ly*, *-ier*, *-iest*	broth					grounded	
						surrounded	
RR			cloudiness	thoughtful		boundary	
multisyllabic words from everyday speech			loudspeaker	thoughtless		unwound	
irregular sounds			proudly	thoughtfully		rewound	
prefixes: *un-*, *re-*, *mis-*			loudly	thoughtlessly			
suffixes: *-ful*, *-able*, *-tion*			unclouded	rethought			
Wt +	sloth	crouched	thundercloud	afterthought		astounding	hourly
words not familiar from everyday speech	frothy	vouch	cloudless	sought		dumbfounded	scour
prefixes: *self-*, *over-*, *after-*, *dis-*, *under-*, *non-*	frothier	slouch		overwrought		foundation	sourpuss
suffixes: *-ward*, *-ness*, *-ship*, *-less*	frothiest	slouchier				fountainless	
		slouchiest				groundless	

O—Other Word Families

Word Family	**ouse**	**out**	**ove**	**ow**	**owl**	**own**	**oy**
Key Word	**house**	**out**	**ove**	**now**	**owl**	**down**	**boy**
YY							
G						down	
GG	house	out		now		brown	boy
		about		how			
B	mouse	pout	love	bow	owl	gown	boys
regular short vowel		pouts	loves	bows	owls	gowns	joy
word families		scout	glove	cow	howl	town	joys
initial consonant		scouts	gloves	cows	howls	towns	Roy
blends/digraphs		snout	dove	wow	growl	clown	toy
final consonant		snouts	doves	brow	growls	clowns	toys
blends/digraphs		spout	shove	brows		crown	
word + *s*		spouts	shoves	chow		crowns	
		trout		chows		drown	
		shout		plow		drowns	
		shouts		plows		frown	
						frowns	
						browns	
BB	houses	pouted	shovel	crowd	growled	clowned	enjoy
word endings (*-ing*, *-es*,	housing	pouting	shovels	crowds	growler	clowning	royal
-ed, *-y*, *-le*, *-er*, *-est*)	housecoat	pouter		crowded	growling	drowned	loyal
two-syllable words	birdhouse	scouted		crowding	howled	drowning	oyster
with regular vowels	doghouse	scouting		bowed	howler	frowned	cowboy
suffixes: *-ing*, *-ed*, *-y*,	lighthouse	shouted		bowing	howling	frowning	
-es, *-le*, *-er*, *-est*	blouse	shouting		plowed	towel	frowner	
	blouses	shouter		plowing	vowel	crowned	
	mousey	doubt		power		brownie	
		mouth		powder		crowning	
		outfit		flowers		downtown	
		outside		shower		downhill	
		without		howdy		slowdown	
		workout		allow		sundown	
		cookout					
		cutout					
		knockout					
R	thousand	outstanding	shoveler	flowerpot		downstairs	employ
three-syllable words		outfield	shoveling	powerful		downpour	employed
three-letter blends			shoveled	showerhead			annoy
suffixes: *-ly*, *-ier*, *-iest*			government	powdery			annoyed
							annoying
RR	housecleaning	mouthwatering	reshoveled	cauliflower		touchdown	enjoyable
multisyllabic words	housekeeper	mouthful	unloved	superpower			corduroy
from everyday speech	houseful	outgoing	unlovable	meow			
irregular sounds		outfielder		uncrowded			
prefixes: *un-*, *re-*, *mis-*		scoutmaster		powerfully			
suffixes: *-ful*, *-able*, *-tion*		South America					
Wt +	trousers	outrageous	loveless	drowsy	fowl	rundown	employer
words not familiar	spouse	doubtless	gloveless	manpower	prowler	townhouse	employee
from everyday speech	spouseless	doubtfully		scowled	scowl		unemployable
prefixes: *self-*, *over-*,		south		empower			joyfully
after-, *dis-*, *under-*, *non-*		sprout		coward			royalty
suffixes: *-ward*, *-ness*,							voyage
-ship, *-less*							

O—with R

Word Family	or/ord	ore	ork	orm	orn	ort/orth
Key Word	**or**	**more**	**fork**	**storm**	**corn**	**sport**
YY						
G						
GG	or					
	for					
B	cord	more	fork	storm	corn	sport
regular *or* word families	lord	before	forks	storms	born	sports
initial consonant blends/digraphs	Ford	core	cork	form	horn	fort
final consonant blends/digraphs		gore	corks	forms	horns	forts
word + *s*		pore	pork		torn	port
		pores	stork		worn	ports
		sore	storks		sworn	sort
		tore	dork		thorn	short
		wore	dorks		thorns	shorts
		chore				snort
		chores				snorts
		shore				
		snore				
		store				
		swore				
		scores				
BB	border	scored	corked	formed	morning	sorted
word endings (*-ing*, *-es*, *-ed*, *-y*, *-le*, *-er*, *-est*)	order	scoring	corking	forming	corny	sorting
two-syllable words with regular vowels	story	scorer	Porky	former	corner	sorter
suffixes: *-ing*, *-ed*, *-y*, *-es*, *-le*, *-er*, *-est*	stories	snored	forklift	perform	Cornflakes	snorted
	forest	snoring	New York	platform	foghorn	snorting
	orbit	snorer		stormed	hornet	sporty
	afford	bookstore		storming	newborn	forty
	horror	explore		stormy	stubborn	shorter
	record	seashore		normal	popcorn	shortcut
	porch	ignore		inform	acorn	shortest
				rainstorm		airport
						comfort
R	sword	forever	corkboard	formula	cornier	portrait
three-syllable words	correcting	adore		thunderstorm	corniest	tortoise
three-letter blends	chorus	adored		uniform	tornado	important
suffixes: *-ly*, *-ier*, *-iest*	porpoise	adoring				reporter
	recorded	ignored				decorate
		ignoring				
RR	orderly	adorable	uncork	normally	California	fortune
multisyllabic words from everyday speech	ordinary	explorer	recork	performance	stubbornly	fortunate
irregular sounds	original	re-explore		information	reborn	fortunately
prefixes: *un-*, *re-*, *mis-*	corduroy	Florida		enormous	unborn	comfortable
suffixes: *-ful*, *-able*, *-tion*	affordable	unexplored				
		Georgia				
Wt +	chord	forecast	snorkel	formal	hornless	forth
words not familiar from everyday speech	forbidden	reforecast	snorkling	informant	thornless	portable
prefixes: *self-*, *over-*, *after-*, *dis-*, *under-*, *non-*	oral	carnivore	snorkler	tormented	ornery	portray
suffixes: *-ward*, *-ness*, *-ship*, *-less*	corridor	exploration	snorkled	reform	ornament	northwest
	corrupt			abnormal	unicorn	shortage
	scorch			brainstorm	ornamentation	assorted
	gorge					assortment
	glory					escorted
						passport

U—Short Vowel Word Families

Word Family	ub	uc/uck	ud	udge	uff	ug	um	umb
Key Word	**tub**	**duck**	**mud**	**fudge**	**puff**	**bug**	**drum**	**dumb**
YY								
G								
GG								
B	cub	duck	mud		puff	bug	gum	
regular short vowel word families	cubs	ducks	bud		cuff	bugs	gums	
	hub	buck	buds		cuffs	dug	bum	
initial consonant blends/digraphs	sub	bucks	suds		huff	hug	bums	
	club	luck	thud		huffs	hugs	hum	
final consonant blends/digraphs	clubs	muck	thuds		bluff	jug	hums	
	stub	puck			bluffs	mug	drum	
word + *s*	stubs	tuck			fluff	pug	drums	
	tub	Chuck			fluffs	rug	plum	
	tubs	cluck			gruff	tug	plums	
		snuck			scuff	drug	slum	
		stuck			stuff	drugs	slums	
		truck			stuffs	plug	swum	
		yuck			puffs	slug		
		trucks				snug		
BB	rubbed	ducked	budding		fluffy	hugged	hummed	number
word endings (*-ing*, *-es*, *-ed*, *-y*, *-le*, *-er*, *-est*)	rubbing	ducking	buddy		fluffed	hugging	humming	numbers
	rubber	ducky	muddy		fluffing	hugger	hummer	crumble
two-syllable words with regular vowels	clubbed	tucked	muddle		puffy	mugged	Hummer	crumbles
	clubbing	tucking	cuddle		puffed	mugging	drummed	rumble
suffixes: *-ing*, *-ed*, *-y*, *-es*, *-le*, *-er*, *-est*	clubhouse	bucking	cuddly		puffing	muggy	drumming	rumbles
	nightclub	bucked	huddle		puffin	tugged	drummer	jumble
	stubbed	buckle	puddle		stuffy	tugging	summer	mumble
	stubbing	bucket	sudsy		stuffed	tugboat	bummer	mumbles
	stubby	clucked	sudden		stuffing	slugged	gummy	tumble
	stubborn	clucking	soapsuds		Buffy	slugger	gumdrop	fumble
	bubble	trucked	study		buffing	snuggle	clumsy	fumbles
	hubby	trucking	thudding		bluffing	plugged	Humpty Dumpty	
	subway	trucker			scuffed	buggy		
	bathtub	lucky			huffy	bugging		
	washtub				muffin	slugging		
					handcuffs	ugly		
R	scrub	struck	suddenly	fudge	puffier	uglier	summertime	thumb
three-syllable words	shrub	buckled	studying	Mudge	puffiest	ugliest		thumbtack
three-letter blends	scrubbed	success		judge	fluffier	luggage		dumb
suffixes: *-ly*, *-ier*, *-iest*	scrubbing			smudge	fluffiest			crumb
				budget	Bufferin			bumblebee
				nudge				umbrella
RR	bubblegum	unbuckled		judging	restuffed	struggled	cucumber	cucumber
multisyllabic words from everyday speech	subscription	successful		nudging	unstuffed	suggestion	medium	
irregular sounds	subtraction	unsuccessful		judges		ugliness	museum	
prefixes: *un-*, *re-*, *mis-*	substitute	unsuccessfully		misjudged		replugged	stadium	
suffixes: *-ful*, *-able*, *-tion*		unlucky				unplugged	Rumpelstiltskin	
Wt +	grubby	plucky	shudder	judgment	scruffy	shrug	fumbling	humble
words not familiar from everyday speech	rubble	huckleberry	fuddy duddy	trudged	duffle bag	shrugged	gumless	slumber
	shrubbery	honeysuckle		grudge		jitterbug	summary	lumberjack
prefixes: *self-*, *over-*, *after-*, *dis-*, *under-*, *non-*	publish			grudgeless			summarize	
	public			smuggled			strum	
suffixes: *-ward*, *-ness*, *-ship*, *-less*	publicity						aquarium	

U—Short Vowel Word Families

Word Family	ump	un	unch	ung	unc/unk	unt	up	us
Key Word	**jump**	**fun**	**lunch**	**hung**	**junk**	**hunt**	**up**	**us**
YY								
G							up	
GG	jump	fun						
		Sunday						
		under						
B	jumps	bun	lunch	hung	junk	hunt	cup	us
regular short vowel word families	bump	buns	bunch	lung	dunk	hunts	cups	bus
	bumps	gun	hunch	lungs	dunks	bunt	pup	fuss
initial consonant blends/digraphs	dump	guns	munch	rung	hunk	bunts	pups	Gus
	dumps	run	punch	rungs	sunk	runt		pus
final consonant blends/digraphs	lump	runs	brunch	sung	chunk	blunt		plus
	pump	sun	crunch	clung	drunk	grunt		
word + *s*	pumps	spun		stung	flunk	grunts		
	clump	stun		swung	gunk	stunt		
	plump				skunk	stunts		
	slump				skunks			
	stump				spunk			
	thump				stunk			
					trunk			
BB	bumped	sunning	lunches	hunger	dunked	bunted	puppy	busses
word endings (*-ing*, *-es*, *-ed*, *-y*, *-le*, *-er*, *-est*)	bumping	sunny	lunched	hungry	dunking	bunting	puppies	bussed
	bumper	sunned	lunching	jungle	dunker	bunter	puppet	bussing
two-syllable words with regular vowels	bumpy	sunset	lunchbox		slam-dunk	hunted	guppy	fusses
	dumped	suntan	lunchroom		flunked	hunting	guppies	fussed
suffixes: *-ing*, *-ed*, *-y*, *-es*, *-le*, *-er*, *-est*	dumping	sunrise	lunchtime		flunking	hunter	yuppy	fussing
	dumptruck	sunburn	bunches		funky	grunted	yuppies	fussy
	pumped	sunlamp	bunching		junky	grunting	upper	husky
	pumping	runny	bunched		junker	grunter	supper	mussel
	pumpkin	runner	punches		chunking	blunter	support	mustard
	clumped	stunned	punching		junkman	bluntest	suppose	mustang
	slumped	bunnies	punched		chunky	until	upset	husband
	stumped	funnies	munching		bunk bed		cupcake	bonus
	stumper	bundle	munches		uncle		hiccup	cactus
	jumping	funnel	crunching		chipmunk		lineup	minus
	jumpy	tunnel	crunched		sunken		backup	mucus
	thumping	until	crunchy				tune-up	virus
	lumpy	punish	crunches				warmup	walrus
	grumpy	thunder	hunched				upon	
	trumpet	hundred	hunches					
R	grumpier	understand	scrunch	young	shrunk		ketchup	suspected
three-syllable words	grumpiest	understood	scrunchy	youngest	junkier		uproar	suspended
three-letter blends	bumpier	unhappy	crunchier	strung	junkiest		supporting	octopus
suffixes: *-ly*, *-ier*, *-iest*	bumpiest	funnier	crunchiest	hungrier	chunkier		upsetting	fussier
	lumpier	funniest		hungriest	chunkiest		uppercase	fussiest
RR	umpire	punishment	crunchiness	unstrung	punctuation		Tupperware	justice
multisyllabic words	trumpeter	unafraid	munchable	restrung			coverup	hippopotamus
irregular sounds	pumpkinseed	uneven					interrupt	ghostbusters
prefixes: *un-*, *re-*, *mis-*	grumpily	unfinished					uptight	
suffixes: *-ful*, *-able*, *-tion*		unimportant					upholstery	
Wt +	triumph	blunder	luncheon	bungle	spunky		corrupt	cluster
prefixes: *self-*, *over-*,	gumption	blundered	luncheonette	bungalow	drunkenness		disrupt	citrus
after-, *dis-*, *under-*, *non-*		fundamental		flung	juncture		erupt	musket
suffixes: *-ward*, *-ness*,		cunning		fungus	junction		uppity	envious
-ship, *-less*					puncture		rupture	

U—Short Vowel Word Families

Word Family	ush	ust	ut	utch	utt
Key Word	**rush**	**must**	**but**	**crutch**	**mutt**
YY					
G					
GG			but		
B regular short vowel word families initial consonant blends/digraphs final consonant blends/digraphs word + *s*	rush	must	cut		mutt
	gush	just	cuts		mutts
	hush	dust	gut		putt
	mush	dusts	guts		putts
	blush	gust	hut		
	brush	gusts	huts		
	crush	rust	nut		
	flush	rusts	nuts		
	slush	crust	rut		
		crusts	ruts		
		trust	shut		
		trusts	shuts		
BB word endings (*-ing*, *-es*, *-ed*, *-y*, *-le*, *-er*, *-est*) two-syllable words with regular vowels suffixes: *-ing*, *-ed*, *-y*, *-es*, *-le*, *-er*, *-est*	rushed	dusted	cutting		putted
	rushes	dusting	cutter		putting
	rushing	dusty	shutting		putty
	blushed	trusted	shutters		butter
	blushes	trusting	nutty		gutter
	brushed	trusty	gutted		clutter
	brushes	rusted	butting		shuttle
	brushing	rusting	butler		stutter
	crushed	rusty	button		
	crushes	busted	donut		
	gushed	gusted	haircut		
	flushes	gusting	peanut		
	usher	gusty	walnut		
	mushroom	crusty	King Tut		
	paintbrush	custard			
	toothbrush	mustard			
	hairbrush	musty			
R three-syllable words three-letter blends suffixes: *-ly*, *-ier*, *-iest*		customer	nuttier	crutch	butterfly
		dustier	nuttiest	crutches	buttery
		dustiest	buttonhole	Dutch	
		rustier			
		rustiest			
		disgusted			
RR multisyllabic words from everyday speech irregular sounds prefixes: *un-*, *re-*, *mis-* suffixes: *-ful*, *-able*, *-tion*	brushable	adjusted	coconut		bellybutton
	unbrushable	adjustable	cuttable		butterfingers
	rebrushed	trustworthy	unbuttoned		butterscotch
		untrustworthy	rebuttoned		
Wt + words not familiar from everyday speech prefixes: *self-*, *over-*, *after-*, *dis-*, *under-*, *non-* suffixes: *-ward*, *-ness*, *-ship*, *-less*	lush	custody	klutz	hutch	utterly
	Mt. Rushmore	illustrator	strut	dutchess	putter
	plush	industry	utmost	clutch	muttered
	thrush	frustration	spluttered		cluttered
		adjust	buttonless		uncluttered
		thrust	gutless		shuttled
					stuttered

U—Long Vowel Word Families with Final *E*

Word Family	ube/upe	ue	ure	use	ute
Key Word	**tube**	**blue**	**sure**	**use**	**cute**
YY					
G					
GG		blue			
B regular long vowel word families initial consonant blends/digraphs final consonant blends/digraphs word + *s*	cube	rule		use	cute
	cubes				flute
	tube				flutes
	tubes				
BB word endings (*-ing, -es, -ed, -y, -le, -er, -est*) two-syllable words with regular vowels suffixes: *-ing, -ed, -y, -es, -le, -er, -est*	tubing	Sue	sure	uses	cuter
	tuber	glue	cure	used	cutest
	super	glues	pure	using	
		true		fuse	
		clue		fuses	
		clues		excuse	
		dues			
		argue			
R three-syllable words three-letter blends suffixes: *-ly, -ier, -iest*	Superman	avenue		reuse	salute
	Superwoman	rescue		useful	Luther
	Superfudge	fuel		amuse	computer
		cruel		accuse	
		arguing			
		truly			
RR multisyllabic words from everyday speech irregular sounds prefixes: *un-, re-, mis-* suffixes: *-ful, -able, -tion*	supervise	tissue	furniture	usable	parachute
	superstitious	blueberry	insurance	reusable	polluted
		rescuing	measure	excusable	unpolluted
		glueable	treasure	misuse	
		statue	remeasure	unusable	
Wt + words not familiar from everyday speech prefixes: *self-, over-, after-, dis-, under-, non-* suffixes: *-ward, -ness, -ship, -less*	tubeless	hue	capture	amusement	brute
	supervisor	influence	immature	transfusion	lute
	unsupervised	issue	surely	abuse	muted
	exuberant	cue	curable	useless	execute
	exuberantly	duel	incurable	uselessly	Lutheran
	superior	clueless	manicure		chute
		overrule			

U—with R

Word Family	ur	url	urn	urse	urt/urth
Key Word	**purple**	**curl**	**turn**	**nurse**	**hurt**
YY					
G					
GG	purple				
B regular *ur* word families initial consonant blends/digraphs final consonant blends/digraphs word + *s*	blur	curl	burn		hurt
	blurs	curls	burns		hurts
	spur		turn		
	spurs		turns		
	fur				
	furs				
	purr				
	purrs				
	burp				
	burps				
	surf				
	surfs				
BB word endings (*-ing, -es, -ed, -y, -le, -er, -est*) two-syllable words with regular vowels suffixes: *-ing, -ed, -y, -es, -le, -er, -est*	furry	curled	turned	nurse	hurting
	hurry	curling	turning	nursing	curtain
	hurried	curler	turner	nursed	turtle
	blurry	curly	burned	nurses	yogurt
	blurred		burning	curse	further
	blurring		burner	cursing	furthest
	burped		sunburn	cursed	
	burping		turnpike	curses	
	bury		turnip		
	sturdy				
	murder				
	turkey				
	turtle				
	hurdle				
	scurried				
	scurry				
	surprise				
R three-syllable words three-letter blends suffixes: *-ly, -ier, -iest*	hurrying	curlier	furnish	nursery	
	surgery	curliest	furnace		
	purchase		turntable		
	surrounded		return		
	splurge				
	survivor				
RR multisyllabic words from everyday speech irregular sounds prefixes: *un-, re-, mis-* suffixes: *-ful, -able, -tion*	burglary	uncurl	furnaces		
	burrito	recurl	furniture		
	Jurassic		returnable		
	hurricane				
	repurchase				
Wt + words not familiar from everyday speech prefixes: *self-, over-, after-, dis-, under-, non-* suffixes: *-ward, -ness, -ship, -less*	curry	hurl	churn	nursemaid	hurtle
	burden	burly	turnout	disburse	blurt
	urged	unfurl	overturned	reimburse	curtsey
	urgent	cur	urn		frankfurter
	turquoise		spurn		turtledove
	burly				
	urban				

Develop and Support an Interpretation Rubric

Ace your state test.

Points Earned	
2	Start your answer with key words from the question and state your interpretation/ opinion in one sentence.
1	Use specific evidence from the text to support your interpretation/opinion. (*"In the text..."*)
1	Tell why this matters to the text or to the world. (*This was important to the story because..." OR "This teaches us something important about life because..."*)
4	**Proficient**

Common Core Standard Reading 1
Read closely to determine what the text says explicitly and to make logical inferences from it; cite specific textual evidence when writing or speaking to support conclusions from the text.

State Test Practice Questions

Character Traits
What is the most important character trait of the main character?
What is the primary motivation of the main character?
What is the most important way the main character changes from the beginning to the end?

Cause and Effect
Identify the most important example of cause and effect.
What is the most important decision the main character makes?

Literary Elements
What is the climax?
What is the primary conflict and why does it matter to the theme?

Literary Devices
Identify the best example of figurative language.
Identify the example of figurative language that most affects the mood or tone.
Identify the example of a sound technique that most affects the mood or tone.

Main Idea
What is the most important part?
What is the main idea?
What would be another good title?

Theme
Explain the lesson or moral.
What was the major theme?

Author's Purpose
Why did the author write this?
What was the purpose of the first paragraph?
Why did the author describe the main character as…?
How did the author try to influence the reader's thinking?

Common Core Standard Reading 2
Determine central ideas or themes of a text and analyze their development; summarize the key supporting details and ideas.

ADVENTURE! Genre Card

Reader:_______________________ Room: __________

Adventure: A Dangerous Journey, A Desperate Task

Sailing on the high seas, trekking through a mountain pass, or surviving on a deserted island, adventures are defined by the intense physical and emotional challenges faced by the characters and the exhilaration of their fight to survive the odds.

Setting

Place
Where does the story take place? Why does this matter?

Time
When does the story take place and why does it matter?

- Time of day or year
- Past, present, or future
- Historical period

Danger
How does the setting threaten the survival of the main character?

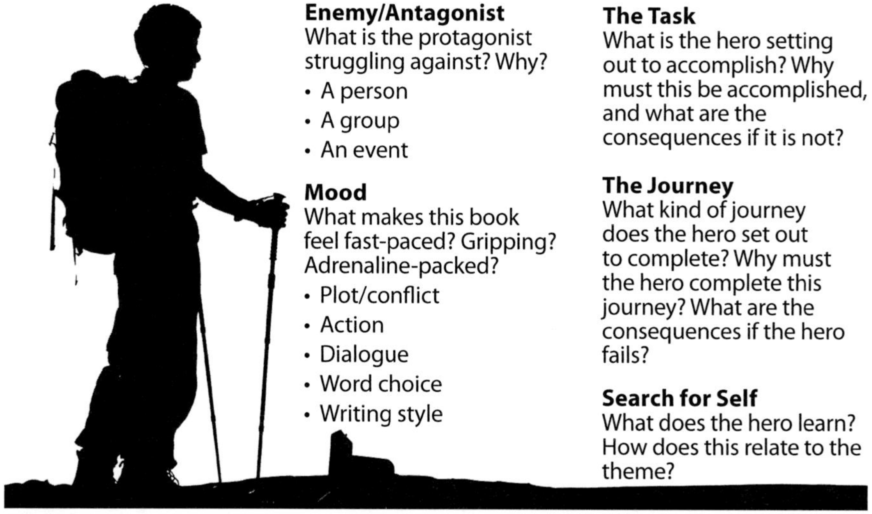

Characters

The Hero
Who is the protagonist or main character? Is s/he more a hero or an anti-hero? Describe his or her:

- Physical characteristics
- Character traits, especially motivations
- Place in society and why it matters

Minor Characters
Identify the minor characters and describe their:

- Motivations
- Relationship to the main character(s)
- Relation to the basic conflict or problem

Enemy/Antagonist
What is the protagonist struggling against? Why?

- A person
- A group
- An event

Mood
What makes this book feel fast-paced? Gripping? Adrenaline-packed?

- Plot/conflict
- Action
- Dialogue
- Word choice
- Writing style

Theme

Author's Purpose
Why do you think the author wrote this book? What was his/her theme, message, moral, or lesson, for you, the reader?

Good vs. Evil
Is it obvious where the good and evil lie in the book, or is it ambiguous? How does this relate to the theme?

Peril
Who is at risk? How is this related to the theme?

- Character
- Community
- Society
- Planet

The Task
What is the hero setting out to accomplish? Why must this be accomplished, and what are the consequences if it is not?

The Journey
What kind of journey does the hero set out to complete? Why must the hero complete this journey? What are the consequences if the hero fails?

Search for Self
What does the hero learn? How does this relate to the theme?

ADVENTURE!

Adventure:

Conflict is at the heart of what makes a good adventure story. Use this organizer to explore how and why authors use different kinds of conflict. Remember to use examples from the text.

	Conflict	Resolution	Author's Purpose or Theme
Character vs. Environment			
Character vs. Self			
Character vs. Character			
Character vs. Society			

Genre Card

Biography

Reader: ______________________ Room: __________

Be prepared to answer the following questions in a live interview speaking as your person:

1. Where are you from? How did that influence you?
2. Tell us about your childhood. What effect did it have on you?
3. What obstacles did you have to overcome? What advantages did you have?
4. Tell us about a turning point in your life.
5. Who are your mentors and/or heroes? Any antagonists?
6. What are your most significant achievements?
7. As a result of your work or accomplishments, how will the world be different?
8. What current issues would/do concern you today and why?

Biography

An account of a person's life written by another person.

Setting

Historical Time
When did this person live? What was going on in the larger world during key stages of this person's life? What influence did these things have on the person?

Geographical Place
Where did this person live? Town? State? Country? Hemisphere? What was the physical environment like? What influence did this have?

Social, Political, and Cultural
What were the social, political, and cultural worlds of this person (family, neighborhood, schools, community, religious group, etc.)? What effect did they have?

Characters

Main Character
Describe this person and their:
- Challenges to overcome/ advantages
- Character traits
- Strengths/ weaknesses
- Major accomplishments

Important People in His/Her Life
What people played a major role in this person's life and how did they influence him/her?

Connection to You
In what ways are you like this person? In what ways are you different?

Questions
If you could meet with this person, what would you ask him/her?

Milestones

Milestones
What were the major milestones in this person's life? Put 10 key events on a timeline. Choose 3–5 key events and explain what effect they had (cause/ effect).

Retell the Life Story
In your own words, tell this person's life story:
- Birth
- Youth
- Adulthood
- Old age/death
- Legacy

Turning Point
Was there any one turning point in this person's life? Explain.

Legacy
What is the major thing for which this person is remembered?

Fantasy

Genre Card

Reader: ____________________ **Room:** ________

Fantasy: Speculative Fiction. What if?

Authors of fantasy create alternative worlds in which to place their characters, their conflicts, and their themes. Choose a fantasy to read. As you read, think about the world the author is creating (physical, social, political, spiritual). Also think about how and why he/she is creating this world. Speculate on the author's theme and intended message for you, the reader.

Setting

Time Period
Is the story set in a medieval world? In an ancient time of gods, myths, and legends? Or is it set in a more modern world? Why?

Place
Does the setting seem to be influenced by a place in our world? Europe? Asia? Africa? Or is it someplace altogether unique?

Magic
What role does magic play in this world? Where does it come from? Who has it? How do they get it? Does it have rules? Why did the author set it up this way?

Society
What is the social hierarchy within the book? Is it a feudal system with kings, nobles, and peasants? A republic with elected officials and social equality? Is there more than one society and, if so, is there conflict between them? Why?

Characters

The Hero
Who is the hero? Did he/she set out to become a hero, or was he/she forced into this role? Describe the following about the hero:
- Physical characteristics
- Place in society
- Strengths
- Weaknesses

Mentor
Is there a mentor or teacher figure in the story? What power does he/she have and where did he/she get it? What influence does he/she have on the hero? Why?

Companions
Does the hero have loyal friends or faithful animals to help accomplish his/her goals? What role do they play? Why?

Enemy
Is there an enemy? What power does he/she have and where did he/she get it? What influence does he/she have on the hero? Why?

Theme

Author's Purpose
Why do you think the author wrote this book? What was his/her theme, message, moral, or lesson for you, the reader?

The Quest
Is there a search for something? The necessity to accomplish something? What is it? How does this relate to the theme?

Good vs. Evil
Is it obvious where the good and evil lie in the book, or is it ambiguous? How does this relate to the theme?

Search for Self
What does the hero learn? How does this relate to the theme?

Basic Conflict
What are the essential conflicts in the book and how do they relate to the theme?

Current Issues
Does anything about the story remind you of an issue in today's world?

Personal Connections
How does the book compare to your life?

Fantasy

Themes & Motifs
Terms
mythic journey
transformation
self-discovery
good vs. evil
pre-industrial civilizations
feudal societies
court intrigue
fate/destiny
invented languages
personification
symbolism
allegory
quest

Character Types
Terms
hero
mentor
apprentice
novice
adept
wizard
mage
paladin
mercenary
enchantress
merchant
tyrant
herald
barbarian
rogue
bard
healer
cleric
minion
dark lord

Fantasy Creatures
Terms
avatar
dragon
dwarf
elf
fairy
familiar
genie
giant
goblin
golem
homunculus
imp
minion
phoenix
troll
unicorn
conquering horde

Fantasy Subgenres
Terms
high fantasy
low fantasy
urban fantasy
epic fantasy
dark fantasy
contemporary fantasy
sword & sorcery (heroic fantasy)
modern fairy tale
historical fantasy
science fantasy
animal fantasy

Key Vocabulary
Terms
realm
haven
ward
fortnight
vigil
honor
armor
bow
citadel
dungeon
hierarchy
saga
chronicle
illusion
feast
cloak
chalice

Genre Card

GRAPHIC NOVELS

Reader: ______________________ Room: __________

Graphic Novels: Combining Art and Text to Tell a Story

Use this organizer to analyze the choices of graphic artists and to plan your own comic.

Key Elements	Conveyed Primarily By...	
	Art	Words
Characters • Physical Characteristics • Motivations/ Emotions • Character Traits		
Setting • Place • Time • Situation		
Plot • Conflict • Rising Action • Climax • Falling Action • Resolution		
Theme • Moral/Message		
Literary Devices • Personification • Metaphor • Idioms • Hyperbole • Symbolism • Mood • Imagery • Irony • Tone • Foreshadowing • Flashback		

GRAPHIC NOVELS

Types of Graphic Literature	Format	Genre	Character Types
illustrated books	inker	informational	hero
comic books	penciler	biography	sidekick
manga	letterer	historical fiction	vigilante
serial	perspective	memoir	villain
adaptation	realistic	superhero	archenemy
	stylized	mystery	nemesis
	sequential	humor	stock character
	line	romance	mutant
	background	adventure	historical
	foreground	fantasy	protagonist
	splash page	horror	antagonist
		science fiction	
		myth	
		traditional tale	

Graphic Style Elements

Sequential Art: The art form used in graphic stories. It uses a series of related pictures that show information about setting, character, action, and events. Each picture moves the reader forward in time through the story.

Panel: A picture with defined borders. Graphic stories usually have a number of panels on each page.

Gutter: The space between each panel.

Speech Bubbles: Bubbles with words in them that show when a character is speaking.

Thought Bubbles: Bubbles (often shaped like clouds—but always different from speech bubbles) that show what a character is thinking.

Captions: Words, usually in boxes, that give reader information that could not be shown in the pictures or dialogue.

Motion Lines: Lines drawn into a picture to show when characters or objects are moving fast.

Sound Effects: Exclamations (usually in larger letters and in different colors than the other words) that show sounds. Some common examples are: POW! BLAM! KABOOM!

POW!

5 Interesting Words or Phrases from This Historical Era Listed in Order of Importance

Word	Definition	Meaningful Sentence	Why Selected
1			
2			
3			
4			
5			

Historical Fiction

Genre Card

Reader: ______________ **Room:** ______

Title ______________

Author ______________

This book is historical because:

This book is fictional because:

	Historical	Fictional
Characters		
Setting		
Events		
Issues Problems Theme		

Things I learned from this author that I might use in my own writing

Genre Card

Horror

Reader: ____________________ **Room:** __________

HORROR: SPECULATIVE FICTION

Horror is an emotion. You know it when you feel it. Authors of horror create an emotional reaction in their readers of fear or dread. They confront our comfortable, everyday lives with something unknown and unknowable, but lurking and horrific. Choose a good horror story to read and ask yourself: *Why do we love horror?*

SETTING/PLOT

Time: When does the story take place and why does it matter?

- Time of day or year
- Past, present, or future
- Historical period

Place: Where does this story take place and why does it matter?

Situation: In our world, the events of this book:

- Could never happen.
- Might happen.
- Could definitely happen.

Source of Horror
Identify and describe the source of horror.

- The unknown
- The supernatural
- A form of evil
- Psychological

What literary devices are used to create the sense of horror?

- Foreshadowing/flashback
- Figurative language

Plot: Describe the rising action, climax, and falling action of the story.

Subplots: Are there subplots? What purpose do they serve?

CHARACTERS

Narrator: Who is the narrator and why did the author decide to tell the story this way?

- 1st person
- 3rd person omniscient
- 3rd person limited
- Reliable or unreliable

Protagonist: Describe the main character's:

- Traits and how they influence the action and theme.
- Place in society and why it matters.

Sources of Comfort
What sources of comfort are available to the main character?

Monster: Is there a monster? In what ways is it:

- Threatening (evokes fear)?
- Disgusting (evokes disgust)?
- Both (evokes horror)?

Effect: How does the source of horror affect the protagonist:

- Morally
- Physically
- Psychologically
- Socially
- Spiritually

THEME

Author's Purpose: Why do you think the author wrote this book? What was his/her theme, message, moral or lesson, for you, the reader?

Basic Conflicts: What are the essential conflicts in the book and how do they relate to the theme?

Good vs. Evil: Is it obvious where the good and evil lie in the book, or is it ambiguous?
How does this relate to the theme?

Love: Do relationships ultimately triumph over the horror? How does this relate to the theme?

Knowledge: What is the role of knowledge and what are the rules for pursuing it?

Search for Self: What does the protagonist learn? How does this relate to the theme?

Search for Meaning: Are the characters struggling with the meaning/purpose of life? What seems to be the author's position?

Genre Card

Horror

Reader: Room:

HORROR: SPECULATIVE FICTION

Horror is an emotion. You know it when you feel it. Authors of horror create an emotional reaction in their readers of fear or dread. They confront our comfortable, everyday lives with something unknown and unknowable, but lurking and horrific. Choose a good horror story to read and ask yourself: Why do we love horror?

SETTING/PLOT

Time: When does the story take place and why does it matter?
- Time of day or year
- Past, present, or future
- Historical period

Place: Where does this story take place and why does it matter?

Situation: In our world, the events of this book:
- Could never happen.
- Might happen.
- Could definitely happen.

Source of Horror
Identify and describe the source of horror.
- The unknown
- The supernatural
- A form of evil
- Psychological

What literary devices are used to create the sense of horror?
- Foreshadowing/flashback
- Figurative language

Plot: Describe the rising action, climax, and falling action of the story.

Subplots: Are there subplots? What purpose do they serve?

CHARACTERS

Narrator: Who is the narrator and why did the author decide to tell the story this way?
- 1st person
- 3rd person omniscient
- 3rd person limited
- Reliable or unreliable

Protagonist: Describe the main character's:
- Traits and how they influence the action and theme.
- Place in society and why it matters.

Sources of Comfort
What sources of comfort are available to the main character?

Monster: Is there a monster? In what ways is it:
- Threatening (evokes fear)?
- Disgusting (evokes disgust)?
- Both (evokes horror)?

Effect: How does the source of horror affect the protagonist:
- Morally
- Physically
- Psychologically
- Socially
- Spiritually

THEME

Author's Purpose: Why do you think the author wrote this book? What was his/her theme, message, moral or lesson, for you, the reader?

Basic Conflicts: What are the essential conflicts in the book and how do they relate to the theme?

Good vs. Evil: Is it obvious where the good and evil lie in the book, or is it ambiguous?
How does this relate to the theme?

Love: Do relationships ultimately triumph over the horror? How does this relate to the theme?

Knowledge: What is the role of knowledge and what are the rules for pursuing it?

Search for Self: What does the protagonist learn? How does this relate to the theme?

Search for Meaning: Are the characters struggling with the meaning/purpose of life? What seems to be the author's position?

© 2010 by American Reading Company®

Poetry

Student:____________________

Room:____________________

1. What is poetry and why does it matter?
2. Name 3 poets you like and tell why you like their work.
3. List and describe 5 different kinds of poetry.
4. Recite one poem from memory.
5. Identify the theme of a poem and support your interpretation with evidence from the poem.
6. Identify and explain the effect of figurative language used in a poem.
7. Identify and explain the effect of sound techniques used in a poem.
8. Identify and explain the effect of structural elements used in a poem.
9. Discuss the author's primary goal and whether or not it was accomplished in a poem you like.

AMERICAN • READING • COMPANY • COMMON CORE STANDARDS

Poetry Vocabulary

Figurative Language

personification

simile

metaphor

hyperbole

symbolism

Types of Poetry: Lyric and Narrative

haiku

limerick

free verse

nursery rhyme

epic

lyric

Structural Elements

syllable

line

line breaks

stanza

verse

rhyme scheme

couplets

Sound Techniques

rhythm

meter

onomatopoeia

alliteration

rhyme scheme

iambic pentameter

What is the subject of the poem?

Who is the speaker?

What is the speaker's attitude toward the subject?

What has the poet done to appeal to your senses?

What effect does the poem have on you as the reader?

What parts of the poem help you to identify the above?

Genre Card

Realistic Contemporary Fiction

Reader: ______________________ **Room:** __________

Comprehension

1. **Plot:** Create a dramatic action timeline of the key events of the plot. Show rising action, climax, falling action, and resolution.
2. **Setting:** Create and label a map showing the most important elements of the setting in the story. Include scale, keys, etc.
3. **Character:** Create a graphic organizer comparing the characters to each other, characters from other books, or people in your life.
4. **Movie Adaptation:** Imagine you have been hired to make this book into a movie. How would the movie be different from the book?
   - Cast: Who would you hire to play which characters?
   - Scenes: Which scenes would you include?
   - Location: Where would you film it?
   - Soundtrack: What music would you use for your opening scene?
5. **Figurative Language:** Find an interesting example in the text of each of the following:
   - Metaphor
   - Simile
   - Personification
   - Idiom
   - Hyperbole
6. **Theme:** What was the book about? If possible, answer with the theme, instead of a plot summary.

Realistic Contemporary Fiction

Stories of characters with normal human powers living in contemporary times in the real world. (Realistic/everyday life fiction, adventure, survival, sports, romance, humor/silly, mystery, and some horror. Horror that plays with the boundaries of reality is speculative fiction.)

Setting

Time: When does this story take place (time of day or year, historical period)?

Place: Where does this story take place (locale, geographical environment)?

Situation
What social, cultural, or political realities is the character living with?

Author's Purpose: How does the setting help the author's purpose?

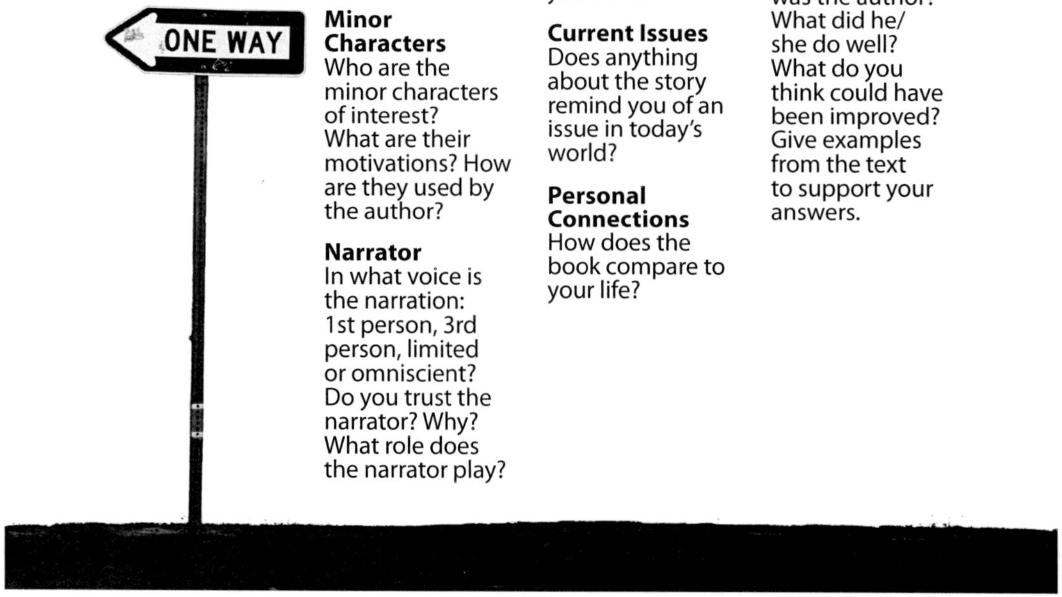

Characters

Protagonist
Who is the main character? Describe his/her traits and motivations using evidence from the story. How do these influence the character's actions and/ or the plot?

Antagonist
Who is the character in conflict or opposition to the main character? What is the conflict? How does this conflict help the author create the theme?

Minor Characters
Who are the minor characters of interest? What are their motivations? How are they used by the author?

Narrator
In what voice is the narration: 1st person, 3rd person, limited or omniscient? Do you trust the narrator? Why? What role does the narrator play?

Plot

Main Events
Outline the key events in the story in chronological order.

Subplots
What subplots are involved? What role do they play?

Conflict
What is the basic problem or conflict? How is it developed? How is it resolved? How does it express the theme?

Climax
What is the climax or turning point in the book? How do you know?

Current Issues
Does anything about the story remind you of an issue in today's world?

Personal Connections
How does the book compare to your life?

Theme

Author's Purpose
Why do you think the author wrote this book in this way? What is the moral, lesson, or message of the story?

Current Issue
Was this book written to comment or explore any contemporary issues? Which ones? Do you agree with the author's portrayal of the issue(s)?

Review
How successful was the author? What did he/she do well? What do you think could have been improved? Give examples from the text to support your answers.

Genre Card

SCIENCE FICTION

Reader: ______________________ **Room:** ________

Twist on Reality

What scientifically plausible, but not yet possible, development defines the story?
- Technological development/aberration
- Scientific discovery
- Natural occurrence
- Social organization
- Other

Which field of science would study this twist on reality?
- Physics
- Biology
- Chemistry
- Sociology
- Anthropology
- Other

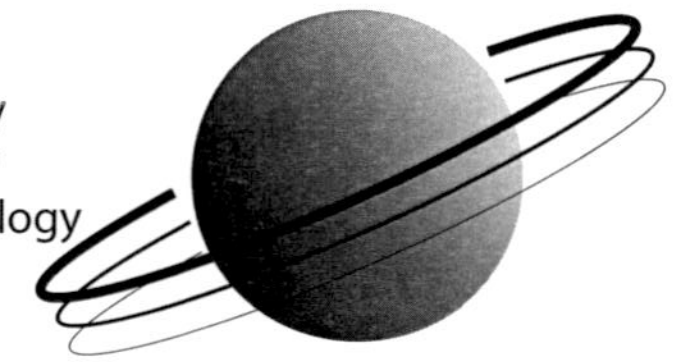

Setting

Time: When does the story take place and how does this help advance the author's purpose?
- Future
- Unknown past
- Alternate present/ parallel universe

Does the twist on reality affect time? How and why does it matter?

Place: Where does the story take place and how does the location advance the author's purpose?
- Earth
- Alien planet
- Outer space

Social, Political, and Cultural
How is the society organized? How does this advance the author's purpose?

Characters

Protagonist: Identify the main character and describe his/her:
- Motivations.
- Traits and how they affect the action.
- Place in the social order.
- Relation to the basic conflict or problem.

Minor Characters: Make a list of the minor characters in the book and describe:
- Motivations.
- Relation to the basic conflict or problem.

Antagonist: What is the protagonist struggling against? Why?
- A person
- A group
- An event
- A force

Species: Are there any species other than humans? Describe their:
- Motivations.
- Traits and how they affect the action.
- Place in the social order.
- Relation to the basic conflict or problem.

Theme

Conflict and Resolution
What is the major conflict/ problem in the book and how is it resolved?

Author's Purpose
What was the theme, message,moral,orlesson?

Utopian, Dystopian, or Somewhere In Between
What seems to be the author's view on the outlook for humanity's future? On human potential?

Search for Meaning: Are the characters struggling with the meaning/purpose of life? What seems to be the author's position?

Morality: Are the lines between good and evil clear or ambiguous?

Love: Do relationships ultimately triumph over difference and fear?

Current Issues: Does anything about the story remind you of an issue in today's world?

Personal Connections
How does the book compare to your life?

SCIENCE FICTION THEMES

Social Commentary
utopia
dystopia
galactic empire
post-apocalyptic life
ultimate fate of the universe
ecological responsibility / stewardship
scarcity & distribution of resources
religious ideologies & conflict
man vs. technology
overpopulation
governments
return to feudalism
hive-like societies
future caste systems
feminism
humanism
totalitarianism

Disasters
pandemic
extinction
alien invasion
nuclear war
dying earth
apocalypse
germ warfare
environmental catastrophe
loss of nonrenewable resources
expanding universe
infertility
asteroid impact
man supplanted by machine
dying sun
new ice age
genocide
black holes

Mind & Identity
bio-implants
bionics
cybernetics
invisibility
life extension and immortality
cloning
cryogenics
memory reprogramming/ removal/editing
posthumans & metahumans
neural implants
nanotechnology
morphing
psionics
telepathy
teleportation
resizing
genetic engineering/ eugenics

Travel and Possible Futures
time travel
parallel universe
alternate history
anachronism
interstellar travel
hyperspace
warp drive/jump drive
wormhole
ansibles (superluminal communication)
FTL (faster-than-light)
Bussard ramjet
space station
space colonization
virtual reality
anti-gravity device
generation ship
solar sail

Traditional Tales

Reader: ______________________ **Room:** __________

Read as many different traditional tales as possible. Use the guide below to discuss the tales you read and plan the tales you write.

Title: ______________________

Subgenre: ______________________

Country of culture of origin: ______________________

Main character(s): ______________________

Minor character(s): ______________________

Setting—time: ______________________

Setting—place: ______________________

Problem: ______________________

Resolution: ______________________

Lesson, moral, or truth taught: ______________________

Symbols used (colors, names, objects, time, etc.): ______________________

____

Figurative language used: ______________________

Patterns: ______________________

1. Rewrite one of the tales from the perspective of a different character.
2. Retell one of the tales to a partner or small group.
3. Find examples of personification, similes, metaphors, and idioms.
4. Create a graphic organizer to compare the tales you have read.
5. Identify patterns you find repeated in the tales.
6. Identify symbols you find repeated in the tales.

Traditional Tales

Traditional Tale Subgenres

Folktale: Passes on wisdom of ordinary people. Often uses animals.

Fairy Tale: Folktale with magic or supernatural.

Myth: Sacred story explaining why the world is the way it is. Usually involves gods, heroes, and supernatural events.

Fable: Short story with a clear moral; usually about animals.

Legend: Based on lives of real kings or heroes who lived before written records. Stories have been passed down and exaggerated over time.

Tall Tale: Has a larger-than-life hero, exaggerated details, and problem or conflicts that are solved in humorous or outrageous ways.

Creation Story: Explains the origin of the earth, its life, and its people.

Pourquoi Tale: Just-so stories. Explains how things came to be the way they are.

Alternative Tale: Updated version of a traditional take with a twist.

AMERICAN • READING • COMPANY • COMMON CORE STANDARDS

Conference Record Form

Level

Student ______________________ Teacher ______________ Room ________

Conf. #	Date	Strengths	Power Goal	Action Plan

Conf. #	Date	Strengths	Power Goal	Action Plan